AF378528

The Irish Face

REDEFINING THE IRISH PORTRAIT

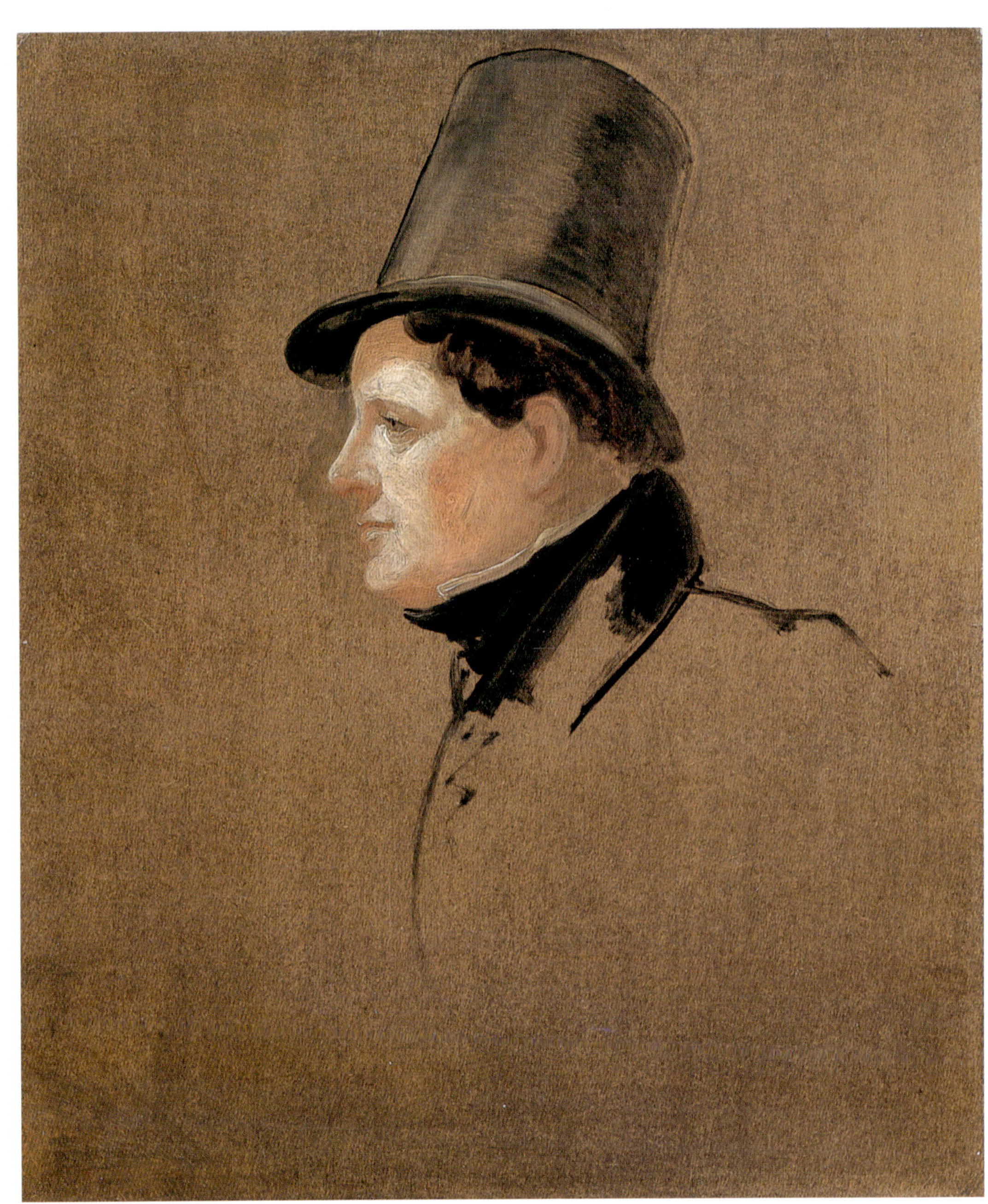

The Irish Face

Fintan Cullen

NATIONAL PORTRAIT GALLERY

Published in Great Britain by
National Portrait Gallery Publications
National Portrait Gallery
St Martin's Place
London WC2H 0HE

For a complete catalogue of current publications,
please write to the address above or visit our website at
www.npg.org.uk/pubs.htm

ISBN 1 85514 290 2

A catalogue record for this book is
available from the British Library.

Publishing Manager DENNY HEMMING
Project Manager and Editor JOHANNA STEPHENSON
Production RUTH MÜLLER-WIRTH
Picture Research CHRISTINA MORGAN and SIMON CONTI
Design PHILIP LEWIS

Printed in Hong Kong

FRONTISPIECE
Daniel O'Connell (1775–1847)
SIR GEORGE HAYTER (1834)
Oil on millboard, 356 × 305mm (14 × 12″)
National Portrait Gallery, London (NPG 4582)

Contents

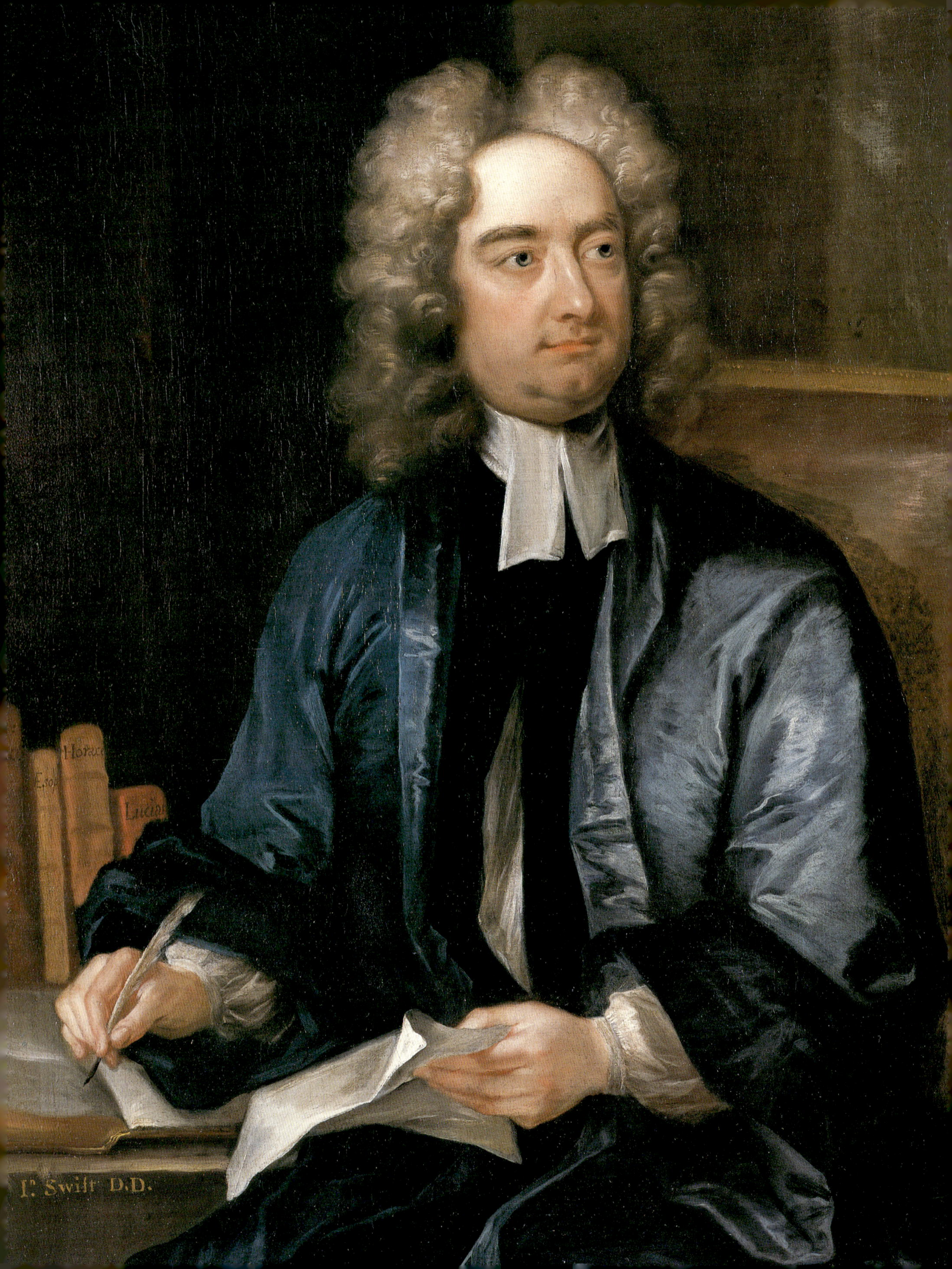
Horac
Esop
Lucian
I. Swift D.D.

IN CALLING THIS BOOK *The Irish Face*, I am aware that readers may feel that some form of anthropological study on the development of an Irish racial type may be on offer. An immediate reading of the subtitle is thus in order. This book is a redefining of what constitutes the Irish drawn, painted, sculpted or photographed portrait from *c*.1700 to *c*.2000. By the word 'portrait' I mean a visual image of a person's face producing a likeness for record that is to be shared with other people, intimates, professional associates and/or the general public. The images discussed here were drawn, painted, sculpted or photographed for posterity and it was expected that they would be appreciated for some time. Most of the images have ended up in museums and public collections and have thus entered the discourse of memory, becoming key visual objects in the nation's perceptions of a particular individual.

David Piper, a former Director of the National Portrait Gallery in London, once wrote a study entitled *The English Face* (1957). In substituting 'Irish' for 'English' in the title I am not attempting to do what Piper did and discuss the subject chronologically and in terms of 'Golden Ages' and avant-garde 'yearnings', or identify a host of artistic geniuses. Instead, it is hoped that the arguments offered in this book are historically specific and contextualised to a degree that they are not culturally contradictory. They are also arranged thematically and the arguments frequently move backwards and forwards in terms of time (though it should be pointed out that chronology usually dictates the flow of the discussion of particular tropes or genres of portraiture).

On re-reading Piper's book I am conscious that a definition of what constitutes the Irish face needs to be offered from the very start. Piper begins his study by refer-ring to the 'British people' and their attitudes to showing their faces. He then goes on to talk exclusively about the English face, although one whole chapter is given over to a Scot, Thomas Carlyle. I hope that such confusions have not crept into this study and that the Irish face, although defined in broad terms is not conceived proprietorially. This book looks exclusively at the role of the portrait in the context of Ireland, while at the same time discussing the Irish presence in portrait produc-tion in London, Rome or further afield, as in the United States of America. Beyond Ireland, London is the key alternative place in any discussion of Irish historical visual material. Reference is thus continuously made to the London-based English tradition in portraiture. A comparative history of the portraiture produced in these islands (incorporating Irish, Scottish, Welsh and English production) has still to be written. But from an Irish perspective, although a quick glance through the illustra-tions of this book may raise a few eyebrows (why so many royal portraits, why George Washington and why David Lloyd George?), it is hoped that the following pages will adequately explain these inclusions and widen our definitions as to the nature of national portraiture in any society or culture.

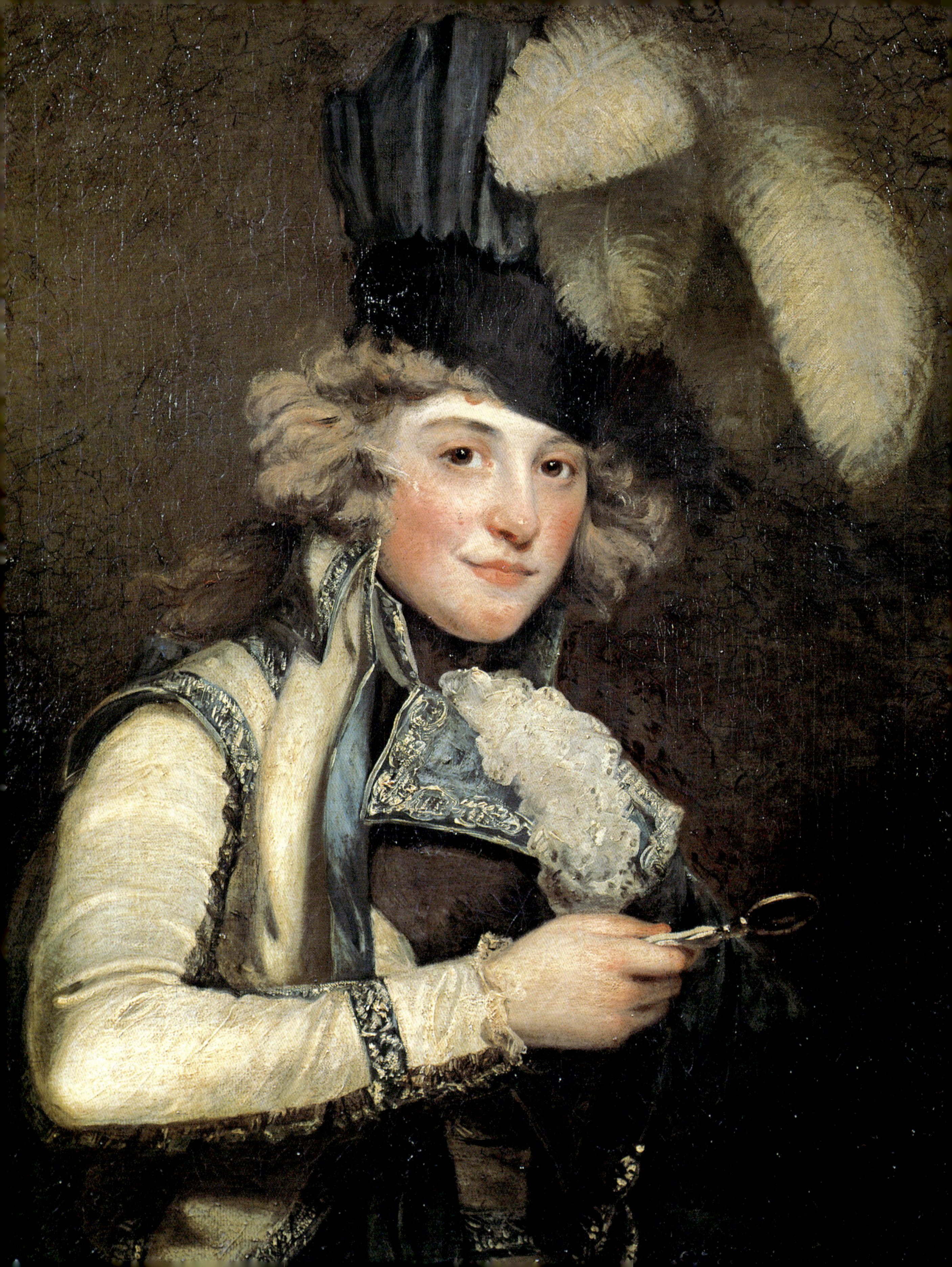

THE IRISH FACE IS the product of many years of musings on the Irish portrait. During that time I have amassed many debts, and I hope that I have remembered to acknowledge most if not all of them. My thanks are extended to the following: Hazel Armstrong, Richard Aylmer, Malcolm Baker, John Bonehill, Síghle Bhreathnach-Lynch, Eileen Black, Margaret Boyd, Barbara Bryant, Anthea Callen, Deborah Cherry, Mary Clark, Jacky Colliss Harvey, Anne Crookshank, Colin Cruise, Tom Dunne, Kate Eustace, Catherine Ford, Roy Foster, Alison Fuller, Peter Funnell, Tony Halliday, Michael Hatt, Denny Hemming, Celia Joicey, Valerie Keogh, Siobhán Kilfeather, Stephen Lloyd, Gráinne MacLochlainn, Edward McParland, Anthony Malcomson, Jan Marsh, Jacquie Moore, Christina Morgan, Peter Murray, Gabriele Neher, Niamh O'Sullivan, Lucy Peltz, Lara Perry, Alexia Petsalis-Diomidis, Marcia Pointon, Charles Saumarez Smith, Desmond Shawe-Taylor, Jim Smyth, Sara Smyth, Nathan Somers, Alan Sommerstein, Johanna Stephenson, Yvonne Thunder, the Comtesse de la Tour du Pin (and her family), Robert Towers, Kevin Whelan and Jeremy Wood.

I am also grateful to the staff at the following institutions: National Portrait Gallery Heinz Archive, London; National Gallery of Ireland Library and Archive, Dublin; Manuscripts Department of the National Library of Ireland, Dublin; National Photographic Archive (National Library of Ireland), Dublin; Tate Archive, London; Government Art Collection, London; and the Hallward Library at the University of Nottingham.

Yet again my family has had to live with this book over weekends and during school holidays – my sincere thanks to them for their patience. Sam Cullen suggested to me the names of the key personalities in today's Ireland, while Ruairí Cullen did the first draft of the Chronology. Felicity Woolf helped in more ways than I can ever record.

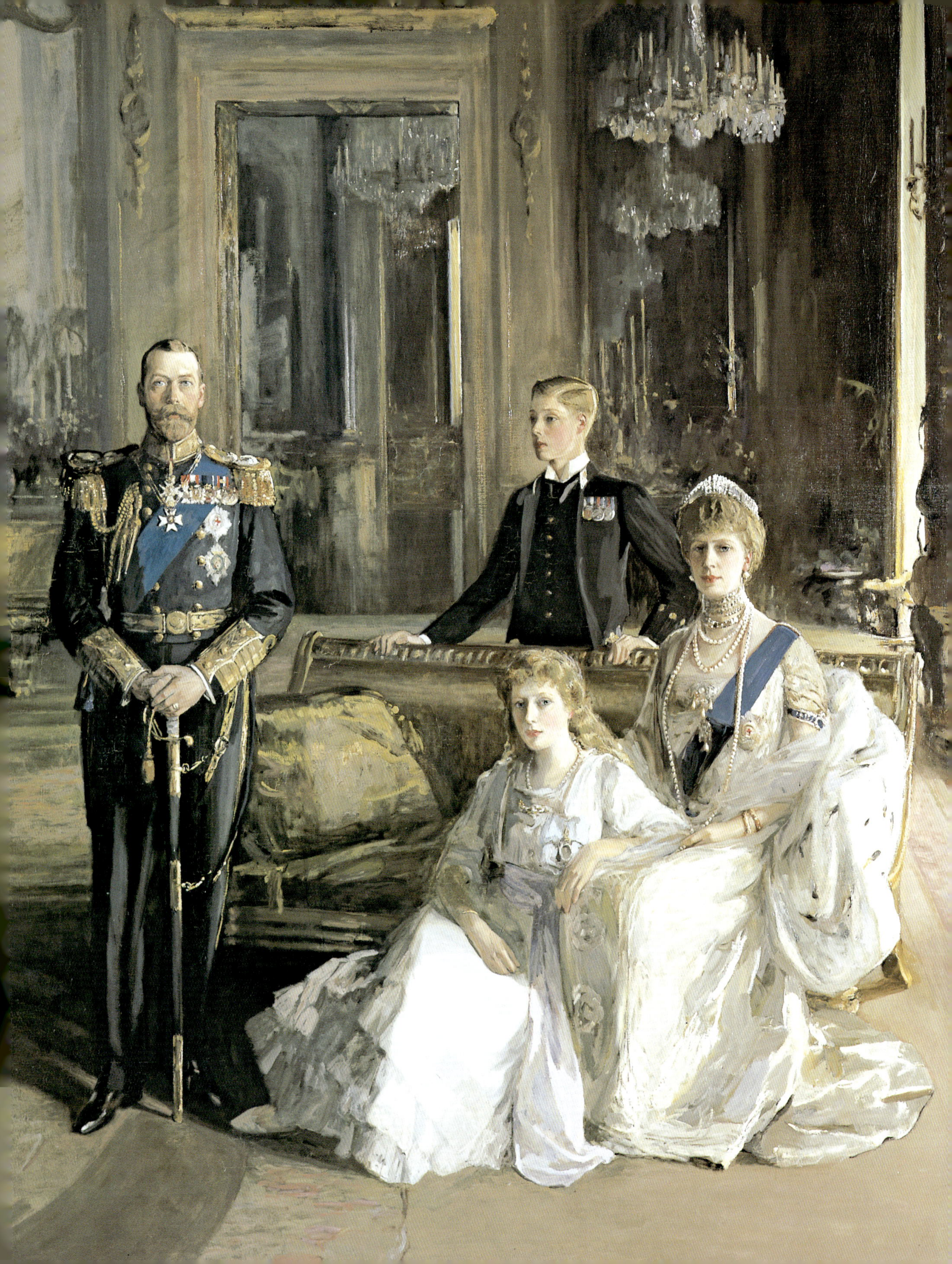

THIS BOOK IS ABOUT the Irish portrait – that is, a thematic analysis of types of portrait that are connected with Ireland. Many are of Irish-born individuals and were produced in Ireland by Irish-born artists; but that is not a key to the Irish portrait as interpreted here. This book also examines portraits of Irish people painted by artists from elsewhere and portraits of non-Irish people (often by non-Irish artists) who had some impact on Ireland. The focus of the book is on the eighteenth and nineteenth centuries, as this was when the genre of portraiture was at its height. The twentieth century repeatedly features, both in terms of actual examples and as a time when the consolidation of collections, such as the Irish portraits in the National Gallery of Ireland, took place. The emphasis in the five chapters is on conventional forms of portrait production, oil on canvas, drawings, engraved illustrated journals, the photograph and the marble bust or the miniature. As the book takes a wide historical period, it is necessary to ascertain the features of a tradition before fully analysing recent examples.

The gender balance of the examples used is heavily weighted in favour of male sitters, although women do feature as prominent case studies in various sections. As will be discussed later in this Introduction (pp.17–18), Lois, the young protagonist in the film *The Last September* (fig.4), is momentarily confronted by family portraits in her uncle's house in Cork during the Anglo-Irish War of 1920. In Chapter 3 Peg Woffington (figs 71–3), a prominent Irish actress on the Dublin and London stages in the mid-eighteenth century, features in a detailed analysis of the relationship between the production of portraiture and the achievement of success (pp.115–18). Equally, the two key institutions to be discussed in this book that have collected Irish portraits since the mid-nineteenth century, the National Portrait Gallery in London and Dublin's National Gallery of Ireland, will be examined in terms of their acquisition or non-acquisition of female portraits, from nineteenth-century writers such as Lady Morgan (fig.13) through to commissioned portraits of a recent Head of State (fig.47). All the same, it is salutary to note that even in its newly restored one-roomed national portrait collection which opened in late 2003, the National Gallery of Ireland can only assemble some ten or so female sitters painted over a four hundred-year period to hang in a group of about fifty men.

What makes a portrait particular to one country or region? Is it possible to define without hesitation a distinctly homogenous portraiture? When two or more cultures are closely interconnected due, for example, to a sustained colonial bond, what effect does this have on the production of portraiture? This book is about national portraiture in as much as it asks the question as to what makes a portrait an *Irish* portrait, what gives a portrait an *Irish* face? That face does not necessarily have to have been native to the island of Ireland; instead, the key focus is on the examination of Irish subject matter in portraiture rather than in arguing for an Irish 'look', a Celtic physiognomy or, in traditional art historical terms, an identifiable Irish school of portraiture.

The driving force behind this particular study is a unique institution, the National Portrait Gallery in London, which owns a large number of hitherto under-explored Irish images or objects associated with Ireland. Many of these feature here, with a discussion of how they have fared as part of the British national collection. It may seem perverse at the start of the twenty-first century, given the present diversity of Ireland's museum and display culture, to view Ireland though the lens of a London-based cultural institution. And indeed it is odd; but then Ireland's relationship with Britain is not that simple. It is the contention of this study that Ireland is not a cultural absolute, nor is it a visually coherent phenomenon. Through at least four centuries of cultural diversity, the Irish portrait has evolved from being a crude indicator of imperial ambition (fig.5) to being a wry post-modernist visualisation (fig.147) of all that unites yet separates so-called 'Irishness' and 'Britishness'. These two images, Marcus Gheeraerts the Younger's Captain Lee of 1594 and John Kindness's Sectarian Armour of 1995, both refer to Ireland but are owned by London's Tate Britain and the Imperial War Museum respectively. Both images are discussed more fully below; for the moment, from the point of view of the history of museum acquisition, it is important to remember that the discussion of the Irish face needs to include an English dimension – and more particularly a London one.

From its early inauguration in the mid-nineteenth century to celebrate people of note and figures of national importance, the National Portrait Gallery has spawned an international series of like-minded institutions from Dublin and Edinburgh to Washington DC and Canberra, Australia. In attempting to keep in tune with the National Portrait Gallery's approach to the examination of the portrait, where the sitter comes first and the artist comes second, where history marginally precedes aesthetics, this book will concentrate on the public portrait. Writing to Lord Ellesmere in 1856, William Gladstone, then Chancellor of the Exchequer, thanked him for the bequest of the so-called Chandos portrait of Shakespeare, which became the first acquisition of the new collection:

> I quite concur in your remarks as to the propriety of making history, and not art, the governing principle for the formation of this gallery, and it is the intention of the government to regulate the selection of trustees or managers by this standard. The authenticity of a portrait, and the celebrity of the

person represented, will be the grounds for the admission of a picture, and not its excellence as a work of art.[1]

Thus less attention is levelled here on the private image or the intimate representation, although in the case of such a famous public icon as Lord Edward FitzGerald (figs 101, 111 and 115), portraits were produced and copies made whose sole currency was private and highly personal: this privileging of the public is not to deny the powerful role of the personal. Instead, a focus on such key topics as the definition of the national portrait, the charting of the political image in Ireland from the eighteenth century to the late twentieth century and an analysis of the portrait of success will reveal the importance of the role of the portrait image in Irish culture.

The obvious and the ambiguous

When we view a relatively recent portrait of the Nobel laureate and poet Seamus Heaney, painted by Edward McGuire in 1973–4 (fig.1), we are untroubled by its cultural components. Commissioned by the Ulster Museum in Belfast when the Irish poet was in his mid-thirties with three highly successful books already published, McGuire's portrait was clearly appreciated by both the poet and his publishers, Faber and Faber, as it appeared on the back cover of Heaney's next volume of poetry, *North*, published the following year.[2] Since then Heaney has become a world renowned figure, while the Dublin-born artist, McGuire, who unfortunately died in his forties, produced a host of comparably stark, confrontational portraits of Irish literary figures often set next to a window thick with wide-leafed foliage. Remembering it some time later in his poem 'A Basket of Chestnuts', Heaney writes that

> Since Edward McGuire visited our house
> In the autumn of 1973,
> A basketful of chestnuts shines between us,
> One that he did not paint when he painted me
>
> Although it was what he thought he'd maybe use
> As a decoy or a coffer for the light
> He captured in the toecaps of my shoes.
> But it wasn't in the picture and is not.
>
> What's there is comeback, especially for him.
> In oils and brushwork we are ratified.
> And the basket shines and the foxfire chestnuts gleam
> Where he passed through, unburdened and dismayed.

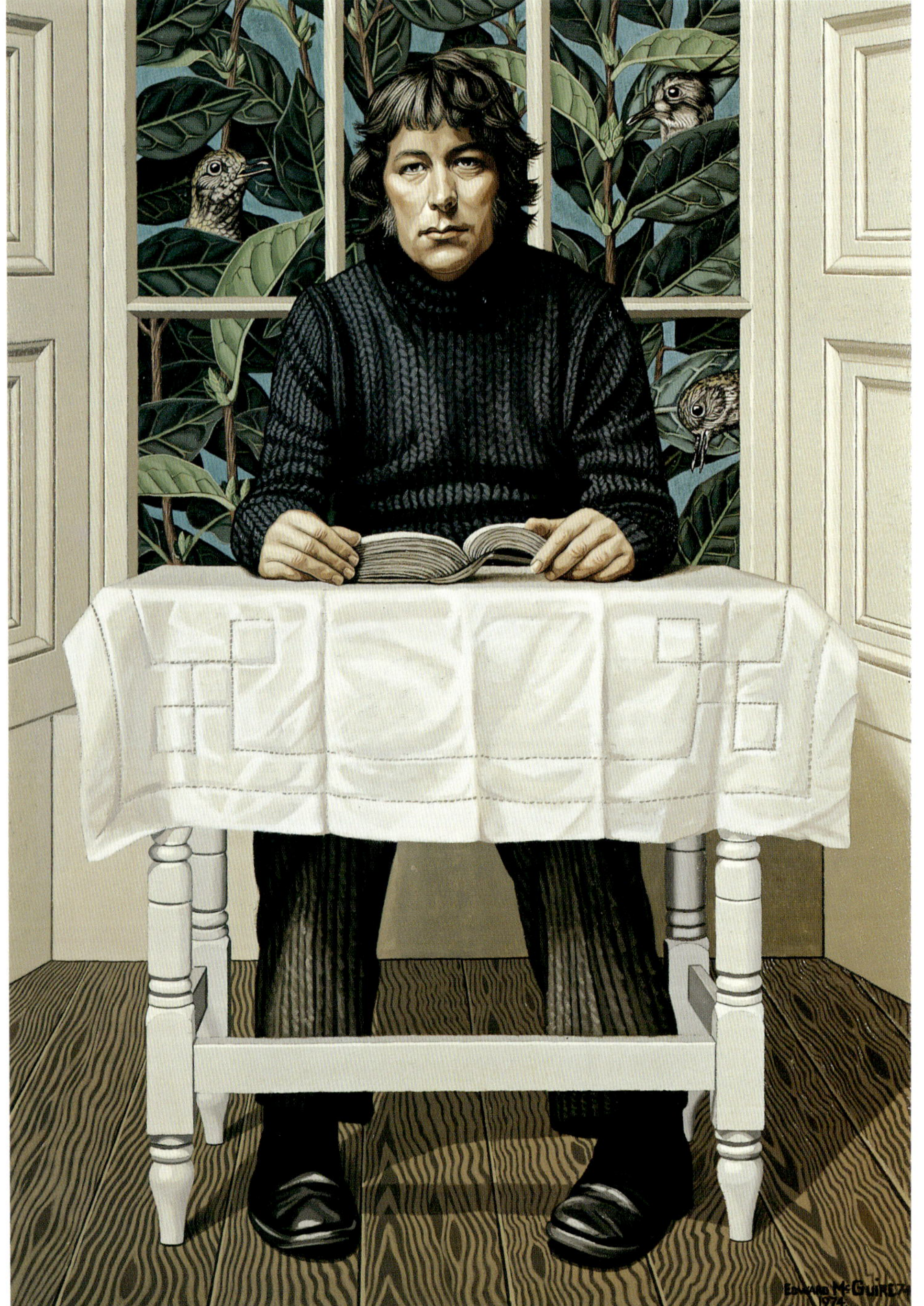

1. **Seamus Heaney**
(b.1939)
EDWARD McGUIRE (1974)
Oil on canvas, 1420 ×
1121mm (55⅞ × 44⅛″)
Ulster Museum, Belfast

The portrait has attracted a range of interpretations. This may be due to the various 'unusual' elements contained in the painting, such as the laurel leaves interspersed with three birds' heads that appear beyond the window behind the sitter: McGuire's 'own kind of phantasmagoria', as Heaney has called this motif. Equally unsettling, once we realise the fact, is that the chair on which the poet presumably sits is not visible.[3] Given the centrality of the pose and Heaney's confident stare, all would agree that the work is indeed highly concentrated and yet there is an air of optimism, despite the fact that Heaney himself has discussed his 'feeling of great wariness' in the early 1970s regarding his situation as a Northern Irish poet publishing with a London-based company. Dorothy Walker has written of the portrait exhibiting a

> tension . . . a fending off of multiple dangers or attackers, a feeling of the siege instinct of the poet's home town, Derry. It is a portrait of the besieged Nationalist poet keeping at bay potential destroyers: British adulation, Unionist resentment, and even the professional envy of poet colleagues.[4]

Meanwhile, the artist Derek Hill criticised the painting as being 'just a wooden carving';[5] although meant as a negative comment, he perhaps put his finger on the way the portrait works. Given its concentrated focus, it is really an icon, a totem of contemporary Ireland. McGuire began the work in autumn 1973, the same year that the Republic of Ireland officially became part of the European Economic Community. The large, casually dressed figure of the poet, his long hair and sideburns framed by the window frame, contrasts with the confined, regulated space of the bay window and the symmetrical patterns on the tablecloth. This portrait can thus be seen as less an image of 'fending off . . . attackers' and more one of a rising Irish literary figure portrayed by an Irish artist during an era of growing confidence in the country's international potential.

Yet the cultural ambiguities of a Derry-born poet living in Dublin, having his portrait painted for a Belfast Museum and his poems published by one of London's leading publishing houses has not gone away. The National Portrait Gallery owns no fewer than seventeen portraits of Seamus Heaney in a variety of media, from oil on canvas to ink drawing to photographs (Dublin's National Gallery of Ireland has only one, a head and shoulder version by McGuire of the larger Belfast painting).[6] When a series of thirteen portrait drawings of Heaney by the Belfast artist Ross Wilson (figs 2 and 3) went on display at the National Portrait Gallery in London in the mid-1990s, the then Director, Charles Saumarez Smith, was challenged by a member of the public as to why portraits of an Irishman had been acquired by a British national collection. Interestingly, he stated that during the entire process of acquisition this issue 'had never at any point entered the discussion'. As for his response to the person in the gallery, Saumarez Smith states that the National

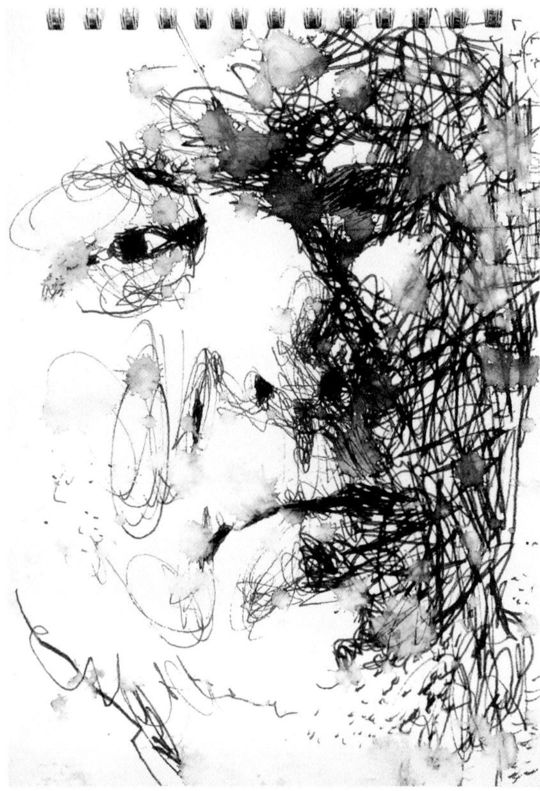

2. **Seamus Heaney** (b.1939)
ROSS WILSON (1994)
Ink and watercolour, 178 × 127mm (7 × 5")
National Portrait Gallery, London (NPG 6262 [4])

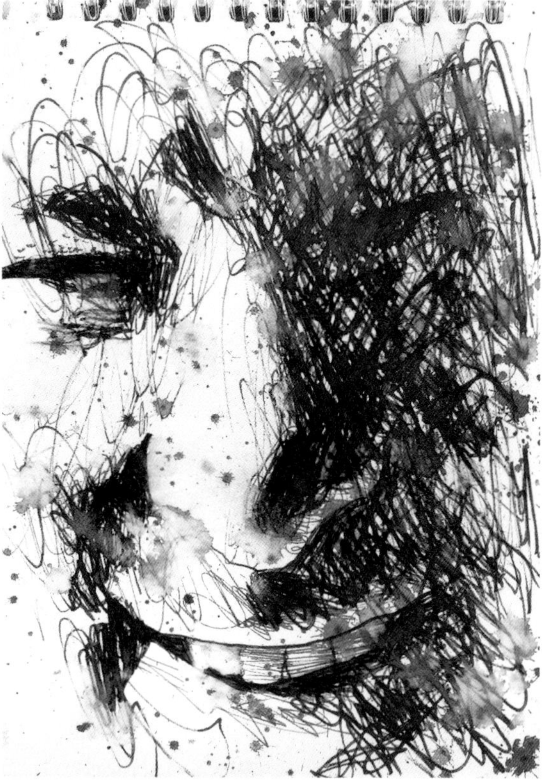

3. **Seamus Heaney** (b.1939)
ROSS WILSON (1994)
Ink and watercolour, 78 × 127mm (7 × 5")
National Portrait Gallery, London (NPG 6262 [11])

Portrait Gallery is 'reasonably liberal about what constitutes a contribution to British national life and, by any standards, a great poet of the English language who has been Professor of Poetry at the University of Oxford can be said to qualify'.[7]

A more ambiguous example of the role of portraiture in Ireland can be found in a 1999 film co-financed by British and Irish companies. In her sensitive if greatly altered film adaptation of Elizabeth Bowen's novel *The Last September*, Deborah Warner and her cinematographer Slawomir Idsiak visualise the peculiar relationship between contemporary inhabitants and past presences represented by family portraits on the walls of an Irish Big House.[8] Set in 1920, the last year of the Anglo-Irish War, the story is of Lois (played by Keeley Hawes), a niece of the owners of Danielstown, County Cork. In one beautifully filmed scene (fig.4) set in the hallway of the Big House, Lois is unexpectedly kissed by her admirer, Gerald, a British soldier stationed nearby in Fermoy. As she takes in the consequences of this act her face is reflected in the glass covering one of the seventeenth-century female portraits hanging in the hall. The juxtaposition of Lois's face and that of her female ancestor is held for some seconds, only to be interrupted by the sounding of the gong for lunch. Later in the film, after events have unfolded and Lois decides to

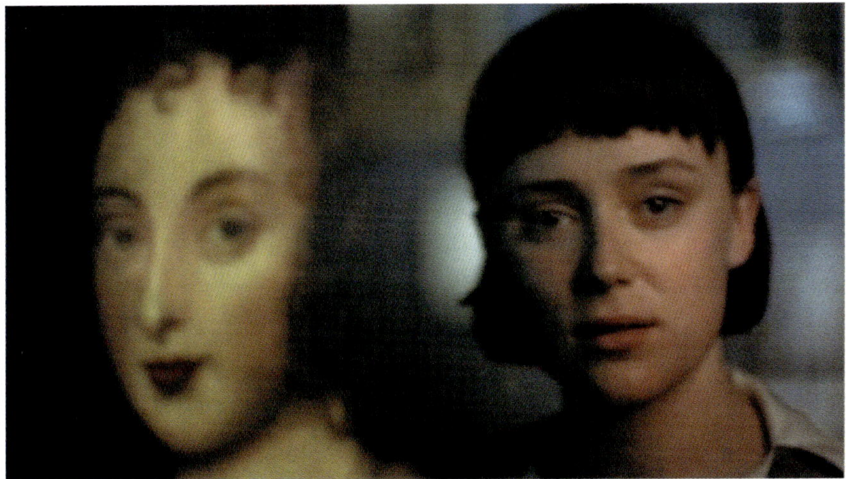

4. **Lois and a seventeenth-century ancestor in**
The Last September (1999)
Directed by DEBORAH WARNER
Trimark pictures

leave Danielstown, we view her departure again reflected in the glazing of another seventeenth-century family portrait, this time a moustachioed male ancestor in a lace collar. Warner is asking us to ponder on how Lois needs to break away from the contemporary world of the Anglo-Irish War and the burdens of history.

Warner's visual juxtapositions are fully justified in that Elizabeth Bowen, in the original novel, frequently refers to the family portraits that decorate the walls of the fictional Danielstown. This Big House, the centrepiece of her narrative, is itself a carefully drawn re-creation of her own home, Bowen's Court, also situated in north County Cork. Not surprisingly, eighteenth- and nineteenth-century portraits had in reality dressed the walls of Bowen's Court: indeed, six family portraits feature as illustrations in her acclaimed historical survey of that house.[9] Towards the end of this autobiographical history, the author discusses a portrait of her grandfather, Robert Cole Bowen, painted in 1881 by a local Cork-based artist and comments on how it hung

> on an end wall of the Bowen's Court dining-room, some way above the chair where he used to sit. Robert confronts all time . . . with a glass-blue stare . . . Below his great father-beard, a beard forked like that of Moses, glints a seal hung from a fob . . . [He] sits before Mr Brenan, the hired artist, in a tolerant lump.[10]

This short passage from *Bowen's Court* (1942) is but a continuation of an earlier concern in *The Last September* (1929), where the author's imaginative description of the relationship between painted images of the past and the reality of the present generation are used to the disadvantage of the twentieth-century Sir Richard and Lady Naylor (Lois's uncle and aunt) and their guests. This subtle use of portraits in the story is exhibited to excellent effect in an early passage describing a dinner scene. The complexity of Bowen's language demands that the whole paragraph be quoted:

> In the dining-room, the little party sat down under the crowd of portraits. Under the constant interchange from the high-up faces staring across – now fading each to a wedge of fawn-colour, and each looking out from a square of

darkness tunnelled into the wall – Sir Richard and Lady Naylor, their nephew, niece and old friends had a thin, over-bright look, seemed on the air of the room unconvincingly painted, startled, transitory. Spaced out accurately round the enormous table – whereon, in what was left of the light, damask birds and roses had an unearthly shimmer – each so enisled and distant that a remark at random, falling short of a neighbour, seemed a cry of appeal, the six, in spite of an emphasis of speech and gesture they unconsciously heightened, dwindled personally. While above, the immutable figures, shedding on to the wash of dusk smiles, frowns, every vestige of personality, kept only attitude – an out-moded modestness, a quirk or a flare, hand slipped under a ruffle or spread airily over the cleft of a bosom – cancelled time, negatived personality and made of the lower cheerfulness, dining and talking, the faintest exterior fiction.[11]

Longevity, Bowen suggests, belongs to the portraits, not to the living. The house with its visual records of its past cancels time and reduces the occupants to the role of perpetrators in a fiction. In *The Last September* the past is always looking over one's shoulder. Equally, as Warner's film so subtly implies, the past, as represented by a portrait, literally reflects the characters in the story; a portrait may only be seen fleetingly, yet it still carries power. The implication of all this is that portraits suggest memories and declare a history. It is that history, the role of the portrait in explaining the past, that concerns this book.

The compact solidity of McGuire's portrait of Seamus Heaney visually complements the robustness of the poet's first few volumes. Equally, the hesitant presence of the family portraits in Bowen's work and in the film adaptation of *The Last September* suggests the author's ambiguous relationship with the land of her birth. Yet both examples are firmly rooted in Ireland. The key to these portraits with regard to their 'Irishness' is the range of views, from the seemingly obvious in the case of the Heaney to the ambiguous in the case of Bowen. A further category is the tentative, images that have not necessarily been consistently discussed in terms of Irish visual history, yet need that connection if the full complexity of their interpretation is to be understood. Two examples will briefly illustrate this additional category: the first is a portrait of an Elizabethan adventurer in Ireland, although the object itself never went nor, in all honestly, needed to go to Ireland; the second is a royal portrait from the early nineteenth century of which there are many versions, one of which can claim 'Irishness' by the fact that it was commissioned by the City of Dublin.

Marcus Gheeraerts the Younger's portrait of Captain Thomas Lee (fig.5) is one of the earliest full-length oil portraits of a known individual affecting an Irish disposition. As has been well argued elsewhere, Tom Lee dresses as an Irish kerne or foot soldier so as to impress the court of Elizabeth I with his potential for negotiating with the

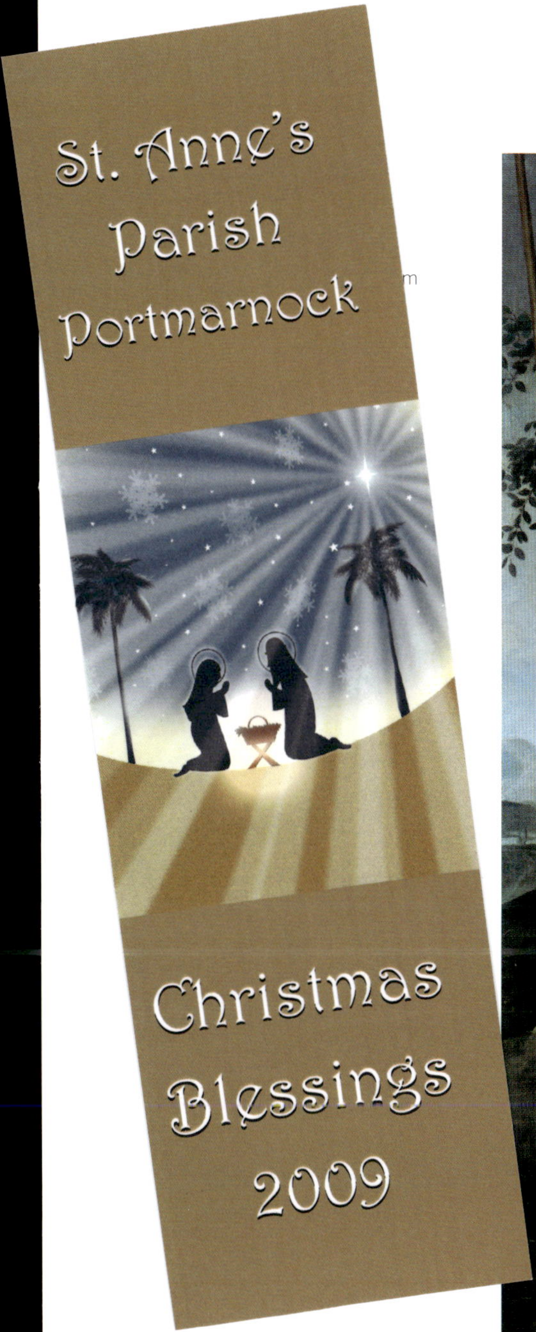

St. Anne's
Parish
Portmarnock

Christmas
Blessings
2009

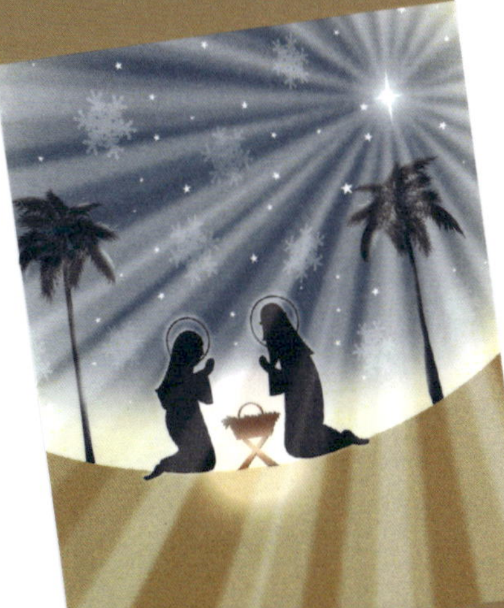

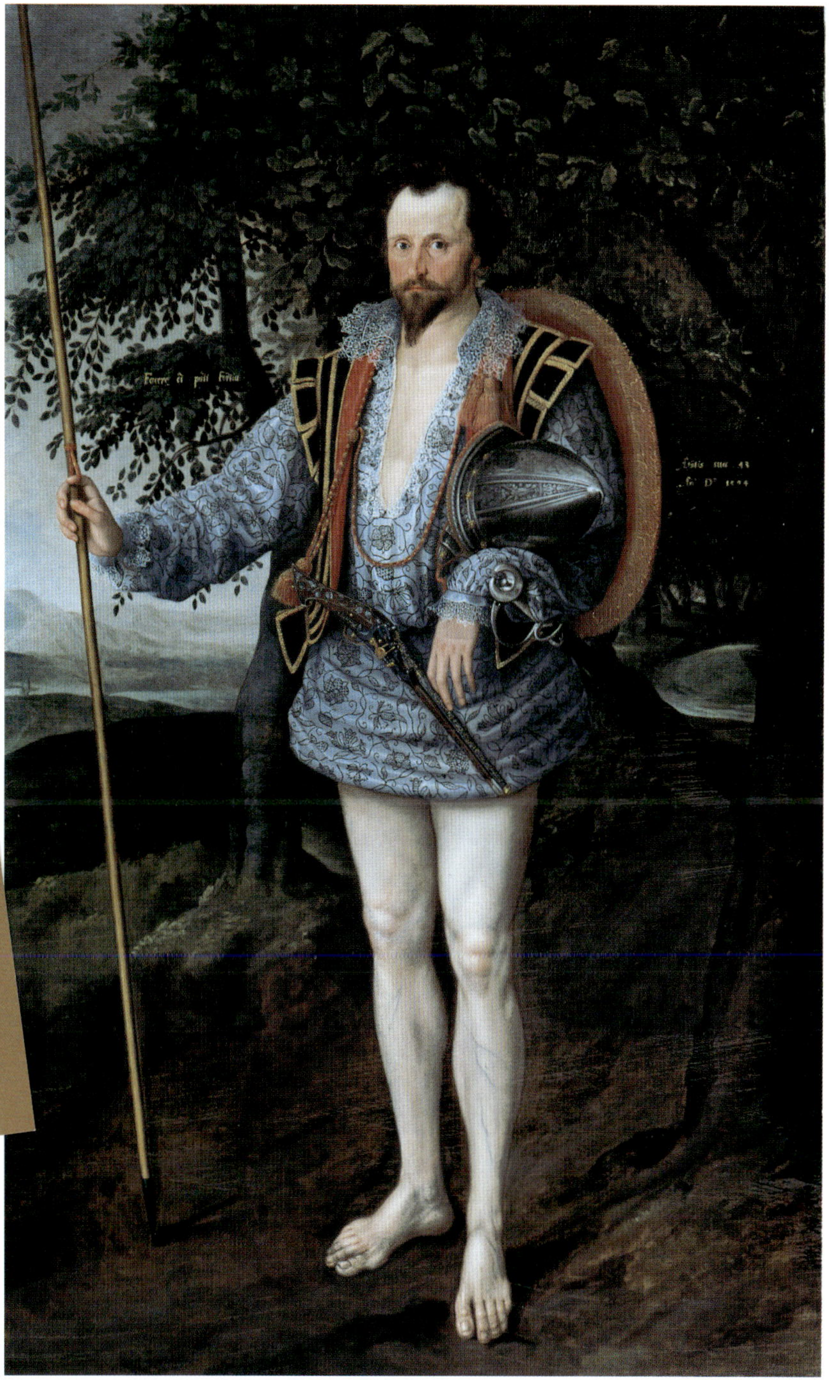

6. **George IV** (1762–1830)
THOMAS LAWRENCE (1818–21)
Oil on canvas, 3048 × 2053mm
(120 × 81")
Dublin City Collection

Although sporting various Royal
Orders, in this portrait the king
is not wearing the collar of the
Order of St Patrick. The king rests
his right hand on the *Table des
Grands Capitaines*, commissioned
by Napoleon but presented by
Louis XVIII to the Prince Regent
in 1817.

native Irish, in particular his old friend, the arch-traitor, Hugh O'Neill, the Earl of Tyrone and leader of the Gaelic confederates in Ulster.[12] Lee, an experienced campaigner in Ireland since at least 1574, presumably requested Gheeraerts to paint him within an Irish landscape, bare-legged in the Irish fashion yet also equipped with an embossed helmet, an elaborate pistol and a beautifully rendered shirt with lace cuffs. Lee also includes a Latin inscription from Livy, which refers to an event that had led to a 'lasting peace'[13] between Rome and the Etruscans, thus implying that he could do the same for Ireland and England. Although this is a painting by a Flemish artist of an Englishman appearing in an Irish disguise, it can still be considered, just like McGuire's Heaney, in terms of the Irish portrait. Focus on Gheeraerts's painting since at least the mid-nineteenth century has been on its iconography of an Englishman in Ireland. A commentator in the *Irish Times* of 1868 was clearly amused that it had been 'vaguely described as "of Ireland"' in the catalogue of the third South Kensington Portrait exhibition. In a description of the picture for his readers back in Dublin, which is clearly tongue-in-cheek, the journalist ridicules Lee's pretentious appearance:

> The way the artist indicates [Lee's] high descent, by showing the 'blue blood'
> in the many visible but by no means varicose veins of his extremely shapely
> legs, is an effort which I would rather leave it to Mr Ruskin to expound … The
> transparent whiteness of [his] garment, the extravagance of the embroidery
> rivet the eyes of the spectator . . . One of the Kings of the Sandwich Islands
> had an idea that a cocked hat and a pair of top boots constitutes full dress . . .
> Lee appears to have thought that a laced shirt was enough to distinguish him
> from Adam . . . so attired it may be supposed, he attended the Drawingrooms
> at the Castle.[14]

More recently, the portrait of Thomas Lee has been on public exhibition at the Tate Gallery for at least a generation. Such exposure has led one historian to comment that its display (along with John Michael Wright's portrait of Sir Neil O'Neill [also owned by Tate Britain, fig.91]) 'give[s] the Irish periphery a hitherto unacknowledged but not undeserved centrality in the Tudor-Stuart experience'.[15]

In early 2002 the National Gallery of Ireland held a small exhibition of royal portraits, mainly based on objects in their collection, entitled *The Monarch's Head*. Portraits of Anne Boleyn, a Hogarth of George III and his family and a life-sized bronze of the same king as a Roman Emperor, which once stood under the dome of the Royal Exchange, now Dublin's City Hall, were displayed with wall panels describing various visits to Dublin by reigning monarchs. The highlight of this exhibition was undoubtedly the English artist Thomas Lawrence's splendid full-length portrait of George IV (fig.6), on loan from the City of Dublin's collection, which was admired by Charles, Prince of Wales, who happened to be visiting Ireland. *The*

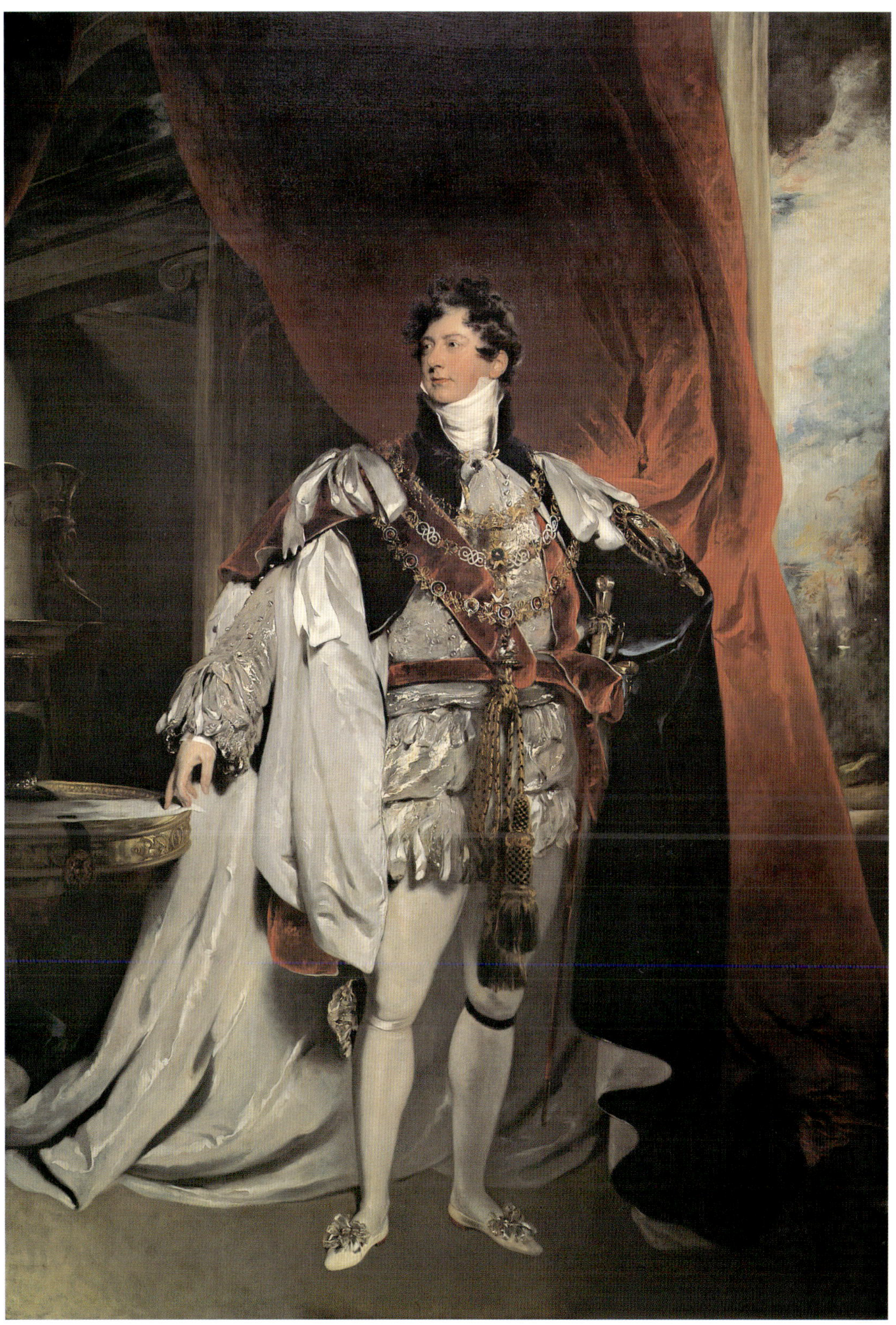

Monarch's Head was the first such exhibition dedicated to the British monarchy held in the National Gallery of Ireland.[16] For the National Gallery to have mounted such a show with confidence and for the heir to the British throne to have visited Dublin freely are testament to the new rapprochement that has developed between Ireland and Britain since the Good Friday Agreement of 1998. And yet the presence of a large number of royal portraits in public institutions may surprise some visitors to Ireland. While taking a guided tour of the State Apartments in Dublin Castle or strolling through the Picture Gallery in Kilkenny Castle, or while viewing the portraits in the dining halls of the Royal Hospital at Kilmainham or of Trinity College Dublin, it will become all too clear that the Republic of Ireland is not short of royal portraits, from Elizabeth I through Charles II to Frederick, Prince of Wales, and a roll-call of Georges.[17]

John Hughes's great memorial in stone to Queen Victoria unveiled in 1908 was originally intended for the forecourt of Leinster House, the then headquarters of the Royal Dublin Society. After 1924, when this fine eighteenth-century house became the seat of the Irish parliament, Victoria's monument was seen as an anomaly and repeated calls were made for its removal. Finally, after forty years overlooking

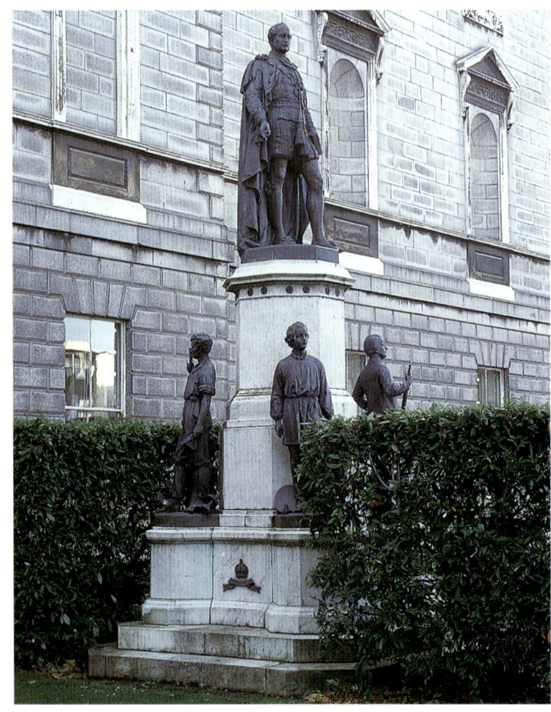

7. **Albert Memorial**
JOHN HENRY FOLEY (unveiled 1871)
Bronze and limestone
Leinster Lawn, Dublin

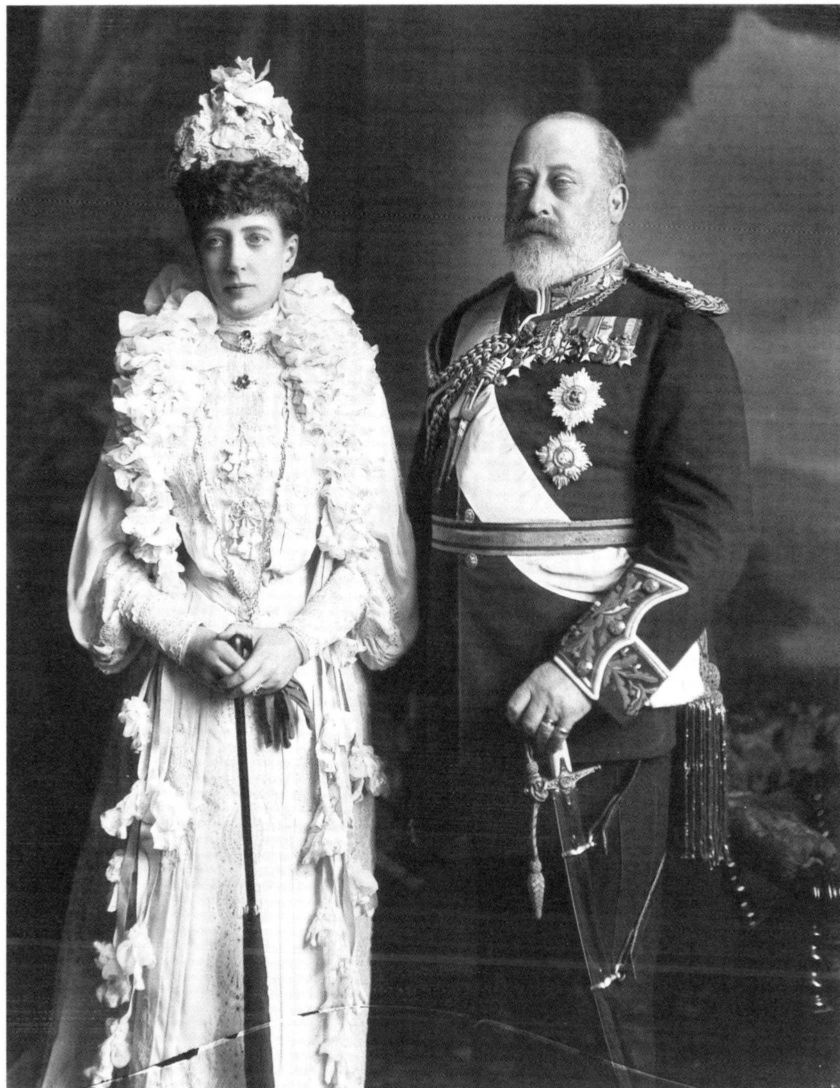

Kildare Street, the monument was condemned to another forty years in storage. In 1987 the figure of Victoria, though this time minus her bronze supports of *Peace, Fame* and *Erin with a Dead Soldier*, was resurrected as a feature outside the Queen Victoria Building, Bicentennial Plaza, Sydney, Australia, a gift of 'the people of Ireland/in a spirit of good will and friendship'.[18] Although Victoria was removed from the front of Leinster House, John Henry Foley's statue of her husband, Albert, the Prince Consort (1872), still stands at the rear, even if somewhat forlorn, tucked next to the Natural History Museum and in a hedge (fig.7). Meanwhile, Victoria and Albert's son Edward VII and his wife Queen Alexandra have the Dublin photographic company of Lafayette to thank for the fine portrait taken during their highly successful visit to Ireland in July 1903 (fig.8). The photograph proved to be 'one of the most reproduced portraits of the year'.[19]

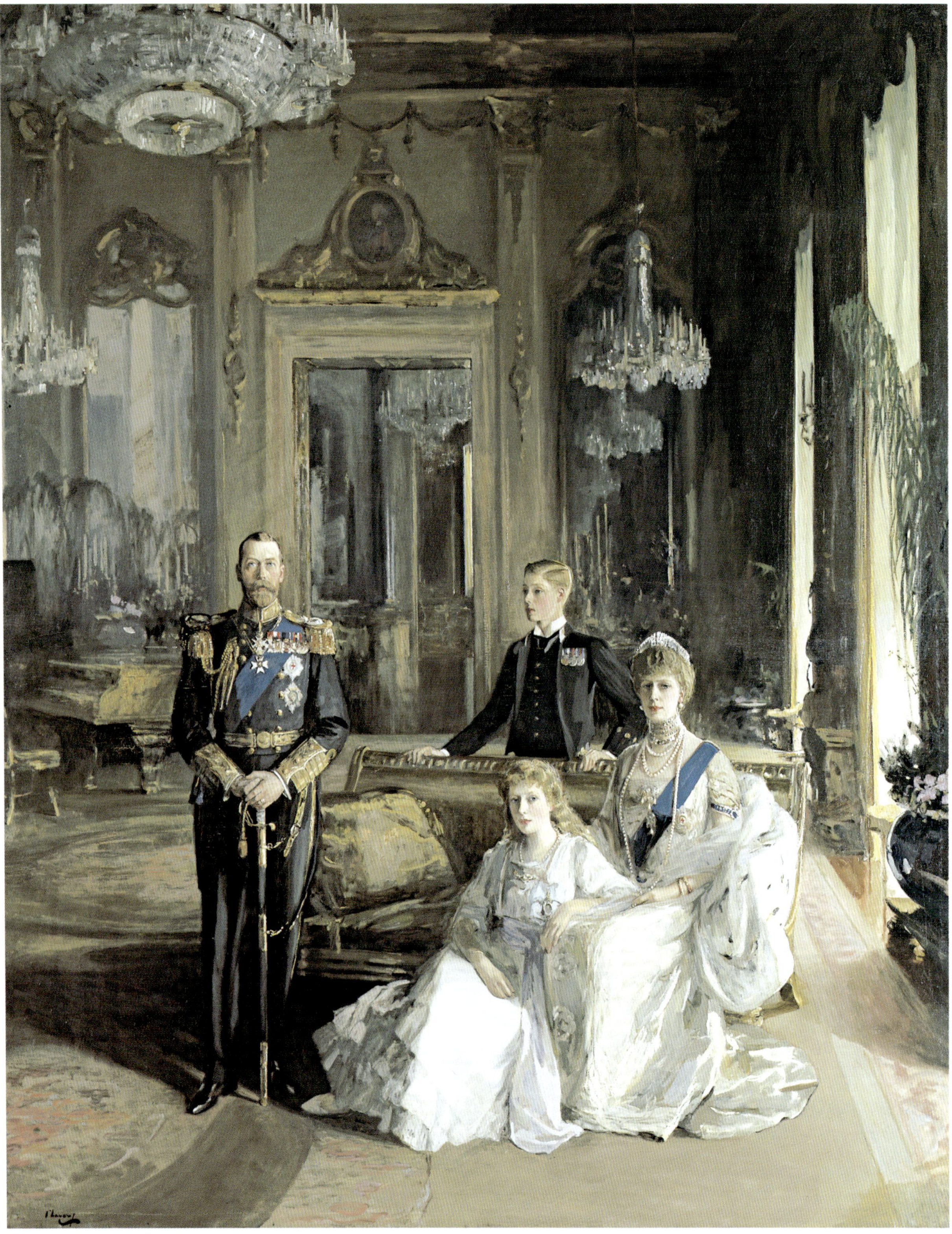

A final Irish contribution to this litany of royal images is Sir John Lavery's large canvas of the family of George V (fig.9) which, unlike the other royal representations discussed here, boasts no relationship with Dublin. Yet this is a portrait by an Irishman who espoused republican values of the last British monarch to rule over the whole of the island of Ireland. The finished version of Lavery's 1913 painting, showing George V with Queen Mary and two of his children amidst the splendour of the White Drawing Room at Buckingham Palace, now hangs in the National Portrait Gallery, London, while a smaller oil study is, appropriately enough, in the artist's home town and can be seen in the Ulster Museum, Belfast. As a man who always played it safe when it came to political divisions, Lavery suggests in his chatty autobiography that he presented the oil sketch of the royal family to Belfast Art Gallery as it then was, in 1919, at the same time as he presented an altarpiece to St Patrick's Church, 'to show the other side that I was not a bigot'.[20]

One should thus not be too surprised to find the portrait by Lawrence of George IV in the collection of the City of Dublin (fig.6). Celebrating the first visit to Ireland by a ruling monarch since James II and VII's ill-fated visit prior to losing the Battle of the Boyne in 1690, the Lawrence was presented to Dublin's Protestant-dominated Corporation by the king in August 1821. Painted just twenty years after Ireland had joined the United Kingdom, this lavish essay in colour and personal pride shows the king dressed in Garter robes but sporting no less than two other collars of distinguished orders. Surprisingly, George failed to get Lawrence to add the collar of the Order of St Patrick to his portrait, given that the king wore the full regalia of this Order at an installation of a Catholic earl, Fingall, along with eight other new knights during his Dublin visit. Shown publicly in Dublin almost a decade later, at the Royal Hibernian Academy's annual exhibition in the summer of 1830, possibly out of respect for the king's death in June of that year, the Dublin royal portrait had not only established, as Kenneth Garlick has discussed, 'the type for the official portraits' of the king; more importantly, its elaborate frame, with a large gold-leafed scroll and inscription, publicly declared its Irish dimension.[21] Indeed, that Irish dimension was a key element in Dublin Corporation's fulsome acceptance of the king's portrait in 1821:

> ... we shall accept, Sire, the boon with thankfulness and joy and cherish it through life as one of the proudest gifts subjects could receive at the hands of their King. As we behold it adorning the Mansion of our Chief Magistrate, it will call to our recollection him who has not been more the Sovereign than the father of his subjects, who when some of the mightiest potentates crouched beneath the stroke of despotism stood undismayed in the midst of surrounding perils ...[22]

The Dublin version of Lawrence's George IV originally hung in the Round Room, constructed behind the city's Mansion House in 1821 specifically for the reception of that monarch during his few days in Ireland. This royal visit was an occasion of civic 'harmony' during a period dominated by the Catholic question: Jacqueline Hill has discussed 'the interdenominational co-operation' in evidence at the 'coronation dinner' that marked the king's visit, while the *Freeman's Journal* commented that 'things look indeed as if we should at last be O N E P E O P L E'.[23] But given a rising Catholic challenge to the Protestant oligarchy, such sentiments soon evaporated and the spirit of 'conciliation' in which the Lawrence portrait had been presented did not survive the nineteenth century. By the early twentieth century, the portrait had become the victim of regime change.

Still hanging on the balcony of the Mansion House Round Room in 1919, Lawrence's George IV overlooked the assembly of the first Dáil Éireann on 21 January to adopt Ireland's Declaration of Independence and ratify the proclamation of the Irish Republic by the insurgents of 1916. Even by August 1921, when the second Dáil was called in the same venue, contemporaneous photographs show that large portraits of former Lord Mayors still decorated the walls along the balcony and, although not discernible in these images, one may presume that Lawrence's portrait presided over the rejection of Lloyd George's first settlement offer as well as the eventual approval of the Anglo-Irish Treaty in January 1922. Seventeen years later, in July 1939, and two years after the passing of a new constitution and the creation of the post of the President of Ireland, Lawrence's portrait of George IV was removed from the Round Room by the then Lord Mayor of Dublin, Caitlín Bean Uí Chléirigh (Kathleen Clarke). As the widow of the executed leader of the 1916 Rising, Tom Clarke, Bean Uí Chléirigh was 'totally opposed to having any royal images in the mayoral residence'. After many years in storage, the portrait was not re-hung in the Mansion House until May 1995, this time in the inner hallway of the residence, where it was unveiled by the Prince of Wales during his first visit to Dublin. And there it hangs today.[24]

Within a few years of Caitlín Bean Uí Chléirigh sending George IV into storage, a similar case of artistic iconoclasm was affecting other royal portraits that had hung for many generations in the former Viceregal Lodge in Phoenix Park. Occupied from 1938 by Douglas Hyde (fig.40), the first President of Ireland, the name of the Lodge was changed to Áras an Uachtaráin (or House of the President). In 1942 the president's private secretary complained that portraits of Victoria and Albert in the Drawing Room were attracting adverse comments from visitors to the Áras. The civil servant involved, Michael McDunphy, specifically requested that inappropriate portraits such as Charles Wellington Furse's splendid three-quarter-length of the 7th Earl of Aberdeen (c.1889–90; fig.10), commissioned in 1886 during his first period of office as Lord Lieutenant and hanging on the Prince's Staircase, should be removed. Aberdeen, who was to return for a second term from 1906 to 1915, was a firm supporter of Home Rule and is shown in pensive mood, wearing a Campbell

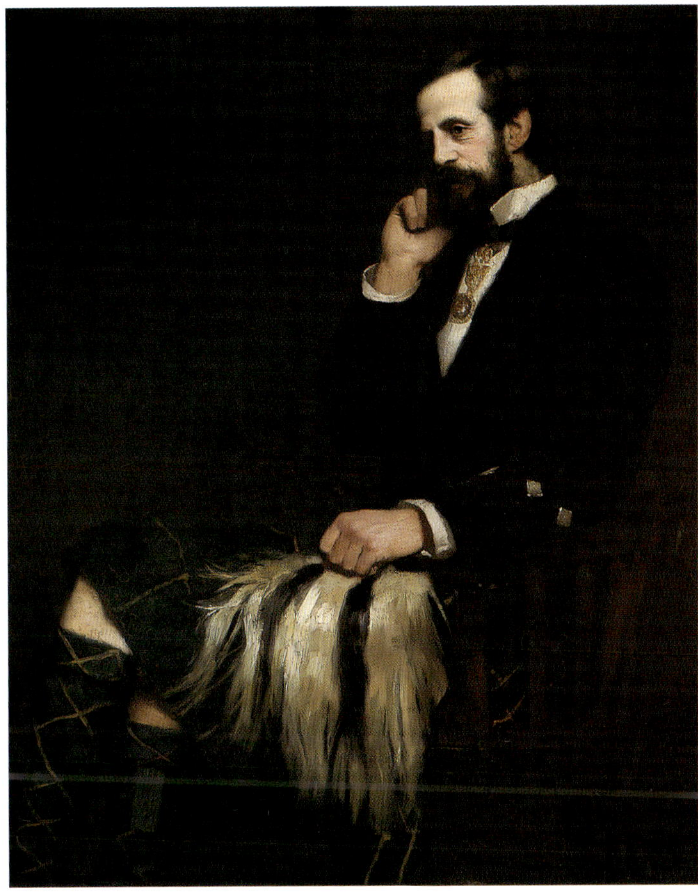

tartan kilt and an impressive sporran as well as the ribbon and badge of the Order of St Patrick. But regardless of aesthetic quality and along with many other portraits, Aberdeen soon joined Victoria and Albert in storage in the Coach House of Dublin Castle.[25]

In their place, Douglas Hyde and his advisers hung a rather indifferent 'pictorial record of Irish history'. Plaster busts of recent Irish leaders hung next to engravings after patriots of the eighteenth and nineteenth centuries. An 1830s engraving after Hugh Douglas Hamilton's late eighteenth-century portrait of Lord Edward FitzGerald (fig.101) is in the collection but so too is Thomas Robinson's large canvas representing the Battle of Ballynahinch (fig.11), a painting that depicts the defeat of Irish rebels in County Down on 12 and 13 June 1798.[26] The mere survival of the painting has led some historians to accept Robinson's declaration of the image's veracity, reading it

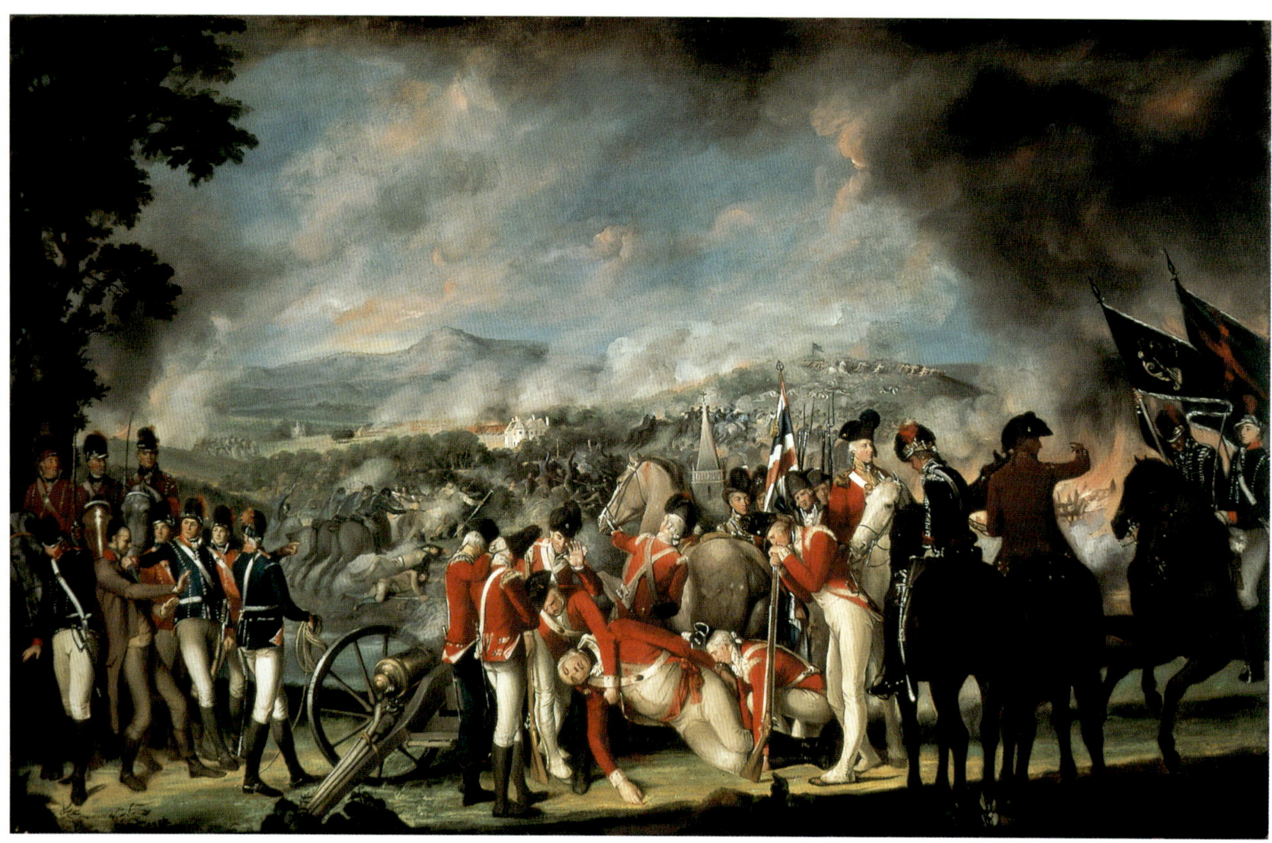

11. **The Battle of Ballynahinch**
THOMAS ROBINSON (1798)
Oil on canvas, 1300 × 2100mm
(51⅛ × 82⅝")
Office of Public Works, Dublin

as being 'unusual in its realism', while recently it has graced a number of book covers as a silent illustration to studies on 1798.[27] The inclusion of such a loyalist oddity in the original Áras collection – and in reaction to its underanalysed portrayal of the rebellion – makes a short discussion of the painting appropriate.

A number of the main figures in Robinson's painting have been identified, thus turning this historical re-enactment into a series of what Robinson called, in an advertisement in the *Belfast News-Letter* of 6 November 1798 which accompanied the exhibition of the painting, a collection of 'many *original Portraits*'. This notice went on to say that the scene, which had only taken place less than four months earlier, 'is a faithful representation of the *Field of Battle and its Events*'.[28] In the centre is the mortally wounded Captain Henry Evatt, adjutant of the Monaghan militia, while on the far right, with his back to us and gesticulating, is Major-General George Nugent, the commander-in-chief of the Northern district. On the far left, surrounded by men from the Irish yeomanry cavalry and militia, we see the arrested United Irish colonel, Hugh McCulloch, a grocer from Bangor, being taken off to be hanged. Beyond, a rout of the United Irish camp on Edenavaddy Hill is taking place, while on the far right two captured 'Liberty' standards, one bearing a yellow harp against a field of green, are about to be presented to General Nugent.

Robinson's painting is clearly reminiscent of Benjamin West's *Death of Wolfe* (1770; National Gallery of Canada, Ottawa) of a quarter of a century earlier, in terms of both theme and composition.[29] In both paintings a British soldier falls to the ground, surrounded by his colleagues, all of whom are deeply affected as if by a personal tragedy; and yet in both, death is at the moment of victory. In West's painting British defeat of the French at Quebec is visualised by gesture on the far left of the canvas, while in the Robinson, Nugent, who is profiled against a burning home-stead, gestures acceptance of the captured United Irish flags. These flags play an important role in underlining a vital visual contrast: military success at Ballynahinch is implied by balancing the group surrounding the doomed McCulloch on the left with the finality of the captured United Irish flags on the right. Colour, too, plays a part in the visualisation of meaning. The red coats of the Irish yeomanry and the blue of the militia dominate the foreground, yet there are subtle inclusions of alter-native colour-coded signifiers. The furled Union flag situated just right of centre distracts us from the green flag on top of Edenavaddy Hill, while McCulloch, the only rebel to be individualised, wears a green kerchief around his neck. It is this piece of subversive clothing that the yeoman grabs as he pulls the United Irishman to the gallows. This spot of green is echoed by the equally 'captured' green of the flags on the far right of the painting. An eye-witness account informs us of the 'wearing of green' at Ballynahinch, 'almost every individual having a knot of ribbons of that colour'.[30] Robinson deliberately reduces the potency of the colour green; his canvas thus becomes a salutary reminder to an Ulster audience of the consequences of rebellion. This message is, of course, strengthened for the specta-tor by the central positioning of the dead captain, a known Orangeman. He in turn is flanked not only by his men but by a field gun and a riderless horse, both of which act as metaphors for British supremacy over the ill-equipped pikemen who lie massacred beyond. Robinson, as a true propagandist for the loyalist cause, focuses our immediate attention on the central figure of the dead Evatt surrounded by weeping soldiers. In reality, the Captain was only one of three men that Nugent lost at Ballynahinch; the rebels, by contrast, lost several hundred.[31]

Despite his claim in the *Belfast News-Letter*, Robinson did not base his composi-tion on any strict fidelity to events as they happened in June 1798: rather, he created a loaded discourse between the opposing sides, the captured McCulloch and his lost standards surrounded by a ruthless military. While the tone of Hyde's original collection at Áras an Uachtaráin may have been predominantly nationalist, the inclusion of Robinson's painting is intriguing due to such loyalist bias. It is thus ironic that just as the President's Office was firing off letters to the Office of Public Works to remove royalist icons of a former Ireland, the State accepted the gift of a canvas mourning the death of an Orangeman and the capture of a rebel.

Sixty years after the bequest of Robinson's *Ballynahinch*, the royal portraits that had been so unceremoniously removed from the Áras have been rescued, carefully conserved and rehung in Dublin Castle. It is thus hoped that we can now begin to broaden our definition of what constitutes an Irish face. It can include McGuire's Heaney (fig.1) and Lord Edward FitzGerald (fig.101) as well as the ostentatious posing of George IV (fig.6) and the features of the dying Captain Evatt in Robinson's canvas. As these various examples show, and when involving the relationship between Ireland and Britain, the approach to the topic of a 'national' portrait is not always as easy as it may seem.

NOTES

1 Quoted in Saumarez Smith, 1997, p.11; see the rest of the Introduction to this book for a very cogent history of the National Portrait Gallery.

2 Black, 2000, p.64; Heaney, 1975, reverse of paperback edn.

3 For a discussion of the painting and the poem see Fallon, 1991, pp.55–6. These three stanzas end the poem as it appears in Heaney, 1991, pp. 24–5.

4 Walker, 1987, p.24.

5 Walker, 1987, p.24

6 The National Portrait Gallery images of Heaney can be viewed on www.npg.org.uk.

7 Retold with permission of Charles Saumarez Smith (2002).

8 *The Last September*, 1999, a Scala Thunder/ Matrix Film Co. Production.

9 Bowen, 1942.

10 Bowen, 1942, p.268, illus. facing p.236. Bowen is referring to James Butler Brenan (1825–89).

11 Bowen, 1998, p.24.

12 Morgan, 1993, pp.132–65. See also Hearn, 1995, pp.176–7.

13 '[Et] facere et pati fortia [Romanum est]' ([Both] to do and endure valiantly [is the Roman way]), spoken by Gaius Mucius Scaevola in Livy's *History of Rome*; see Morgan, 1993, p.143.

14 *The Irish Times*, 15 June 1868.

15 Morgan, 1993, p.160. The Wright painting may have been painted in Dublin: see Crookshank and Glin, 2002, p.20.

16 Le Harivel, 2002; for Prince of Wales's visit see *The Irish Times*, 15 May 2002.

17 See Kennedy, 1999; Fenlon, 2001; Crookshank and Webb, 1990.

18 Quoted in Whelan, 2003, p.201; for Hughes see also Murphy, 2001, pp.38–43.

19 For Lafayette see Pepper, 1998, pp.6–7 and Chandler, 2001, pp.86–9.

20 Lavery, 1940, p.208; for the Royal Portraits see also McConkey, 1984, p.73 and McConkey, 1993, pp.121–2.

21 Garlick, 1989, p.194; Levey, 1979, no.33. The scroll reads: 'His Majesty, King George IV th. Presented to the Corporation of Dublin by his Most Gracious Majesty in commemoration of his visit to Ireland AD 1821. Painted by Sir Thomas Lawrence, RHA [*sic*].'

22 Gilbert, 1889–1944, vol.17 (1916), p.363. My thanks to Mary Clark, Dublin City Archivist, for this reference. A year later, in 1822, Dublin Corporation requested their 'highly dignified countryman', the recently victorious and Irish-born Duke of Wellington, to sit for his portrait 'to be placed in the Mansion House near to that of our beloved King as a lasting testimony of our high esteem and approbation' (Gilbert, 1889–1944, vol.17 [1916], pp.437–8).

23 Hill, 1997, pp.321–3.

24 Mary Clark, Dublin City Archives, email communication 3 September 2002. For a photograph of an early meeting of Dáil Éireann in Keogh Collection, National Library of Ireland (KE 219) see National Library of Ireland, 2002, dated under 1921.

25 File P1149 National Archives, Dublin, Michael McDunphy (Douglas Hyde's Private Secretary): 'Recommendations re removal of paintings from the Áras in 1939–40s', 17 August 1942 (written to Office of Public Works). My thanks to Jacquie Moore for this reference. McDunphy's letter refers to a dozen portraits: the Victoria portrait was by John Partridge and that of Albert by John Lucas, see Kennedy, 1999, pp.53–7 (illustrated); for the Aberdeen portrait see pp.34–6.

26 *Art in State Buildings 1922–1970*, p.19; McDunphy, 1945.

27 Crookshank and Glin, 1969, p.61 (entry by Thomas Pakenham). As a book cover, among others, see Pakenham, 1969, and Pakenham, 1997; also, Bardon, 1992.

28 Quoted in *Irish Portraits*, p.60; for Robinson see also Crookshank and Glin, 2002, pp.172–4.

29 For West's painting (1770) see von Erffa and Staley, 1986, no.93, pp.211–13.

30 James Thomson, then a boy of twelve, quoted in Bardon, 1992, p.235; see also Pakenham, 1969, pp.227–8.

31 Thomas Bartlett, 'Defence, Counter-Insurgency and Rebellion: Ireland, 1793–1803', in Bartlett and Jeffery, 1996, p.282.

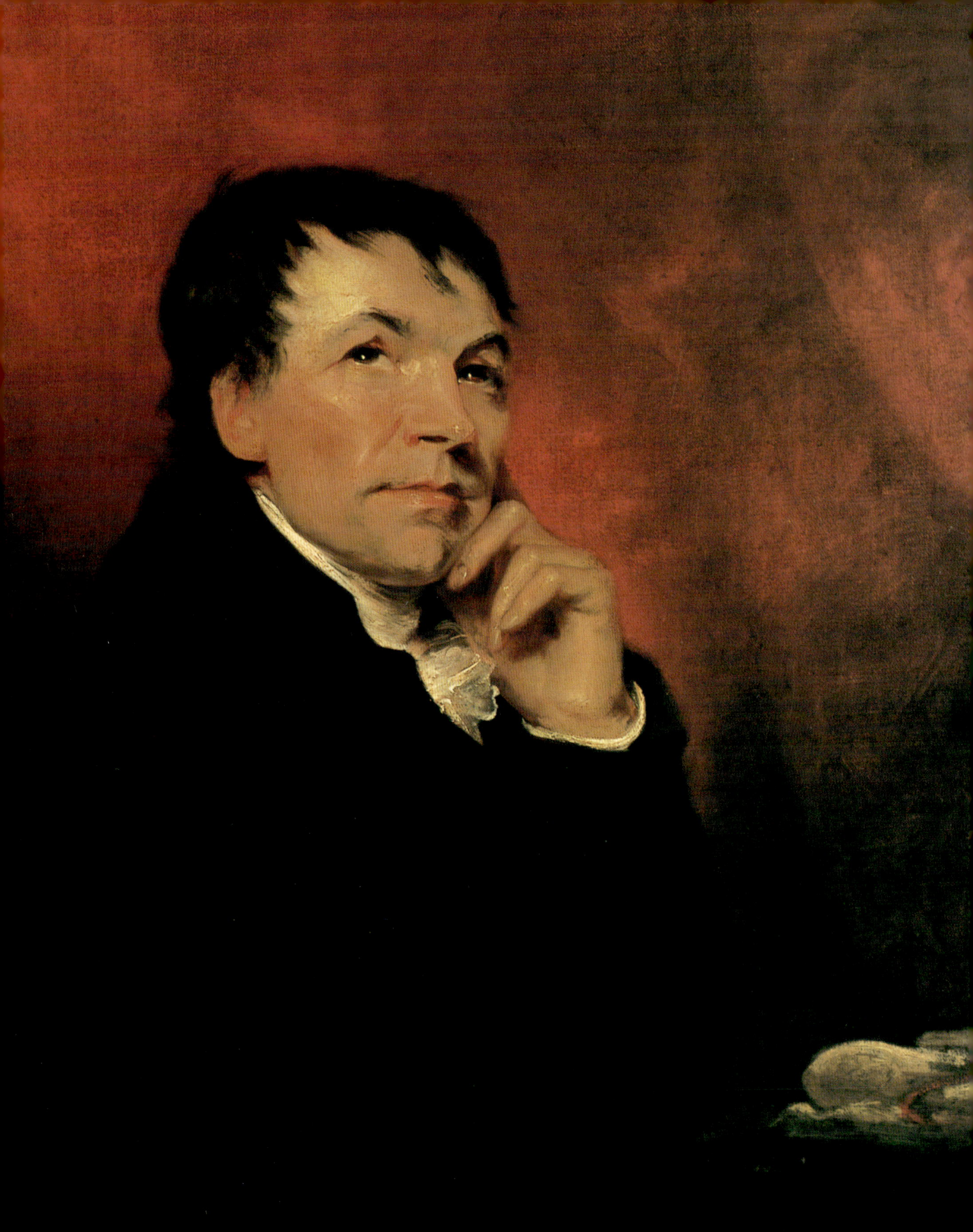

IN THE EIGHTEENTH and nineteenth centuries Ireland followed England in terms of the dominance of portraiture over all other forms of exhibited art. Portraits made up the largest percentage in any exhibition in Dublin prior to the founding of the Royal Hibernian Academy in 1824 and continue to hold a key position in that institution's annual show even today. While discussing the aesthetic motivation behind his hanging policy in the Academy's Gallagher Gallery, Liam Belton RHA, the academician who presently hangs the summer show, says that:

> In the past I tended to keep all the portraits together as it [the show] becomes more cohesive; but then lately I put unusual portraits among other works. One needs an element of surprise, something dynamic: it can't be too formulaic.[1]

In the nineteenth century four of the nine presidents of the Royal Hibernian Academy were portraitists. One of them, Stephen Catterson Smith (1806–72), a Yorkshire-born painter, gave up a respectable business in London, where his clients had included the royal family, to become portrait painter to the Lord Lieutenant of Ireland, a post he held for almost thirty years (as well as being President of the Royal Hibernian Academy on two occasions).[2] In addition to the display of contemporary portraits at such venues as the annual Royal Hibernian Academy show, historical portrait exhibitions became a popular adjunct to the many large-scale industrial exhibitions held in both Cork and Dublin from 1852 and 1853 respectively, after the initial success of London's Great Exhibition of 1851. In the early years of these exhibitions, historical portraits were hung with other examples of Irish art. But in 1872, at the *Dublin Exhibition of Arts, Industries, Manufactures and Loan Museum of Works of Art*, held in Earlsfort Terrace, a display of 630 portraits was included which has been interpreted by Cyril Barrett and Jeanne Sheehy as the 'nucleus of a national portrait gallery'.[3] The official catalogue carried a ringing endorsement of the venture:

> On the walls of the National Portrait Gallery the History of Ireland, from distant ages down to our own times, is now vividly portrayed . . . [they] cannot fail to render this National Department one in which every Irishman must feel a special pride and interest.[4]

Although it has been suggested recently that the idea of a national portrait gallery 'is a fundamentally English-speaking concept', shared by London, Edinburgh,

Dublin, Washington DC and most recently Canberra, Australia, Ireland has never actually enjoyed an independent national portrait collection.[5] The 'nucleus' that was evident in 1872 metamorphosed into a subsection of the National Gallery of Ireland that had been founded in 1864. Under the guidance of Henry Doyle, second Director of the Gallery, a portrait collection was formed. Doyle was himself a portrait painter; he also happened to buy some of the Gallery's important early Old Master paintings, such as works by Fra Angelico, Titian and Rembrandt. In 1872 he applied to the Treasury for a grant to establish an Irish National Portrait Gallery but was refused. All the same, by 1875 he had set aside a room in the Merrion Square building 'for the display of Irish portraits [which] was called the National, Historical and Portrait Gallery. There were 160 exhibits . . . and a catalogue published for a penny'.[6] Within a decade the National Gallery of Ireland had established quite a viable collection of national portraits and moved into a bigger apartment. By 1907 the space allotted to the Irish Portrait Collection was greatly increased to one room for portrait prints and 'a fine suite of octagonal rooms in the new wing of the gallery' to house oil portraits, miniatures and drawings.[7]

Back in 1872, the popularity of the idea of 'national portraiture' was such that the Dublin photographic firm of William Lawrence published a *List of Photographs of National Historical Portraits* from the Dublin Exhibition which offered the public some 300 images, including such romantic subjects as Lord Edward FitzGerald (fig.101) and his wife, Lady Pamela, after exhibited oils by Hugh Douglas Hamilton and George Romney. Photographs after John Comerford's miniature of Robert Emmet (fig.132), on loan from his family in New York, were also available. In addition, an independently published *Handbook* to the 1872 portrait exhibition written by Percy FitzGerald attempted to define the Irish portrait. In a suitably romantic flourish, the author defines the Irish interpretation of the genre as the representation of a 'struggle'. He then goes on to identify various virtues that distinguish Irish genius such as 'versatility', 'wit', 'readiness' and 'humour':

Few countries can show so much variety in their mental production, such dash and brilliancy, or toast such a company of men and women celebrated in every department. The Scotch may bring their sober and thrifty wares to an alien market and dispose of them there to the best advantage; and were a gallery of Scottish worthies collected, we would feel ourselves awed by the piercing and reflecting glances, the sharp twinkling eyes, the solemn sagacity which would beam from the frames. Respect and admiration would certainly be present, though interest and sympathy might be wanting. But with the Irishman of fame, some hard-fought battle of life, some tale of interest or adventure, some history, odd, eccentric, sad, humorous, or even astonishing, will be found associated. This is owing to the condition of the Irishman of

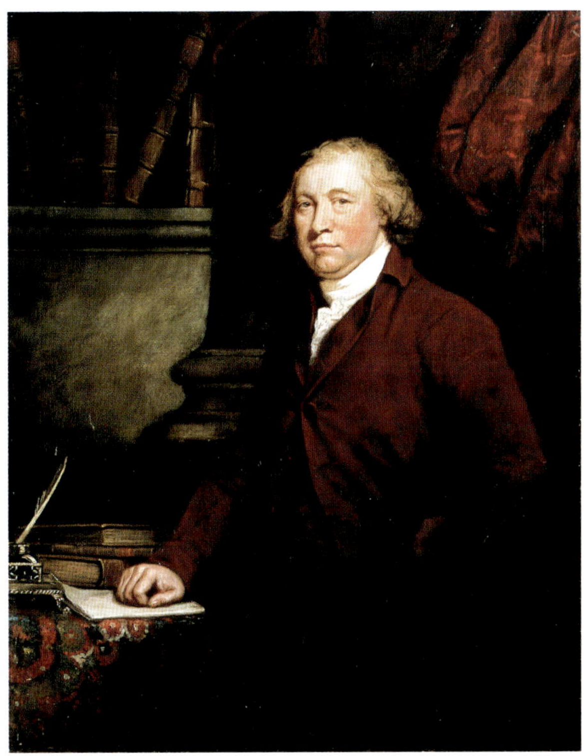

12. **Edmund Burke** (1729–97)
JAMES BARRY (C.1774)
Oil on canvas, 1270 × 990mm (50 × 39″)
National Gallery of Ireland, Dublin

Purchased in London for the National Gallery of Ireland in 1875, Barry's
portrait of his patron had been commissioned in 1772 by Burke's friend
Dr Brocklesby. The artist produced a number of other portraits of Burke,
the most important being fig.63, now in Cork.

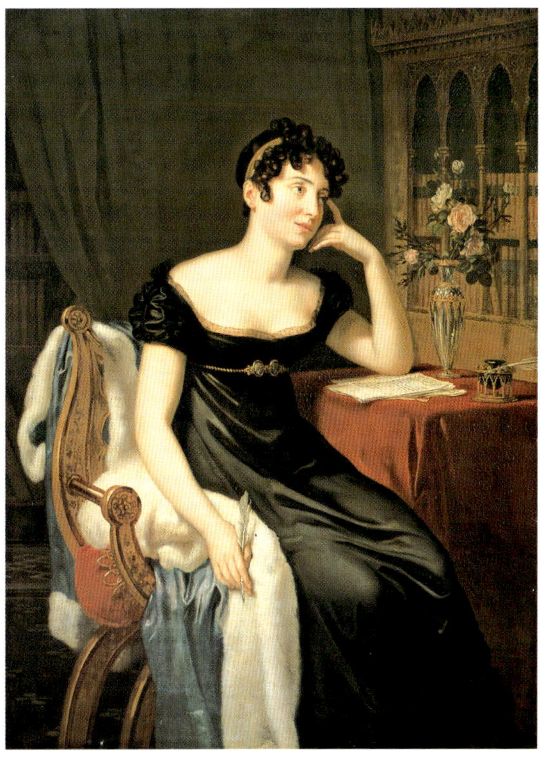

13. **Sydney Owenson, Lady Morgan** (C.1783–1859)
RENÉ BERTHON (1820s)
Oil on canvas, 1300 × 980mm (51⅛ × 38⅝″)
National Gallery of Ireland, Dublin

Painted in Paris by a pupil of Jacques Louis David, this highly
flattering representation of the novelist was offered in 1860 to
the newly established National Portrait Gallery in London. After
a perfunctory rejection by Lord Stanhope, first Chairman of the
NPG, the painting was accepted by Dublin's National Gallery.

genius having formerly had to take his wares to a (comparatively speaking) foreign market, and to struggle desperately under all the disadvantages of being a stranger.[8]

As Dublin's new national portrait collection developed in the 1870s, its political spread was relatively even. James Barry's serious portrait of the statesman Edmund Burke (fig.12) was an early purchase balanced by the more relaxed air of the novelist Sydney Owenson, Lady Morgan, as painted by the French artist René Berthon (fig.13). Superficially, both of these early acquisitions satisfy Percy FitzGerald's defining characteristic of the Irish portrait as representing a 'struggle', albeit not necessarily in the manner he intended. Purchased in 1875, Burke's portrait had been commissioned a hundred years earlier by Burke's close friend Dr Richard Brocklesby. The actual painting of the portrait took Barry some two years, due to the sitter's busy political schedule, much to the artist's annoyance. Although a late nineteenth-century commentator such as FitzGerald is happy to conjure up an image of the 'painter of genius, like Barry, struggling for a bare crust',[9] the facts of this particular commission were less to do with artistic 'struggle' and more to do with a mutual intransigence that seems to have set in between both sitter and artist. In an interesting exchange of letters dating from 1774, the long drawn-out minutiae of the sittings become apparent. Towards the end of the correspondence, Burke apologises to the artist:

> I waited on you exactly at half an hour after eleven, and had the pleasure of finding you at home; but as usual so employed as not to permit you to under-take this disagreeable business . . . Much as it might flatter my vanity to be painted by so eminent an artist, I assure you that, knowing I had no title to that honour, it was only in compliance with the desire (often repeated) of our common friend, that I have been so troublesome. You, who know the value of friendship, and the duties of it, I dare say, will have the goodness to excuse me on that plea.[10]

In keeping with the 1872 *Handbook*'s alignment of Irish portraiture and 'struggle', the bequest to Ireland shortly after the writer's death in 1859 of Berthon's portrait of Lady Morgan (fig.13) had more to do with finding a home for this large full-length painting than the romanticisation of exile which FitzGerald refers to as the 'condi-tion of the Irishman of genius'. In fact, this 1860 bequest 'to the Irish nation' predates the actual foundation of the National Gallery, but its acquisition by Dublin may well have been a reaction to the portrait having been rejected by the National Portrait Gallery in London. Philip Henry Stanhope, 5th Earl Stanhope and first Chairman of the London National Portrait Gallery, was fully justified in turning down the offer of the portrait from the author's family because, having only died in 1859, the romantic novelist did not satisfy the newly laid down ten-year rule. But in a letter to the London Gallery's Secretary and later its first Director, George Scharf, Stanhope underlined his opposition to including the author of *The Wild Irish Girl* by stating 'that the fame of Lady Morgan is much too slight – much too flimsy if I may so express myself – for the admission of her likeness into the chief National Collection'.[11] As Lara Perry has usefully suggested, Stanhope's dismissal of Lady Morgan's fame may have been due to his disregard for women novelists, but it might also have been tinged by a wish to distance his Gallery from what Morgan had called her 'Irish histories'. This series of Irish novels published between 1806 and 1827 had attempted, according to Tom Dunne, 'to promote the liberal Protestant leadership of the new Catholic democracy, and the consolidation of the imperial relationship'. Yet it had also spawned what Morgan herself called 'a genuine Irish novel'. Recalling *The Wild Irish Girl* in the preface of a new popular edition in 1846, the author claimed that it began a literary tradition 'founded on national grievances and borne out by

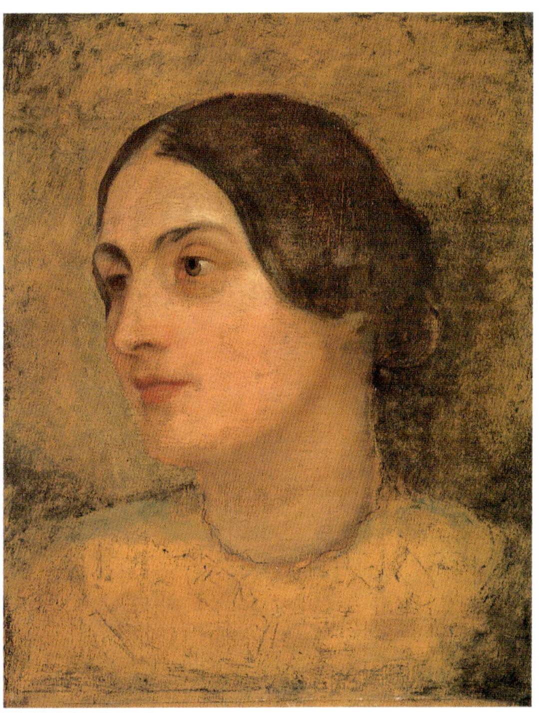

14. **Caroline Norton** (1808–77)
GEORGE FREDERICK WATTS
(1850)
Oil on canvas, 420 × 330mm
(16½ × 13″)
National Gallery of Ireland,
Dublin

Watt's unfinished sketch shows
the London-born granddaughter
of celebrated poet and novelist
R.B. Sheridan. Daniel Maclise
used her as a model for a
painting of *Erin*, as well as the
personification of Justice in a
mural in the House of Lords
(1845–7).

historic fact'.[12] Clearly Stanhope had no wish to introduce such a contentious discourse into his fledgling collection.

While not suitable for the 'chief National Collection' in London, Berthon's portrait of Lady Morgan was deemed acceptable to the periphery. Ireland's acceptance of this full-length grand romantic portrait of a lady of letters may well have been enlightened, but the portrait was to remain the only one of its type and gender for many years to come. Apart from a few modest roundels of other women writers, most notably Caroline Norton by G.F. Watts (fig.14), presented in 1887, the gender balance of the early decades of the Irish national portrait collection was defiantly male.

Reynolds's full-length portrait of the Irish aristocrat, Charles Coote, 1st Earl of Bellamont (fig.15), was purchased from Christie's in 1875, while within a decade the 4th Duke of Leinster would present a three-quarter-length of Bellamont's brother-in-law, the rebel Lord Edward FitzGerald (fig.101), whose iconography is discussed at length in Chapter 4. Meanwhile, portraits of major nineteenth-century Irishmen trickled into the collection, from images of politicians such as the Duke of Wellington (fig.16) and Daniel O'Connell (fig.17) to Lady Morgan's successors in developing the Irish novel, writers John Banim (fig.18) and William Carleton.

A few years later, between 1887 and 1888, the portrait collection was greatly increased by the acquisition of almost three hundred prints from the John Chaloner Smith collection. This great cache of largely mezzotint portraits included important works by major European contributors to the art of engraving such as the

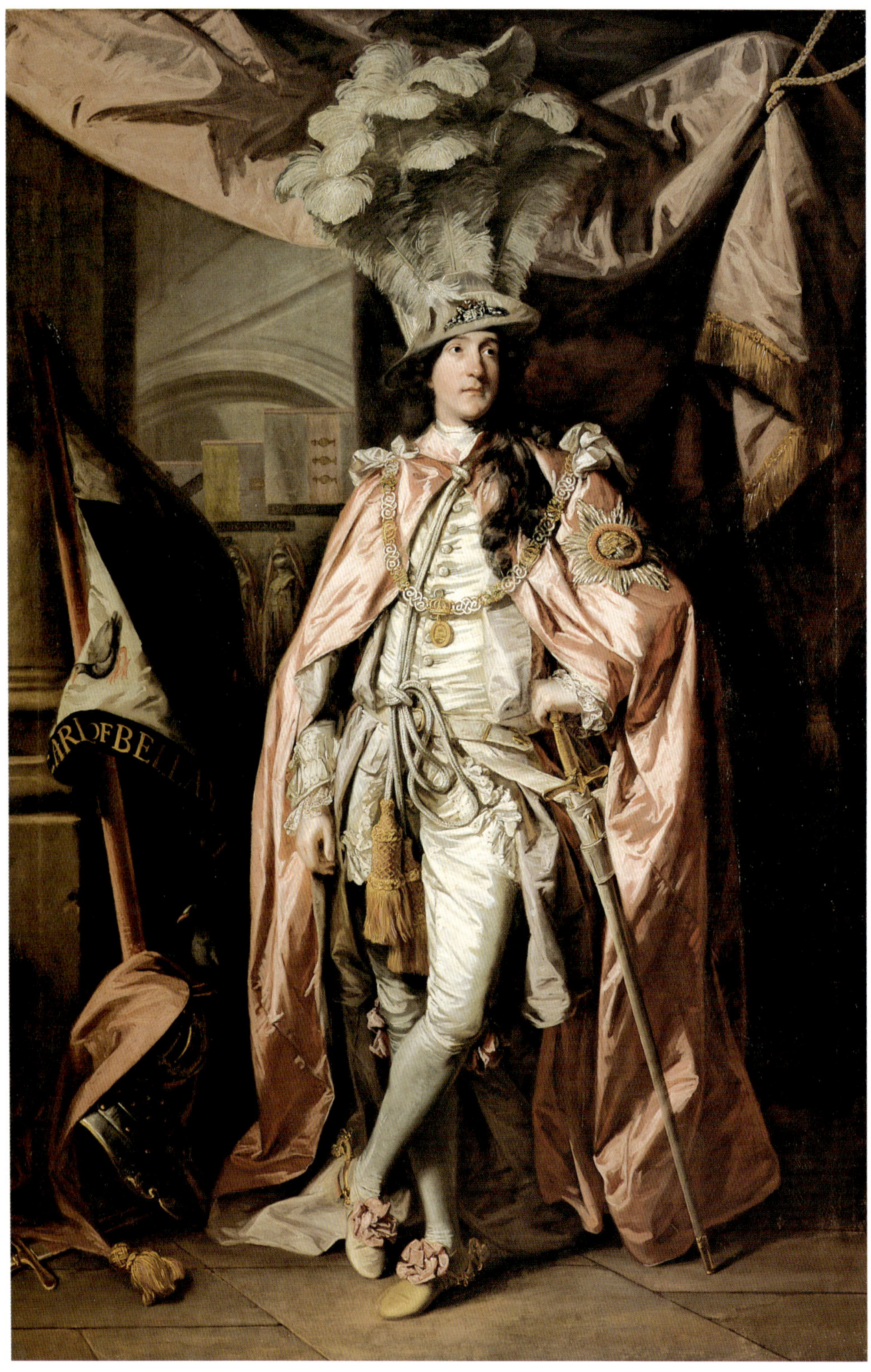

EARL OF BELLA

15. **Charles Coote,**
1st Earl of Bellamont
(1738–1800)
JOSHUA REYNOLDS (1773–4)
Oil on canvas,
2450 × 1620mm
(96½ × 63¾")
National Gallery of
Ireland, Dublin

16. **Arthur Wellesley,**
1st Duke of Wellington
(1769–1852)
JOHN LUCAS (1842)
Oil on canvas,
970 × 740mm
(38⅛ × 29⅛")
National Gallery of
Ireland, Dublin

Born in Ireland, Wellington
acted as Chief Secretary for
Ireland; as Prime Minister
he saw the passing of
the Bill for Catholic
Emancipation.

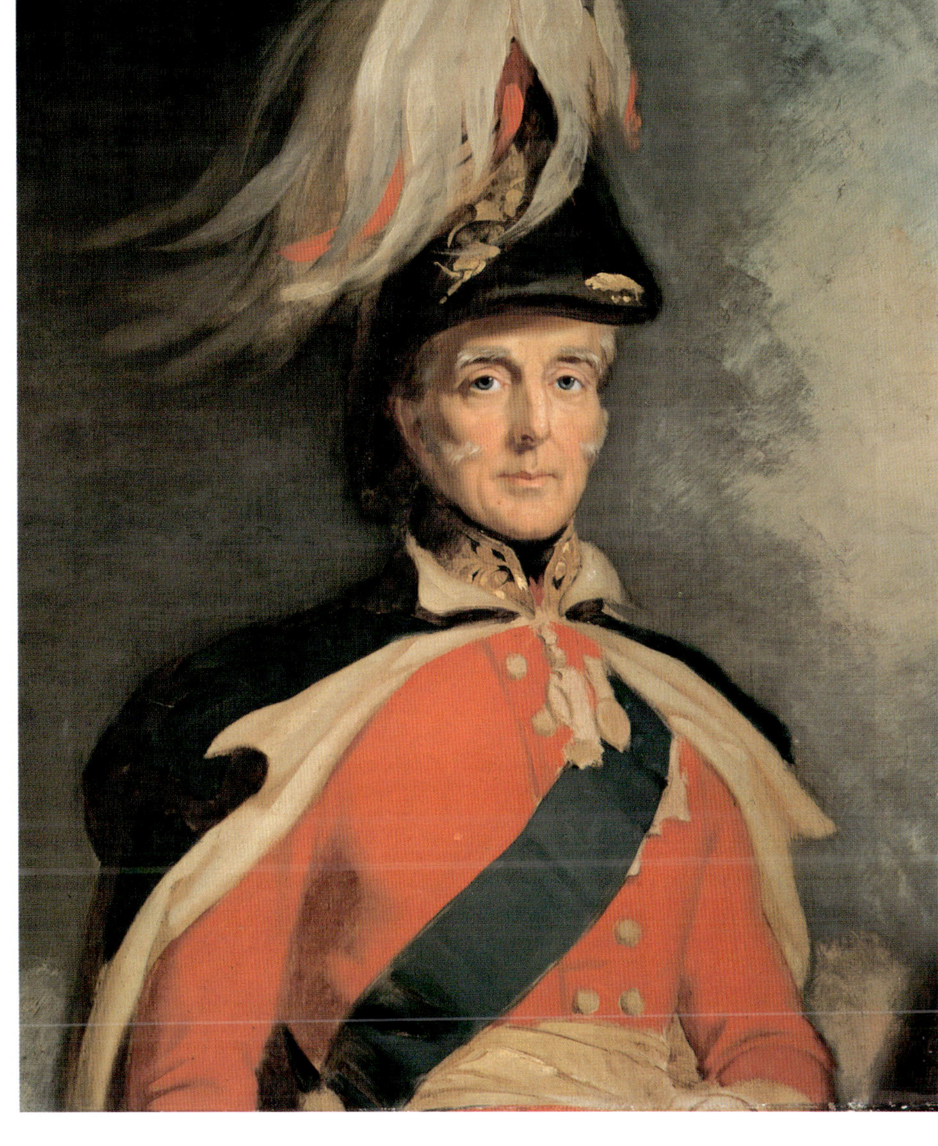

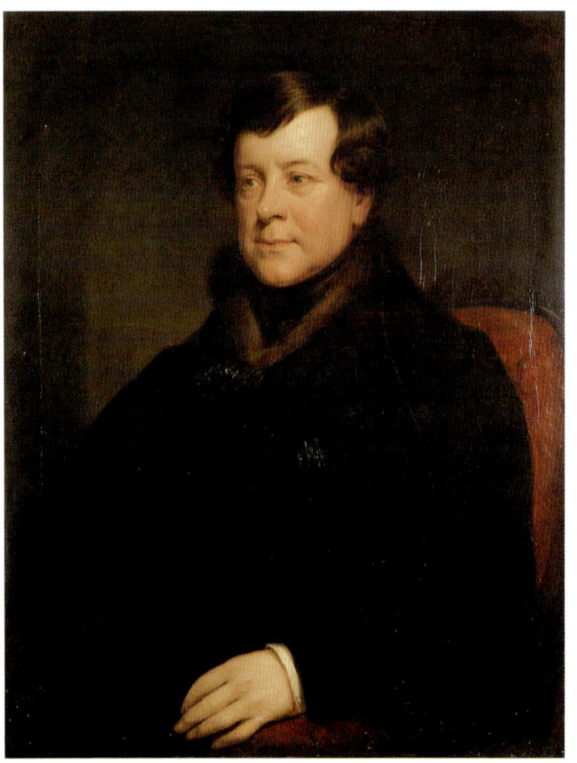

17. **Daniel O'Connell** (1775–1847)
GEORGE MULVANY (c.1840)
Oil on canvas, 900 × 700mm (35 × 27⅝")
National Gallery of Ireland, Dublin

Given his status as nineteenth-century Ireland's great political populiser, O'Connell's iconography is large. It extends from formal oil portraits by artists such as Mulvany and David Wilkie to colossal street monuments by John Henry Foley, as well as wood and ceramic figurines.

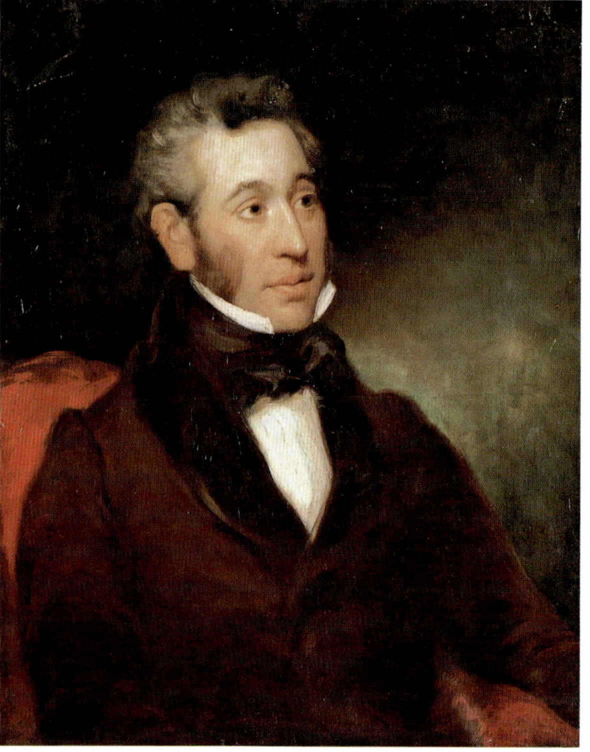

18. **John Banim** (1798–1842)
GEORGE MULVANY (c.1840)
Oil on canvas, 740 × 610mm (29⅛ × 24")
National Gallery of Ireland, Dublin

A product of the Irish middle classes and greatly influenced by Walter Scott, Banim's novels such as *The Boyne Water* (1826) achieved success in England despite their rather lengthy expositions on Irish history.

Dublin-born James McArdell (figs 19–21), who is discussed again in Chapter 2. Many of McArdell's sitters in the Chaloner Smith collection are of Irish interest, and when the collection was shown in Dublin at the 1872 portrait exhibition it was praised by Percy FitzGerald in his *Handbook*, despite the fact that the 'selection of mezzotints . . . are a melancholy record of the departed glories of the country'.[13] Such an opinion suggests that the purchase of this mezzotint collection can be viewed as a late nineteenth-century exercise in Georgian nostalgia, but in the context of establishing a national portrait collection it was also a curatorial act of national re-appropriation. Added to that, the purchase was sponsored in part by a gift of £1,000 from a member of the Guinness family as the Treasury in London had 'refused a special grant for the purpose'.[14]

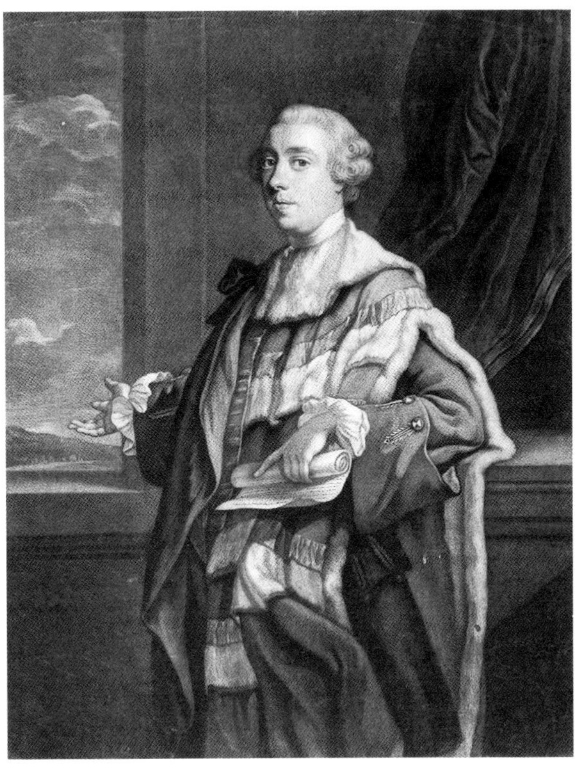

19. **James FitzGerald, 20th Earl of Kildare** (1722–73)
JAMES MCARDELL after JOSHUA REYNOLDS (1754)
Mezzotint, 358 × 260mm (14⅛ × 10¼")
National Portrait Gallery, London (NPG D14788)

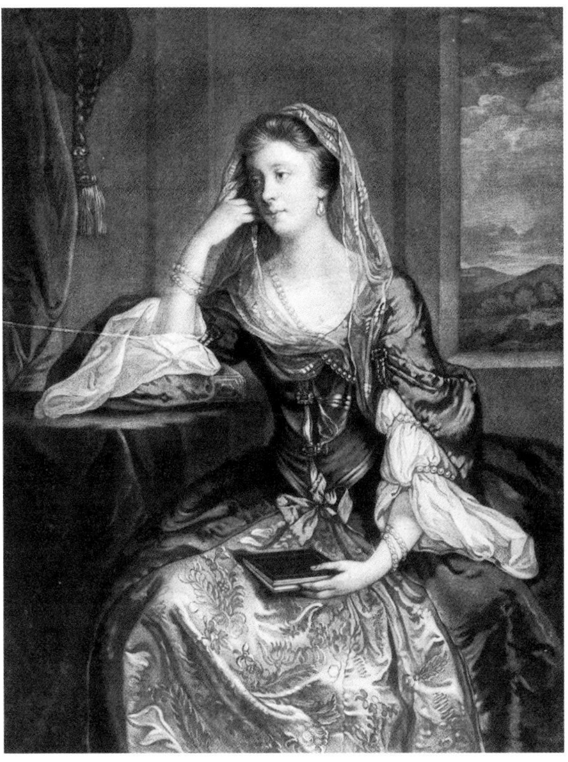

20. **Emily, Countess of Kildare,
wife of 20th Earl of Kildare** (1731–1814)
JAMES MCARDELL after JOSHUA REYNOLDS (1754)
Mezzotint, 346 × 248mm (13⅝ × 9¾")
National Portrait Gallery, London (NPG D5060)

Examples of the 'departed glories' of Ireland in the eighteenth century included portraits of successful Irish actors, such as Peg Woffington (fig.71) and James Quin (fig.21), both after original paintings by London-based artists, as well as grand artistocratic figures such as the Earl and Countess of Kildare, the parents of Lord Edward FitzGerald, both by McArdell after oil portraits by Joshua Reynolds (figs 19 and 20). The prints after Irish artists included the wonderful *Self-Portrait* by Thomas Frye published in 1760 (fig.22) and a splendid series of mezzotints after Hugh Douglas Hamilton's famed pastel ovals of Irish politicians and writers of the 1770s.[15] This collection of mezzotints after Hamilton was reinforced around the same time by the acquisition of four pastels which included portraits of Irish eighteenth-century members of parliament (fig.23).[16]

Given the gradual formation of this rich collection of Irish portraiture, why, one must ask, was an Irish National Portrait Gallery not funded in the 1870s by the government in Westminster? The Gallery's director, Henry Doyle's ambitions were admirable. He wished to establish an inclusive collection, with images of 'eminent Irish men and Irishwomen, but also statesmen and others who were politically or

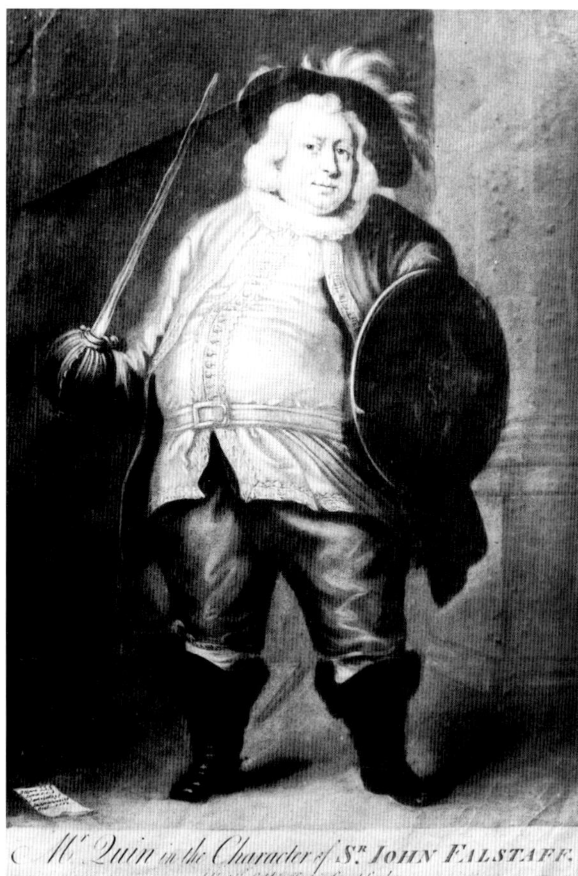

21. **James Quin** (1693–1766)
JAMES McARDELL after FRANCIS HAYMAN (?)
Mezzotint, 356 × 253mm (14 × 10″)
National Gallery of Ireland, Dublin

The celebrated Irish-born actor is shown as Sir John Falstaff in
Shakespeare's *Henry IV*. The Dublin-born McArdell produced many
mezzotints of actors and also reproduced portraits of aristocratic
sitters after oil paintings by Joshua Reynolds.

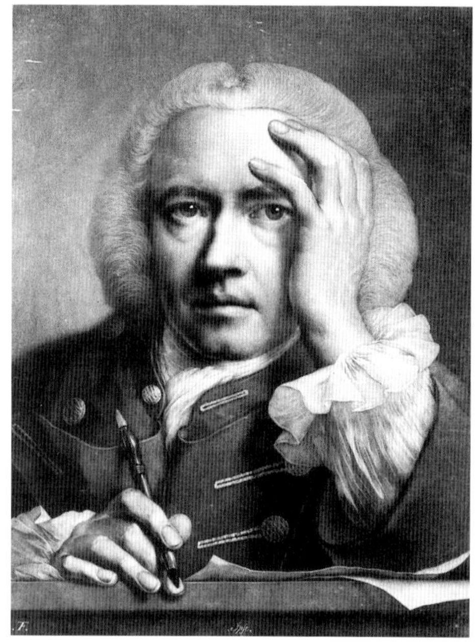

22. **Self-Portrait**
THOMAS FRYE (1760)
Mezzotint, 56 × 352mm (2¼ × 13⅞″)
National Portrait Gallery, London
(NPG D11284)

Thomas Frye produced portraits in all mediums – oils,
pastel and miniature – but is best remembered for his
extraordinary series of mezzotint heads dating from 1760.

socially connected with Ireland, or whose lives serve in anyway to illustrate her
history, or throw light on her social or literary, or artistic records'.[17] One practical
explanation may be the fact that although it had been founded in 1856, the National
Portrait Gallery in London was still in temporary accommodation thirty years later
in the mid-1880s. The present site in St Martin's Place was not opened to the public
until 1896. As one of the nations making up the United Kingdom of Great Britain
and Ireland, it would perhaps have been unseemly for Ireland to receive public
funding when the imperial capital was still deficient in terms of an adequate home
for the national collection of portraits. By contrast, Edinburgh did create its own
Scottish National Portrait Gallery in 1882, but only after an anonymous private
benefactor had offered a stunning £10,000.[18]

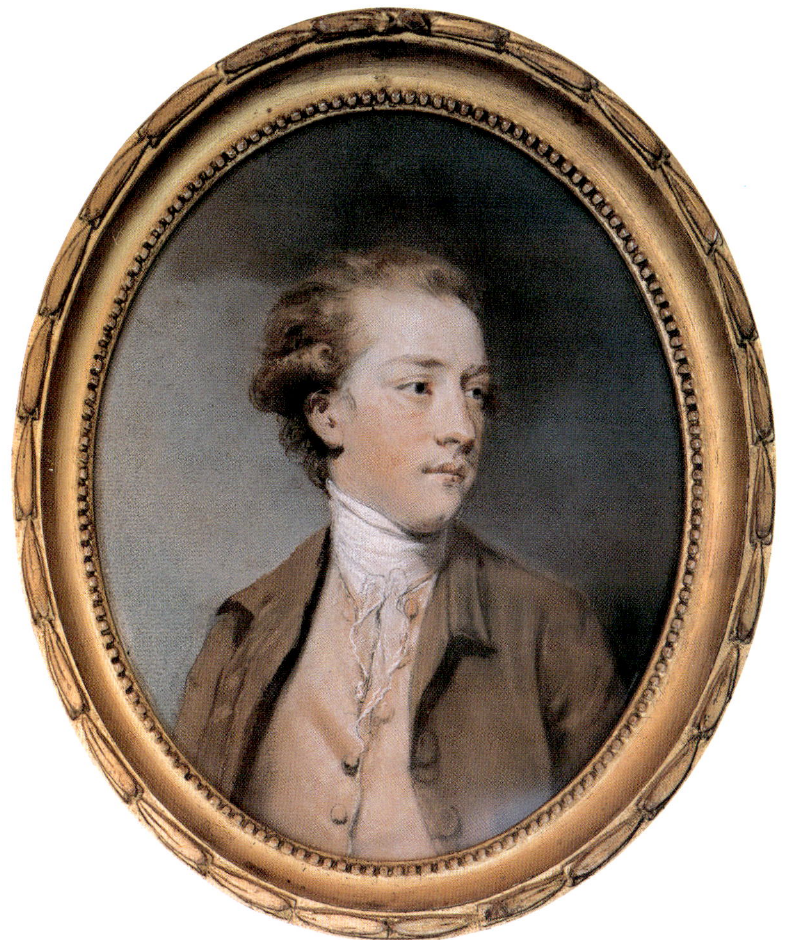

23. **Denis Daly MP** (1747–91)
HUGH DOUGLAS HAMILTON (1770s)
Pastel on paper, 241 × 203mm (9½ × 8″)
National Gallery of Ireland, Dublin

'Eminent Irishmen' in London

In writing to the Treasury in 1872, Dublin was only asking for £2,000. The Treasury's reply to Doyle reminded him that such a 'proposal is in fact to create at the public expense a separate National Portrait Gallery for Ireland'. This could not be tolerated, as

> provision is already made by Parliament for a National Gallery of Portraits of distinguished personages where eminent Irishmen are represented indiscriminately with Englishmen and Scotchmen and that it would materially lessen the importance and interest of this general and essentially National Collection if separate and competing Galleries were to be established in Dublin and Edinburgh confined respectively to portraits of Irish and Scotch celebrities.[19]

Cautious as ever about spending, the Treasury was right. 'Eminent Irishmen' were represented in the London Gallery, hanging alongside their fellow English, Scots and even Welsh subjects of the crown. Some Irishmen had been in the collection

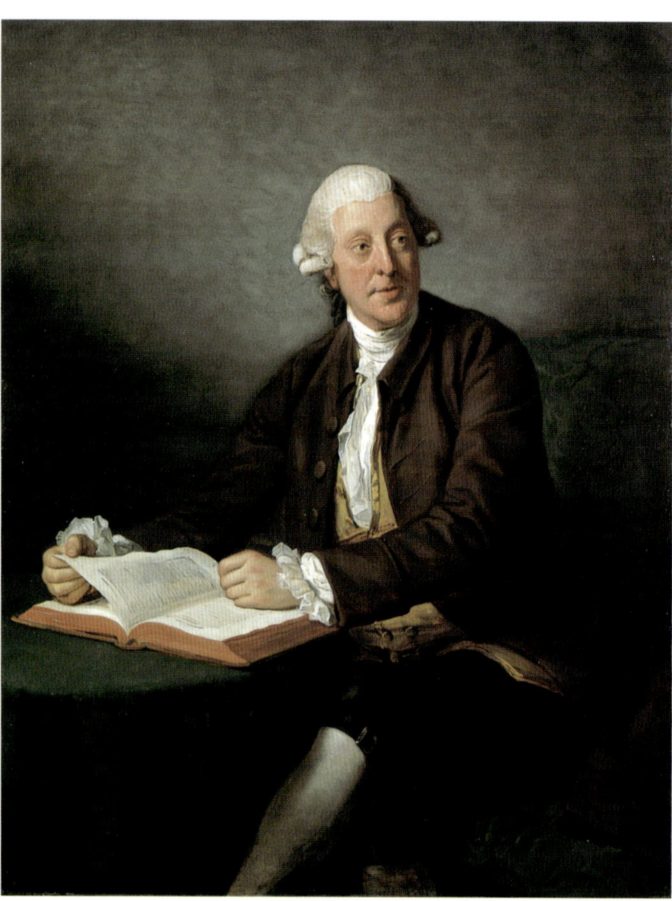

24. **Arthur Murphy** (1727–1805)
NATHANIEL DANCE (1777)
Oil on canvas, 1270 × 1016mm (50 × 40″)
National Portrait Gallery, London (NPG 10)

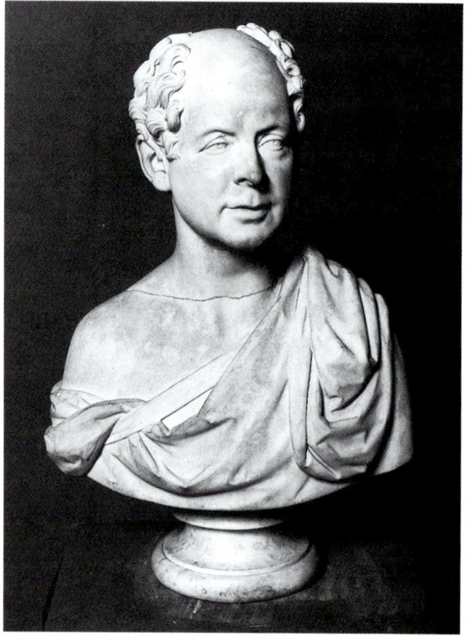

25. **Thomas Moore** (1779–1852)
CHRISTOPHER MOORE (1842)
Marble bust, ht 610 mm (24″)
National Portrait Gallery, London (NPG 11)

Celebrated in the nineteenth century as Ireland's
national poet, Thomas Moore's fame rested on
his *Irish Melodies*, which began appearing in 1808.
A friend of Lord Byron, he later wrote a life of
the poet as well as of Lord Edward FitzGerald.

from almost the very beginning but, as we have seen with the saga of Berthon's portrait of Lady Morgan, no 'eminent' Irishwomen were to be acquired until the gift of a late portrait of the actress Peg Woffington in 1881 (fig.72). While a few of the Irish names that appear in the early lists of the National Portrait Gallery's collection may now no longer resound through history, others have lasted the course. One of the more obscure is perhaps the playwright Arthur Murphy, whose portrait by Nathaniel Dance (fig.24) entered the collection in 1858, two years after the founding of the Gallery. Less obscure is the poet Thomas Moore, whose bust in marble by his fellow countryman Christopher Moore (fig.25) was bought in 1861. In a letter of the previous year to George Scharf, the first Secretary and Keeper of the National Portrait Gallery, the sculptor listed five busts of Irishmen that he had in hand 'of distinguished characters . . . [who] might not be considered unworthy of Places in [such a] Noble and Patriotic Institution'. The Trustees only bought the bust of the poet whom the sculptor had referred to as 'the poet of all nations'.[20] But such purchases did not go unnoticed. Given the newness of the national collection of portraiture, the *Art Journal* was puzzled by the inclusion of Murphy, a long-forgotten eighteenth-century writer. 'We do not deny', the *Journal* wrote, 'that in a Gallery of British Worthies a time may come for Arthur Murphy, – but his time is not yet. Nay, it is a long way off.'[21] Perhaps to the further bafflement of the *Art Journal*, only a few years later the Gallery purchased yet another portrait of an eighteenth-century Irish playwright, John O'Keeffe (fig.26), who is shown holding a copy of his comic opera *The Agreeable Surprise* (1781).

A few decades later, in 1899, Scharf's successor Lionel Cust articulated London's approach to Irish sitters by refusing to transfer portraits of Murphy and O'Keeffe to the Dublin Gallery on the grounds that 'it could be hard to claim that [their] fame . . . was gained in Ireland'.[22] There was a strong element of truth in this statement in that

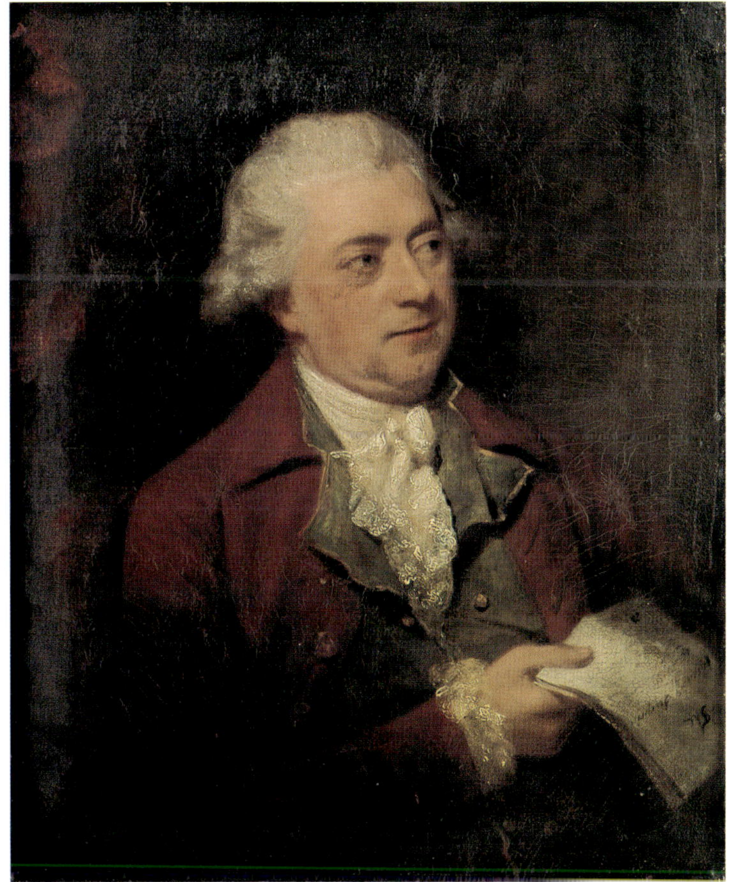

26. **John O'Keeffe** (1747–1833)
THOMAS LAWRANSON (1782)
Oil on canvas, 758 × 637mm
(29⅞ × 25⅛")
National Portrait Gallery,
London (NPG 165)

Painted by a little-known Irish
artist, the Dublin born O'Keeffe
was trained as a painter in
Dublin but went on to become
a popular playwright: his *Wild
Oats* is still performed today.

Murphy's comedies such as *Wild Oats* (1791) had been and, throughout the nineteenth century, were still popular on the London stage. A recent history of the Irish theatre claims that by 1800, twenty years after his first major success, O'Keeffe had enjoyed '1,200 performances of his plays in London'.[23] The decidedly English provenances of the two portraits may also have influenced Cust's argument. As a friend of Dr Johnson and David Garrick, Murphy's portrait had once been owned by Mrs Thrale/Piozzi while a friend of O'Keeffe's daughter had written in 1863, prior to the painting's acquisition by the National Portrait Gallery, that it had 'never been out of the possession of Mr Keefe and his daughter'.[24]

Cust applied a similar defence for a portrait of Father Theobald Mathew, the Apostle of Temperance (fig.27) who, 'irrespective of his place of birth' (Ireland), was comparable (surprisingly) with Lord Castlereagh as being of 'national' interest (that is, pertaining to the United Kingdom) and thus 'the portraits should be placed here'.[25] Earlier, in the 1860s, the acquisition by the Trustees of the National Portrait Gallery of the portrait of Father Mathew had met with conflicting views. The small head-and-shoulder portrait by the now forgotten Edward Leahy had been exhibited at the Royal Academy of Arts in 1847, having been painted from the life in Cork a year earlier. It was offered by the artist to Scharf in 1865 and its representation of a popular social reformer clearly overruled the doubts of at least one prominent trustee of the National Portrait Gallery. In a letter to his fellow colleagues, Thomas Carlyle wondered how Mathew, 'author merely of a temporary row against whisky in various quarters, can have solid claim to a place among the great men of the British nation'.[26] As proof of such a claim, some months later the *Irish Times* ran a story on the London Gallery 'in Connection with Ireland'. The newspaper announced the National Portrait Gallery's purchase of the portrait of Father Mathew and related how:

> near to George Street [London], where the portraits are collected, a number of Irish labourers are working at the erection of the new Foreign and India Office, and Mr Leahy happened to pass the spot with the portrait while the men had struck down work for dinner. They recognised the picture under his arm, and crowded round the delighted artist, asking leave to have a sight of it. He gladly showed it to them, but they were so pleased with it that Leahy could hardly get away from among them with his prize.[27]

Suitably armed with such anecdotes when referring to the National Portrait Gallery's collection of portraits of 'eminent Irishmen', the Treasury official who wrote to Henry Doyle in 1872 may also have been thinking of recently acquired self-portraits of Irish artists such as Nathaniel Hone and James Barry (fig.62) or portraits of famous ecclesiastics such as the Catholic Oliver Plunkett (fig.28) and the Anglican Jonathan Swift (fig.78). The painting of Plunkett, the Archbishop of Armagh, has been dated to around the time of his execution for High Treason in

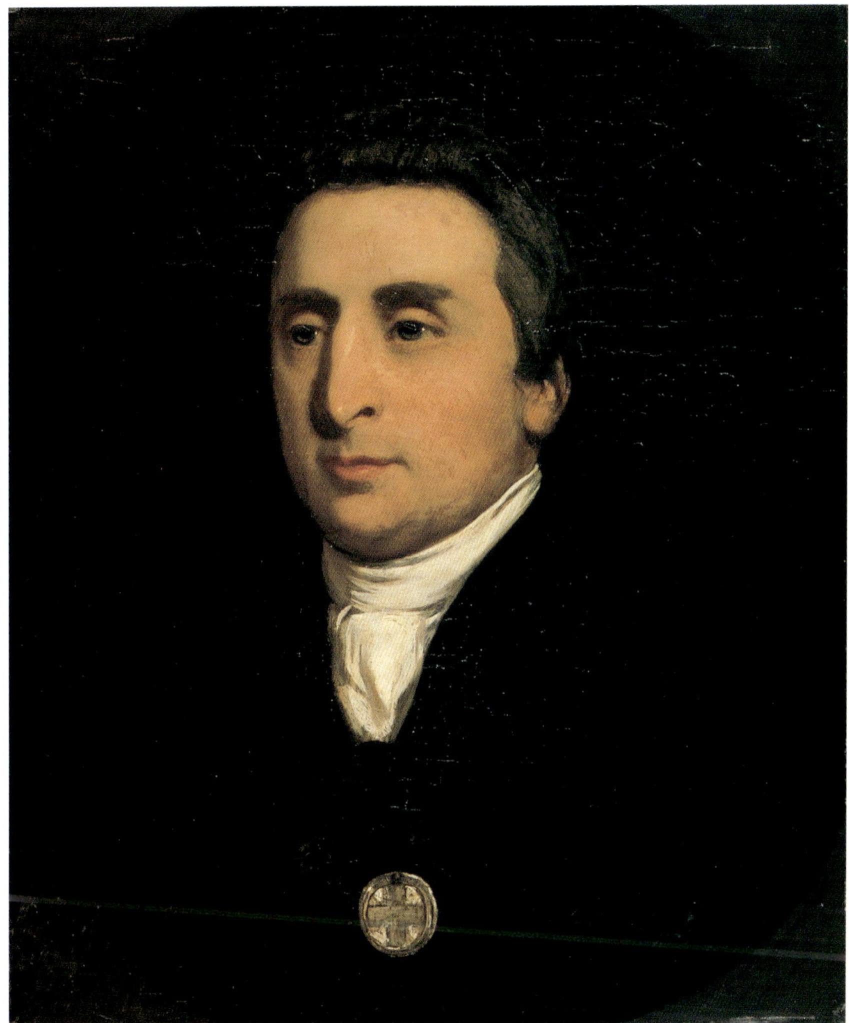

1681. Attributed to the Irish artist Garret Morphey, who painted for a recusant market in England, the portrait of Plunkett displays a range of Catholic objects from a hand-held crucifix, the primatial cross behind, a mitre, a book and a blood-stained knife (possibly suggesting torture).[28] The National Portrait Gallery portrait of Jonathan Swift is again by an Irish artist, Charles Jervas. Painted in Dublin *c.*1718, while Swift was Dean of St Patrick's, it was owned in the early nineteenth century by the Irish peer Lord Moira (fig.100), whom we will meet again in Chapters 3 and 4.[29] Although denied money from the Treasury, in 1875 Doyle was able to buy a head and shoulder version of one of Jervas's many portraits of Swift, which was soon supplemented in the Chaloner Smith purchase by mezzotints after Francis Bindon.[30] The case of Swift is but one of a number of examples of the Dublin Gallery acquiring portraits of sitters associated with Ireland that were already represented in the London collection. In the eyes of a Treasury civil servant such double expenditure would have been seen as seriously unnecessary.[31]

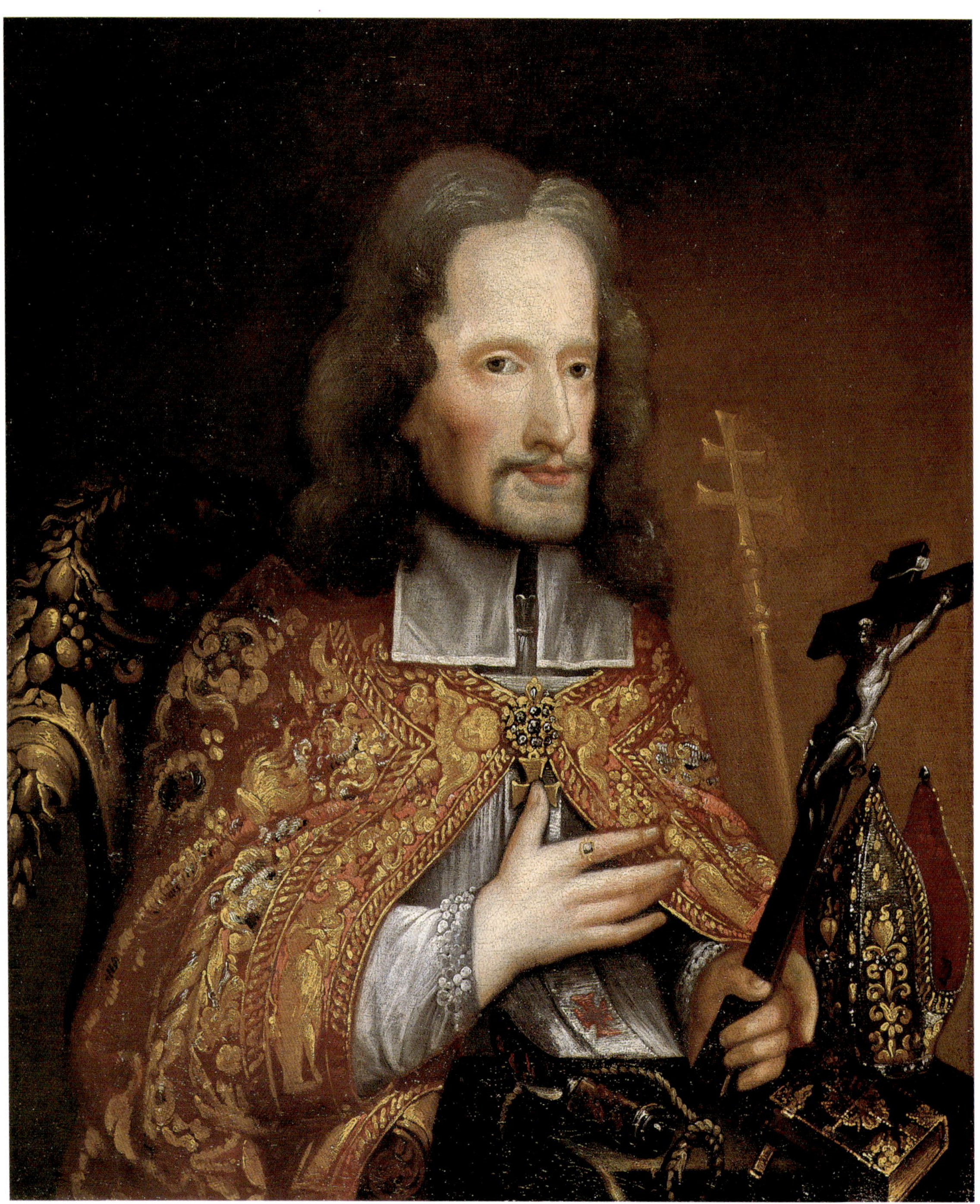

Another reason why London did not want to pay for an Irish National Portrait Gallery may be the fact that, as Marcia Pointon points out in her thoughtful account of the origins of London's National Portrait Gallery, 'the relationship between military commemorative art and national portraiture underlies the foundation of all national portrait galleries'.[32] Pointon cites early nineteenth-century efforts to establish such a gallery in London in the light of the Napoleonic Wars, and later the need to commemorate those who served in the Crimean War. The problem with Ireland was that military commemoration was not so straightforward. Which side of the military divide would capture the attention of the visitor to the gallery, the imperial soldier or the Irish rebel? The nationalist newspaper, the *Freeman's Journal* criticised the National Portrait Gallery in London for giving too much attention to those 'whose imperial services were more marked than their Irish feelings'. Not enough attention, they claimed, was paid to those 'who have helped to adorn our literature, art, and science, or have served the country in other ways'. In an equally critical tone, the more usually unionist *Irish Times* disparaged London's display of 'warriors and statesmen whom Ireland has reared for English purposes'.[33] Looking at acquisitions made by the London Gallery in the 1880s, the Irish press may have been thinking of portraits of Irish-born Westminster statesmen such as Edmund Burke (NPG 655, 854) and Richard Brinsley Sheridan (NPG 651), or of Irish-born military heroes such as the commander of the British forces during the two Sikh wars, Field-Marshal Hugh, Viscount Gough (NPG 805). But in fact the arts had not been ignored. As the previous analysis of the early acquisitions of the National Portrait Gallery shows, portraits of Irish-born actors, writers and artists, from Peg Woffington to random eighteenth-century playwrights to such luminaries as James Barry and Tom Moore, were also part of the collection. What the newspapers perhaps did not wish to admit was that those who had made it into the National Portrait Gallery, like so many Irishmen and women of all generations and all walks of life since the eighteenth century, had decided to forge their careers in England. Equally, the Dublin newspapers usefully forgot that their own city had relatively recently erected statues by the celebrated Irish sculptor John Henry Foley to both Burke (1868, outside Trinity College) and Gough (1874–80, on horseback, Phoenix Park).[34]

Due to Scotland's more assimilated state in the nineteenth century, as well as her more public embrace of military imperialism, the establishment of a portrait gallery in Scotland was not a politically contentious issue but one merely slowed down by finance.[35] Thomas Carlyle, who is credited as a founding figure of the London National Portrait Gallery and became a trustee in 1857, had earlier been a strong advocate of the establishment of a national collection of portraits in his native Scotland. In a letter of 1854 to David Laing of the Society of Antiquaries of Scotland, Carlyle had expressed his views on the value of national portraiture:

It has always struck me that Historical Portrait Galleries far transcend in worth all other kinds of National Collections of Pictures whatever; that in fact they ought to exist . . . in every country, as amongst the most popular and cherished National Possessions: – and it is not a joyful reflection, but an extremely mournful one, that in no country is there at present such a thing to be found . . . I hope you in Scotland, in the 'new National Museum' we hear talk of, will have a good eye to this, and remedy it in your own case.[36]

As a vocal advocate of the notion of the Hero, Carlyle stressed the highly charged attraction of the historical portrait to a sensitive viewer:

any representation, made by a faithful human creature, of that Face and Figure, which *he* saw with his eyes, and which I can never see with mine, is now valuable to me, and much better than none at all . . . Often I have found a Portrait superior in real instruction to half-a-dozen written 'Biographies', as Biographies are written; or rather let me say, I have found that the Portrait was a small lighted *candle* by which the Biographies could for the first time be *read*, and some human interpretation be made of them.[37]

In examining other writings by Carlyle on hero worship, Paul Barlow has usefully concluded that such views encouraged the creation of 'a space [that] engendered direct human contact through each image. By collecting historical portraits the gallery would connect the modern viewer to the humanity which animates cultural and historical developments: nation would be recognised as community.'[38]

For Westminster to foster such an emotive bond between the present and the past in the context of Ireland, and in particular in the realm of political or military portraiture, was highly unlikely. Three notable events that would pave the way for 'a generation of upheaval in land ownership, religious ascendancy and nationalist politics' occurred in the years leading up to the Treasury's refusal of Doyle's request for funds to establish a distinctly Irish Portrait Gallery. These events included the disestablishment of the Anglican Church of Ireland in July 1869, followed in May 1870 by Isaac Butt's founding of the Home Rule movement, and terminating a few months later with Gladstone's first Land Act. The upheaval began to manifest itself in the 1874 elections when 'Home rule', as Roy Foster has pointed out, 'was subscribed to by a spectacular fifty-nine MPs'.[39]

Doyle's correspondence with the Treasury continued into 1873 but seems to have come to a close with a stinging riposte from Whitehall on 9 May. While acknowledging the 'marked success of the Loan National Portrait Gallery', the Treasury was of the opinion that:

local, and not imperial, liberality is the proper source from which such collections should be created and maintained . . . as soon as the central Government oversteps the limit of those objects which are common to all, and enters into the field of local claims, there is no logical termination to its interference, and the result is, and cannot but be, that all genuine local interest, such as consists in action and sacrifice, is destroyed or survives only in the shape of appeals for aid.

This country furnishes, happily, many more men who are entitled to live in its records than it is possible to commemorate in its capital, and it is for private and local munificence to extend such records beyond the point at which they become too numerous or too partial for the state to provide.

For these reasons, my Lords regret that they cannot agree to recede from their former decision.[40]

The Treasury letter states only too clearly the problems faced by a portrait gallery within an imperial framework: 'no one', it says elsewhere in the letter, 'however eminent, sees more than a very limited part of all that goes to make up the greatness of the state'. And that 'limited part', the truly 'imperial' part, is the role of what the Treasury referred to earlier as the 'National Gallery of Portraits' situated in 'the capital of a great empire'. In such an imperial vision, Ireland is peripheralised and turned into the 'local'.

If, as Carlyle implied, portraits could evoke emotive responses, they could also lead to a situation where, as a contemporary verse put it, 'Tender, pathetic, grave, gay, humorous, every / feeling of the heart, every quality / of the mind may be excited by portraits'.[41] Such excitement conjured up by Irish national history, and more particularly by military commemoration in an Ireland that was hell bent on Home Rule, was indeed seriously problematic. As has been pointed out, a portrait of the 1798 rebel Lord Edward FitzGerald (fig.101) was presented to the National Gallery of Ireland in 1884. The Duke of Leinster's gift of Hugh Douglas Hamilton's three-quarter-length late eighteenth-century oil portrait of FitzGerald was matched that same year by a gift from another member of the FitzGerald family of a miniature of the sitter by Horace Hone (see fig.111).[42] As the examination of the political portrait in Chapter 4 shows, the portraits of Hamilton and Hone became the visual sources for nationalist reproductions of the handsome United Irishman throughout the nineteenth century. For the government to refuse to support the creation of an institution displaying such commemorative material was indeed not at all surprising.

A final reason for the failure to create a separate National Portrait Gallery for Ireland was the lack of an identifiable key individual who embodied national great-ness. Again, as Pointon has discussed with regard to the setting up of London's

National Portrait Gallery, the Chandos portrait of Shakespeare 'held a symbolic position . . . it was the Gallery's first acquisition and its first gift . . . [while] the founders of the American National Portrait Gallery [in the 1960s] required a portrait of George Washington, Father of the Nation, to justify the gallery's aspirations' (fig.29).[43] In the 1870s and 1880s, when a national portrait collection was being created, Ireland had no such unifying figure, no Father, let alone Mother, of the Nation. In the pre-independent Ireland of the late nineteenth century an individual such as the rebellious FitzGerald was clearly not acceptable, while statesmen like Edmund Burke (fig.12) or Henry Grattan, of whom portraits were acquired in the early years of the National Gallery of Ireland, were not in the same league as such representatives of their respective nations as Shakespeare or Washington. In the 1880s the only likely candidate was Daniel O'Connell, who had enjoyed a European

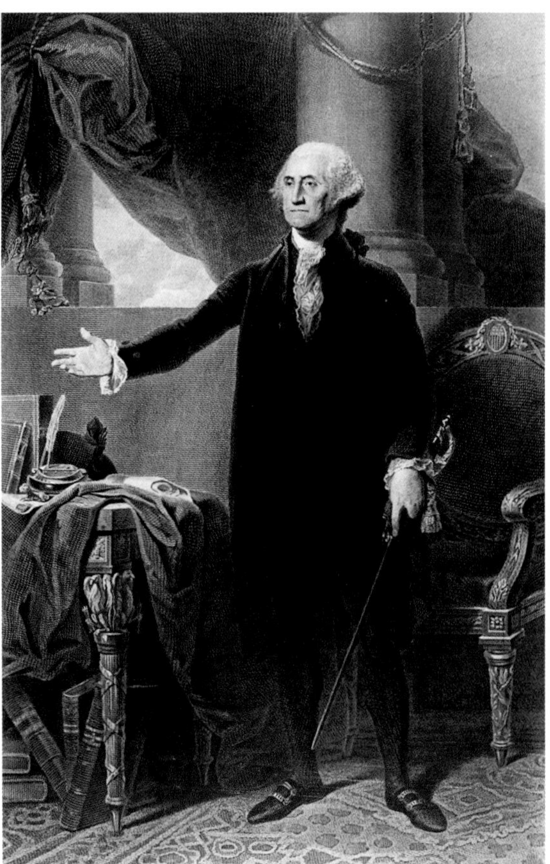

29. **George Washington**
(1732–99)
JAMES HEATH after
GILBERT STUART (1800)
Engraving, 500 × 330mm
(20 × 13")
British Museum, London

The 'Lansdowne' portrait of Washington is so called because the original oil painting (1796, National Portrait Gallery, Smithsonian Institution, Washington DC) was sent to the Marquis of Lansdowne by a wealthy Philadelphian. It was first engraved in London by Heath and published on 1 January 1800.

reputation and whose portrait by Mulvany (fig.17) entered the Dublin collection in the same year as Hamilton's portrait of Lord Edward.

Yet at the same time one must remember that the twenty-year-long saga of the creation of an O'Connell monument in the centre of Dublin is a salutary indication of the contemporaneous inability of the Irish general public to agree on one individual national figure. The monument of the 'Liberator' is more than just the story of what has been referred to as 'the most important sculptural commission of the nineteenth century in Ireland'. It was also 'the only statue of a Catholic erected on the streets of Dublin in the nineteenth century'.[44] The ceremony surrounding the laying of the O'Connell foundation stone in August 1864 was followed by intense unionist anger and serious rioting in Belfast at what was seen as a privileging of the Catholic figure, as well as general resentment at recent political and economic Catholic gains. Hatred of the specific memory of O'Connell was made manifest in the burning of his effigy, 'clothed in the garments like those in which the Irish agitator, when in the flesh, was wont to enclose himself', as one Orange pamphleteer put it.[45] Many years later, a few days after John Henry Foley's three-tiered monument was unveiled in 1882 (and only two years before the National Gallery of Ireland purchased Mulvany's oil of O'Connell), anti-Protestant outbursts by nationalists led to stones being thrown at the early eighteenth-century monument to William III on Dublin's College Green, while 'anti-O'Connellites' had to be warned by the *Freeman's Journal* 'of the need to behave with propriety'.[46] Taking into account such public disagreements as to who in nineteenth-century Ireland was worthy of celebration, it is not surprising to learn of the general under-representation of the Irish amongst Victorian worthies. W.E. Vaughan has estimated that the Irish possibly account for only 11 per cent of *Dictionary of National Biography* 'subjects born between 1800 and 1870'.[47]

As the nineteenth century came to an end, the inadequacies of the Irish portrait collection in Dublin were still apparent. The *Freeman's Journal* saw it as 'one of the most interesting places in Ireland to visit', yet there was a need for it to be 'more national than cosmopolitan'. This Catholic-liberal newspaper suggests that in attempting to create 'a really extensive gallery of national portraits', 'artistic considerations' must be set aside in favour of completeness, where even 'a copy is better than nothing'.[48] The newspaper recommended that pictures 'of Irish interest' in the National Portrait Gallery (and in other London locations such as the Garrick Club and at the South Kensington Museum) should be moved to Dublin, and cites such historical desirables as Oliver Plunkett, Henry Grattan, J.P. Curran, Daniel O'Connell and Samuel Lover. The article ends with the view that the present array of images in Merrion Square is but a 'nucleus' and that the 'collection of national portraits proceeds altogether too slowly'. In fact, within a year things had begun to happen. In 1897, the oil on canvas portrait of Plunkett (fig.28) purchased by London back in

1868 was transferred on loan to Ireland where it was to remain a most popular exhibit in Dublin for many years.[49] The *Freeman's Journal* may not in fact have been aware that Dublin already had portraits of Grattan, O'Connell (fig.17) and Lover, while within the next twenty years the National Gallery of Ireland acquired no fewer than four oil portraits, as well as a death-mask of the late eighteenth-century lawyer John Philpot Curran (figs 32–5).

Such journalistic criticism made little or no impression on the curator, Ellen Duncan, who in 1907 described the collection for the *Burlington Magazine*, her focus being on its 'charm' and lack of overcrowding.[50] A more detached visitor in 1914 was Charles Holmes, then Director of the National Portrait Gallery in London, who not only gave an account of his visit in his autobiography, but annotated his personal copy of the Dublin 1908 *Catalogue of Pictures* with both comments and very astute pencil drawings of the portraits that caught his eye (figs 30 and 31).[51]

Holmes's saunter around the Dublin Gallery is amusing yet opinionated. In comparing the London and Dublin collections he found curatorial similarities but also major cultural differences. A contemporary portrait of Anne Boleyn is the 'same as ours', while a version of Reynolds's portrait of Oliver Goldsmith is 'much better than ours!!' as is the bust by Christopher Moore of Tom Moore (fig.25). John Lewis's portrait of Peg Woffington (fig.73) is 'a poor thing but more lusty and human than any other portrait I have seen'. J.P. Curran by Hugh Douglas Hamilton (fig. 33) is 'rather stodgy', while the same artist's portrait of Lord Edward Fitzgerald (fig.101) is 'a dull heavy picture'. A square-framed miniature of FitzGerald by Horace Hone which corresponds to the oval of the same sitter in London (fig.111) is described as 'a poor thing and very plebeian; hair redder than in the oil'. Holmes is equally scathing of the Lady Morgan portrait (fig.13) that his own institution had refused over fifty years earlier, condemning it as representing 'a coarse woman'. Despite the fact that Holmes's extensive sketching in the Dublin catalogue may suggest a cultural sympathy with the Irish collection, he later reveals that although he 'spent many hours making notes and sketching portraits', he 'could not get a likeness':

> The Irish facial proportions were quite different from the English, and needed a different thumb-nail formula. In the True native type, the broad nostrils come in the middle of the face, the upper lip is immense, the jaw and cheek-bones broad, the forehead low, as if some race, pre-Celtic, aboriginal, almost anthropoid.[52]

Such a comment takes us back to the earlier remarks made by both Lord Stanhope in 1859 and the Treasury official in 1873. Holmes is unable to get his head round the Irish: they are just different, both culturally and also physiognomically. His comments appear in his autobiography of 1936, and by that date such racist formulations with regard to the Irish were becoming somewhat threadbare. But in

JOHN PHILPOT **CURRAN**,

Born at Newmarket, co. Cork, 24th July, 1750. He was educated at Trinity College, was called to the Bar in 1775, and quickly made his reputation as a brilliant orator. He sat in the Irish Parliament for Kilbeggan and Rathcormac, speaking and voting with the Popular Party but was not a member at the time of the Union. In 1806 he was made Master of the Rolls, a post which he held until 1814. He died in London 14th October, 1817.

520. **OIL PICTURE**, by SIR THOMAS LAWRENCE, P.R.A.

2 ft. 5 in. H.; 2 ft. w.

Half length, seated; full face. Black coat and white stock

Exhibited at the British Institution in 1849.

From the collection of Sir Robert Peel, Bart. Sold, with other pictures from the Drayton Manor Collection, at Robinson and Fisher's, London, 10th May, 1901. Purchased by Lord Iveagh, and by him presented to the Gallery.

545. **OIL PICTURE** painter unknown.

2 ft. 5 in. H.; 2 ft. w.

Half length, to right; in black coat; his arms folded across his body. He holds a paper in his right hand.

Purchased in 1903.

MEZZOTINT, by JOHN RAPHAEL SMITH, after the picture by SIR THOMAS LAWRENCE in the possession of Earl Grey (C. S., 50, i.)

From Chaloner Smith collection.

COLOURED PRINT, Caricature, "*The Master of the ScRolls.*" Published by M'Cleary, 32 Nassau-street, Dublin.

JOHN, LORD **CUTTS**,

Second son of Richard Cutts, of Arkesden, Essex; born in 1661. In 1686 he was serving under Charles, Duke of Lorraine, against the Turks, when he distinguished himself by his bravery at the siege of Buda. He came over to England with William of Orange as Lieutenant-Colonel of an English Regiment. He accompanied William to Ireland, was at the battle of the Boyne, and for his services at the siege of Limerick, was created Baron Cutts of Gowran, in 1690. He afterwards served in Holland, being Brigadier-General at Steinkirk, and by his brave conduct and coolness under fire at the siege of Namur, acquired the name of " The Salamander."

30. **Catalogue of Pictures and other works of art in the National Gallery and the National Portrait Gallery, Ireland** (1908)
CHARLES J. HOLMES (1914)
Pencil sketches of John Philpot Curran
Page size 140 × 210mm (5 ½ × 8 ¼")
National Portrait Gallery, London (NPG Archives)

LORD EDWARD **FITZGERALD**.

A younger son of James, 1st Duke of Leinster; born in London 15th October, 1763. He entered the army in 1780 and served in America, but was dismissed in 1792 owing to his expressed sympathy with the Revolution whilst on a visit to Paris. He joined the United Irishmen, and in 1796 went to Hamburg for the purpose of negotiating with the French Government for armed assistance to Ireland. In the following year he assumed the military leadership of the United Irishmen to assist by arms the independence of Ireland; but his designs being known to the Government his arrest was ordered. He succeeded for some time in evading capture, but on 17th May, 1798, the house in Thomas-street in which he was hiding was entered by soldiers, and in the struggle to effect his arrest he was wounded by a pistol shot, and being removed to Newgate, died from the effects of his wound on 4th June, 1798. He married the famous Pamela, by whom he became great grandfather to Mr. George Wyndham.

195. **OIL PICTURE**, by HUGH DOUGLAS HAMILTON.

4 ft. 1 in. H.; 3 ft. 1½ in. w.

Three-quarter length, standing; in cut-away green coat with brass buttons, red neckerchief, and buff pantaloons.

This picture was painted for Lord Edward's mother, the Duchess of Leinster, and remained in her possession after her second marriage, descending after her death to her daughter, Mrs. Beauclerk. From the latter's grandson, Mr. Aubrey de Vere Beauclerk, of Ardglass, it was purchased by the Duke of Leinster. It was engraved as frontispiece to Moore's "Life of Lord Edward Fitzgerald."

Presented by Charles William, 4th Duke of Leinster, in 1884.

2156. **WATER-COLOUR MINIATURE**, by HORACE HONE.

Similar to a miniature by Hone at Carton; both perhaps after the bust portrait by Hamilton at Carton.

Presented in 1884 by Lieut.-Colonel William H. D. FitzGerald, son of Lord William FitzGerald.

31. **Catalogue of Pictures and other works of art in the National Gallery and the National Portrait Gallery, Ireland** (1908)
CHARLES J. HOLMES (1914)
Pencil sketches of Lord Edward FitzGerald
Page size 140 × 210mm (5 ½ × 8 ¼")
National Portrait Gallery, London (NPG Archives)

the eyes of the by then retired third Director of the National Portrait Gallery, and with such a weight of evidence against them, the Irish did not automatically qualify for admittance to what Stanhope had defined as the 'chief National Collection', nor could they benefit from what the Treasury had seen as 'imperial liberality'.

Capturing authenticity

In his notes on the Dublin collection Holmes had commented upon and drawn three heads of the Irish lawyer and politician John Philpot Curran (fig.30); two are oils, the 'stodgy' one by Hamilton and a 'poor caricature' now attributed to James Petrie, and the third a death mask. Such a concentration of portraits of one sitter was an early feature of the display in Dublin and encouraged discussion as to the accuracy of one image over another.[53]

In 1936 the recently resigned Director of the National Gallery of Ireland, Thomas Bodkin, in an attempt to analyse the subject of an Irish portrait collection, compared the formalised rules drawn up by the National Portrait Gallery in London

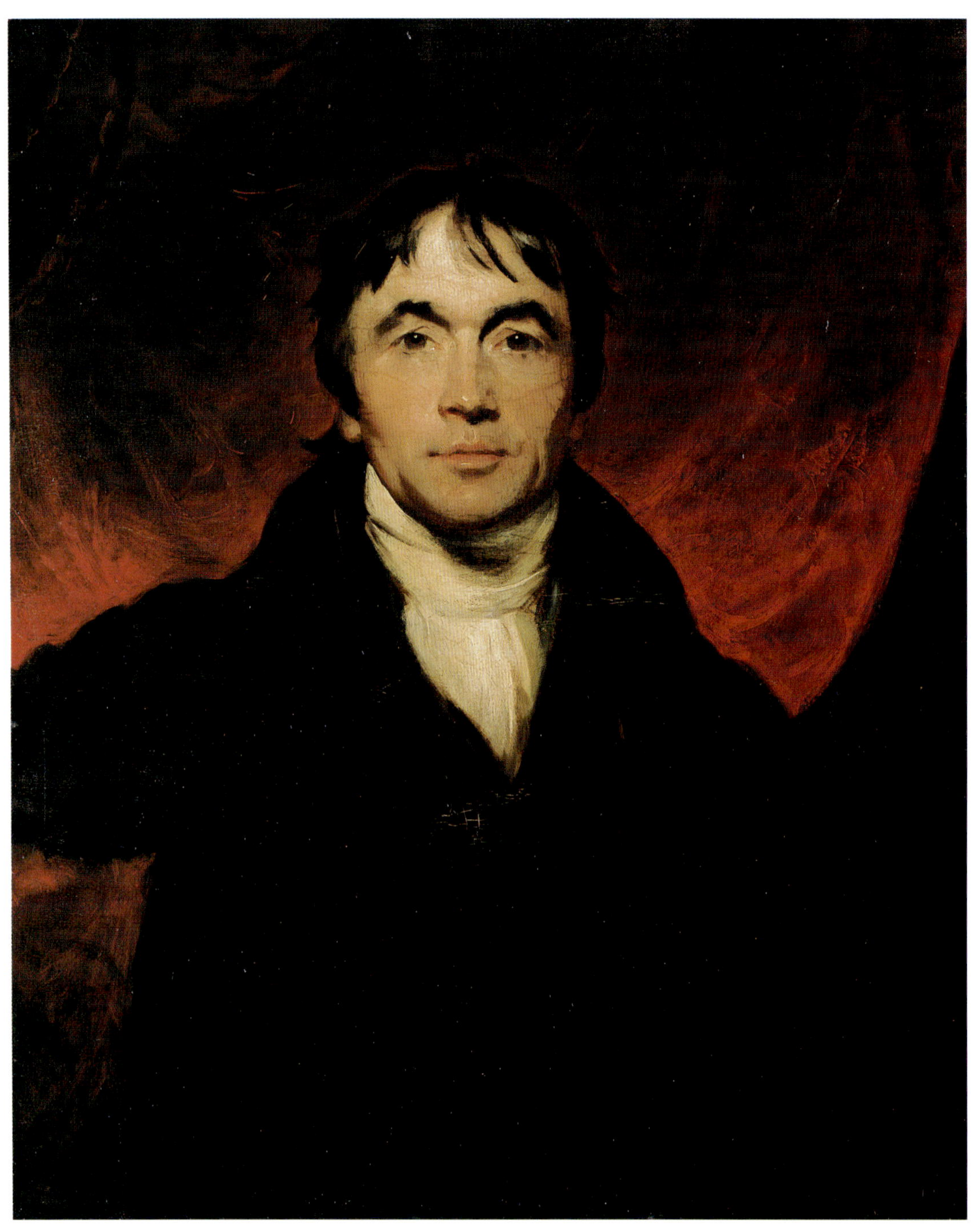

32. **John Philpot Curran** (1750–1817)
THOMAS LAWRENCE (c.1807)
Oil on canvas, 730 × 610mm (23¾ × 24″)
National Gallery of Ireland, Dublin

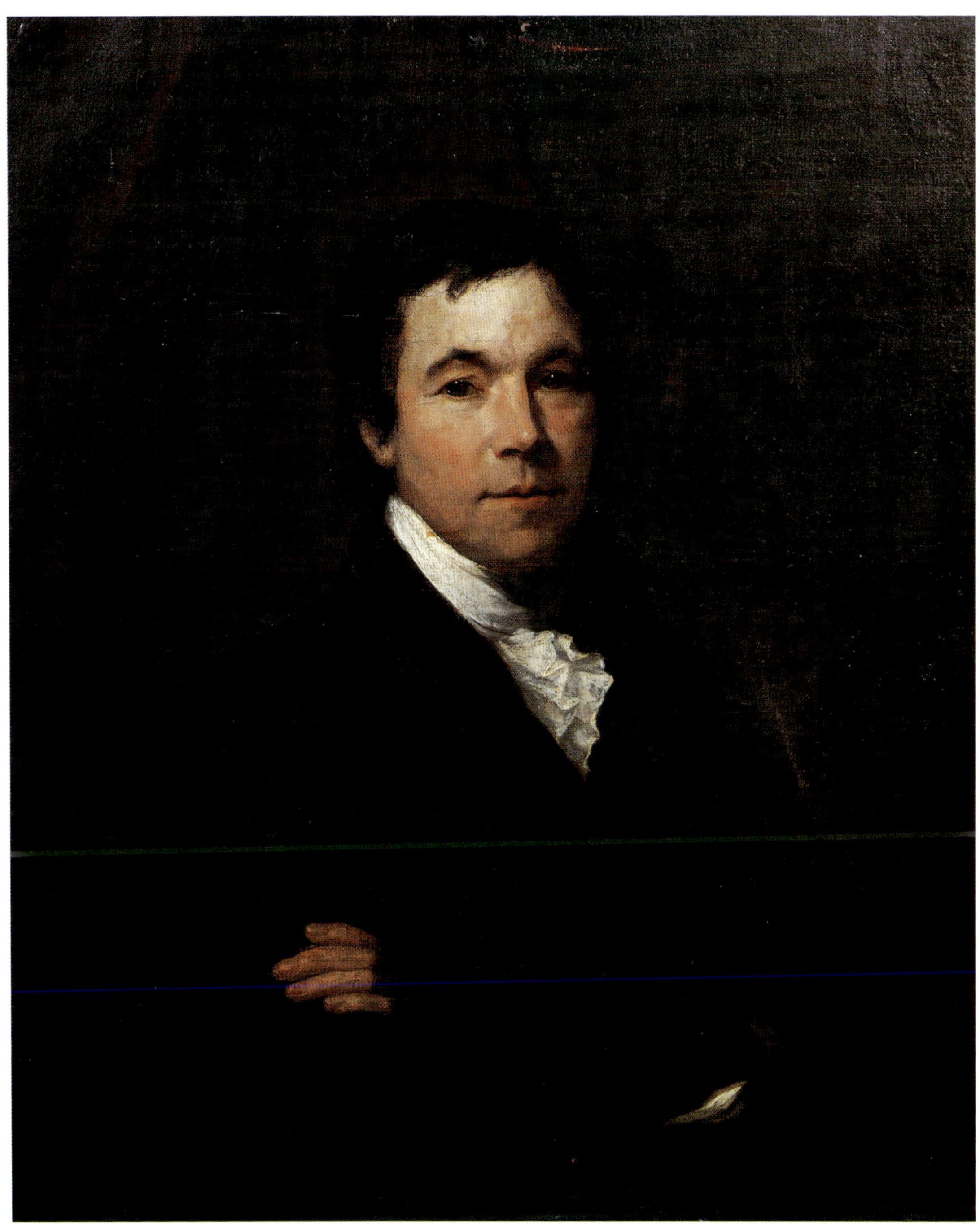

33. **John Philpot Curran** (1750–1817)

Oil on canvas, 762 × 635mm (30 × 25″)
National Gallery of Ireland, Dublin

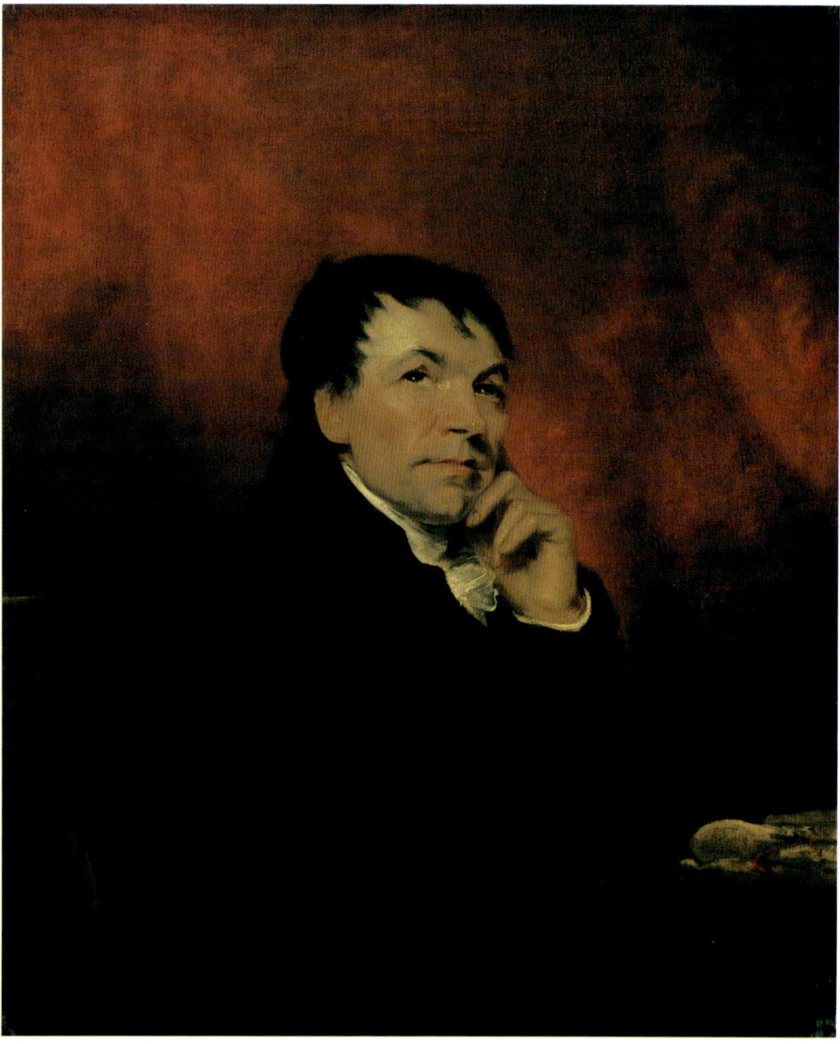

with the more relaxed approach of 'the Irish authorities [who] have refrained [perhaps wisely, he adds] from definite regulations, and consider each case on its merits as it arises'.[54] While not a fan of the segregation of portraits into special collections, Bodkin goes on to highlight some of the key issues regarding the formation of national collections of portraits, namely the need for posterity, celebrity and authenticity. These three issues are discussed throughout this book.

Focusing on various portraits of Curran, Bodkin argues that with regard to subsequent posterity Curran was not a problem: he should be in a portrait gallery of Irish worthies. His defence of Wolfe Tone and other United Irishmen, his opposition to the government patronage system and his famed oratory have given him an important place in Irish ascendancy history. Bodkin refers to Curran's 'protean character', an attraction that made him the subject of many nineteenth-century biographies.[55] The connection between the quantity of textual references to an individual and the inclusion of visual records of them in a portrait gallery is an important aspect of establishing their national legitimacy: if posterity is not a problem, what of authenticity? The fact that well-known individuals will probably have been portrayed on a number of occasions throughout their lives suggested a dilemma for Bodkin:

> What varied notion might be formed about Napoleon from a single portrait of the lean young lieutenant of artillery at Toulon, or one of the stocky emperor on the eve of Austerlitz, or one of the bloated and melancholy exile on Saint Helena! It may almost be said of any celebrity's portrait 'never the hour and the place and the sitter together'.

So how do you choose, Bodkin wonders, how do you decide which is the most authentic image? He goes on to analyse a variety of portraits of Curran, illustrating his article with eight images of his subject. He starts off his discussion with the Thomas Lawrence portrait in the National Gallery of Ireland (fig.32) which dates from *c.*1807 and once hung at Drayton Manor, Staffordshire, as part of the famed gallery of political portraits collected by Sir Robert Peel, Tory Prime Minister in the 1830s and 1840s and once Chief Secretary for Ireland. The Lawrence, Bodkin says, is full of 'striking dignity in a moment of authentic inspiration' and he compares it with the contemporaneous portrait also in the Dublin collection by Hugh Douglas Hamilton (fig.33) which is 'not without charm, though completely lacking in force'; a further portrait by an unidentified artist (possibly William Owen) is in the National Portrait Gallery, London (fig.34). As far as Bodkin is concerned, the accuracy with which these three paintings fulfil their roles as portraits can only be verified, rather bizarrely, by the existence of Curran's death mask (fig.35). 'The high, arched eyebrows; the wide, mobile mouth; the fine oval of the jaw' as seen in the death mask are all 'unmistakably apparent in each of the oil paintings'. This, according to Bodkin, proves that all three oils are portraits of Curran. In the previous century in Ireland, others had played with this science of comparison. Sir William Wilde, for example, intent on finding visual proof of Swift's insanity, found an exact correspondence between 'the side of the head and ear' by comparing a portrait by Rupert Barber (a pastel now at Bryn Mawr College) with 'a cast taken after his death and preserved in Trinity College'.[56]

Bodkin's main problem is that with the preponderance of oil paintings or engraved portraits of such a subject as Curran, one can never know what a person really looked like: thus the portrait gallery is a frustrating institution.[57] He ends his article in a literalist and rather weak fashion by advocating a preference for photography as a recording tool for the faces of what he calls 'our . . . great men', as it will better serve 'the scientific needs of historians and biographers' rather than 'the journeyman painter' whose work has proved 'so detrimental to the cause of art in Great Britain'.

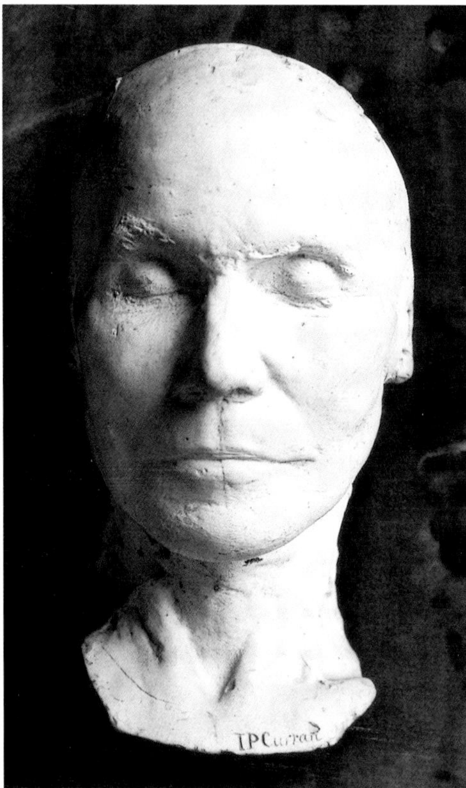

35. **John Philpot Curran**
(1750–1817)
ANONYMOUS (1817)
Plaster, ht 320mm (12⅝")
National Gallery of Ireland,
Dublin

By contrast, the critic Percy FitzGerald contributed a useful account of Lawrence's portrait of Curran (fig.32) to his *Handbook* for the 1872 Dublin exhibition. For FitzGerald, portraiture is essentially about 'character', not accuracy:

The tradition runs, that [Lawrence's] head of Curran was 'dashed in' with all speed, instead of adopting his usual leisurely deliberation. Lawrence had first painted Curran as an ordinary sitter, but happened to meet him at dinner shortly after. He told Curran that he had <u>not</u> painted him, did not know what he was, and must paint him again. The result was most striking. The colouring, too, and general handling, all show the same vigorous character, though an objection perhaps might be made to the blue, which wants the depth and lustre of Gainsborough's than which it is brighter in tone.[58]

In analysing national portraiture, Bodkin had missed the point. The rationale behind a national portrait collection is not just the accuracy of the features of a subject as captured on an individual canvas or marble bust; rather, it is what the portrait represents. Portraits convey meaning and history based on what they suggest for the society in which the portrait is seen. Lawrence knew this when he changed his portrait of Curran from that of 'an ordinary sitter' into a 'vigorous character': national portraiture is not just about the quality of the medium used to capture the likeness.

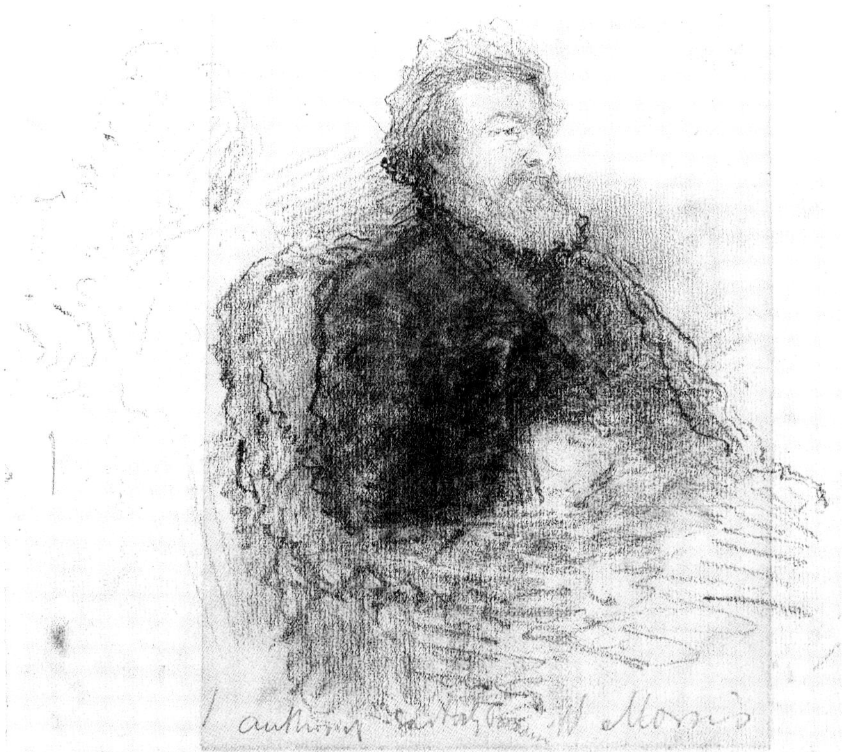

36. **William Morris** (1834–96)
JOHN BUTLER YEATS (1886)
Pencil on paper, 168 × 190mm
(6⅝ × 7⅓")
National Gallery of Ireland, Dublin

The modern Irish portrait

In 1901 the painter Sarah Purser organised in Dublin a two-man exhibition of works by the portraitist John Butler Yeats and the landscapist Nathaniel Hone (not to be confused with the eighteenth-century portrait painter). The importance of this exhibition for reviving an interest in recent Irish art has long been recognised.[59] What has not been stressed sufficiently is the fact that, leaving aside Hone's undoubted talents as a landscape painter, the exhibition of Yeats's portraits was the first retrospective display in Ireland of contemporary portraits. Throughout the nineteenth century the Royal Hibernian Academy mounted annual exhibitions which always included portraits. Despite the precedent set by the previously discussed 1872 display of historical portraits, it was not until the 1901 exhibition that Dublin was asked to reflect on the role of portraiture in contemporary Ireland. Yeats showed sixty-three objects, the majority being portraits. They ranged from three-quarter-length oils to small pencil sketches and included representations of members of his family, close friends and members of the Contemporary Club in Dublin (figs 36, 39). This somewhat eccentric club was founded in 1885 and attracted members who were sympathetic to Home Rule and interested in the discussion of up-to-date issues.[60] Membership of such a group gave Yeats access to a wide array of interesting people whose portraits he sketched. In many ways the pencil drawings that he

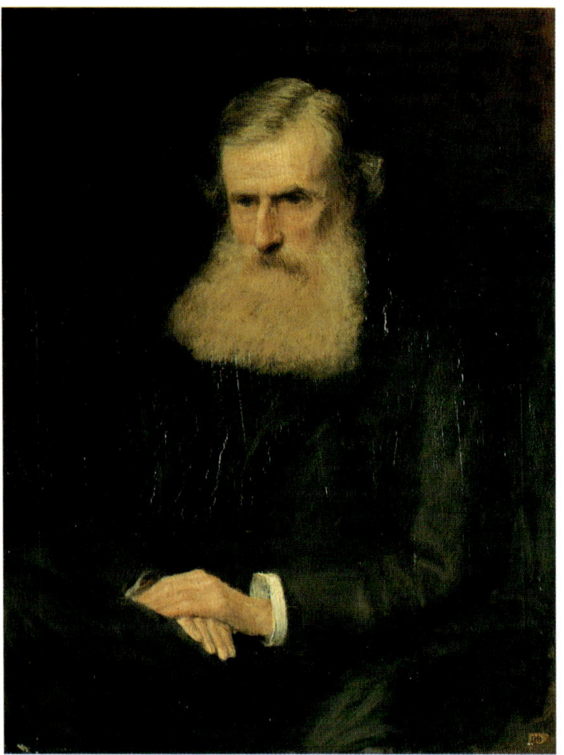

37. **John O'Leary** (1830–1907)
JOHN BUTLER YEATS (1891)
Oil on canvas, 910 × 710mm (35⅞ × 28")
National Gallery of Ireland, Dublin

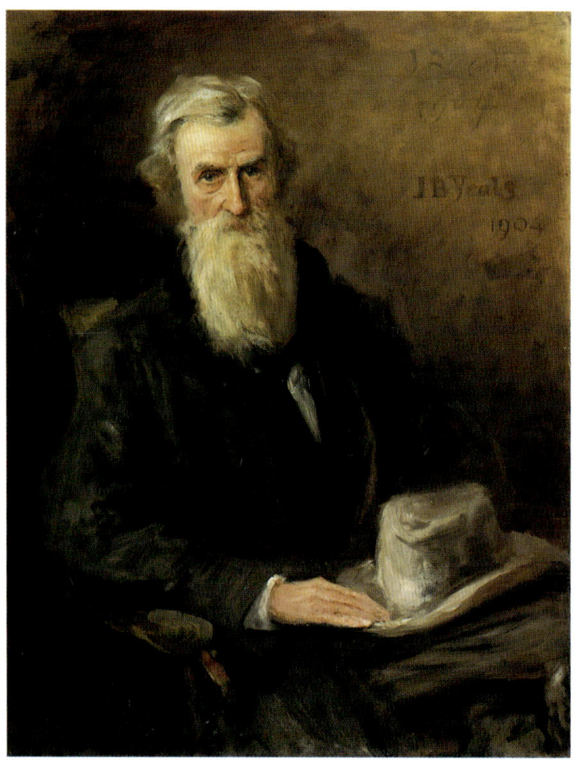

38. **John O'Leary** (1830–1907)
JOHN BUTLER YEATS (1904)
Oil on canvas, 1120 × 870mm (44⅛ × 34¼")
National Gallery of Ireland, Dublin

produced of leading thinkers and political agitators are as sympathetic in execution as George Frederick Watts's contemporaneous yet arguably more illustrious Hall of Fame of leading Victorians. Yeats's drawing of William Morris (fig.36) may not have the same bravura of technique as Watts's oil portrait of Morris of 1870 (NPG 1078), but it conveys an espousal of the English artist's theory of creativity based on friendship. In admiration of Watts, Yeats observed that 'the genius of portrait painting is largely a genius for friendship, at any rate I am quite sure that the best portraits will be painted where the relation of the sitter and the painter is one of friendship'.[61] Despite such utterances, the production of a series of portraits of living persons with whom the artist was personally acquainted was nothing new. Joshua Reynolds had done the same thing back in the eighteenth century when he painted his literary and artistic friends, amongst whom the Irish were a prominent feature: Edmund Burke, Oliver Goldsmith and, as we will discuss later, the engraver James McArdell (fig.49). The difference now, in the early twentieth century, was that, as Paul Barlow has shown in writing about Watts, sitters 'had to be dead before portraits could enter the collection [of the National Portrait Gallery]. By the time Watts's work entered the gallery, it represented another lost cultural community, like that of Reynolds's literary friends.'[62]

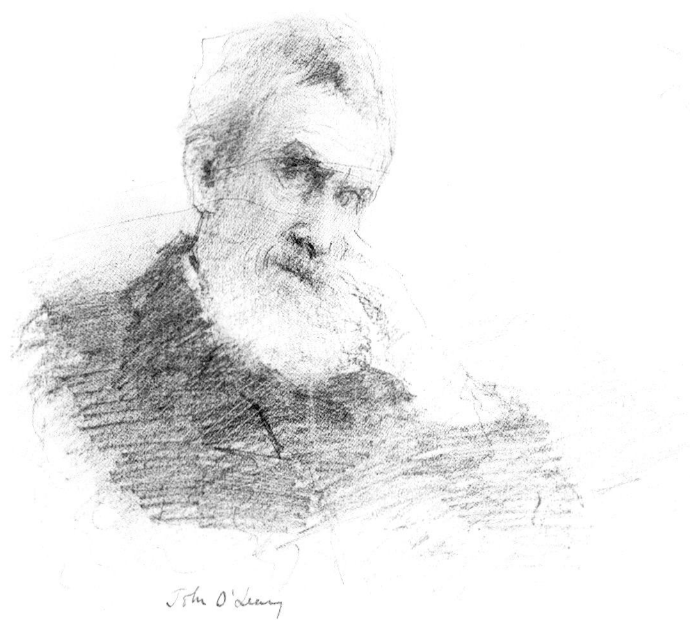

39. **John O'Leary** (1830–1907)
JOHN BUTLER YEATS (1886)
Pencil on paper, 168 × 220mm
(6⅝ × 8⅝")
National Gallery of Ireland,
Dublin

Yeats also suffered as a result of this stipulation. He produced portraits of Dublin's intellectual life but the collection of portraits in Merrion Square, only a short walk from Yeats's studio in St Stephen's Green, was a mausoleum to history, not to modern life. His sitters had to be dead before they found rest in the National Gallery of Ireland. The old Fenian John O'Leary, whom Yeats first drew at the Contemporary Club in 1886, did not have to wait that long as his oil portrait by Yeats of 1891 (fig.37) was presented by the National Literary Society within a year of his death in 1907. A second oil (fig.38) was presented in 1926 in memory of the New York lawyer and collector John Quinn.[63]

In attempting to create a comparable Hall of Fame for Dublin, albeit on a far smaller scale, Yeats was following this Victorian precedent yet giving Ireland something it had never had before. In exhibiting a range of contemporary portraits, he displayed the power of portraiture to exhibit meaning. In this case the meaning was in the people Yeats chose to paint and draw, members of his artistically driven family, liberal scholars and cultural activitists such as O'Leary, Douglas Hyde, George Russell ('Æ') and Edward Martyn. The artist described the

technique of portrait painting [as] mainly a technique of interpretation; to get to the colour, to model the face adequately, this to the practical hand is comparatively easy; to so paint that people should, perforce, see the particular shape of brow or eye that interest the painter, here is the true difficulty, here the true enjoyment and exquisite triumph of the painter.[64]

So Yeats included O'Leary amongst his gallery of friends in the 1901 exhibition and in fact actually exhibited two portraits, a pencil sketch (possibly fig.39) and an oil (definitely fig.37). The oil of O'Leary was much lauded by the archaeologist

George Coffey in the *Daily Express*, who thought it 'a great portrait' and 'probably the finest portrait painted by an Irish artist in recent years'.[65] As a figure who was to exert an enormous influence on the artist's son, W.B. Yeats, it is worth examining the representations of O'Leary to see what exactly it was that led to such praise and to estimate the impact of contemporary portraiture on early twentieth-century Dublin.

In 1924 Thomas Bodkin isolated Yeats's major quality as a 'bent for the intellectual rather than the sensuous', going on to claim that the artist's portraits of O'Leary, Standish O'Grady, Æ and John Millington Synge 'have an air of mingled intimacy and dignity that no other portrait painter of modern time surpasses'.[66] Bodkin may have been more enthusiastic than other critics, but the 'intimacy and dignity' of many of Yeats's portraits are striking features of his oeuvre. At the same time it is worth noting that the *Irish Times* of 1901 had commented that Yeats was 'fortunate in having as his sitters so many distinguished and interesting personages'.[67] This merging of visual intimacy with a dignified aura in his distinguished sitters is Yeats's major contribution to portraiture and it is particularly apparent in the images of O'Leary. Through his rapid technique in both drawings and oils Yeats captures an excellent likeness and offers great visual delight, but he also conveys surprising psychological insight. At the same time, in a sitter such as his old Fenian friend, Yeats is dealing with a national subject, in this case a former felon imprisoned back in the 1860s for journalistic subversion.[68] As such his many portraits, in the context of the Irish cultural revival of *c*.1890–*c*.1910, collectively exhibit a new-found confidence in visualising a national personality. The portraits of O'Leary, all of which date from this twenty-year period, can be read as national portraits.

Roy Foster has suggested that Yeats's portraits of O'Leary, combined with his son's autobiographical memories and poetry, 'fixed O'Leary as the type of heroic – and ancient – republican'. Foster goes onto say that to Yeats *père et fils* O'Leary represented a kind 'of free-thinking Catholic intelligentsia', and that he 'indicated ways' in which they 'could belong to the new Ireland: a world where like-minded people of both religious traditions could share a pride in an ancient culture, rather than remember the conflicts and dispossessions of the past'.[69] In looking at the pencil sketch and oil exhibited in 1901 (figs 37 and 39) and then moving on to what is by far the best of the O'Leary images, the 1904 oil (fig.38), one sees how the artist focuses on what W.B. Yeats was to call the 'great authority'. This is conveyed, as Yeats suggested, through O'Leary's 'distinguished head', 'long imprisonment, his association with famous figures of the past [and] his lofty character'.[70] Hilary Pyle has discussed the 1904 portrait as an amalgamation of the earlier portraits, a concentration on alertness of mind and serious thinking.[71] Their seriousness of purpose together with, in particular, the implied accessibility of the 1904 image portray an Irishman who has overcome adversity, yet is also in his seventy-fourth year, ready to join in continued debate. The accessibility of the 1904 portrait is visually implied by the large scale of the canvas, which stretches the torso and head aided by the rectangular box of the beard. The eyes stare out at the viewer and invite communication, just as the carefully placed hand with its long delicate fingers acts as a kind of gesture of approach. Equally, the outdoor coat and hat suggest a public man and not just the old-time private friend of the artist. The declamatory signature and date of '1904' round off a portrait that has all the confidence of an artist, but at the same time a country that is finding its way in a new century.

The 1904 portrait of O'Leary was commissioned by the American lawyer John Quinn and exhibited that year along with five other portraits by Yeats at an Irish exhibition organised by the Irish collector Hugh Lane in the Guildhall, London. Perhaps aware of the unfulfilled nature of the National Gallery of Ireland's historical collection, and equally aware of the cultural luminaries living in Dublin at the time, Lane commissioned Yeats to paint portraits of a host of prominent Irish figures.[72] Although after a short time William Orpen had to take over the series due to Yeats's impossibly slow working methods, Lane's commission is an important indication of the nation's need to celebrate itself in portraiture. Given the literary and cultural developments that were occurring in Ireland from the 1890s through to the early years of the twentieth century, Lane's initiative brought the visual arts into the centre of intellectual activity.

When eventually Lane's Municipal Gallery of Modern Art opened at 17 Harcourt Street, Dublin, in 1908, his catalogue listed three pages of 'Portraits of Contemporary Irishmen and Women', many of which were his own gift to the city. Yeats contributed oils of Douglas Hyde, co-founder and first President of the Gaelic League (fig.40), playwright John Millington Synge (fig.41), W.B. Yeats and the Abbey Theatre actor W.G. Fay. His rival William Orpen was represented by various portraits of political figures, from the radical Michael Davitt (fig.43) to the more establishment figure of Sir Anthony MacDonnell (fig.42), like Davitt a native of County Mayo, but by contrast a former Lieutenant-Governor in India and Under-Secretary for Ireland since 1902.[73]

Yeats's O'Leary of 1904 (fig.38) is a national portrait in that it evokes a country in transition, but at the same time it is not a radical image. In the late 1890s O'Leary was involved in a range of advanced nationalist activities, most notably the centenary commemorations for the rebellion of 1798, but as F.S.L. Lyons has said, he was 'a monument to an antique style of nationalism'.[74] The 1904 portrait, with its stoic stare and straight-backed assurance, has all the qualities of W.B. Yeats's often repeated comment that O'Leary's head was 'worthy of a Roman coin'.[75] Over the years of the Revival the various portraits of O'Leary enjoyed wide public display and attention, from exhibition at the Royal Hibernian Academy in the late nineteenth century to success in Dublin in the 1901 exhibition, and further afield with appearances at London's Guildhall in 1904 and at the New York Independent Artists' exhibition of

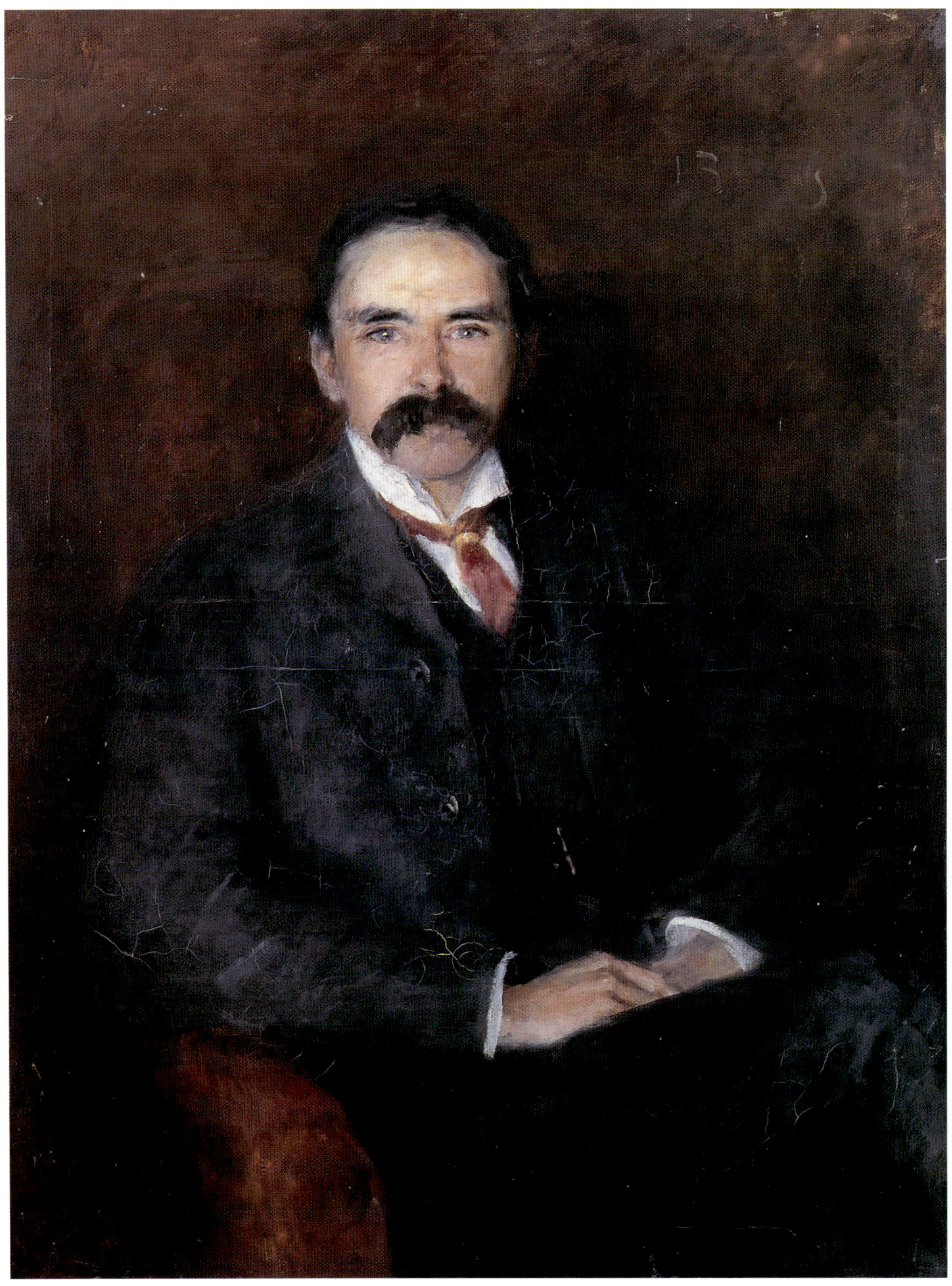

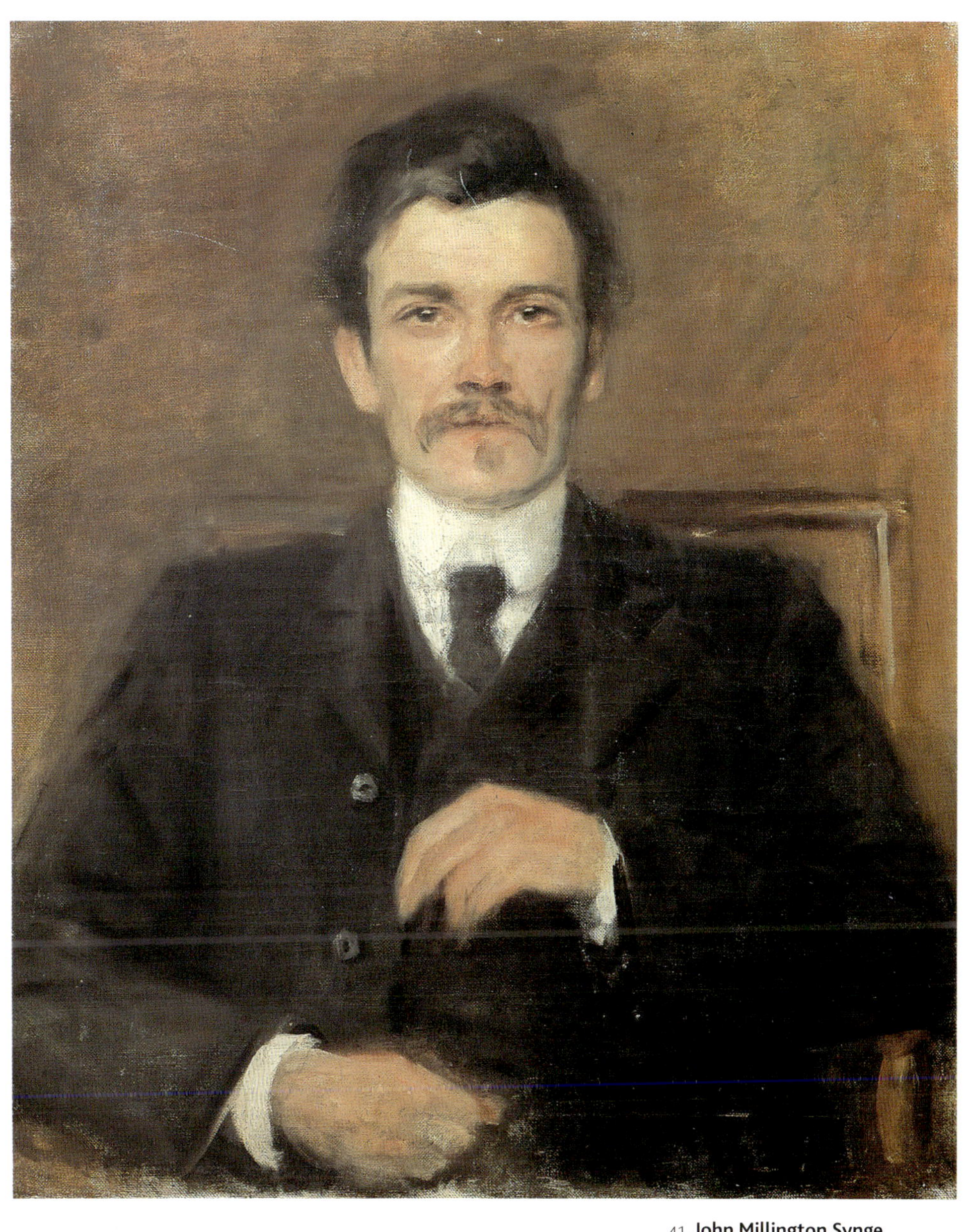

41. **John Millington Synge**
(1871–1909)
JOHN BUTLER YEATS (1905)
Oil on canvas, 737 × 610mm
(29 × 24″)
Dublin City Gallery, the Hugh Lane

OPPOSITE
40. **Douglas Hyde** (1863–1947)
JOHN BUTLER YEATS (1903)
Oil on canvas, 1100 × 850mm
(43¼ × 33½″)
Dublin City Gallery,
the Hugh Lane

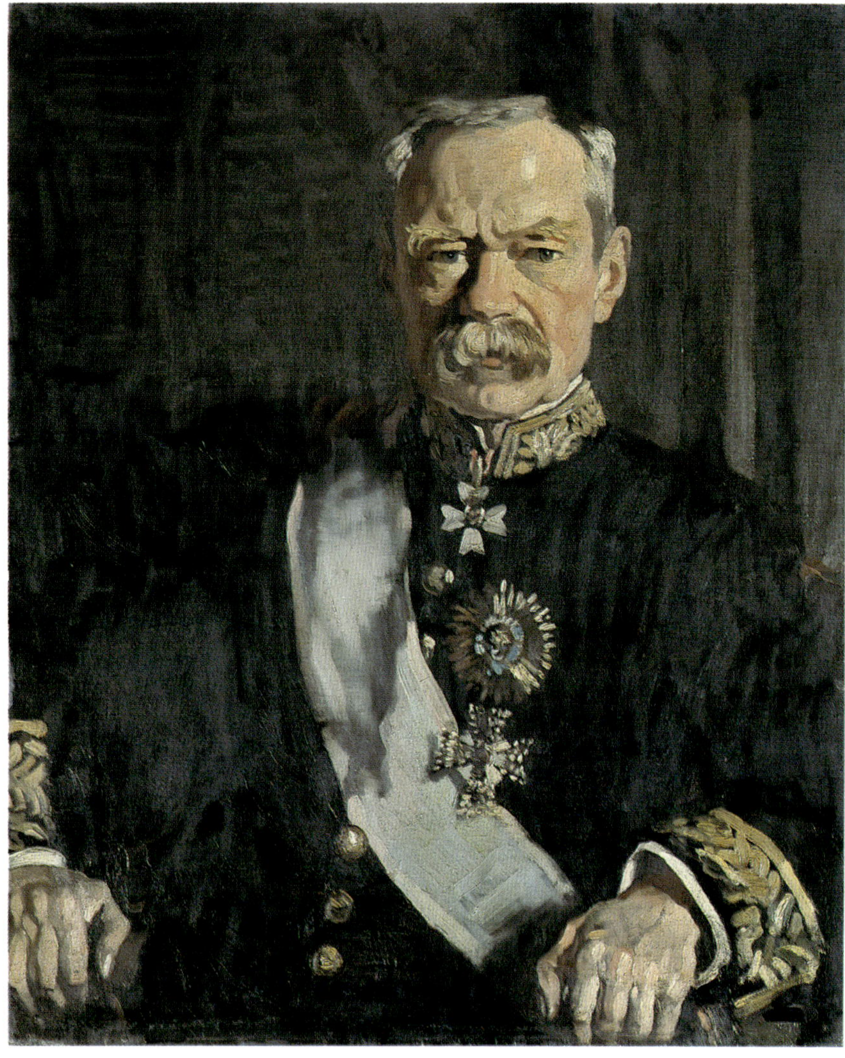

1910. In the mid-1920s, a few years after Independence, Quinn's collection of Yeats's oils returned to Ireland, and six portraits of Revival figures (O'Leary, Standish O'Grady, Æ, W.B. Yeats, George Moore and Douglas Hyde) were presented to the National Gallery of Ireland by Mr C. Sullivan in memory of John Quinn. One can interpret this act at that particular moment as central to reinforcing a sense of nationhood[76] and as such it can be argued that portraiture frequently plays the political card, even in this case when the portrait is that of a moderate (O'Leary), and most particularly so during a period of rapid political and cultural change.[77]

If this is the case, Ireland is not dissimilar from other nations. It is instructive to compare, for example, an examination of a national image during a similar period

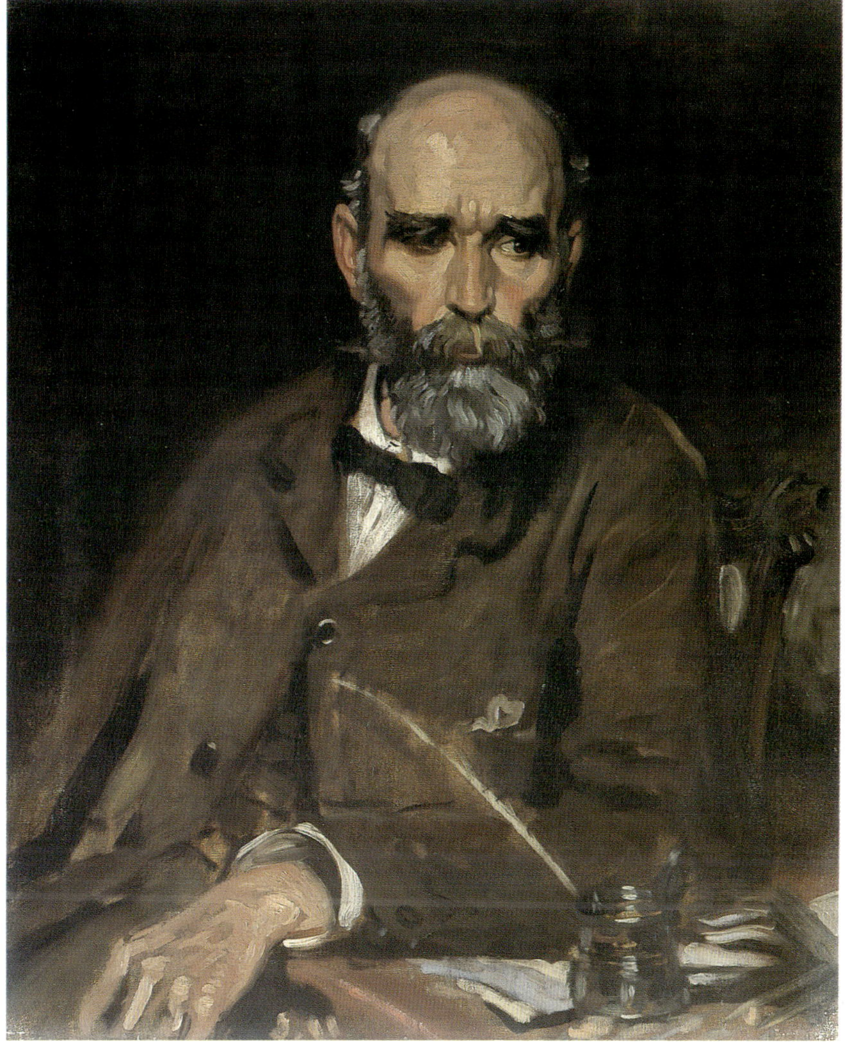

of change in eighteenth-century America. In his survey of American painting, art historian Jules Prown offers a succinct analysis of a late eighteenth-century portrait by the Connecticut artist Ralph Earl, which echoes the discussion here. Earl's 'subdued' portrait of the politician Roger Sherman (fig.44) is painted in a 'sober and restrained style' that 'reinforces awareness of the character of the sitter, a self-made man who worked his way up . . . to become . . . a Senator'. Prown concludes by suggesting that form, the 'primitive quality of the angular portrait' and historical fact about the sitter, 'strength, spare toughness and moral rectitude', merge in the portrait by Earl to create 'an unforgettable symbol of the spirit of independence and the will to achieve and preserve it that marked the establishment of the United States of America as a self-reliant federal republic'.[78]

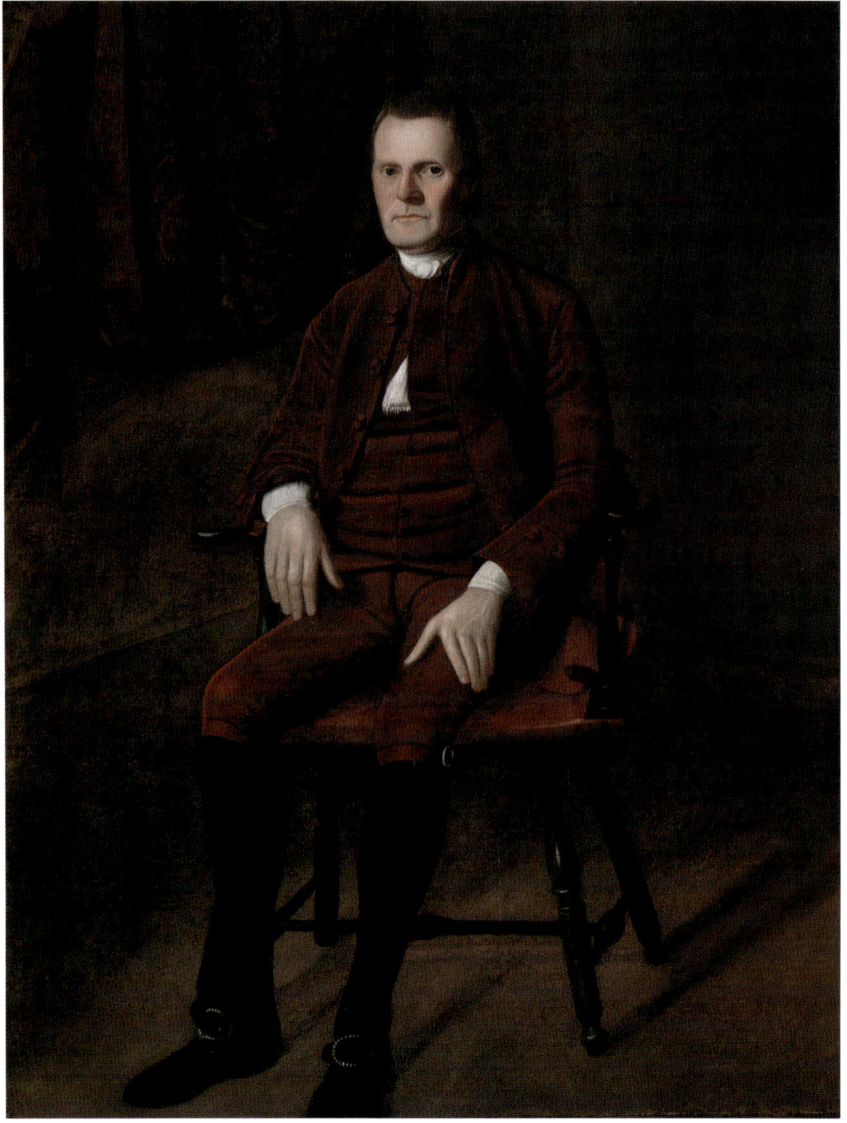

This form of visual analysis, what Prown calls 'style as evidence',[79] makes us consider what America was becoming in the immediate aftermath of 1776. Earl's portrait of a plain man in a plain setting painted in a plain style says a lot about the society that produced it, despite the fact that Sherman 'was one of only two men . . . to sign the Declaration of Independence, the Articles of Confederation, and the Federal Constitution, the three major documents of American independence'.[80] The similarity that needs to be drawn between an image such as Earl's Sherman of 1777 and Yeats's O'Leary of 1904 is that these paintings of seemingly benign statesmen can also be read, when sufficiently contextualized, as icons of national advancement. Both Sherman and O'Leary were of a privileged elite with access to major movers and shakers of their respective eras. Yet they were also moderates

whose portraits are historical documents that suggest their quiet influence on
events as succinctly as any letter or treaty.

Later developments in national portraiture

The collecting of portraiture in Ireland has, of course, not been confined to the
National Gallery of Ireland. The updating of the catalogue of portraits in Trinity
College, Dublin, published by Anne Crookshank and David Webb in 1990 to correspond with the quartercentenary of the College runs to over 340 objects.[81] The
Ulster Museum in Belfast has been collecting portraits since its foundation, and
more recently has commissioned portraits that have attained national status, such
as Edward McGuire's 1974 canvas of Seamus Heaney (fig.1). Other portrait commissions have followed, most particularly the celebrated musicians James Galway (by
Carol Graham, 1988) and Barry Douglas (Tom Phillips, 1989–90).[82] In terms of
portraiture, the Belfast collection specialises in personalities relevant to Ulster
history and culture and has benefited hugely from the generous bequest of around
thirty pictures by Sir John Lavery in 1929. As discussed in Chapter 5 below, Dublin
too gained from Lavery's generosity, but Ulster received just as wide a range of
individuals. The Roman Catholic Cardinal, Michael Logue (fig.85), who reappears in
Chapter 3, cohabits here with portraits of the Grand Masters of the Orange Lodge
and even Sir Edward Carson, until 1921 leader of the Ulster Unionist Party.[83] Lavery's
donation coincided with the opening of the new Museum and Art Gallery on
Belfast's Stranmillis Road and was occasioned, as he said himself, by the fact that
'I was born in Belfast' and 'that they had built a gallery there, but had no pictures
to put in it'.[84]

Although portraiture in the traditional sense has dwindled internationally as
an art form, recently Ireland has had the unique boast of supporting what must be
one of the few national self-portrait collections in the world.[85] While differing from
the famous Uffizi collection of artist's self-portraits founded in Florence in the
seventeenth century in that it is limited to artists connected with one country, the
collection is comparable in its bizarre range. It is also comparable in that it grows
out of an academic tradition.

Situated along the Corridoio Vasariano that connects the Uffizi Gallery with the
Pitti Palace, the Italian self-portrait collection was formed by Cardinal Leopoldo
de'Medici as a means of restoring cultural prestige to Florence in reaction to the
tangible threat of Rome. In time the Gallery acquired self-images from a range of
celebrated artists, both native Italians such as Annibale Carracci and foreign visitors
such as Diego Velázquez.[86] In 1805 the Florentine authorities accepted a self-portrait
by the Irish artist Hugh Douglas Hamilton (fig.45) when the then Director of the

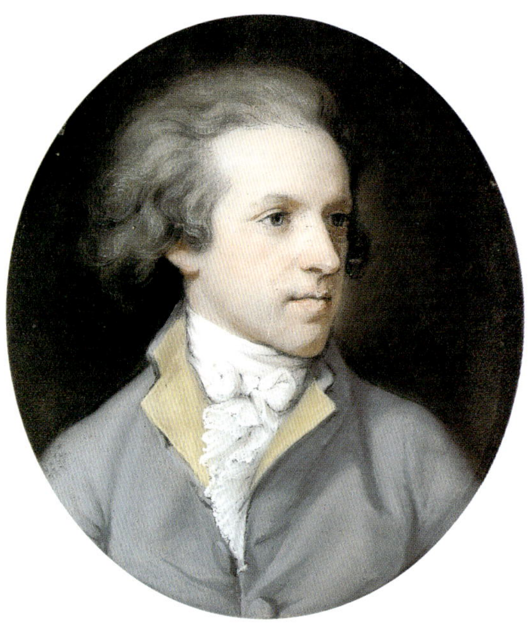

45. **Self-Portrait**

(c.1785)
Pastel, 220 × 200mm (8⅝ × 7⅞")
Uffizi Gallery, Florence

Uffizi, Tommaso Puccini, wrote to Maria Louisa Bourbon, Queen Regent of Tuscany, thanking her for bequeathing a pastel portrait. He pointed out to the queen that he had known Hamilton in Rome some years before and had always thought the Irish artist to be 'il quale non ebbe pari nel passato secolo nell' arte di trattare i pastelli'.[87] In praising Hamilton's contribution to eighteenth-century pastel painting Puccini was also celebrating the aim of such a portrait collection: the celebration of artistic genius and traditional forms of representation. A contemporary and compatriot of Hamilton's not represented in the Uffizi is James Barry. Despite the fact that he produced some of the most interesting self-portraits in the second half of the eighteenth-century (figs 58, 62 and 63), Barry's short stays in Florence in 1766 and again in 1770, combined with his combative personality and his general dislike of portraiture as an art form, would have discouraged any contribution.[88] It is probably not surprising to learn that John Lavery happily supplied the Uffizi with a three-quarter-length self-portrait when he was asked in 1910.[89]

When it was set up in 1982, the Irish Self-Portrait Collection, which is now owned by the University of Limerick, derived its core collection from portraits owned by a local journalist/collector who had been closely advised by Thomas Ryan, the Limerick-born President of the Royal Hibernian Academy. Espousing traditionalist academic views, Ryan has stated that the painter must have 'competence in drawing, a painterly ability with regard for tonal values and compositional harmony and balance'.[90] In 1989 Patrick Doran, the curator of the National Self-Portrait Collection, wrote of how since its foundation it 'has been enriched by the annual addition of a number of works, the year average being fourteen'.[91] One of those additions is Louis le Brocquy's head (fig.46) which is signed 1982. Le Brocquy's watercolour stands out from the banal traditionalism of so much of the Limerick collection in terms of its desire to confront what Dorothy Walker has called 'the head-cult of the Celts in which the magic box of the skull was thought to be the domain of ancestral spirits'.[92]

Unfortunately, the Irish Self-Portrait Collection has few works of comparable interest to the le Brocquy, with the exception perhaps of contributions from Mary FitzGerald and Rita Duffy. A recent review in the contemporary Irish art journal *Circa* sums up the problems faced by such collections in the twenty-first century:

> This collection is beginning to lose what little vitality it started with. The reason this vitality has vanished in the collection lies solely in its inability to recognise that art has changed since the collections inception in 1981 [*sic*] and that art no longer necessarily hangs on a wall or sits on a plinth. Such physical justification for art's existence is archaic.[93]

Le Brocquy's *Study of Self in Watercolour* (fig.46) is suspended in space with the lack of outline around the head creating an ambivalence that he himself has articulated as a 'stillness'.[94] There is little here of the Renaissance conventions of time and progress, realism and perspective. As such, le Brocquy is going beyond the academic norms of the traditional self-portrait and offering more of a presence than a reality. As many have observed, this idea of 'presence' is central to le Brocquy's great series of 'Heads'. Presence is also evoked in the fact that the artist continuously repeats these heads. Since 1975 he has produced many variations on the heads of major Irish modernist writers such as W.B. Yeats, James Joyce and Samuel Beckett, which suggest the tradition of the icon and thus by implication a semi-religious array of saints, if not a deity. As one recent critic has suggested,

> In their modernity . . . in the spareness of their isolation within space, and in the central position which they occupy, they become invested with a pronouncedly hieratic quality. They float within our vision, potentially hypnotic, as in much religious imagery from all cultures.[95]

The same is true of his own *Study of Self in Watercolour*. Le Brocquy has not distracted himself with any more than a few such self-images, but as a group the 'Heads', both his own and those of other Irish artists, can be seen as a major late twentieth-century contribution to the national portrait.

This chapter began with a discussion of the origins and development of a National Portrait Gallery for Ireland. Henry Doyle's late nineteenth-century dream of an independently existing collection never really expanded beyond an ad hoc assemblage of portraits umbilically attached to the body of the National Gallery of Ireland. Until now, and certainly over the past century, the status of this collection has been ill-defined. Up to the 1970s, Dublin's national portraits could be viewed in an uninspiring and old-fashioned display that resembled photographs of the National Gallery of Ireland a century earlier. Then for a few decades many of the key

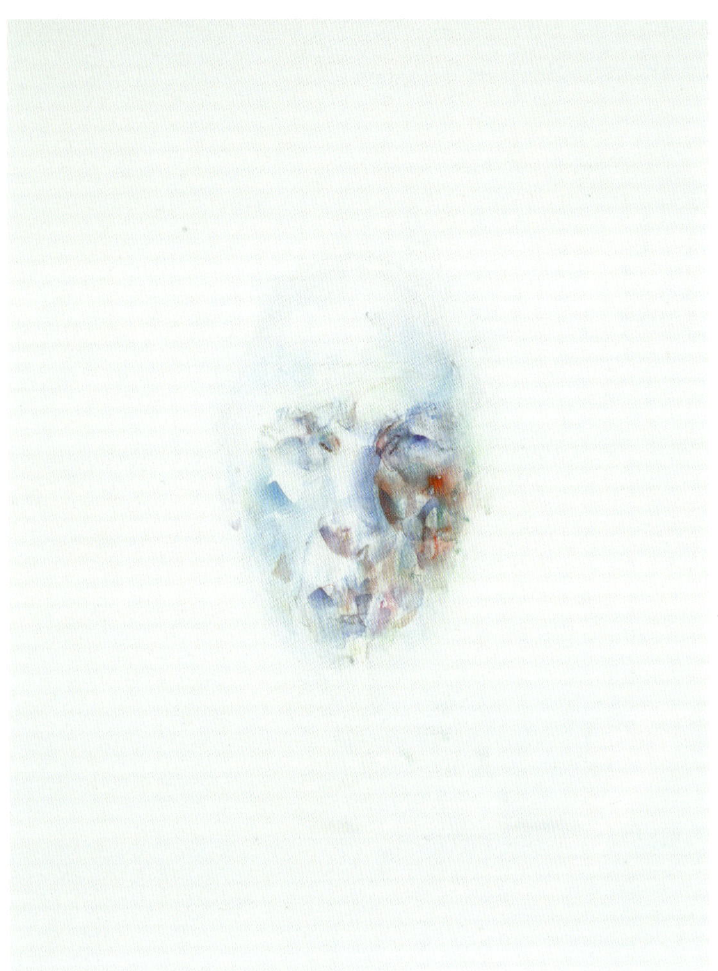

national portraits (for example, images of Lord Edward FitzGerald, fig.101 and Edmund Burke, fig.12) were on extended loan and banished to semi-oblivion in ill-lit rooms in Malahide Castle, north of Dublin city. More recently with a combination of increased funds and a welcome confidence in Ireland's variegated history, a policy on national portraiture has been articulated. Assisted by funds from corporate Ireland, a series of portraits of prominent Irish personalities have been commissioned and exhibited in Merrion Square. The first was Mark Shields's portraits of Mary and Nicholas Robinson, unveiled in December 1998 (fig.47); the latest is a portrait by le Brocquy of the international pop star Bono.[96] It is also to be welcomed that the newly established National Portrait Gallery display in the National Gallery of Ireland will now attempt to convey the confusions and frustrations, as well as the engaging complexities, involved in attempting to define the national portrait. The presence of Ireland's seventh president (and her spouse) and Ireland's most illustrious pop star are fitting additions to the story of the Irish national portrait.

OPPOSITE
47. **Mary** (b.1944) **and Nicholas Robinson** (b.1946)
MARK SHIELDS (1998)
Oil on canvas, 2830 × 1220mm (111⅜ × 48")
National Gallery of Ireland, Dublin

This double portrait was commissioned by Irish Life and Permanent as the first in a series of national portraits. Mary Robinson was seventh President of Ireland from 1990 to 1997 and most recently UN Commissioner for Human Rights. Nicholas Robinson is a lawyer, cartoonist and architectural historian.

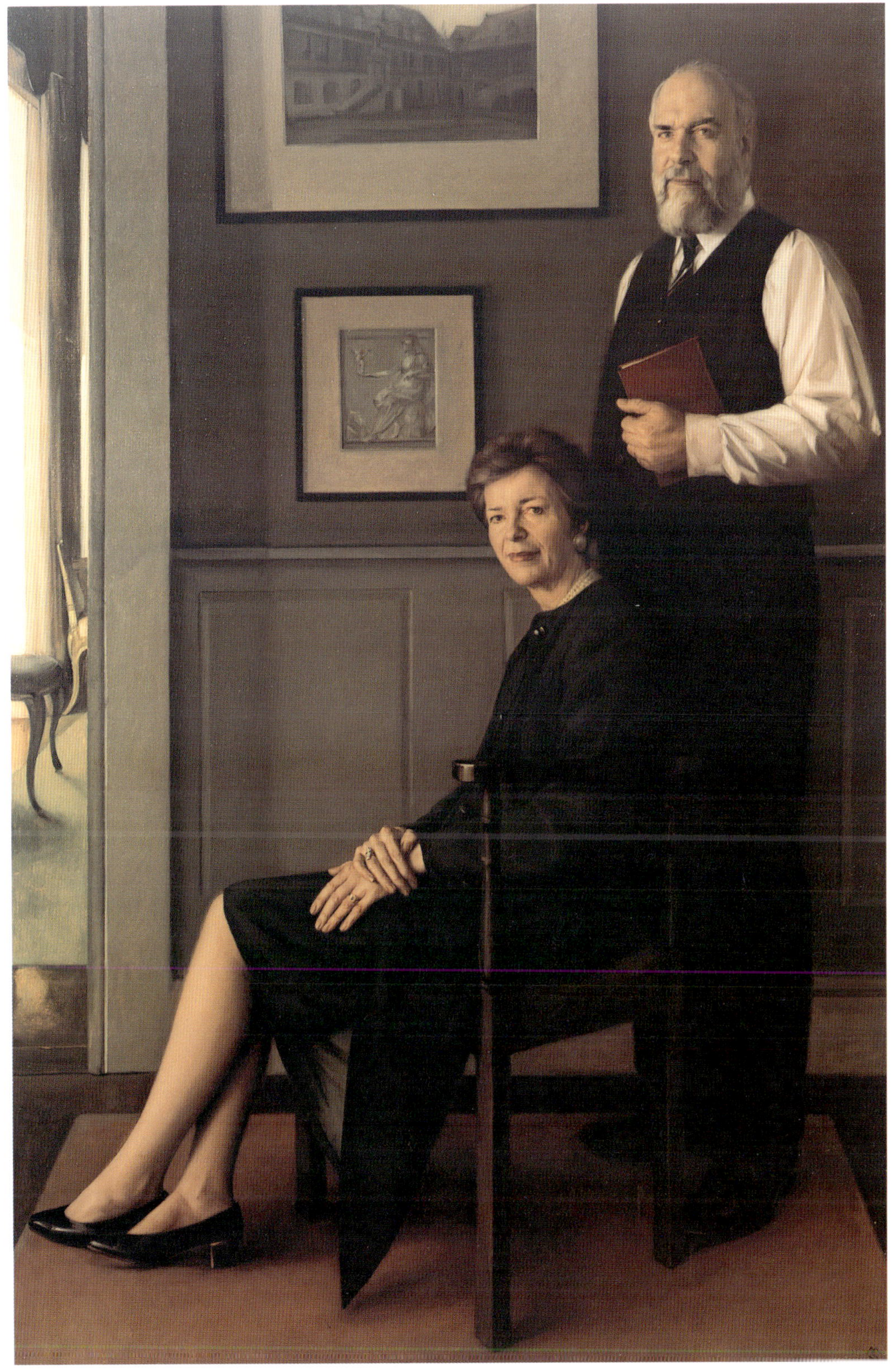

1 Liam Belton RHA in conversation with Elaine Fallon, RHA Marketing Officer, to coincide with the 173rd RHA annual exhibition, May–June 2003, www.royalhibernianacademy.com.

2 Kennedy, 1999, pp.44–5.

3 Barrett and Sheehy, 'Visual Arts and Society, 1850–1900' in Vaughan, 1996, p.442.

4 Edward Lee, Introduction, *Official Catalogue*, 1872.

5 Pointon, 1994, p.51. The National Portrait Gallery of Australia only opened its doors in May 1998, see www.portrait.gov.au. Canada plans to open a Portrait Gallery in 2004–5, see www.portraits.gc.ca.

6 Caffrey, 2000, p.33. For the National Gallery of Ireland's early purchases see Homan Potterton, Introduction, *National Gallery of Ireland*, 1981, p.xix.

7 Duncan, 1907, pp.6–7.

8 FitzGerald, 1872, p.10; see also Lawrence, 1872; Elliott, 2003, p.182.

9 FitzGerald, 1872, p.11.

10 Quoted in Cullen, 2000, p.184; see also Pressly, 1981, p.72 and Figgis and Rooney, 2001, pp.70–3.

11 NPG Archive, Chairman's letters to the Secretary, envelope 4, 20-c-3, letter from Stanhope to Scharf, 11 Dec. 1859.

12 Perry, 1998, pp.237–9; Dunne, 1988, pp.73, 76. See Perry's forthcoming study, *Beauties: Women, History and the Nineteenth-Century National Portrait Gallery*, Aldershot.

13 FitzGerald, 1872, p.64. See Chaloner Smith, 1883.

14 Homan Potterton in Le Harivel, 1988; *Catalogue of Pictures and Other Works of Art in the National Gallery and National Portrait Gallery, Ireland*, Dublin, 1898, p.215.

15 Le Harivel, 1988, p.167 (NGI 10,465); pp.194–7 (NGI 10,233, 10,294, 10,182, 10,153).

16 Le Harivel, 1983, p.232 (David La Touche, NGI 7237; Denis Daly, NGI 6993).

17 Doyle, 1882, p.114.

18 Smailes, 1985, pp.15–21.

19 NGI Archive, Administration, 1869–99, Box 2: letter from William Law, HM Treasury to the Board of Governors, NGI, 30 Dec. 1872. See Síghle Bhreathnach-Lynch, 'A National Gallery for Ireland: Issues of ideological significance', in Stewart, 2002, pp.230–48. I am most grateful to Dr Bhreathnach-Lynch for directing me to this material.

20 NPG Archive, Register Packet 117, letter from Christopher Moore to George Scharf, 6 Aug. 1860. The other busts were of the 1st Lord Plunket, J.P. Curran, Lord Jeffreys and Sir Ian Mackintosh.

21 Paul Barlow, 'Facing the past and present: the National Portrait Gallery and the search for 'authentic' portraiture', in Woodall, 1997, p.231 (quoting the *Art Journal*, 1858, p.243).

22 NGI Archive, Administration, 1869–99, Box 2, letter from Lionel Cust to Walter Armstrong (Director of NGI), 30 Jan. 1899.

23 Morash, 2002, p.72.

24 NPG Archive, Register Packet 10; Walker, 1985, vol.I, pp.375–6.

25 NGI Archive, letter from Lionel Cust to Walter Armstrong, 30 Jan. 1899. Robert Stewart (1769–1822), Viscount Castlereagh, had been acting and then official Chief Secretary of Ireland, 1797–1801; later became Foreign Secretary (1812–22), in which capacity he attended the post-Waterloo conference in Vienna.

26 NPG Archive, Register Packet 199, letter from Leahy to Scharf, 8 May 1865; letter from Carlyle to NPG Trustees, 7 June 1865.

27 *Irish Times*, 20 Oct. 1865.

28 Piper, 1963, pp.279–80; Fenlon, 1991–2, pp.135–48; Crookshank and Glin, 2002, p.16.

29 Piper, 1963, pp.337–8.

30 Figgis and Rooney, 2001, pp.309–10; Le Harivel, 1988, pp.29–30.

31 Another example of a double purchase is Robert Devereux, 2nd Earl of Essex, Lord Lieutenant of Ireland in 1599 and favourite of Elizabeth I. London bought a head-and-shoulders portrait attributed to Marcus Gheeraerts the Younger in 1864, while Dublin acquired an even better three-quarter-length by William Segar in 1886; see Strong, 1969, pp.115–16.

32 Pointon, 1993, p.229.

33 *Freeman's Journal*, 3 Oct. 1896 and the *Weekly Irish Times*, 10 Apr. 1897; my thanks again to Síghle Bhreathnach Lynch for this reference.

34 See Whelan, 2003, chap.3: 'Contested identities and the monumental landscape'. In 1957–8 the Gough monument was blown from its pedestal and is now on view in the grounds of Chillingham Castle, Northumberland; see Whelan, 2003, pp.207–12 and Murphy, 1996, pp.41–2.

35 See Cullen, 1993, pp.58–73 and Smailes, 1985.

36 Quoted in Smailes, 1985, p.160.

37 Quoted in Saumarez Smith, 1997, pp.11–12.

38 Barlow in Woodall, 1997, pp.227–8.

39 Foster, 1988, pp.398–9.

40 NGI Archive, Administration, 1869–99, Box 2, Treasury letter signed R.R. Whingam(?), 9 May 1873.

41 Tiffin, 1867, p.95 quoted in Pointon, 1993, p. 227.

42 Caffrey, 2000, pp.98–9; Walker, 1985, vol.I, pp.182–3.

43 Pointon, 1993, pp.241–2. See also Pointon, 1994, pp.63–4.

44 Murphy, 1995, p.155; Murphy, 1994, p.204.

45 Quoted in Boyd, 1969, p.47. For background see Bardon, 1992, pp.350–2; see also Fintan Cullen, 'Union and Display in Nineteenth-Century Ireland', in Arnold, 2004, pp.111–33 and Murphy, 1996, p.22.

46 Murphy, 1994, p.205.

47 Vaughan, 1989, pp.794–9.

48 *Freeman's Journal*, 3 Oct. 1896, p.5. See also Bhreathnach-Lynch in Stewart, 2002, p.244.

49 NGI Archive, letter from Lionel Cust to Walter Armstrong, 26 Feb. 1897; Duncan, 1907, p.11. A portrait of Plunkett after Morphey has been in the Siena Convent, Drogheda, since 1722, see McDonnell, 1995, no.11. For a recent examination of the cult of Plunkett see Kilfeather, 2002.

50 Duncan, 1907, pp.6–20.

51 The NPG Archive holds Holmes's annotated *Catalogue of Pictures and Other Works of Art in the National Gallery of Ireland and the National Portrait Gallery, Ireland*, Dublin, 1908.

52 Holmes, 1936, pp.310–11.

53 As can be seen from the images of Curran listed in the page from Holmes's copy of the NGI *Catalogue* (fig.30), the Hamilton (fig.33) is not listed as it only entered the collection the year the *Catalogue* was published; equally, the death mask was not presented until 1912. In 1914, Holmes may also have seen on display the mezzotint image of Curran after Lawrence (now NGI 10,058) and a caricature (NGI 11,867). For the Hamilton and Petrie portraits see Figgis and Rooney, 2001, pp.180–2, 386–8.

54 Bodkin, 1936, pp.246–51.

55 The National Library of Ireland online catalogue lists at least twelve biographical accounts in the nineteenth century, with the most recent being 1958.

56 FitzGerald, 1872, p.34. The Barber is illustrated in colour in Crookshank and Glin, 2002, p.87; in the nineteenth century it was owned by a member of the Le Fanu family in Bray, County Wicklow: see Strickland, 1913, vol.I, p.22. Swift's death mask is illustrated in Fox, 1986, p.131.

57 For Curran's iconography see Walker, 1985, vol.I, p.140; Figgis and Rooney, 2001, pp.110–1, 180–2, 383–8. Paul Barlow discusses the issue of authenticity and portraits of Thomas Carlyle in Woodall, 1997.

58 FitzGerald, 1872, p.30.

59 Kennedy, 1991, pp.6–7.

60 Murphy, 1978, p.140. See also Cullen, 1987, p.54 and *passim*. Many of the sketches are now in the National Gallery of Ireland, see Le Harivel, 1983, nos 6078–83 and 7357–65.

61 Quoted in Cullen, 1987, p.23; see Yeats, 1918, pp.79–80.

62 Barlow in Woodall, 1997, p.236.

63 For Yeats's portraits of O'Leary see Pyle, 1997, pp.66, 76, 82 and 118; Murphy, 1978, p.141 and Cullen, 1987, pp.82–3.

64 Quoted in Cullen, 1987, p.23, again from Yeats, 1918, pp.79–80.

65 Murphy, 1987, p.233; Pyle, 1997, p.82.

66 Bodkin, 1924; Cullen, 1987, p.20.

67 E.J.G., 'Loan exhibition of Paintings by Mr Hone RHA and Mr Yeats RHA', *Irish Times*, 21 Oct. 1901; Cullen, 1987, p.20.

68 For further discussion of Fenian portraits see Chapter 5, pp.203–5.

69 Foster, 1997, pp.42–3.

70 Yeats, 1972, p.52.

71 Pyle, 1997, p.118.

72 Murphy, 1978, pp.271–2 and Cullen, 1987, p.29; see also Temple, 1904.

73 Friends of the National Collections of Ireland, 1984, pp.17–19. The other artists included in this 1908 exhibition were Antonio Mancini, Sarah Purser, H. Harris Brown and Count Dunin Markievicz. For Lane's 'Prefatory Note' to the *Illustrated Catalogue* see Cullen, 2000, pp.248–51.

74 F.S.L. Lyons, 'The Watershed, 1903–7', in Vaughan, 1996, p.117.

75 Yeats, 1972, p.42.

76 Foster, 2003, p.302.

77 This point is further developed in Chapter 4 below.

78 Prown, 1969, p.35.

79 See Prown, 2002.

80 Prown, 1969, p.35.

81 Crookshank and Webb, 1990. The previous catalogue, Strickland, 1916, had been produced by the author of the great *Dictionary of Irish Artists*.

82 Black, 2000.

83 McConkey, *Lavery*, 1993, chap.9 and Black, 2000, pp.56–7; for a list of bequests to Irish collections see Lavery, 1940, pp.254–7.

84 Lavery quoted in McConkey, 1984, p.219 n.56, *Belfast Newsletter*, 10 Dec. 1929.

85 Finlay, 1989.

86 Prinz, 1971 (vols 2 and 3 deal with the Italian and non-Italian collections respectively); Haskell, 1980, pp.403–4.

87 Translated as 'he who was unsurpassed in the art of pastel drawing in the previous century'. Archivio Soprintendenza alle Gallerie, Florence, MS 196, Filza XXXII, 49: letter from Tommaso Puccini to Queen Maria Louisa Bourbon of Tuscany (Florence), 21 Sept. 1805; see Prinz, 1971, p.222 and *Firenze e l'Inghilterra*, 1971, p.55.

88 Pressly, 1981, pp.8, 15.

89 Lavery, 1940, pp.155–6, illus.; a half-length variation on the Uffizi painting dating from 1928 is in the collection of the Museums and Galleries of Northern Ireland: see Black, 2000, p.57, and illus. in Ó Cuív, 2000, p.120.

90 Finlay, 1989, p.230.

91 Finlay, 1989, p.8.

92 Walker, 1997, p.63.

93 Sam Walsh, *Circa Art Magazine*, 93, autumn 2000, p.54.

94 Quoted in Kearney, 1988, p.201.

95 Smith, 1996, p.45; le Brocquy also produced an oil *Study of Self* in 1987: Smith, 1996, p.103, no.96.

96 My thanks to Síghle Bhreathnach-Lynch and Valerie Keogh of the National Gallery of Ireland for information on the Irish Life and Permanent Portrait Series. Others awarded with a national portrait have been Olympic gold medallist Ronnie Delaney (by James Hanley, 2000); broadcaster Gay Byrne (by John Kindness, 2000) and T.K. Whitaker, civil servant and economist (by Thomas Ryan, 2002).

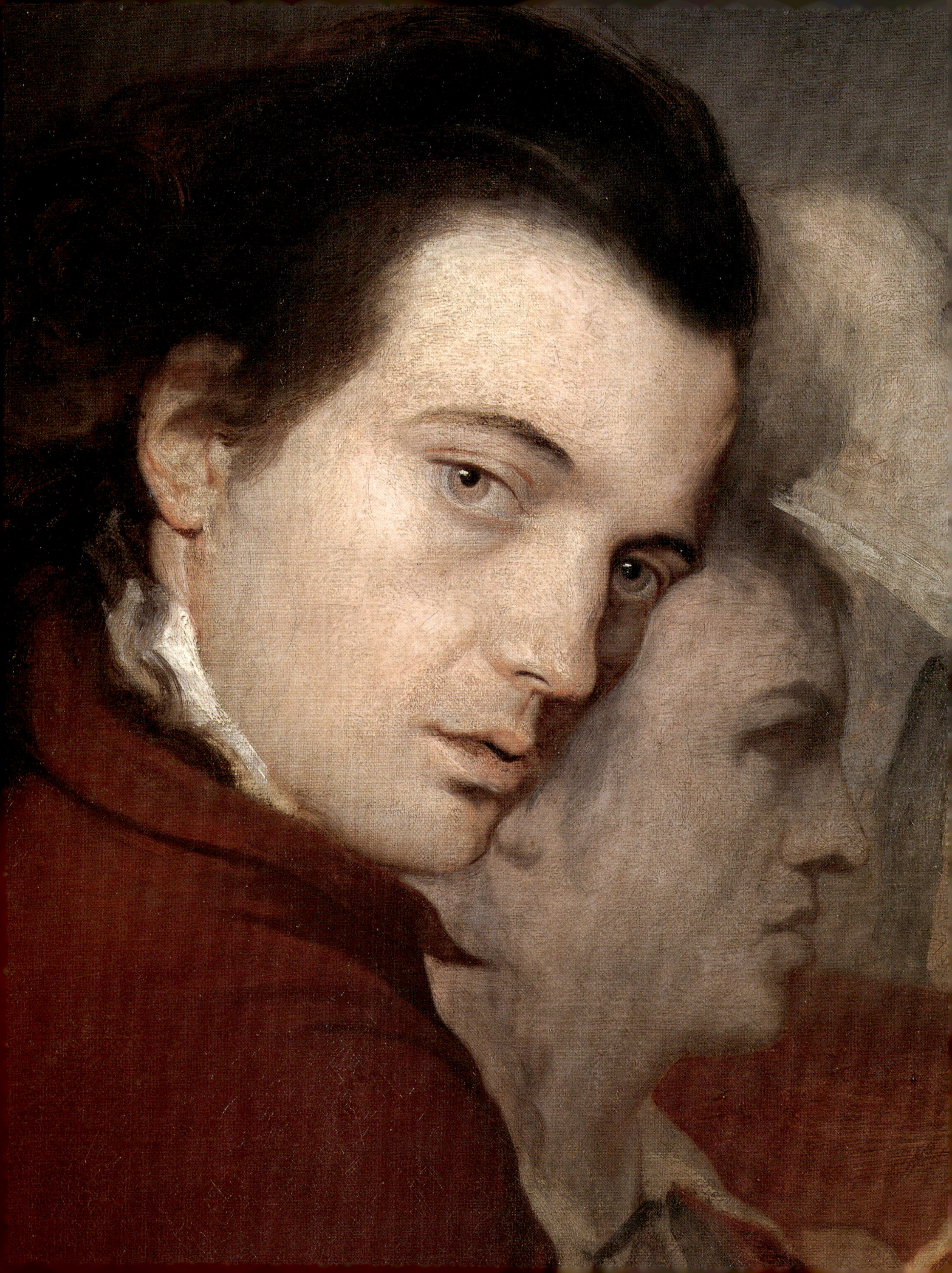

THE FOCUS OF this chapter is on a series of case studies that explore different types of portrait-making in a variety of media.[1] The link between them is that they all relate to the production of an Irish portrait abroad, while all examples are from the eighteenth century. In all cases the artists and their sitters are preoccupied with visualising the power of a prevailing establishment. Attitudes to such an establishment do of course vary, from the passively celebratory to the more potently confrontational. The former are examined through a range of examples: the result of the artist being in the right place at the right time, as in James McArdell's mezzotints after Reynolds (figs 19, 20, 48) or Hugh Douglas Hamilton's portraits of the exiled Stuarts and other Grand Tour images painted in Italy (figs 55, 56).

The portrait may, on the other hand, be the product of economic migration from early eighteenth-century Ireland (fig.57) and a sign of financial and social advancement within a world of changing fortunes. John Trumbull's portrait of Patrick Tracy portrays a man who had for many years helped the British Empire from his position as a New England merchant until it proved more judicious to do otherwise. Yet, as with James Barry's *Self-Portrait* (fig.58), the production of the portrait can also exhibit signs of aggression and hostility. Although very much within the traditions of the European self-portrait, Barry's image is not just about the artist himself, but also about the plight of the Irish Catholic in Hanoverian London. The major link between all these examples is that they illuminate the making of portraits which we can call 'Irish' within a now articulated space that will remain broad.

An Irish scraper

In Chapter 1, when discussing the formation of a national collection of portraits in Dublin in the late nineteenth century, reference was made to the acquisition of prints by James McArdell from the Chaloner Smith collection of mezzotint reproduction engravings (figs 19–21; see p.40). The mezzotint allowed a wider audience to enjoy the products of fashionable portraiture, and McArdell was a central figure in its revival in London in the 1750s. A Dublin-born engraver, he moved from Ireland to London in 1746 and was to dominate the production of engravings after artists such as Joshua Reynolds for the next two decades. His rise to fame was prodigious.

In 1754, still only in his mid-twenties, he produced his first mezzotint after a Reynolds portrait, *Lady Charlotte Fitzwilliam* (fig.48), the result of the portrait artist's only speculative printing venture. Writing to the sitter's mother, the Countess Fitzwilliam, Reynolds requested 'the liberty of having a Mezzotinto Print [made] from it'. He went on to 'beg the favour to know what is to be writ under the Print'. Eventually, McArdell's richly textured print was lettered: 'J. Reynolds pinxt J. Mcardell fecit. Lady Charlotte Fitz-William. Publish'd by J. Reynolds . . . 1754.'[2] In time, Reynolds returned the plate to the engraver who, with confidence in his own creative powers, put his London address on the third state.[3]

McArdell was soon enlarging the engraved plate to produce bigger mezzotints; he encouraged a group of fellow-Irish engravers to follow him to London and thus spawned what David Alexander has termed 'The Dublin Group' of mezzotint scrapers.

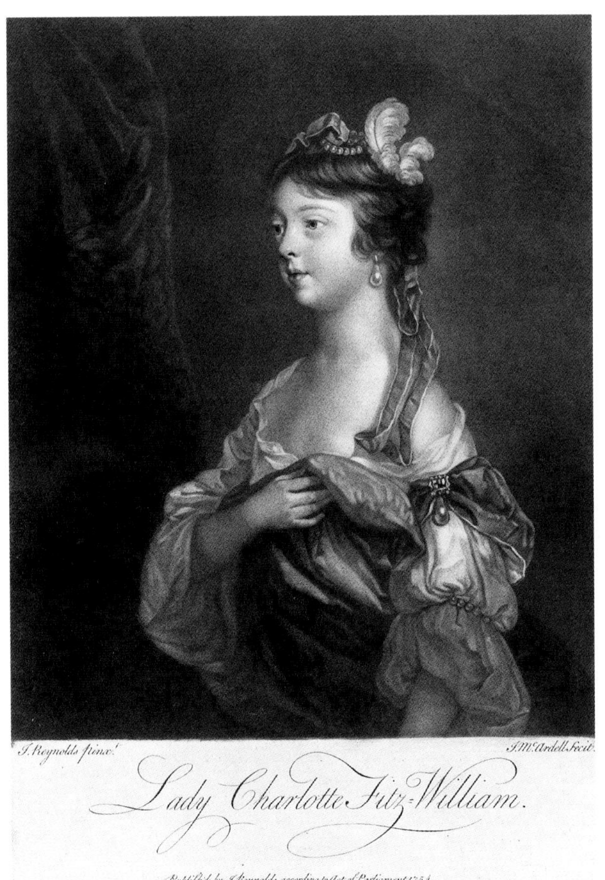

48. **Lady Charlotte Fitzwilliam (later Lady Dundas)** (1746–1833)
JAMES McARDELL after
JOSHUA REYNOLDS (1754)
Mezzotint, second state,
326 × 225mm (12⅞ × 8⅞")
British Museum, London

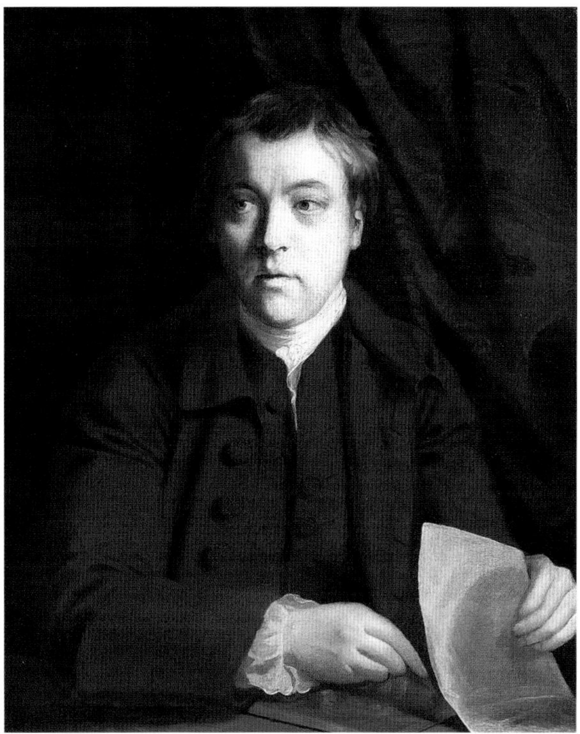

49. **James McArdell** (1728/9–65)

Oil on canvas, 749 × 623 cm (29½ × 24½")
National Portrait Gallery, London (NPG 3123)

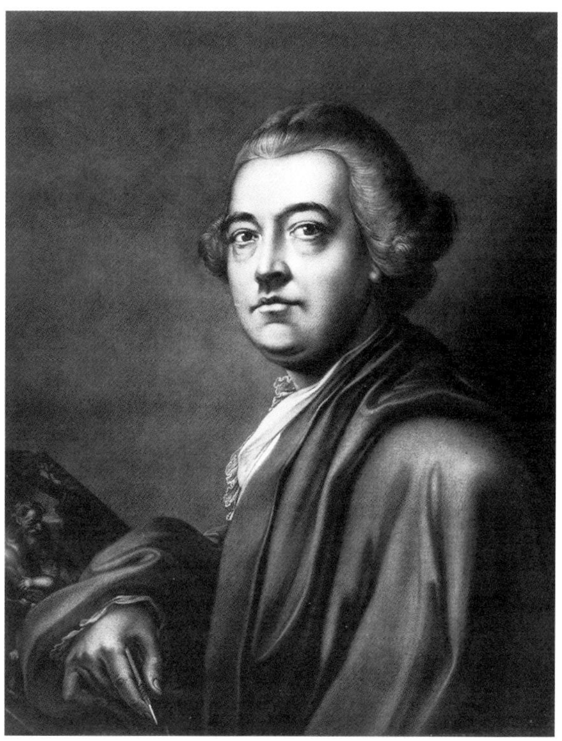

50. **James McArdell** (1728/9–65)

Mezzotint, 406 × 327mm (16 × 12⅞")
British Museum, London

In Alexander's words, 'up to 1775 the great majority of mezzotints after Reynolds were engraved by the Irish engravers, which reflects their dominant position'.[4]

Working in London at an opportune time, James McArdell is a perfect example of the émigré seizing the moment and raising his status such that Reynolds could later say, while turning over a number of McArdell's prints, 'By this man, I shall be immortalised'.[5] Indeed, the author of the book of memoirs from which these words are taken, J.T. Smith, an acquaintance of Reynolds and onetime Keeper of the Department of Prints and Drawings at the British Museum, also remarked:

> Fortunate are those collectors who can boast of proof-impressions from the portraits of Sir Joshua: they of themselves form a brilliant school of Art, not only for the grace displayed in their attitudes, but also for the grandeur of their chiaroscuro.[6]

Reynolds produced an oil portrait of McArdell possibly dated to about 1756,[7] which deserves comparison with McArdell's own self-portrait of a few years later (figs 49 and 50). The latter is now only known through a mezzotint engraved by Richard Earlom in 1771, while the original drawing by McArdell was produced in 1765, the year of his early death at the age of thirty-seven. In both the Reynolds's oil and Earlom's print the artist is shown at work on a copper plate. Produced a few years after the publication of the print of Lady Charlotte Fitzwilliam, the oil is a portrait of a close colleague: he shows an informal McArdell, the Irishman caught in the act of creation; his hand scrapes at the plate while he looks up, distracted, his lips parted. One is reminded of some of Reynolds's other informal portraits of artists and writers who were also his friends. His earliest portrait of Samuel Johnson, for example (NPG 1011), dates from within a year of the portrait of McArdell. He, too, has been captured in distracted mood with his mouth slightly agape, with pen in hand as opposed to the Irishman's burin. John Kerslake suggests that, as 'no references to payment occur in [Reynolds's] ledgers', McArdell 'may never have had a formal appointment'.[8] As such, the McArdell portrait, like the larger Johnson canvas, was probably uncommissioned and was more a sign of friendship than any formal financial arrangement. The extent of that friendship is nicely summed up in Northcote's well-known anecdote of McArdell asking Reynolds to advise him on a portrait print of Rubens. The Irish mezzotinter asked Sir Joshua

> to inform him particularly of the many titles to which Rubens had a right, in order to inscribe them properly under his print ... Dr Johnson happened to be in the room with Sir Joshua at the time, and understanding MacArdell's inquiry, interfered rather abruptly, saying, 'Pooh! Pooh! put his name alone under the print, Peter Paul Rubens: that is full sufficient, and more tha[n] the rest'. The advice of the Doctor was accordingly followed.[9]

The friendly exchange of images such as that between Reynolds and McArdell was not uncommon. In the 1770s Reynolds's other great Irish friend, Oliver Goldsmith, would write to his brother saying, 'I will shortly send my friends over the Shannon some mezzotinto prints of myself and some more of my friends here, such as Burke, Johnson, Reynolds and Colman'.[10] By comparison, the engraved print portrait by Earlom (fig.50), based on a lost drawing by McArdell, is altogether more public. The now more formally bewigged and thus more publicly presentable mezzotinter unhesitatingly displays his work in progress, a plate with Van Dyck's *Time Clipping the Wings of Love*, while he looks out at the viewer fully confident of his powers. McArdell had exhibited his engraving after Van Dyck's painting at the Society of Artists' exhibition in London in 1760, and it is one of over two hundred mezzotints he produced after artists other than Reynolds. Whereas the oil portrait of McArdell is a private homage to an important personage in Reynolds's artistic environment, the mezzotint by Earlom after McArdell has more to do with the Dublin artist's awareness of his own career – one not necessarily entwined with that of the future first President of the Royal Academy of Arts.

A final example of where McArdell's career was going is suggested by the appearance of one of his mezzotints of Queen Charlotte, wife of George III, in the background of an Irish family portrait of the mid-eighteenth century. Recently

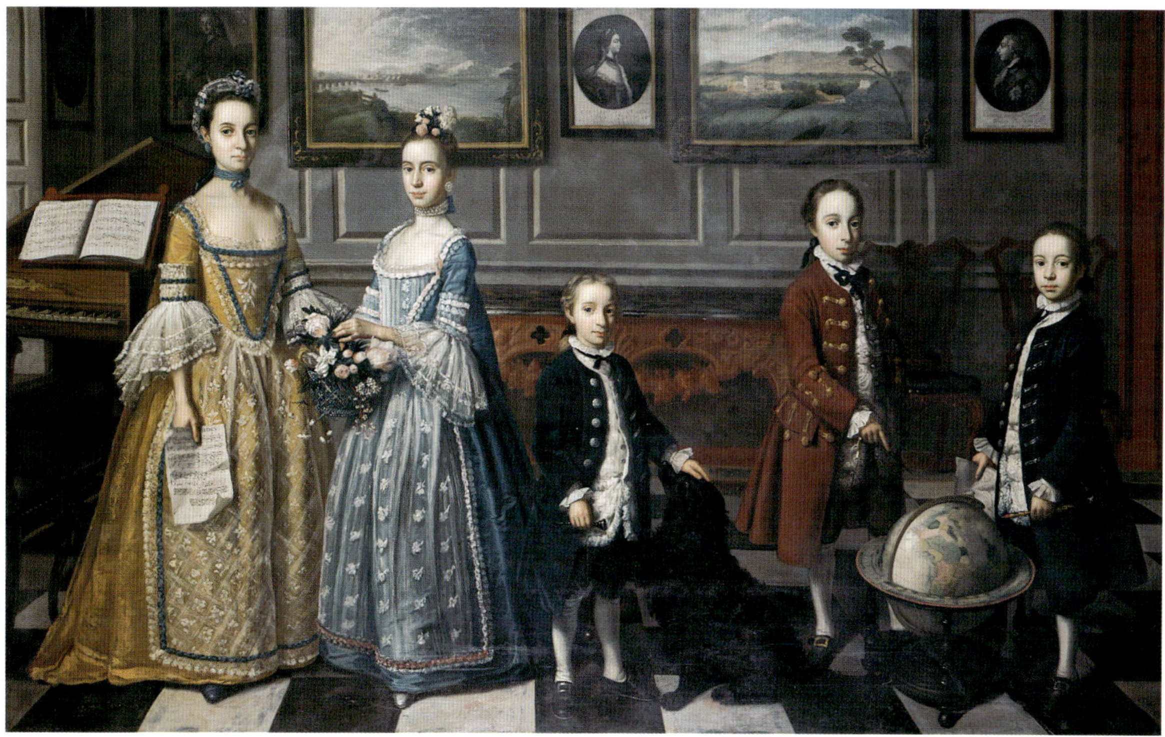

51. **The Family of Thomas Bateson Esq.** (1705–91)
Attributed to
STRICKLAND LOWRY (1762)
Oil on canvas, 1637 × 2640mm
(64½ × 104")
Ulster Museum, Belfast

attributed to the English-born artist Strickland Lowry, the large canvas of the Bateson family (fig.51) of 1762 shows the five children of Thomas Bateson, a wealthy Belfast merchant, standing on the chequered floor of the hall of their home, Orangefield, County Down.[11] In the centre, behind the youngest child and his dog and flanked by landscapes of Long Bridge, Belfast and Orangefield itself, is McArdell's profiled head of the queen, published in the very year that the painting was inscribed (on the harpsichord on the left): 'Londini fecit 1762'. McArdell's royal portrait, which seems to be either the first or second state of the print as later states are slightly different, is a companion to an earlier mezzotint after Jeremiah Meyer of the king, on the far right.[12] Another mezzotint, a portrait of Pitt the Elder, is discernible on the far left. This, too, is a product of the Dublin Group, being a 1756–7 print by Richard Houston after William Hoare's portrait of 'the Great Commoner' (NPG 128). Houston (c.1722–75), who had accompanied McArdell from Dublin to London in 1746, went on to gain fame for his reproductive prints after Rembrandt and contemporary English artists.[13]

In its composition and in its genderised iconography, Lowry's portrait group is conventional in the extreme. The girls stand on the left, next to the harpsichord, while one holds music and the other flowers; the boys stand on the right with the eldest son and heir (Thomas Bateson, 1752–1811) pointing at the globe to indicate future travel and experience; a second son holds a porte-crayon and some paper to suggest wholesome industry and drawing, while the youngest pats a black spaniel, symbolic of fidelity. The prints by the London-based Irish 'tinters' act as a backdrop to this interior portrait of a loyal Belfast family, indicating that although eighteenth-century Irish portrait artists had a currency in the home market, it was one that was filtered through their success in the more competitive world of the metropolis.

Global players

Reynolds's relationship with the Irish predates his friendship with McArdell by a few years and, as we will see, it also anticipates his fractious relationship with James Barry by about two decades.[14] One single canvas painted in Rome by the young Joshua Reynolds in 1751 (fig.52) conveniently brings together a range of Irish 'milordi' who passed through Italy in the mid-eighteenth century. Painted as a parody of Raphael's *School of Athens*, the Reynolds canvas was commissioned by Joseph Henry of Straffan who sprawls across the steps in the centre. Henry takes on the character of Diogenes and holds a book entitled *Larry Grog*, which has been identified by Cynthia O'Connor as referring to Larry Grogan, the author of a popular ballad about 'an artless young man just come from the schoolery'. Behind Henry is his uncle Joseph Leeson, seen in profile looking through an eye-glass, who takes the place of Plato in Raphael's original composition. Leeson's son, the beaky-nosed Joseph Junior, looks on three heads to the right of his father. The nouveaux riches Leesons derived their money from brewing; Leeson senior gradually moved up the social ladder, acquiring a seat in the Irish parliament in 1743, the year before he travelled to Italy. In time he gained a peerage (1756), eventually becoming Earl of Milltown in 1763. Thomas Dawson, the first Viscount Cremorne, appears in the bottom right, while the Earl of Charlemont appears in the bottom left, playing the recorder in an impromptu orchestra made up of companions from Scotland, England and Wales. Finally, Charlemont's tutor, Edward Murphy, sits at a table in the centre foreground.[15] Instead of re-creating the classical perfection of Raphael's interior, Reynolds's *Parody* uses a Gothic backdrop which, as Edgar Wind has suggested, indicates barbarism and ridicules 'with one stroke both the neo Roman and the neo Gothic tastes'. Reynolds's Gothic setting also produces what Wind saw as 'an atmosphere of obscurantism singularly suited' to the futile debates of the milordi; the Gothic is also a signifier of a specific racial background, given the northern European origins of these Irish and British cognoscenti.[16]

Commissioned by an Irishman and including no fewer than six Irish visitors to Rome, Reynolds's *Parody* appeared only a few years before Charlemont began his celebrated argument over payment with Giovanni Battista Piranesi. This quarrel was centred on the Irish aristocrat's original agreement to sponsor the Italian's etchings, *Le Antichità Romane*. The connection between Reynolds's *Parody* and the Piranesi commission is that the former is the most elaborate portrayal in the form

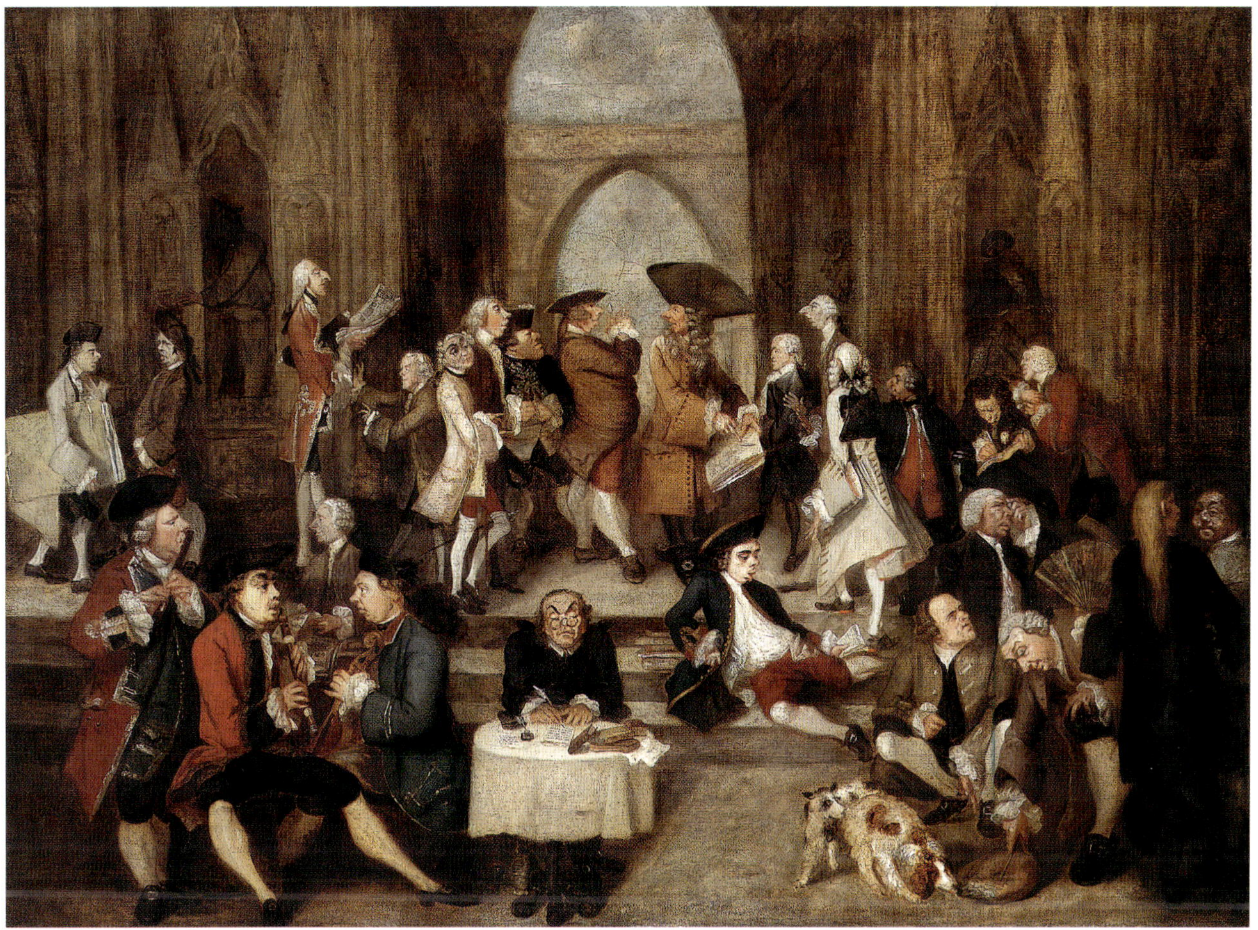

52. **Parody of School of Athens**
JOSHUA REYNOLDS (1751)
Oil on canvas, 970 × 1350mm
(38¼ × 53⅛")
National Gallery of Ireland, Dublin

of portraiture in the eighteenth century of Irishmen at the centre of metropolitan Europe, while the latter's frontispiece to volume I of *Le Antichità* (1756) is one of the century's most emphatic verbal statements in a visual medium of a confident Irishness. The frontispiece proudly declares Charlemont's origins: 'Regni Hiberniae Patricio' (nobleman of the Kingdom of Ireland), which in turn is illusionistically embedded in an antique architectural framework that includes Charlemont's family crest. As such, despite the ensuing saga of graphic defacement that the dedications were to undergo, one must read this frontispiece and Reynolds's *Parody* as examples of the Irish periphery successfully penetrating the metropolitan centre.[17]

That success was further achieved through representation by Pompeo Batoni, semi-official painter of Grand Tourists in Italy from the 1740s to the 1780s. The importance of his Irish and British patrons in establishing and maintaining his fame has long been recognised. Some years ago, Anthony M. Clark established that of the 265 or so surviving Batoni portraits, 75 per cent or roughly 200, are of sitters from these islands with approximately 160 being English while the remainder come

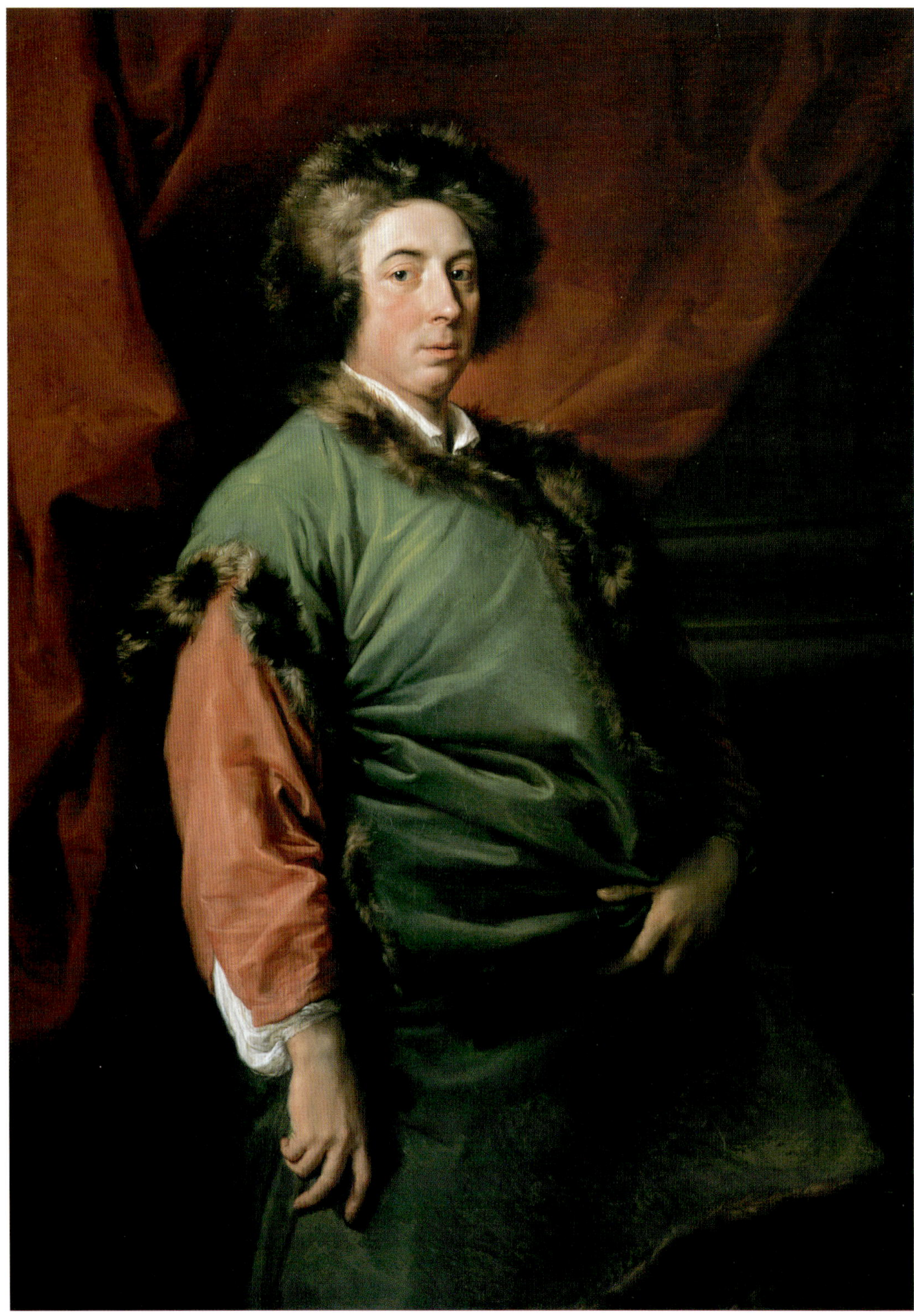

**53. Joseph Leeson, later
1st Earl of Milltown** (c.1711–83)
POMPEO BATONI (1744)
Oil on canvas, 1370 × 1020mm (54 × 40⅛″)
National Gallery of Ireland, Dublin

Enjoying a successful real estate and
brewing fortune, Leeson was on the Grand
Tour in 1744–5 when he was painted by
Batoni. Although he was not elevated to
the peerage for another decade, Leeson's
eccentric domestic dress and general
demeanour give him the air of a confident
member of the European elite visiting Rome.

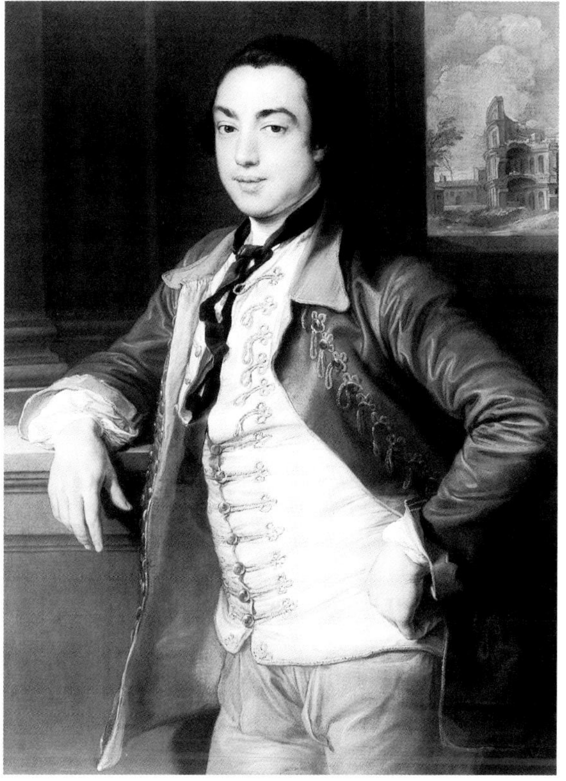

**54. James Caulfeild, 4th Viscount Charlemont
(later 1st Earl of Charlemont)** (1728–99)
POMPEO BATONI (1753–6)
Oil on canvas, 978 × 737mm (38½ × 29″)
Yale Center for British Art, Gift of Paul Mellon, 1974

from Ireland, Scotland or Wales. Irish sitters dominate the final group of forty
portraits, with some eighteen men and at least two Irish women painted by the
Italian artist. A group of Irish gentlemen were in fact Batoni's earliest patrons.[18]
They included the Leesons (fig.53), who appear in Reynolds's *Parody*, and Joseph
Leeson's kinsman Joseph Henry, as well as Thomas Dawson.[19]

A few years later, between 1753 and 1755, Batoni painted Lord Charlemont (fig.54)
and in time went on to paint a host of other travelling Irish aristocrats. Painted when
Charlemont was in his mid-twenties and still a Viscount, the Batoni shows an
assured young man who had already extensively toured the eastern Mediterranean
and would in time create one of the most important art collections in Ireland. This
is a particularly fine example of the type of Grand Tourist portrait that Batoni would

continue to develop for another thirty years. The sitter leans in relaxed pose against a classical plinth and is dressed in an elaborate Hussar-like suit decorated with gold-frogged fastenings.[20] The beautifully painted black neck ribbon bounces off the pure white of the waistcoat, while the sitter's rich red lips are echoed in the jacket collar, cuffs and the breeches. In the right-hand corner Batoni offers a view of the Colosseum, a monument that soon became the standard backdrop for Grand Tourist portraits.

LATE EIGHTEENTH-CENTURY JACOBITISM?

If Charlemont's fracas with Piranesi boldly visualises an Irish presence in Rome to a degree that is only passively hinted at by Batoni, the Irish contribution to late eighteenth-century pan-European political concerns is further exemplified by a group of portraits of the exiled Stuarts by an Irish artist in the mid-1780s. Hugh Douglas Hamilton's series of portraits of the last of the Jacobites, the final legitimate members of the royal family of Stuarts (figs 55 and 56), are also the last in a line of

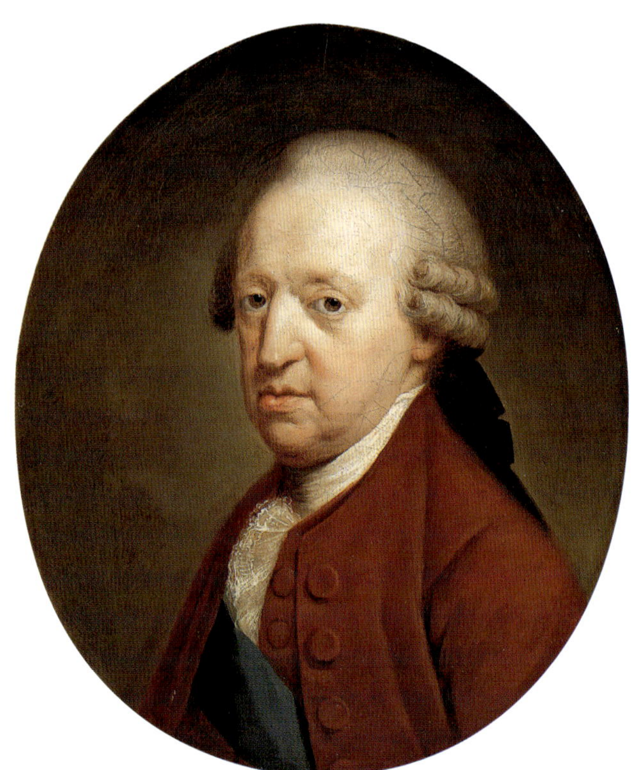

55. **Prince Charles Edward Stuart** (1720–88)
HUGH DOUGLAS HAMILTON (1785)
Oil on canvas, 248 × 219mm (9⅞ × 8¾")
National Portrait Gallery, London (NPG 376)

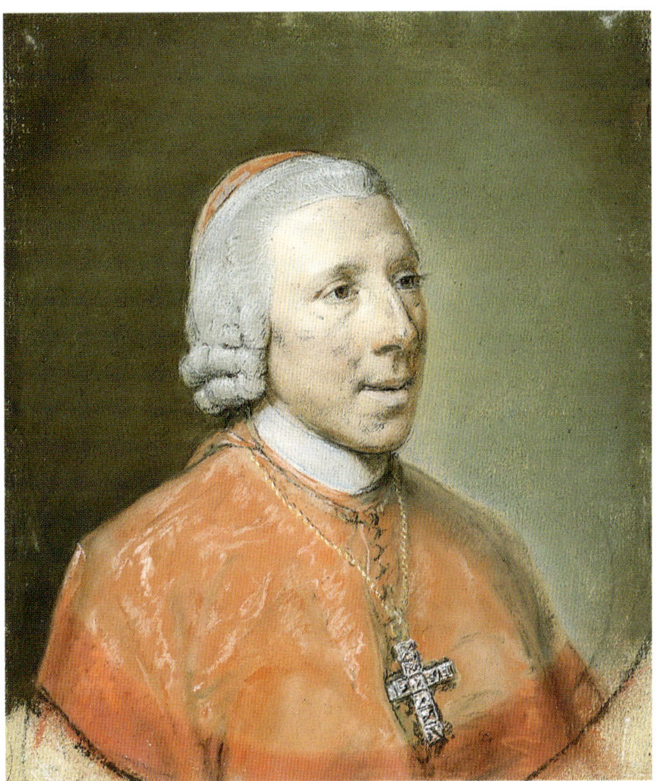

56. **Cardinal York** (1725–1807)
HUGH DOUGLAS HAMILTON
(1786)
Pastel, 245 × 216mm
(9⅝ × 8½″)
National Portrait Gallery,
London (NPG 378)

Jacobite portraits that go back at least a hundred years. Reference was made in the
Introduction (p.20) to John Michael Wright's late seventeenth-century portrait of
the Irish Jacobite Sir Neil O'Neill (fig.91); the image will be discussed again in
Chapter 4 in the context of the development of the political portrait in Ireland.
A scion of the O'Neills of Shane's Castle, County Antrim, Sir Neil 'was mortally
wounded when attempting to prevent William of Orange from crossing the Boyne'.
In Wright's portrait of about a decade earlier we see an assured image of a warrior
equipped with an exotic array of weaponry, accompanied by a henchman and a
mastiff. Wright's painting of a Jacobite sympathiser has been referred to as 'the most
important portrait of an Irishman painted in the seventeenth century'; it is also one
of many Irish portraits of aristocratic followers of James VII and II to have survived
the religious intolerances of the eighteenth century.[21]

Hamilton's Jacobites of the 1780s focus on Charles Edward Stuart, grandson of
James VII and II, and known to history in the more popular guise of Bonnie Prince
Charlie. During his extended decade in Italy Hamilton spent two years in Florence
(1783–5) where he studied and drew from the antique statues at the Uffizi, was
elected to the Accademia del Disegno, painted many oil and pastel portraits of Irish
and British Grand Tourists and sketched a pastel self-portrait (fig.45) now hanging
in the Corridoio Vasariano. He also managed to visit the Stuarts in exile in Prince
Charles's San Clemente Palace.[22] As painted by Hamilton and now in his sixties, the
Young Pretender was no longer the handsome young prince from 'over the water'

but a tired old man who would be dead from an excess of alcohol by 1788. While in Florence, Hamilton also drew the prince's daughter, Charlotte, who went by the title of the Duchess of Albany; a short while later, in Rome, he painted Charles's brother, Henry, Cardinal Duke of York (fig.56).[23] The authenticity of the likenesses was verified by Sir William Forbes, a Scottish visitor to Rome in 1792:

> Two original & excellent likenesses of the unfortunate Charles Stuart, Count of Albany & and his brother, the Cardinal Duke of York, painted by a Mr Hamilton . . . In his study I found the portraits which I went to see. They are of a middle size considerably larger than large miniatures but much below the size of three quarter pictures, extremely well painted. The likeness of the Cardinal I could perfectly judge afterwards when I saw him himself.[24]

The Stuart portraits of the above three sitters attributable to the Irish painter total about sixteen separate images.[25] Copied miniature versions, most probably by another hand for placement on snuffboxes or similar surfaces, may account for at least an extra three, bringing the total to a possible nineteen portraits of the exiled later Stuarts by Hamilton.

Given the large number of Stuart portraits that Hamilton painted and the potential political ramifications of portraying the late eighteenth-century remnants of the Jacobite threat, can we see these images as more than a chance commission by an established foreign painter in Italy in the mid-1780s? In all the known portraits of Charles, the old prince wears a Garter ribbon and in some (for example the Scottish National Portrait Gallery and Dundee versions) the Garter jewel is more visible than in others. Charles had inherited the jewel from his father, James, the Old Pretender, who had received it from his father, James VII and II; he in turn inherited it from his brother, Charles II, and originally from their father, Charles I. Eventually, at the death of Cardinal York, the last of the Stuarts, in 1807, the jewel was bequeathed to the Hanoverian line, 'in gratitude', as Michael Levey has suggested, 'and in recognition finally of the reality'.[26] That reality was that the Stuarts were now a spent force. While Charles declares his royal identity in Hamilton's portrait, his brother the Cardinal is in ecclesiastical garb wearing a *mozzetta*, a skull cap and an episcopal cross; the Duchess of Albany is in profile with a jewelled diadem and a lace trim to her bodice. Despite the abundance of Stuart images attributed to Hamilton and his status as a major Irish artist, there is surprisingly only one recorded cache of Hamilton's Stuart portraits in Ireland from the late eighteenth century. The Balfour family at Townley Hall, County Louth, maintained until relatively recently at least one version each of Hamilton's portraits of Charles and his brother; by contrast, Dublin's National Gallery of Ireland did not acquire an authentic Stuart portrait (an oil on canvas version of the Cardinal York portrait) until 1982.[27]

Why then did Hamilton produce so many portraits of this trio and what have they got to do with the Irish face? John Kerslake suggests that the subject of Stuart portraiture is 'devilled by their practice of commissioning copies, in a good many cases for propaganda purposes'.[28] But by the mid-1780s what was the propaganda for? By that date the Jacobite cause was well and truly dead. From an Irish point of view, as Breandán Ó Buachalla and Éamonn Ó Ciardha have recently shown, the Jacobite tradition had been long and worrisome to those loyal to the Hanoverian succession.[29] From the late seventeenth century, Ireland had maintained a 'fatal attachment' to the exiled house of Stuart and portraits played a role in perpetuating this connection. Writing from Vienna in 1737 to James VIII and III, the Old Pretender in Rome, Owen O'Rourke, one of the Irish Wild Geese, reported how a local Jacobite agent (a Mrs Hamilton, known by the pseudonym of 'Lucy') was searching for representations of Prince Charles, then about seventeen years old:

> She can gett noe good painter to come to copy the prince's picture … and that to send it abroad and consequently seen, may give room for Hanoverian spys to make some buzle…[30]

Fifty years later, and by the time Hamilton was painting his portraits of Charles and his brother, this European-wide connection no longer mattered. The 'Gordian knot of Jacobitism', as Ó Ciardha has pronounced, 'was finally loosed by the death of James [VIII and III] in January 1766'; in not recognising Charles as Charles III, Pope Clement XIII ostensibly cut off all European Catholic support for the Stuarts.[31] Although lingering mid-eighteenth-century support in Ireland for the Jacobite cause has been identified as encouraging agrarian protest and anti-clericalism, there is no evidence in Hamilton's carefully organised career that he would have sided with a seditious political cause. Painting in Florence and Rome in the mid-1780s, he had left Ireland in about 1765 and by 1769 was painting portraits of George III and his family that are still at Windsor. In 1792, only a few years after Hamilton painted his portraits, Edmund Burke ridiculed any lingering fears amongst Irish Protestants of a Stuart threat when he conjured up the preposterous image of the pope wishing to 'absolve his majestie's [George III] subjects [the Irish] of their allegiance, and send over the Cardinal of York to rule them as his viceroy'.[32]

Paul Kléber Monod has suggested that Hamilton's paintings of Charles (fig.55), with 'large drooping eyes, pouting lower lip and sagging chin, convey a sense of pathos' recalling 'the image of the "man of sorrows", the royal martyr Charles I'.[33] Although Hamilton's oval portrait may superficially suggest, for example, a 1649 etching of Charles I by Wenceslas Hollar where the executed king prominently displays the star of the Garter, in the light of Charles Edward's defeat at Culloden in 1746, as Laura Lunger Knoppers has rightly suggested, 'Charles I as Jacobite icon faded with the fading of the military threat. Divine-right ideology could not be sustained indefinitely in the face of military defeat and diplomatic failure'.[34] Hamilton's Stuart portraits and their variations may have been produced with propaganda in mind, but it was a damp-squib form of propaganda. No one really cared any more about the last of the Stuarts: Hamilton's portraits are a perfect example of an artist responding to the requirements of his patrons, supplying copies for friends and repeating a successful formula. The century-long Irish involvement with Jacobite imagery had come to an end.[35]

MAKING GOOD IN AMERICA

As the representation of travellers on the Grand Tour makes abundantly clear, the aristocracy and landed gentry dominated Irish portraiture in the eighteenth century. A cursory look through the list of identified portraits in the first volume of the catalogue of *Irish Paintings in the National Gallery of Ireland* reaffirms this view.[36] To gain a sense of an alternative clientele for portraiture we need to continue our search for the Irish portrait abroad. John Trumbull's fine portrait, dating from 1784–6, of the successful Massachusetts-based merchant Patrick Tracy (fig.57) is a case in point. Tracy was an Irish-born entrepreneur who set up a successful shipping business in Newburyport, north Massachusetts, and in 1789 left an estate 'valued at slightly more than £3,739, a considerable sum for the time'.[37] Having emigrated from Ireland some seventy years earlier and learned his sea skills on ships sailing between New England and the West Indies, Tracy is an example of the Irishman who profited from the British Empire in America. In terms of his career as a merchant, his emigration in the second decade of the eighteenth century was an astute move. In Ireland merchants were seriously disadvantaged with regard to trade with America and the West Indies, as everything was 'dominated by English merchant houses, English intermediaries, and English capital'. By contrast, British North America, which included such towns as Newburyport, 'dominated exports from the islands to Britain'. In 1770, two years before Patrick Tracy was appointed a Justice of the Peace in Newburyport, maritime trade between North America and the West Indies was worth in excess of £800,000.[38] In time Tracy was in a position to build a brick mansion as a wedding present to his son, and to give financial support to the Revolutionary forces.

Trumbull's portrait of Tracy was probably painted in London and based on a miniature likeness supplied by Tracy's son. It shows a bewigged man in his seventies leaning on a large anchor. Over to the left are a barrel and bales of goods, one of which is stamped with Tracy's monogram, 'PT', while the sea, this successful merchant's livelihood for well over half a century, is an appropriate background. The foreground is decorated with oyster and other seashells. Although Trumbull's painting exhibits a number of anatomical inconsistencies, its focus on a mariner

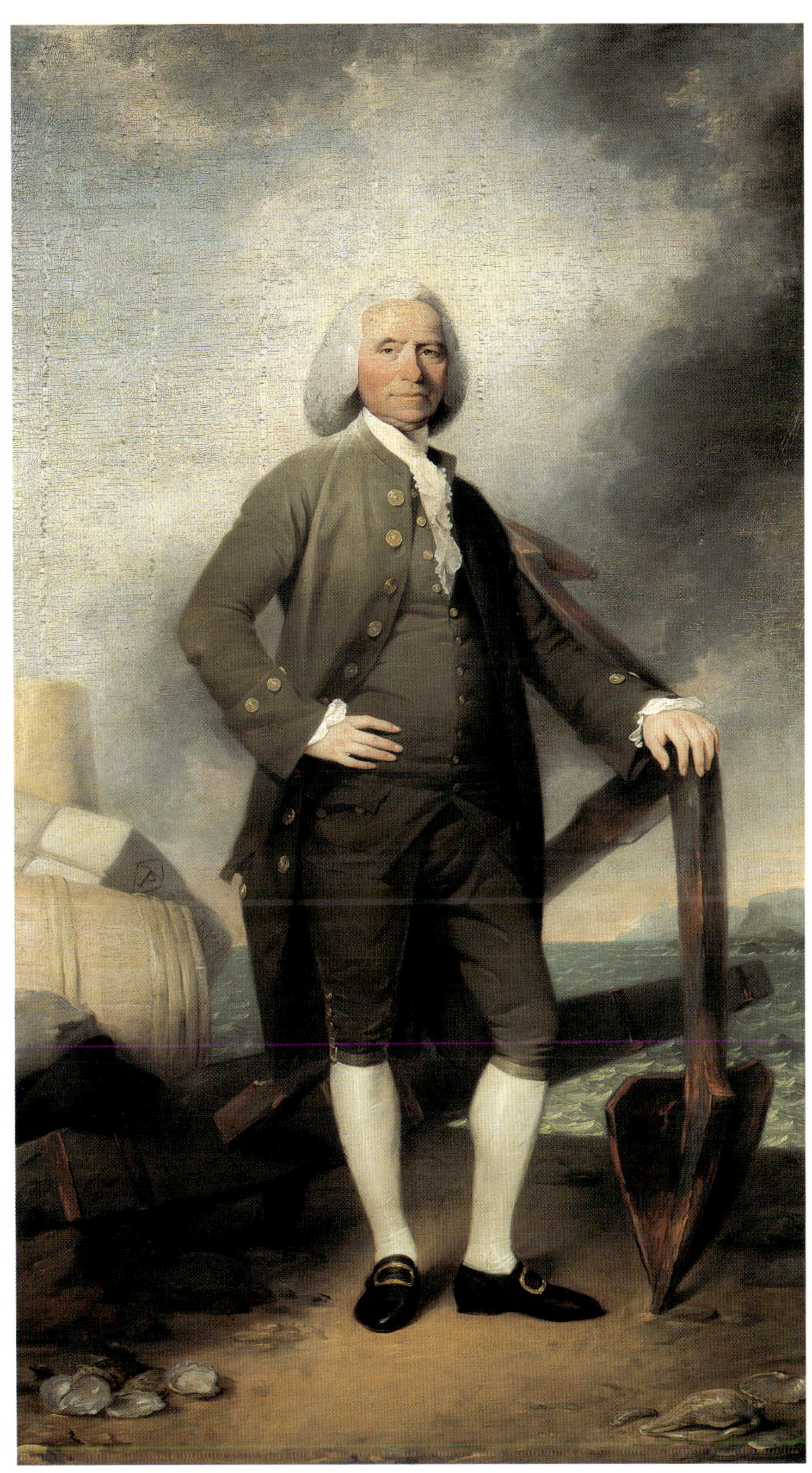

57. **Patrick Tracy** (c.1711–89)
JOHN TRUMBULL (1784–6)
Oil on canvas, 2325 × 1337mm
(91½ × 52⅝")
National Gallery of Art,
Washington DC

and merchant makes it a welcome antidote to the host of aristocrats that dominate eighteenth-century Irish portraiture. Despite the fact that it was not painted from the life, Trumbull's portrait of Tracy is comparable in its scale and ambition to Ralph Earl's *Roger Sherman* (fig.44) of a decade earlier. Earl's picture is perhaps more direct in its approach and plainer in style, but both suggest straightforward men who have weathered the upheavals of revolution and, although from different cultural backgrounds, they are united in their recorded contributions to the political process that led to the Continental Congress in Philadelphia.[39]

Irish middle-class success often did not reveal itself in portraiture. It was not until the late nineteenth century and the portraits of Walter Osborne that a sustained representation of Irish middle-class achievement emerged. Back in the eighteenth century, newly wealthy men such as Joseph Leeson, who inherited a brewery fortune, passed on the business so that he could concentrate on becoming an aristocrat. Dressed in a fur-lined *robe de chambre* with a matching fur hat, and backed by deep red drapery with the traditional column peeping through, Batoni's portrait of Leeson (fig.53) gives us no clue as to the sitter's origins. This is a man who has socially arrived. Trumbull's Tracy of forty years later does not hesitate to indicate the source of the sitter's success, although the painting's visual language is not unrelated to that of the earlier work. Tracy's solidly upright stance, his graceful poise and his metropolitan dress conceal his immigrant past. The marine and merchant associations indicate his achievement, but only in the same way that fashionable English portraitists such as Thomas Gainsborough had been using nautical imagery in naval portraits for quite some time. Like his compatriot, Leeson, of a generation earlier, Tracy has arrived: his pretensions may not be aristocratic or Italianate but there is the same concern with self-fulfilment that is the essence of commissioned portraiture.

James Barry's *Self-Portrait*

Like his predecessor James McArdell, Cork-born James Barry was another Irish artist whose life and work impinged on the fame of Sir Joshua Reynolds. Both Barry and Reynolds produced self-portraits of themselves around the year 1780 (figs 58 and 59). Unlike many other forms of portraiture, self-portraiture removes the contractual arrangement between client and artist: the painter is both the subject and the interpreter. But in keeping with the political tone of so much Irish portraiture, it is useful to examine Barry's self-image in terms of its representation of a Catholic Irishman in an age of cultural exclusion. It is only the head that dates from 1780: the surrounding details date from 1803, over twenty years later.[40]

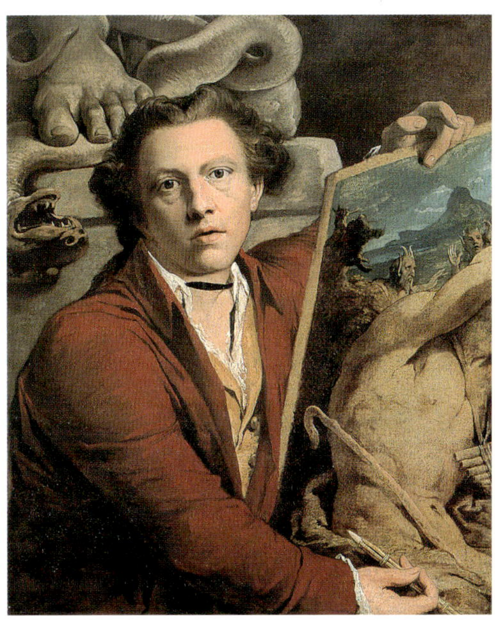

58. Self-Portrait
JAMES BARRY (1780–1803)
Oil on canvas, 760 × 630mm (30 × 25″)
National Gallery of Ireland, Dublin

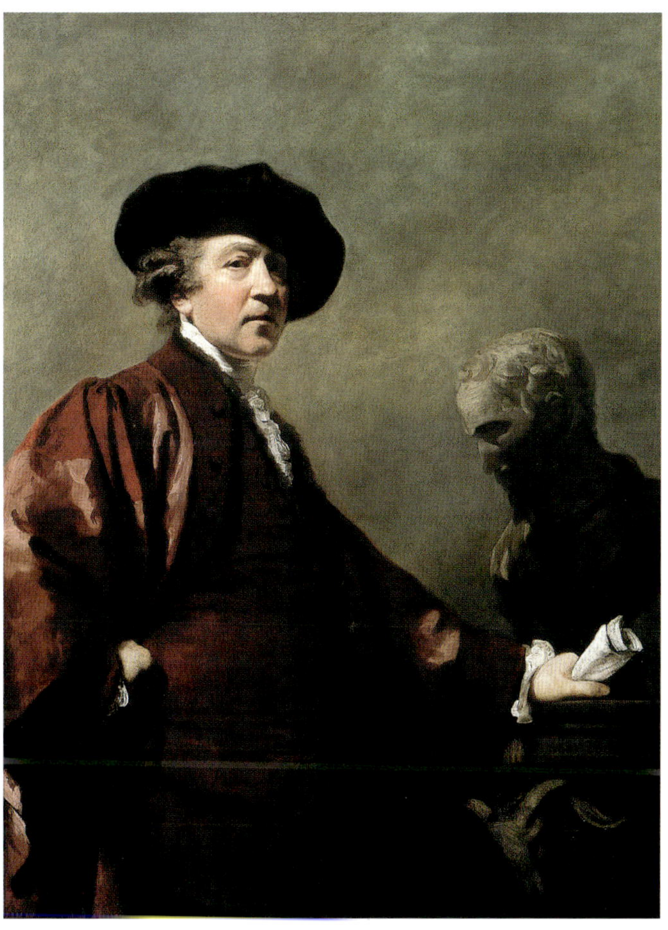

59. Self-Portrait
JOSHUA REYNOLDS (1780)
Oil on canvas, 1016 × 1523mm (40 × 60″)
Royal Academy of Arts, London

Between 1777 and 1781 Barry was working on a huge cycle of murals on the theme of *The Progress of Human Culture and Knowledge* for the Great Room of the Society of Arts (later the Royal Society of Arts, John Adam Street, off London's Strand).[41] He included his self-portrait in the bottom left-hand corner of one huge canvas, *Crowning the Victors at Olympia* (fig.60). In this depiction of Ancient Greece Barry assumes the character of the fifth-century BCE artist Timanthes, shown holding one of his paintings, a representation of the Cyclops. The artist (Barry/Timanthes) sits at the feet of a statue of Hercules crushing the serpent of Envy. The later *Self-Portrait* (fig.58), now in the collection of the National Gallery of Ireland, was originally executed as a study for the larger mural.

In his *Self-Portrait* of 1780 (fig.59) Reynolds paints himself in the robes of a Doctor of Civil Law from Oxford University, an honour he received in 1773. Some seven years later he recorded this event and subsequently commissioned Valentine Green to produce a mezzotint after his oil painting; this was published in December 1780. On completion, Reynolds presented the oil portrait to the Royal Academy of Arts.

In both these eighteenth-century self-portraits the viewer is led to consider the artists in relation to creative figures from the past: Barry's references are to Ancient Greece, while Reynolds, through his use of fur-trimmed robes and a velvet hat against an empty background, reminds us of Rembrandt's self-portraits. Equally, just as Barry in the Society of Arts mural places himself as a legendary Greek artist balanced between two art works (Timanthes' painting of the Cyclops and a statue of Hercules), so too Reynolds leans elegantly on a plinth supporting a sculptured bust-portrait by Daniele da Volterra of that 'Hercules of the Renaissance', Michelangelo. Barry looks back to antiquity while Sir Joshua limits his references to modern masters, one from the sixteenth century, the other from the seventeenth. Furthermore, both self-portraits were painted for learned societies in London, the Royal Academy and the Society of Arts: both suggest a self-conscious calling to attention of artistic antecedents, as well as a confident assertion of the artist's place in history. Valentine Green's engraving after the Reynolds emphasised the intellectual accomplishments of the sitter in its inscription, 'President of the Royal Academy, Member of the Imperial Academy at Florence, Doctor of Laws of the Universities of Oxford and Dublin, and Fellow of the Royal Society'.[42] Equally, the inscription on Barry's later (1792) engraving of *Crowning the Victors,* which included his self-portrait, informed us that he was 'Professor of Painting to the Royal Academy'.[43] But the similarities end there.

Both Reynolds and Barry were staunch advocates of the superiority of history painting over portraiture and landscape. They both wrote extensively on this topic, Reynolds in his famous fifteen *Discourses on Art* delivered to the students of the Royal Academy of Arts between 1769 and 1790 and well known to students of eighteenth-century aesthetic theory.[44] Barry's writings are less well known but no less prodigious: between 1775 and 1801 he published numerous public letters, pamphlets and descriptive catalogues of his works, as well as delivering lectures as Professor of Painting, also at the Royal Academy of Arts.[45] Reynolds, it can be argued, failed to stick to the strict principles he outlined in his lectures to the Royal Academy and happily made his name, his considerable fortune – a grand house and studio in Leicester Fields (now by London's Leicester Square) – and gained his knighthood as first President of the Royal Academy. His posthumous status within the canon of British artists is celebrated and largely unchallenged. Barry, by contrast, was a much criticised and somewhat marginalised figure who specialized in edifying history subjects and, despite having money in the bank (as was learned posthumously), lived alone and in squalor. William Blake, one of Barry's few contemporary defenders, wrote of him in relation to Reynolds: 'while Sir Joshua was rolling in Riches, Barry was Poor & Unemploy'd except by his own Energy'.[46]

The comparisons continue: Reynolds was sociable and gregarious while Barry was awkward and cantankerous. Reynolds was eager to help young artists and, through his *Discourses*, set about constructively intellectualising the role of the artist in late eighteenth-century England. Barry, by contrast, was a loner who cared little about communicating directly with his students and whose voluminous writings are often full of an aggressive and hectoring tone of little immediate appeal. Just as Reynolds enjoyed the benefits of a successful portrait practice, so Barry wrote continuously of the negative dominance of the portrait in English art and strongly condemned it. Despite the fact that Barry produced one of the most fascinating self-portraits by an Irish or English artist in the late eighteenth century, his public pronouncements on the art form are tinged with vitriol. The problem was that to Barry, painting portraits of others was not an intellectual exercise; painting portraits of himself was another matter. In his introduction to *An Account of a Series of Pictures, in the Great Room of the Society of Arts* of 1783, he states that 'the sole painting of these portraits, comparatively contemptible as it has appeared to people of elevated minds . . . is notwithstanding the means amongst us . . . by which is obtained a fashion, a fortune, and upon true commercial ideas, a rank and consequence'.[47]

A contemporary biographer, Anthony Pasquin, who published an eccentric history of the *Artists of Ireland* in 1796, gives an indication of the public view of Barry and his attitude to portrait painting in his short account of the artist:

When this inconstant man had returned from Italy, and was much depressed in circumstances and in spirit, and it was generally supported that he was sinking for want of a patron, the late *Duke of Northumberland*, with becoming nobleness, invited the disconsolate artist to dine with him; and during the repast at Northumberland House, the discourse ran upon the distribution of the painting around the room; among which was the inimitable effort, by *Titian*, of the Carnaro family. 'How Mr. Barry, do you approve of the placing of these pictures?' said his Grace. 'Oh, very well, my Lord Duke; but there is a capital place at the bottom there, in a side light, which is unoccupied.' 'I mean that vacancy to be filled by a production from your pencil, Sir; which I request you to finish as soon as possible. I wish the subject to be taken from the history of England; but shall leave the selection, the size, and the price, to be fixed by yourself; and have only this to add, that you will contrive to introduce a master of the Horse in the grouping, and draw my portrait in that character.' After this instruction the parties separated; and in the ensuing week his Grace called upon the artist repeatedly, who was uniformly denied. At length the Duke, fatigued by such caprice, sent him a letter by his servant, desiring to speak to him; when the inflated *James Barry* was pleased to express himself thus: 'Go to the Duke, your master, friend, and tell him from me, that if he wants his portrait painted, he may go to the fellow in Leicester-fields; for that office shall never be fulfilled by me.'[48]

Pasquin indicates that the Irish artist was the subject of severe artistic criticism as well as personal abuse. One of the issues regarding his reputation that needs greater emphasis is the role of religion in his life and work. An examination of his Roman Catholicism reveals the importance he gave to his religion on a personal level, and also the effect it had upon his art, particularly the reworked *Self-Portrait*.

Born a Roman Catholic in Cork in 1741, Barry remained devout throughout his life. Although the Penal codes levelled against Catholics in both Ireland and England were not as all pervasive as has been popularly believed – more a series of what Tom Bartlett has called 'petty oppressions' – there was throughout the eighteenth century a vigorous anti-Catholicism that acted as an effective control mechanism.[49] Although originally a friend and protégé of such an eminent figure as Edmund Burke (fig.12) and, as suggested by Pasquin, the beneficiary of patronage from such grandees as the Duke of Northumberland, Barry was always aware of the disadvantages of his religious affiliation. Equally, it is clear from some assessments of Barry written after his death that he was victim of a form of discriminatory discourse not levelled at his contemporary, Sir Joshua Reynolds. In 1810, four years after Barry died, Richard Payne Knight published a critique of his collected writings in the *Edinburgh Review*. Ethnicity and religious denomination feature prominently in Payne Knight's comments:

He was a man of a naturally vigorous and active mind, tinctured with Enthusiasm even to the verge of insanity; and, long before he had acquired any practical skill whatsoever in the art which he professed, <u>could talk the matter well</u>. It was this, probably, much more than his picture of St Patrick . . . which recommended him to the favour and patronage of Mr Edmund Burke: for that picture, whatever might have been the impression of its comparative

merit in an exhibition at Dublin, must have been but a wretched performance, unless his art suddenly forsook him in subsequent works which we
have seen.[50]

Payne Knight exhibits at least two prejudices: the stereotypical view that the Irish
have a tendency to overuse language (Barry, Payne Knight says, 'could talk the matter
well') and his opinion of the impossibility of art of any quality having been produced
in Dublin half a century earlier. Later, Payne Knight addresses the artist's religion:

Barry, in his religion, was a zealous, and, in some respects, bigotted
Romanist, – though his writings breathe nothing but universal toleration.
Minorities, indeed, in religion as well as politics, are always friends to liberty;
but, from some opinions quoted by his biographer concerning the perni-
cious effects of 'the growth and multiplicity of sects, and of allowing everyman
to think for himself in matters of doctrine and faith, and to expound the
scriptures as may suit his ambition or interest' (vol.2, p.333), we may safely
infer that he would not have been a very indulgent leader of a triumphant
majority.[51]

Seven years later, in 1817, William Hazlitt's entry on Barry in the *Encyclopaedia
Britannica,* says much the same thing:

His mother being a zealous Catholic, the son could not avoid mixing at times
in the company of priests resident at Cork, who pointed out to him books of
polemical divinity, of which he became a great reader, and for which he
retained a strong bias during his lifetime. He was said at one time to have
been destined for the priesthood, but for this report there is no authority. He,
however, always continued a Catholic, and in the decline of life manifested
rather a bigotted attachment to the religion of his early choice.[52]

Accused by two prominent, Protestant, English literary critics of the period of
being a zealot, as well as being a bigoted and intolerant Romanist, Barry's reputation and his adherence to Catholicism were certainly the subject of much abuse.
Modest support for him did occasionally surface. Not surprisingly, Blake had something to say:

WHO will Dare to Say that Polite Art is Encouraged or Either Wasted or
Tolerated in a Nature where The Society for the Encouragement of Art
Suffer'd Barry to Give them his Labour for Nothing, A Society Composed of
the Flower of the English Nobility & Gentry . . . Suffering an Artist to Starve
while he Supported Really what They, under Pretence of Encouraging, were
Endeavouring to Depress.– Barry told me that while he Did that Work, he
Lived on Bread & Apples.[53]

Over in Ireland, a year after Barry's death, Watty Cox, a radical Dublin publisher, in his newly founded *Irish Magazine,* which he initially seemed to want to call *The Irish Catholic Magazine,* offered a more crudely partisan form of support. Cox wrote that:

> Mr Barry, was allowed to be one of the greatest Painters in the World . . . [and] has been without his consent, by English writers, quoted as a proud example of British genius, and actually acclimated as a British growth[.] Mr Barry was born in Cork, and educated for the priesthood in the Catholic church, but his unequalled talents for painting were more properly applied to what his great mind was intended for, and we know he was not only not an Englishman, but the very reverse in the most extensive meaning of the word, that he disdained the name, the feeling and character which it assumes, that he was Irish, all and entire Irish, and felt so sensibly for Ireland's wrongs, and such was his abhorrence of her enemies, either as detractors or traytors, that neither rank or talents however eminent, numbered among his country's persecutors, could be honoured with an introduction to his house or company.[54]

All of these judgements on Barry have elements of truth. He does seem to have been 'a man of vigorous and active mind', as Payne Knight observed, his attachment to his religion seems to have been constant and he was certainly self-obsessed. But it is the tone of Payne Knight's and Hazlitt's attacks that should be noted. Barry is labelled a 'zealot' and a 'bigotted Romanist', although Payne Knight qualifies these accusations by saying that his 'writings breathe nothing but universal toleration'.[55] Taking this observation further, how can the artist's 'Romanist' preoccupations be reconciled with his equally tolerant writings? Barry, it should be pointed out was exceptional amongst his artistic contemporaries in London, apart from Reynolds, for the abundance of his published writings. Some answers to the posthumous accusations of Payne Knight and Hazlitt may be found by examining the final version of Barry's self-portrait in the context of his writings.

The role of religion was never far from Barry's thoughts[56] – although the subject was not favoured by British taste in the late eighteenth century and as such did not feature prominently in the culture of representation. As a Protestant nation unified by its anti-Catholicism,[57] Britain had a fear of the religious icons which dominated the churches and abbeys of the absolutist Roman Catholic countries across the Channel. As a young man Barry had enjoyed a number of years living and studying in Italy and, as his letters and writings show, he was greatly impressed by the ceremonies and trappings of Catholic church ritual. It is thus not surprising to find in his *Crowning the Victors at Olympia* (fig.60) a sustained visualisation of religious ceremony. Barry plays here with deliberately Roman Catholic themes but, surrounded as the artist was by a dominant Anglicanism, they are expressed in arcane details based on extensive classical learning. The scene is Greece in the fifth century BCE:

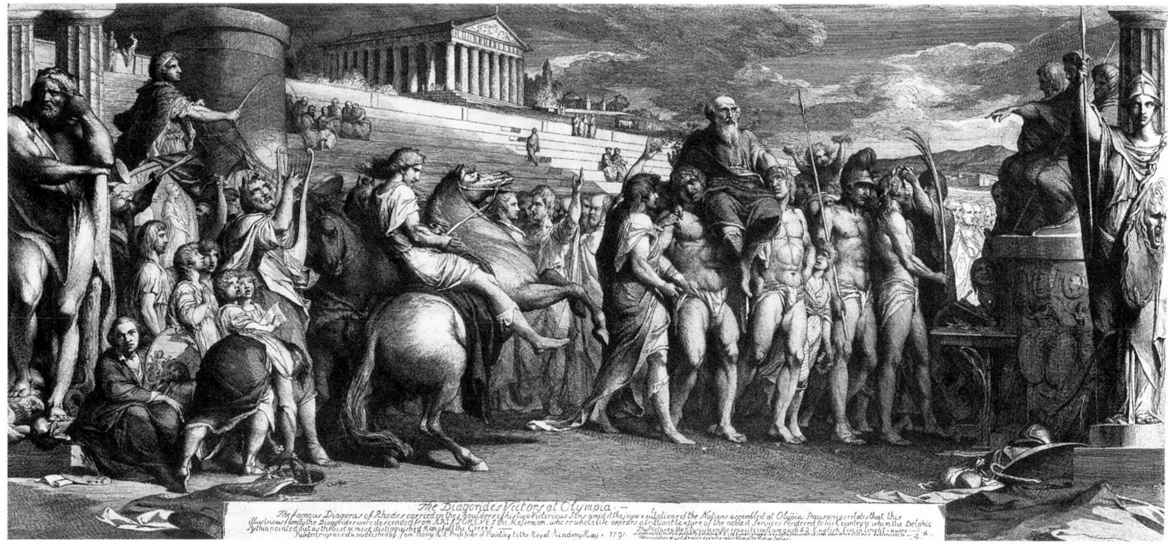

Diagores of Rhodes, a former champion, is carried aloft by his two sons, both of whom have just won competitions and are about to be awarded their prizes by the judges on the far right. Barry had read a 1749 dissertation by Gilbert West drawing similarities between the 'Olimpick Games' and Roman Catholicism. According to William Pressly, 'The power of excommunication was wielded by both Hellanodick [or Judge] and Pope, while Extreme Unction, the palm, and the crown of martyrs were common to both.'[58] In the prize-giving one of the judges crowns a champion and presents a palm. In his later writings Barry 'was to extend this analogy when he compared the papal states to the sacred territory of [Greece]'.[59] He dedicated his etching of this scene in 1795 to the 'Papal Government in Rome, Mother and gracious Protector of the Laudable Arts and of Genius'.[60]

In this context Barry's inclusion of his own self-portrait in this painting, as discussed above, is doubly significant. In the character of the classical Greek artist Timanthes, he is accompanied in this far left corner of the composition by fellow heroes Hiero of Syracuse, the winner of the chariot race, and the poet Pindar, playing his harp.[61] Barry thus includes himself in a carefully orchestrated homage to the Papacy: by placing himself at the far end of the mural from the representation of the proto-papacy he invites the viewer to balance one with the other. We have seen that the figure of Barry/Timanthes sits beneath a statue of Hercules crushing the serpent of Envy: Hercules had also been interpreted since Renaissance times as a Jesus-like figure, trampling sin and deceit. Through his physical proximity to this paragon the painter, holding aloft his art, benefits from these Christian analogies.

In the early summer of 1780, as Barry was working on his great murals in the Adelphi off the Strand, only minutes away in Westminster and further east in the City, the anti-Catholic Gordon Riots raged. The houses of prominent proponents of the Catholic Relief Act were burnt down and seriously damaged. One such victim was Barry's friend and sometime patron Sir George Savile, the instigator of the first Catholic Relief Bill, who appears in another of Barry's great canvases,

60. **Crowning the Victors at Olympia**
JAMES BARRY (1792)
Etching and engraving (black ink),
420 × 926mm (16½ × 36½")
British Museum, London

The Distribution of Premiums in the Society of Arts (fig.61).[62] As a vice-president of the Society of Arts Savile had earlier strongly supported Barry in his efforts to get permission to decorate the Great Hall. Edmund Burke, Barry's other great patron and a parliamentary colleague of Savile's is also included in the *Distribution*. Burke had frequently spoken out against what he called an anti-Catholic 'poison' which was being circulated from Church of England pulpits. In the wake of the Gordon Riots, he claimed that the blame for the deaths, arson and violence perpetrated by the mob lay more at the feet of the establishment than with the rioters themselves. The political establishment and the Anglican Church were the real fosterers of hate. 'We ought', he claimed, 'to reflect that an Offence, which in its Cause is National, ought not in its Effects to be vindicated on individuals but with a very well tempered severity'.[63] It was during this period of intense anti-Catholic feeling, from the passing of the Catholic Relief Bill in June 1778 to the Gordon Riots two years later, that Barry was painting his murals. Burke's articulation of a 'National' cancer behind such anti-Catholicism points to Barry's cycle as an attempt to visualise, on a large scale and in a public place, a national problem: that of religious intolerance and, in Barry's reckoning, England's error in turning away from Rome.

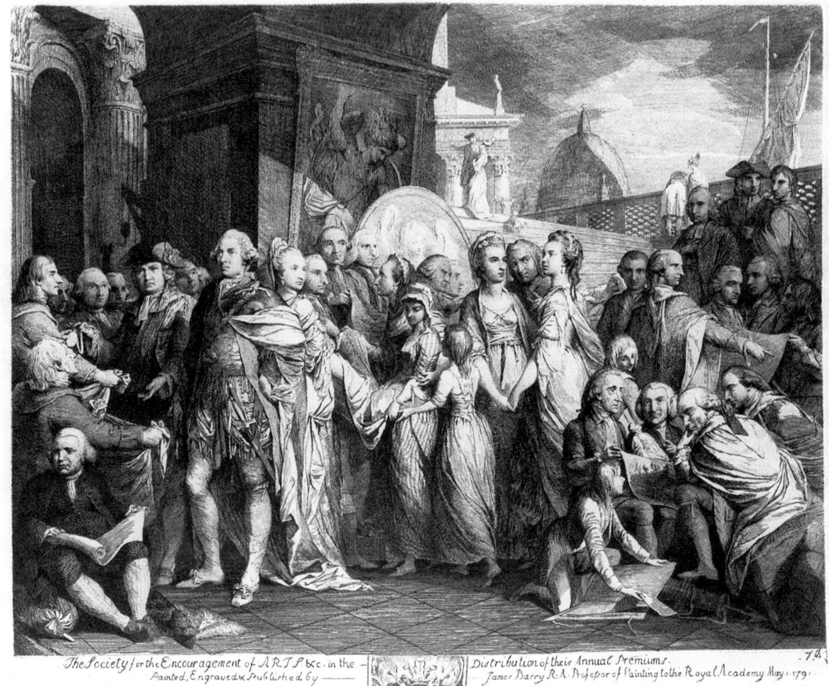

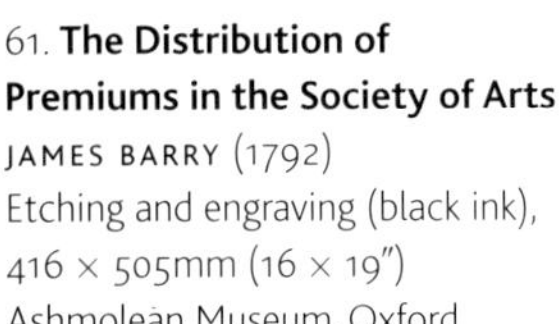

61. **The Distribution of Premiums in the Society of Arts**
JAMES BARRY (1792)
Etching and engraving (black ink),
416 × 505mm (16 × 19")
Ashmolean Museum, Oxford

This scene of the annual awards offered by the Society of Arts shows the Prince of Wales (left, in Garter robes) surrounded by public benefactors. Sir George Savile appears three heads to the right of the Prince, while Burke is on the far right, next to a sculpture of a Grecian mother.

Barry's *Self-Portrait* (fig.58), begun, as we have seen, in 1780, must be read in the light of these preoccupations. His life was one of swimming against the tide and of affirming his religious convictions, while at the same time emulating Greek artistic and cultural achievement. Is the *Self-Portrait,* in both its original 1780 context and its rejuvenation in 1803, an accusation against an unreformed political and ecclesiastical establishment, represented by the serpent's head? The accusation levelled is one of intolerance combined with repression, that 'Offence' which as Burke had suggested, 'in its Cause is National'.

By the time he completed this modest-sized canvas, in 1803, Barry was over sixty and no longer looked as young or as virile as he appears here. Instead, he left the head unaltered and dispatched the reworked portrait to the Society of Arts, which in 1804 had requested a self-portrait to appear as a frontispiece to a volume of its *Transactions.*[64] Conceived during a period of intense religious unease, can we connect this *Self-Portrait* with the artist's own religious beliefs? At the same time, given the fact that it was not actually completed until 1803, three years before he died, how does the painting fit into Barry's creation of his own biography? Throughout his career he produced many self-portraits: in Rome, in 1767, he had painted an image (fig.62) of a young, ambitious artist accompanied by colleagues studying the Torso Belvedere, seen here in the upper right-hand-corner of the painting. (It is worth pointing out that the Torso Belvedere appears again in the later *Self-Portrait* as a model for the torso of the Cyclops.) Back in London, in 1776, he exhibited at the Royal Academy a dramatic double portrait of himself and Burke (fig.63), the latter in the guise of Ulysses fleeing the cave of Polyphemus.[65] Barry looks to his patron for guidance, the older man's finger raised in a possible gesture of instruction. Four years later, in 1780, Barry produced a brooding close-up, the head and shoulders oil sketch now in the Victoria and Albert Museum, possibly an earlier study for the Society of Arts mural.[66] But it is in the later self-portrait now in the National Gallery of Ireland (fig. 58) that Barry offers a more penetrating commentary on himself and the connection between religion and art. Here light draws the eye directly to the face, especially his well-lit left cheek and forehead. On the left, Envy whispers in Barry's ear. The viewer's eye is drawn from left to right, past Barry's eyes to the top right-hand corner, where the artist's hand rests on his painting within a painting. Drawn back again to the lighted face, the eye plunges downwards via the black neck ribbon and the line of Barry's shirt and waistcoat. A cross-shape is thus created, dividing yet connecting the two art works displayed. Balanced between Envy and a lost masterpiece of antiquity, and connected by the sign of the cross, Barry suggests a choice.

In the context of choice, Barry in 1783 suggested a clue as to his way of thinking. In discussing the statue of Hercules in the Society of Arts mural, he wrote:

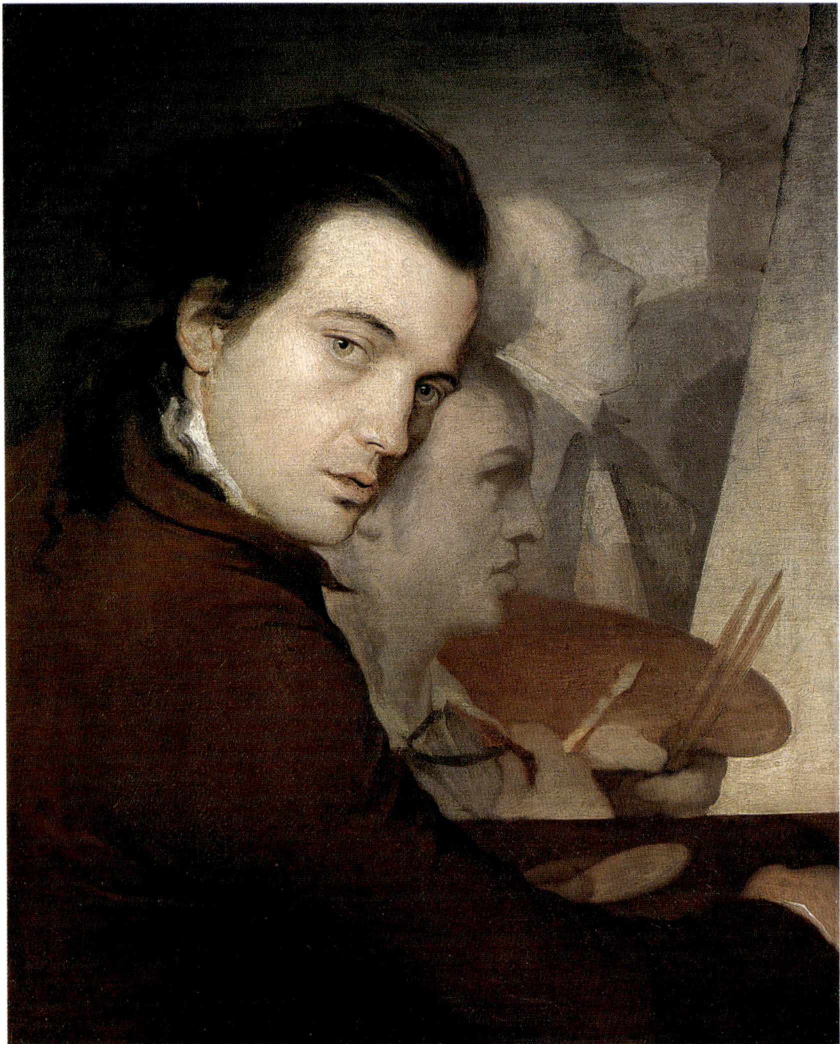

Envy should continually haunt and persecute the greatest characters; though for a time, it may give them uneasiness, yet it tends on the one hand to make them more perfect, by obliging them to weed out whatever may be faulty, and occasions them on the other, to keep their good qualities in that state of continued unrelaxed exertion, from which the world deserves greater benefit, and themselves in the end, still greater glory.[67]

In this *Self-Portrait*, Barry's own awareness of his personal greatness is perfectly expressed. Envy whispers in his ear while he, the successor of Timanthes, carries on working – shown here, he is actually in the process of drawing a heroic image. Indeed, the subject that Barry paints echoes what Pliny said of the Greek painter's art: 'He painted a hero which is a work of supreme perfection, in which he included the whole art of painting male figures.'[68] John Barrell and others have discussed

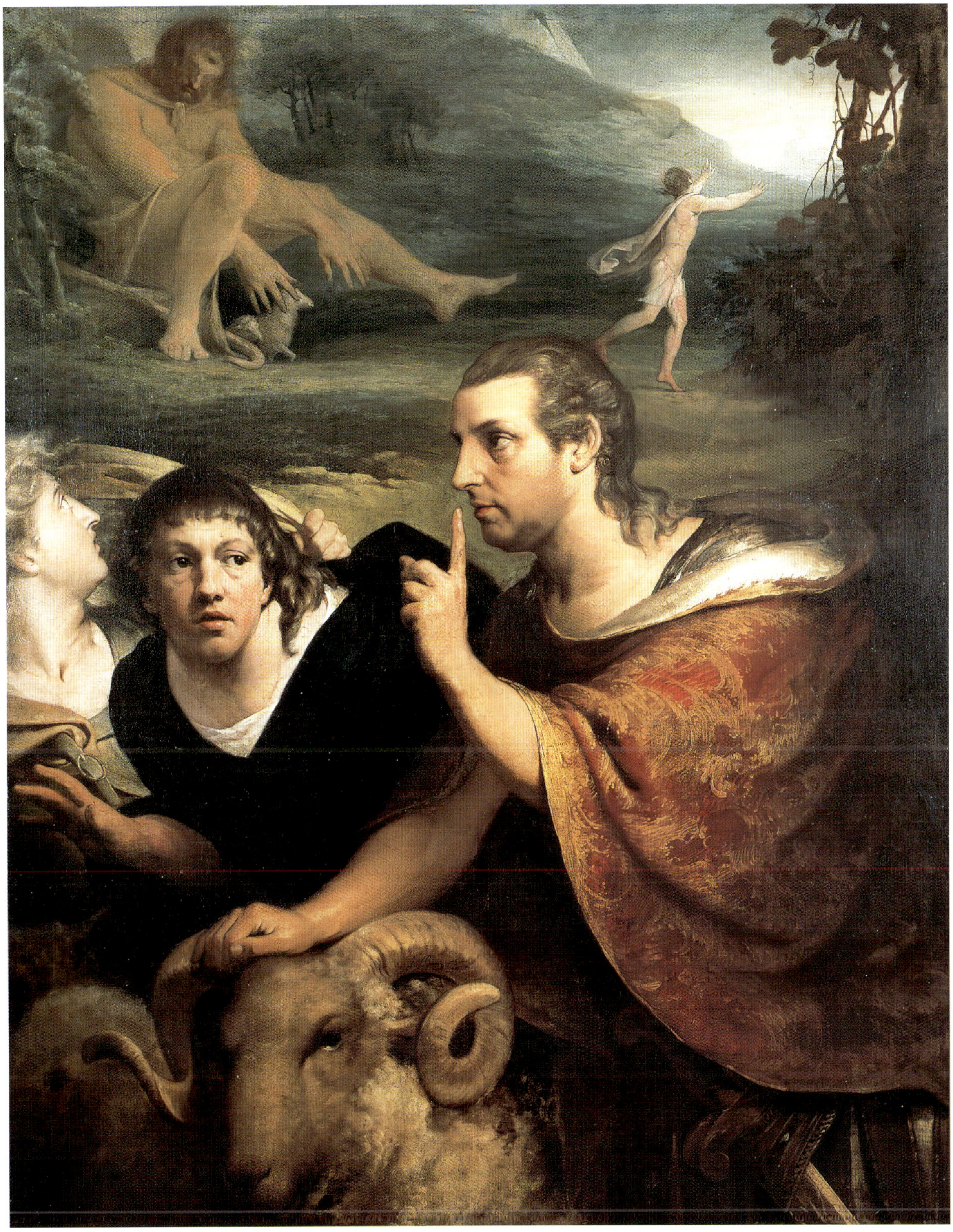

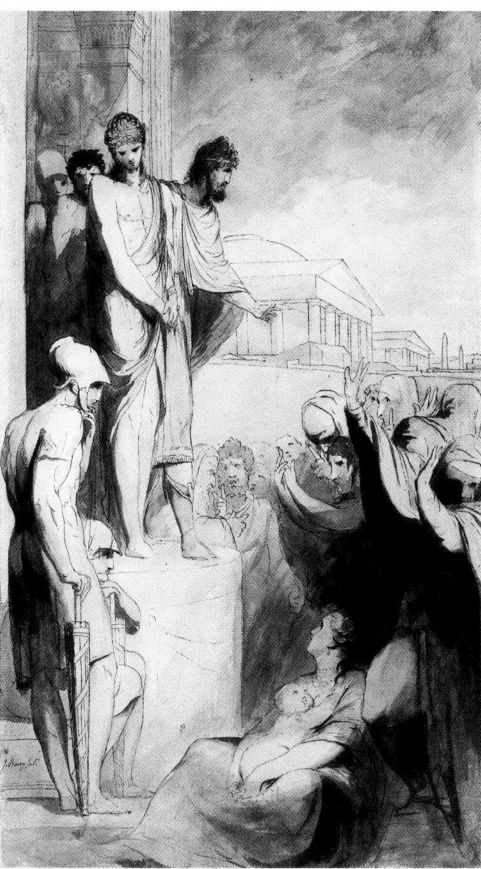

64. **Study for 'Ecce Homo'**
JAMES BARRY (C.1773)
Pen and brown ink and brown wash,
445 × 261mm (17½ × 10¼")
British Museum, London

Barry's use of the representation of Envy as a vindication of his greatness against the petty rivalries and gossip inherent in such an institution as the Royal Academy where he had held the Professorship of Painting from 1782 until his expulsion in 1799.[69] But the composition of the *Self-Portrait* suggests a wider accusatory tone: the 'cause is National', to use Burke's phrase.

On occasion, Barry's self-preoccupation led him to take on a Jesus-like role. In his 1776 double-portrait with Burke (fig.63), Barry's brow is dotted with perspiration, 'a highly unusual detail', as Pressly points out, that in the visual arts is traditionally associated with the Jesus of the Passion.[70] The later *Self-Portrait* (fig.58) foregoes the sweaty brow but echoes divine representations in its declamatory forwardness. Barry pushes his form very close to the picture plane, as if to say, 'Behold the Man'. We are asked to recall the visual tradition of the 'Ecce Homo', where Jesus was presented to the Jewish populace by Pontius Pilate. In the 1770s an attempt by a number of artists, including Barry, to decorate the interior of St Paul's Cathedral had been thwarted. Barry's original idea was to paint an 'Ecce Homo', but the scheme came to nothing and all that remains is a pen and ink drawing (fig.64).[71] But the idea of the 'Ecce Homo' did not disappear from Barry's consciousness. In the late *Self-Portrait* he balances himself between what we might call 'suffering endured',

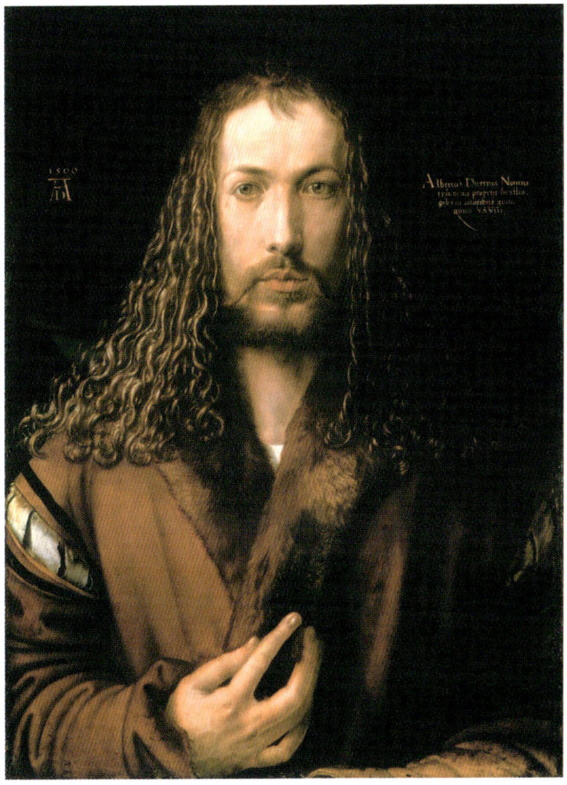

represented by the serpent of Envy, and 'redemption', implied by the painting on the right. Art has a rejuvenating potential: it lives on after human death. Thus mortality on the one hand and everlasting fame on the other both neatly frame the artist. It is no surprise to learn that the iconographic title of *Ecce Homo* was occasionally used by artists producing self-portraits during the Renaissance and beyond, Albrecht Dürer being perhaps the most famous example.[72] Unlike Barry, Dürer in his self-portrait of 1500 now in Munich (fig.65) does not indulge in esoteric Christian symbolism; instead, the German plays with visual analogies of the representation of God. As Joseph Koerner has argued, Dürer's portrait utilises the tradition of Jesus-like 'strict frontality, a hieratic symmetry and systematized proportionality'. Yet equally, Dürer stresses the autonomous nature of the self-portrait, 'a form or subject of painting which [he] can be said to have invented for the North'.[73] In both the Dürer panel and the Barry canvas, at least one of the artist's hands is prominently displayed and the eye is compositionally led back to the face. This conjoining of the face and hand is, of course, a key feature of Western portraiture, but in Barry's case it acts as both a personal and political message. The Irish artist's right hand holds a porte-crayon, the instrument of creation, which is in turn visually echoed by the explicitly phallic staff that emanates from the Cyclops's groin. Ultimately, in Barry's self-portrait as Timanthes both potency and strength are emphasised, defiant in the face of late eighteenth-century anti-Catholicism: the Penal codes are seen, as has been said, as merely a 'petty oppression'.

1 The discussion of the variety of portraits produced in the eighteenth century has been the hallmark of many recent studies on the genre of portraiture: see Pointon, 1993; Pullan, 1994; Moore and Crawley, 1988; West, 1995; West, 1996; Lovell, 1987; Woodall, 1997.

2 Letter of 14 July 1754, Ingamells and Edgcumbe, 2000, pp.17–18.

3 Mannings, 2000, Text, p.171. See Clifford, Griffiths and Royalton-Kisch, 1978, p.42, no.101.

4 Alexander, 1973, p.81.

5 Recalled by J.F. Nollekens, see Smith, 1829, vol.II, p.213.

6 Smith, 1829, vol.II, p.223.

7 Kerslake, 1977, vol.I, p.175.

8 Kerslake, 1977, vol.I, p.175; for the Johnson portrait see Penny, 1986, p.240 and Mannings, 2000, p.280.

9 Northcote, 1819, vol.I, p.231.

10 Alexander, 1973, p.79, quoting Malcolm C. Salaman, *Old English Mezzotints*, The Studio, London, 1910, p.32; George Colman was a London theatre manager.

11 Black, 1991, pp.46–8.

12 The McArdell was published by John Bowles and Son and Robert Sawyer, London, in 1762: see O'Donoghue and Hake, 1908–25, vol.I, p.410, no.36.

13 Alexander and Godfrey, 1980. For Pitt, later Earl of Chatham, see Kerslake, 1977, vol.I, pp.45–7.

14 Reynolds's relationship with Irish sitters and patrons has been the focus of a number of recent studies, e.g. Cullen, 1997, pp.84–90; Pointon, 1997, chap.2; Coleman, 1995, pp.131–6.

15 Ingamells, 1997, p.484; Benedetti, 1997, pp.51–7; O'Connor, 1999, pp.114–16. The identification of Murphy as the figure in the foreground has been questioned by Sergio Benedetti and Fionnuala Croke in 'Unpublished letters of Edward Murphy and Lord Charlemont', in McCarthy, 2001, p.62.

16 See Mannings, 2000, p.491.

17 See Cullen, 2000, pp.167–9 and pls 14–15.

18 Clark, 1985, pp.43, 46.

19 Benedetti, 1997, pp.20–25, 57.

20 *Pompeo Batoni and his British Patrons*, 1982, pp.36–7.

21 For O'Neill's demise see Ó Ciardha, 2002, caption to pl.9. This art historical opinion is offered by Crookshank and Glin, 2002, p.20. For Irish (and English) Jacobite portraits by Garret Morphy (c.1655–1715/16) see Figgis and Rooney, 2001, pp.364–77 and Fenlon, 1991–2, pp.135–48. Jacobite portraits in Kilkenny Castle are also discussed in the more recent publication, Fenlon, 2001, pp.73–4 (portraits of the 2nd Duke of Ormonde) and p.93 (a portrait of 'The Old Pretender' after Antonio David).

22 For Hamilton in Italy see Cullen, 1984, pp.176, 200–01; Ingamells, 1997, pp.451–2; Crookshank and Glin, 1997, pp.63–9.

23 For the Stuart portraits see Kerslake, 1977, vol.I, pp.3, 38–45, 323–8, vol.II, pls 109–25, 925–38. Claims have been made for Hamilton's authorship of portraits of Charles's wife, Louisa Maria von Stolberg (NPG 377: Kerslake, vol.I, pp.2–3) but on stylistic grounds I am doubtful; also, she and the prince were living apart during Hamilton's stay in Florence and they formally separated in 1784.

24 Sir William Forbes, 2 Dec. 1792, quoted in Figgis and Rooney, 2001, p.168; National Library of Scotland, Forbes MSS 1539–1545, vol.II, p.378.

25 In addition to the NPG and NGI catalogues, see *Scottish National Portrait Gallery Catalogue*, 1977, no.622, p.136; *Dundee City Art Gallery, Catalogue of Paintings*, 1973, pp.58–9; Cullen, 1984, pp.168, 200–01. See also Nicholson, 2002, pp.90–92 and Tayler, 1950, pp.100, 115.

26 Levey, 1964, p.25.

27 Figgis and Rooney, 2001, pp.166–8.

28 Kerslake, 1977, vol.I, p.348.

29 Ó Buachalla, 1996; Ó Ciardha, 2002.

30 Letter from O'Rourke to James, 7 Dec. 1737, quoted in Nicholson, 2002, p.30.

31 Ó Ciardha, 2002, p.365; see also Mac Craith, 1998.

32 Edmund Burke, *A Letter to Sir Hercules Langrishe*, Dublin, 1792, p.50, quoted in Ó Ciardha, 2002, p.368.

33 Monod, 1989, p.91. Monod makes a number of errors in his discussion of the Hamilton portraits, from stating that the artist was Scottish to misidentifying the location of one Prince Charles portrait to Towneley Hall, Lancashire when it was in Townley Hall, County Louth.

34 Laura Lunger Knoppers, 'Reviving the martyr king: Charles I as Jacobite icon', in Corns, 1999, p.284; the Hollar image is reproduced in the same book, accompanying John Peacock's article, 'The visual image of Charles I', p.210.

35 Ó Ciardha illustrates his book with a host of Jacobite portraits between pp.224–5. One of the most interesting is pl.33, a Stephen Slaughter conversation piece of c.1745 showing two Irishmen raising a glass to 'the king over the water' (private collection).

36 Figgis and Rooney, 2001, pp.475–7.

37 Information on the dating and origins of this portrait are taken from Cooper, 1982, p.116.

38 Thomas Bartlett, '"This famous island set in a Virginian sea": Ireland in the British Empire, 1690–1801' and Jacob M. Price, 'The Imperial Economy, 1700–1776', in Marshall, 1998, pp.258, 90.

39 For more on Sherman's involvement with the American Revolution see Kornhauser, 1991, p.109, and for Tracy's contribution see Miles, 1995, pp.299–303.

40 For Reynolds see Penny, 1986, pp.287–9 and Mannings, 2000, Text, p.51, no.21; for Barry's *Self-Portrait* see Pressly, 1981, chap.9.

41 See Pressly, 1981, chap.4.

42 Penny, 1986, p.117.

43 Pressly, 1981, p.273, no.19.

44 Reynolds, 1981 edn.

45 Barry, 1809 edn.

46 Blake's 'Annotations to Reynolds's *Discourses*', see Reynolds, 1981 edn, p.284.

47 Barry, 1809 edn, vol.ii, p.306

48 Pasquin, 1796, pp.48–9.

49 Thomas Bartlett, '"A weapon of war yet untraced": Irish Catholics and the Armed Forces of the Crown, 1760–1830', in Fraser and Jeffery, 1993, pp.66–85.

50 Payne Knight, 1801, p.294.

51 Payne Knight, p. 322; Payne Knight is quoting from Fryer's two-volume *Works* of Barry (1809).

52 Hazlitt, 1937 edn, vol.18, p.126.

53 Quoted in Pressly, 1981, p.202.

54 *Irish Catholic Magazine*, Dec. 1807, p.58.

55 Payne Knight, 1801, p.322.

56 Barrell, 1986, chap.2 and Luke Gibbons, '"A Shadowy Narrator": History, Art and Romantic Nationalism in Ireland 1750–1850', in Brady, 1991, pp.99–127; for a response to Gibbons see Tom Dunne, '"One of the Tests of National Character": Britishness and Irishness in paintings by Barry and Maclise', in Stewart, 2002, pp. 260–90. For Gibbons's more recent comments on Barry see Gibbons, 2003, chap. 2.

57 Colley, 1992, chap.1.

58 Pressly, 1981, pp.92–101.

59 Pressly, 1981, p.100.

60 Pressly, 1981, p.277, no. 28.

61 For Barry's account of his inclusions see Barry, 1809 edn, vol.ii, pp.422–4.

62 Pressly, 1981, pp.86–7.

63 Quoted in Haydon, 1993, p.240.

64 Pressly, 1981, pp.191, 241–2, no.67.

65 Pressly, 1981, pp.238–9, no.48. The self-portraits are briefly discussed in Cullen, 1997, pp.33–5; see also Luke Gibbons, '"Into the Cyclops Eye": James Barry, Historical Portraiture, and Colonial Ireland', in Cullen and Morrison, forthcoming.

66 Pressly, 1981, p.240, no.64.

67 Barry, 1809 edn, vol.ii, p.331.

68 Pressly, 1983, p.38, quoting Pliny, *Natural History,* Book xxxv, p.74.

69 Barrell, 1992, p.208.

70 Pressly, 1983, p.33.

71 Pressly, 1981, pp.42–5, 246, no.10.

72 See Woods-Marsden, 1998, p.37.

73 Koerner, 1986, pp.414, 416–17; see Koerner, 1993, chaps 4–8.

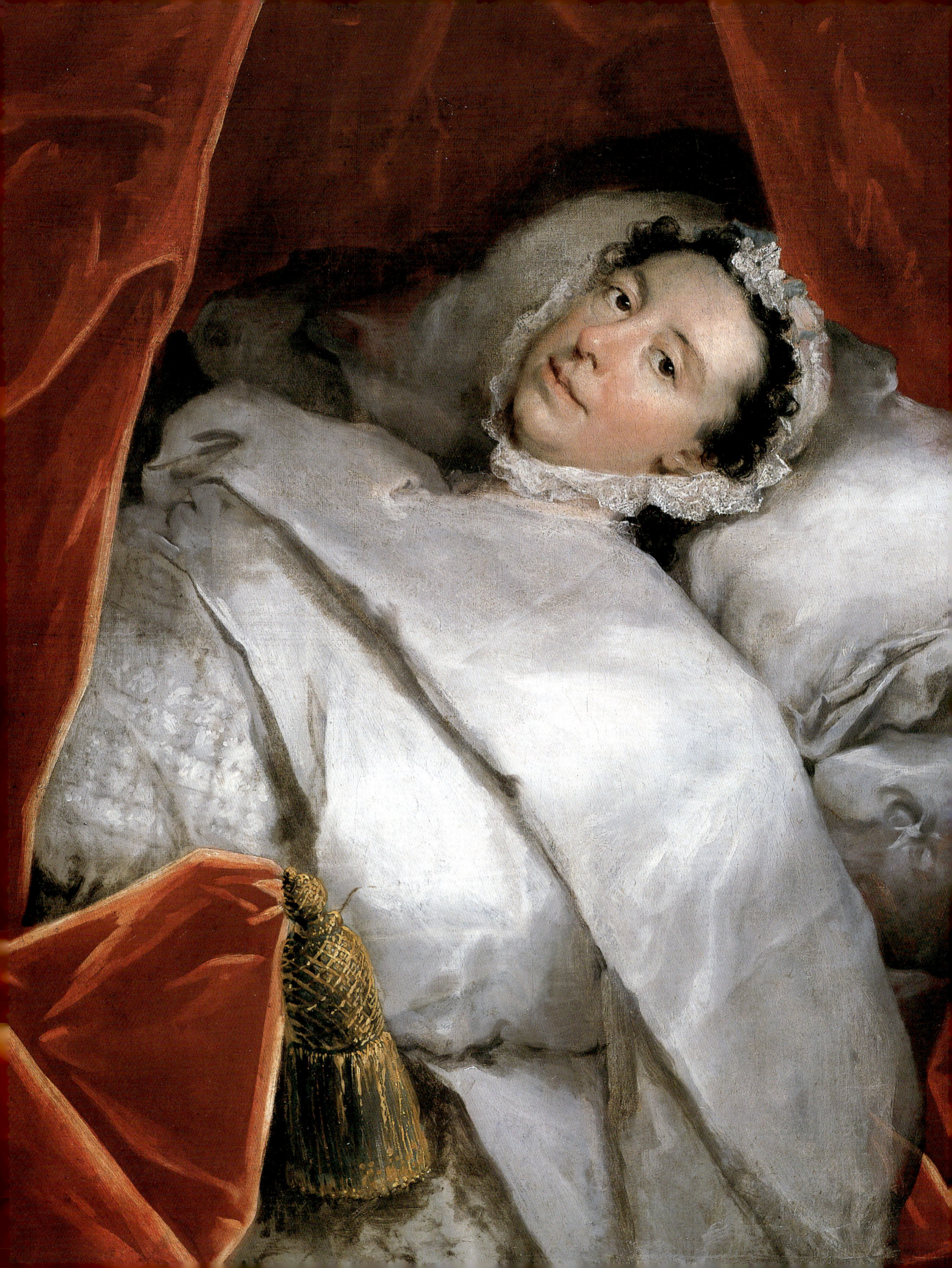

A KEY ELEMENT in producing portraiture is to record individual achievement. Defining success is not so easy. Rather than attempting to chart the wide range of Irish achievement over three centuries, this chapter concentrates instead on the portrayal of success, both at home and abroad, in just two areas: the theatre and the church, again with an emphasis on the eighteenth century.

The widespread accessibility of the image in the last fifty years has made fame more achievable than ever. From Andy Warhol's 'fifteen minutes' to the participation of the otherwise 'ordinary' individuals on the internationally varied versions of the television phenomenon *Big Brother*, the delights of instant recognition are within imaginable reach. Ireland is as involved in this development as any other developed nation. Indeed, more than at any time in Irish recorded history, many outside the island can now name a host of Irish celebrities who have made it on the international stage. There is little trouble in recognising pop or film stars such as Bono and Liam Neeson (figs 66 and 67), while others will nod at newspaper photographs and television footage of sporting stars such as Roy Keane and Sonia O'Sullivan. But what of the historical precedents to this contemporary explosion of visual success? By looking back at eighteenth-century Irish celebrations of fame in London and Dublin, we will see that the picturing of the rock star Bono with 'the world's most powerful man', as *The Guardian* newspaper referred to President George W. Bush (fig.66), is not an especially new phenomenon.

Wearing his distinctive sunglasses, Bono's constant pictorial presence in newspapers and on television screens has meant that he has transcended the world of rock promotion shots and album covers. His well-chronicled meetings with world leaders, especially recent Presidents of the United States of America on behalf of financial relief for Third World debt and Aids-related concerns, have turned him into one of the most successful lobbyists of his generation. The fact that a Dublin singer 'with no surname', as *The Guardian* puts it, is in a position to affect American policy on foreign aid, is indeed a bizarre situation. Bono's friend Bob Geldof, another Dublin-born rock singer and activist, has commented that

> the main thing [Bono's] got is access because of his fame – and the only route I was prepared to go was one that would move the political agenda . . . It's embarrassing and pathetic that people who have celebrity have access, but if that's the case, let's fucking use it, you know?[1]

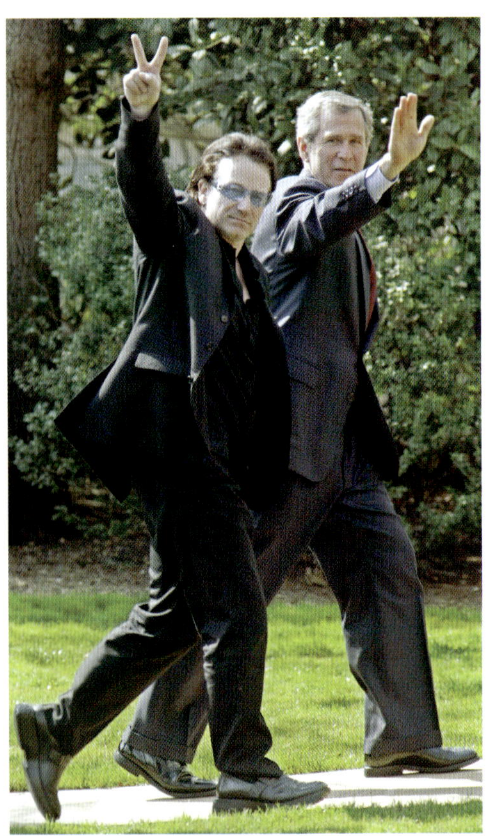

66. **Bono** (b.1960) **and George W. Bush** (b.1946)
ALEX WONG (2002)
Photograph Getty Images

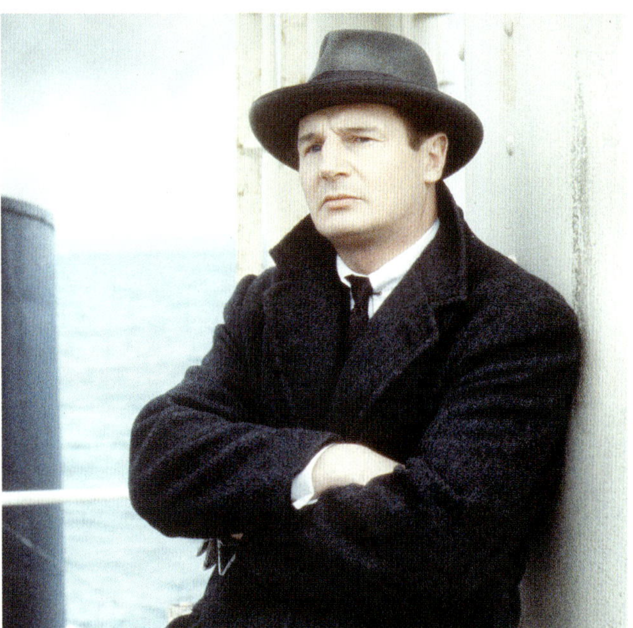

67. **Liam Neeson** (b.1952) **as Michael Collins**
Michael Collins, directed by NEIL JORDAN (1996)
Warner Brothers

The Bono/George Bush photograph of early 2002 (fig.66) maintains the bizarre contrast between the two men on their way to discuss international debt. The besuited, well-groomed President is accompanied by an open-shirted rock singer wearing a ring in each ear; to quote Geldof again, Bono 'is the pop star of record' who is also 'an exceptionally clever man, and he's also a paddy, so he's very verbal. He [is] . . . jesuitical'.

In examining the representation of success there is frequently an element of surprise at who actually becomes a celebrity. The following eighteenth-century examples allow us to burrow beneath the surface of the image, from a highly successful actor to ecclesiastics both Anglican and Roman Catholic. By examining how such unlikely candidates for success as a Dublin street urchin turned actor and a late eighteenth-century Roman Catholic priest turned Anglican charity preacher spawned an array of visual images, a common bond will emerge between, for example, Peg Woffington (fig.73) and Walter Blake Kirwan (fig.76). That bond has nothing to do with any character similarities between the two people, but is all about how portraiture was used to celebrate success. It is about tracing links between the production of portraits and the portrayal of life as a public performance.

Playing the part

The representation of the Irish actor is multitudinous. Actors by definition live in a world of masks and deception and their art is based on making us believe that they are someone else. Just as images of film stars are widely accessible today in newspapers and magazines, so too portraits of successful actors were widespread from the eighteenth century. Today, a film still of Liam Neeson playing Michael Collins (fig.67) reminds us of the actor's appearance, and also of Neil Jordan's epic, 'the most important film made in or about Ireland in the first century of film'.[2] Equally, the many portraits of Peg Woffington and later Charles Macklin, who enjoyed huge fame on the Dublin and London stages in the eighteenth century, indicate Irish success stories of two hundred years ago. The manner in which Woffington dealt with her fame and her visual representation will be discussed in greater detail below; Macklin had to overcome extreme prejudice in England due to his Irish accent.[3] Eventually, however, he was much praised as a comic actor, going on to become famous for his portrayal of Shylock in the *Merchant of Venice*, a role he played for almost forty years. Numerous paintings and prints show him in this role: some are single portraits where he pleads his case in the dramatic trial scene, while others show him with his daughter, Maria, who frequently played opposite him as Portia.[4] In 1773, at the somewhat advanced age of about seventy-four, Macklin chose to move from Shakespeare's comedies to the more tragic roles of Macbeth and Richard III. This caused a riot, leading Macklin to take some members of the audience to court. This is the context for Johan Zoffany's painting now in Tate Britain, London (fig.68).[5] Macklin stands left of centre, wielding a rather sketchily painted knife; the actor Matthew Clarke in the character of Antonio, his naked chest exposed, stands to the right, while in the centre Portia played by Maria Macklin grasps her father's wrist. Off to the left is the trial judge, the Duke of Venice. What distinguishes this representation of Macklin as Shylock over all the other known representations of scenes from the play is the highly personalised nature of the Irish actor's orchestration of the image. Macklin agreed with Zoffany not only that his real daughter should be depicted in the character of his stage daughter in Shakespeare's play, but also, in the light of Macklin's court case, William Murray, 1st Earl of Mansfield and Lord Chief Justice, who was presiding judge at the real trial of 1774–5, sits on the far left in the guise of the Duke. Although left unfinished and seemingly unpurchased when Zoffany moved on to India in 1783, this large painting is a grandiose statement by an Irish actor in London intent on salvaging his reputation. In May 1775 Mansfield had ruled in Macklin's favour, stating that:

> If, from malice, ill-will, or resentment, a number of people are ungenerous
> enough to take advantage of the situation a poor Actor is in, being at their
> Mercy upon the Stage to deprive him of his bread, and insult him, not upon

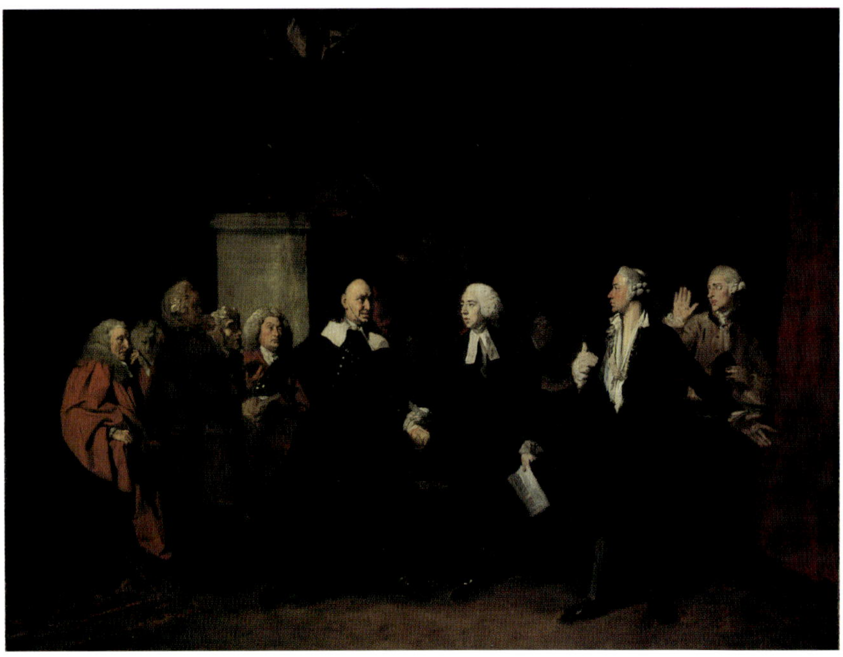

any offence arising out of the play, but from malice and conspiracy against the person who is the Actor, to strip him of the means of living, that is a strong ground of action, which may be brought by him.[6]

Another male Irish actor, this time in the nineteenth century, William Charles Macready was born in England of Irish parentage and rose to the position of undisputed Shakespearian actor from c.1820 to 1851. His father had been a jobbing actor who specialised in Irish stage roles, but Macready benefited, like so many other Irish 'on the make', from the fact that his father conveniently changed religion and sent his son to a public school. By the age of twenty-eight, as John Jackson's portrait of 1821 illustrates (fig.69), Macready was in a position to commission a portrait of himself in medieval costume as the dying monarch in Shakespeare's *Henry IV Part II*, a role he had played at Drury Lane Theatre 'in celebration of the Coronation of George IV'. He was a friend of the Irish artist Daniel Maclise as well as of Charles Dickens, who referred to them as 'the two Macs', although both of them had attempted to reduce the 'barbarous savage ring' of their Irish prefix by conflating it with the paternal surname.[7] Despite such apprehension with regard to Celtic prefixes, it did not prevent Macready from being painted by Maclise in *Macbeth and the Weird Sisters*, which was exhibited at the Royal Academy in 1836. The painting was to enjoy a continued exhibition history for another twenty years in London, Dublin and Edinburgh.[8]

A key figure in this pantheon of Irish thespians on the London stage was Dorothy (or Dora) Jordan. Although born in London, Jordan grew up in Dublin and 'spoke of herself as Irish', indeed, years later the Prime Minister, Lord Melbourne, told the young Queen Victoria of how he remembered her as having 'beautiful

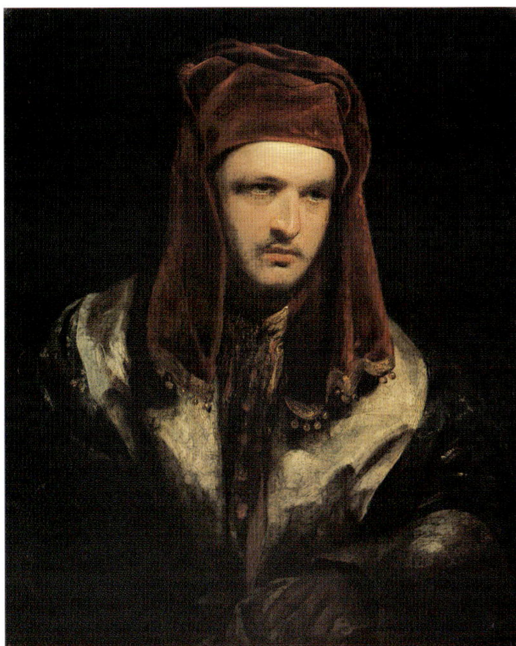

69. **William Charles Macready** (1793–1873) **as Henry IV**
JOHN JACKSON (1821)
Oil on canvas, 910 × 616mm (36 × 24¼")
National Portrait Gallery,
London (NPG 1503)

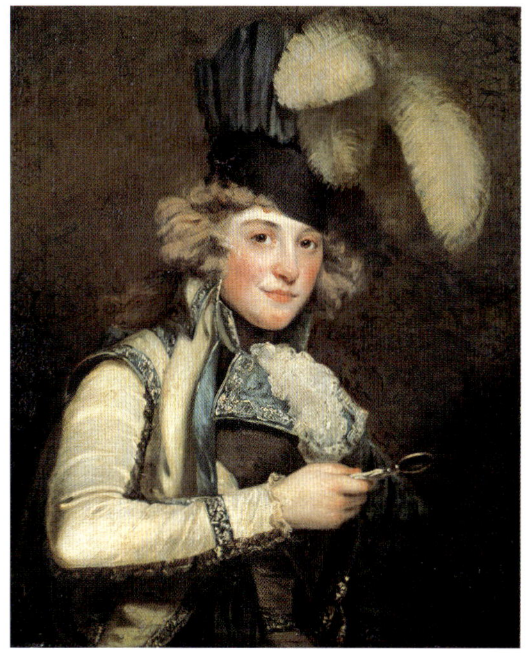

70. **Dorothy Jordan** (1762–1816) **as Hippolita in Colley Cibber's** *She Would and She Would Not*
JOHN HOPPNER (C.1791)
Oil on canvas, 749 × 622 cm (29½ × 24½")
National Portrait Gallery, London (NPG L174)

Disguised in male costume, Dora Jordan played this role in 1785–6. The portrait was painted at the commencement of her long relationship with the future King, William IV. Appropriately, the portrait now hangs next to Martin Archer Shee's full-length of her lover.

enunciation. She was an Irish girl'. In time, like her Irish predecessor Peg Woffington, she excelled in 'breeches parts': that is, roles that asked her to dress as a man. John Hoppner painted her in two such roles and William Beechey at least once, as Rosalind in *As You Like It*, dressed in 'yellow knee breeches'. In Hoppner's Viola in *Twelfth Night* (Kenwood House, London; Royal Academy 1796) she appears as the disguised Cesario in a military uniform, while around 1791 the same artist painted her in a comparable role 'as the dashing Hippolita who disguises herself as an army officer to win her lover' in Colley Cibber's *She Would and She Would Not* (fig.70).[9]

Peg Woffington had gained great renown many decades earlier, playing Sir Harry Wildair in Farquhar's *The Constant Couple*, and was painted in the role in a half-length oil now in the Harvard Theatre Collection. 'She always conferred a Favour upon the Managers', wrote one eighteenth-century theatre historian, 'whenever she changed her Sex, and filled their Houses'.[10] In male parts both Woffington and later Jordan were celebrated for their elegant legs and delicate ankles, though when it came to portraiture these features were cautiously avoided. Despite these visual omissions, the cross-dressed actress, as Gill Perry has suggested, 'was restrained in

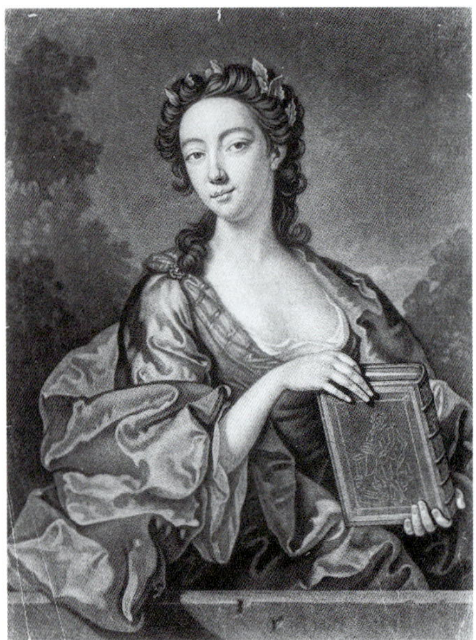

71. **Peg Woffington** (c.1718–60)
JOHN FABER, JNR after JOHN GILES ECCARD (1745)
Mezzotint, 325 × 230mm (12¾ × 9″)
National Portrait Gallery, London (NPG D4872)

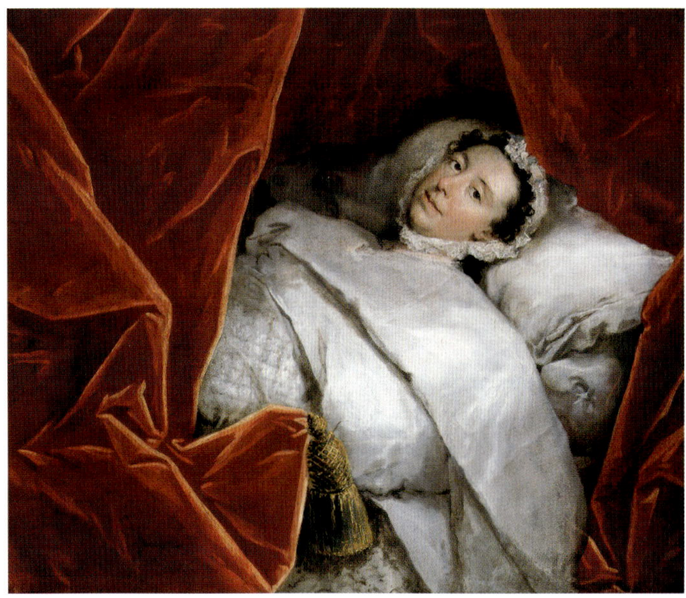

72. **Peg Woffington** (c.1718–60)
ANONYMOUS, possibly by PIETER VAN BLEECK (c.1758)
Oil on canvas, 902 × 1067mm (35½ × 42″)
National Portrait Gallery, London (NPG 650)

favour of a more thoroughly feminized effect playing on the continuities between the obvious delicacy of the actress's features and the ornamental richness of her clothing'. An 'erotic charge' was thus present in the juxtaposition of 'masculine disguise' and '"natural" femininity'.[11] The half-length portrait of Jordan as *Hippolita* was exhibited at the Royal Academy in 1791, an exhibition that took place just as news of the latest infatuation of the Duke of Clarence (the future William IV) was beginning to hit the London newspapers. Sporting a tall blue and black ostrich-plumed hat to complement her highly rouged cheeks, the actress wears a silk coat with a lace shirt-frill that cascades over her disguised bosom. About to raise her eyeglass, Jordan takes a hurried side-glance at the viewer. When exhibited in Somerset House in 1791, sexual ambiguity tinged with celebrity gossip would have increased the element of 'desire' provoked in the spectator, of whichever gender or sexual persuasion.[12] Such ambiguity was also evident earlier in the century when Peg Woffington had appeared in male clothing. Contemporary comment suggests that pleasure amongst the spectators was clearly uppermost:

> When first in Petticoats you trod the Stage,
> Our Sex with Love you fir'd, your own with Rage!
> In Breeches next, so well you play'd the Cheat,
> The pretty Fellow, and the Rake compleat –
> Each sex, were then, with different Passions mov'd,
> The Men grew envious, and the Women loved.[13]

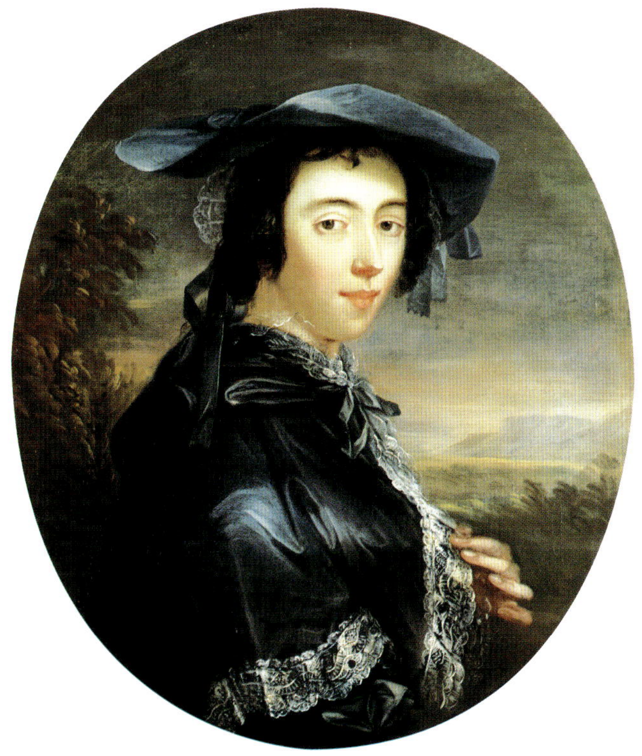

73. **Peg Woffington** (c.1718–60)
JOHN LEWIS (1753)
Oil on canvas, 760 × 633mm
(29⅞ × 24⅞")
National Portrait Gallery, London
(NPG 5729)

These examples demonstrate that the representations of the successful Irish actor in London between 1740 and 1840 were wide-ranging. On the one hand there are the sexually provocative images of women in breeches parts, in the case of Woffington and Jordan, while for the men we find confident defences of personal integrity in the person of Macklin or patriotic displays of monarchial support in the example of Macready.

To return to Woffington, here we encounter not only the most celebrated Irish actress of the eighteenth century but, conveniently for a study of the Irish portrait, a sitter who enjoyed a wide iconography. One reference book on eighteenth-century stage personnel lists no less than eighty-one separate portraits of Woffington in both oil and print media.[14] The focus of our study is on just three images (figs 71–3) which encapsulate a neat conflation of her visual portrayal from about the 1740s to her death in 1760. A mezzotint dating from 1745 by John Faber after John Giles Eccard's painting (fig.71) shows her half-length, 'as a comedienne' with laurel in her hair and a volume of Shakespeare in her hands. She is wide-eyed and confident, her face softly contoured (Walpole disparagingly referred to her as 'Irish-faced')[15] while her cleavage is surrounded by a rich array of billowing silk. The painting by John Lewis, of which there are two versions, one in London (fig.73) and one in Dublin, is signed and dated 1753. Here she appears in a feigned oval, wearing a cape and a bonnet against a landscape of distant mountains. Painted in Dublin while Woffington appeared at the Smock Alley Theatre, she is depicted by the resident scene painter: it is thus most probable that the landscape may represent stage scenery. The final image (fig.72) is the most extraordinary of the three. It is not known for certain who painted this image of Woffington but it has been dated to the last three years of her life, as she collapsed on stage in May 1757 while performing Rosalind in *As You Like It* and soon took to her bed.

The colonial body

Despite her notoriety for cross-dressing, the abundant images of Woffington rarely show her in such male roles. Although the situation had sufficiently changed by the 1790s, when Dora Jordan was a leading London actress, in the 1740 and 1750s visual representation demanded a less ambiguous approach. In Eccard's and Lewis's portraits (figs 71 and 73) the actress's femininity is stressed above all else. On stage she nightly revealed her charms and sexuality and in time, given the fashion for actors' biographies, it was expected that she would do the same in print. When eventually, in 1760, an anonymous edition of Woffington's *Memoirs* was published, it appears 'to have provided soft-core pornography for a considerable audience'.[16] The visual evidence suggests much the same story. In oil on canvas or in engraved sheets of paper Woffington looks delectable, with her oval face, large eyes and delicate hands. The focus on the sexuality of the actor is not unusual in eighteenth-century representation, but such an emphasis is heightened when we remember Woffington's Irish origins. Irish male actors suffered jokes about their 'extraordinary sexual prowess' and were the most frequent focus of sexual stereotyping, but Irish women did not go uncommented. In one play of 1729 the audience is told that 'hibernians are men of great natural parts', while in 1765 we learn that English women love 'Irish Commodities – Commodities of large and generous Growth'.[17] It is thus not surprising to find that Woffington's so-called *Memoirs* is littered with sexually titillating passages that create a similar commodification of the actress:

> Peggy Woffington was at her Father's Death no more than ten years of Age, and her Sister eight years younger than herself. Even at that tender Age, she discovered Beauties which surprized and enchanted. An irresistible Grace appeared in her minutest Actions, and over her Whole Frame was diffused such a pleasing *Je ne scais quois*, as struck the Spectators with Wonder and Delight. Her Eyes were black as Jet, and while they beamed with ineffable Lustre, at the same Time, revealed all the Sentiments of her Heart, and shewed that Natural Good Sense, tho' improved by Education, resided in their fair Possessor [. . .] Her Cheeks were vermilioned with Nature's best *Rouge*, which, like the Lilies and the Roses, blended in Sweet Conjunction,

were striving for Preference, and outvied all the laboured Works of Art. [. . .]
Her Breasts, which just then began to pout, and declared the Woman, were
ravishingly delicate and inexpressibly pleasing.[18]

Siobhán Kilfeather has commented on how Woffington's *Memoirs* is 'interesting for
. . . [its] acknowledgement of the sexual vulnerability of children'.[19] This is indeed
true in the piece just quoted, but in terms of Woffington's fame by 1760, the year she
died, when turning to the visual appearance of the mature actress in a painting or a
mezzotint, the male spectator would have searched for the now 'pouted' breasts, the
dark eyes and the red cheeks. Indeed, the *Memoirs* go on to remark: 'If then, such was
her Portrait at her then tender Age, what must it have been, when, matured by Time,
the tender Plant ripened into the full Glow of expanded Beauty?'[20]

Eccard's print of *c.*1745 and Lewis's painting (which was also turned into a
mezzotint by Michael Jackson) of some eight years later, along with the many other
representations of the actress, satisfy such searchings. Woffington is made visually
'available' just as the *Memoirs* inform us of her deflowering, when 'within a fortnight
of Eleven' by 'the vigorous BOB', who, though 'a Lad of some Spirit . . . [was]
possessed of True Hibernian Assurance'. The text describes the ensuing foreplay in
terms that echo the cut and thrust of so many mid-eighteenth-century stage performances: 'She darted a Look of Anger, mixed with Majesty . . . B. regarded not her
Frowns, but imprinted a Kiss on her Sweet Lips'. Finally, after 'taking her in his
Arms, threw her on the ****** Oh happy Bob!!! ****** *Hic MS. est Valde deflendus*'.[21]

The focus here is on male domination: male prowess is being celebrated and
Woffington submits. She and her visual imagery thus fall under the power of the
male spectator. Her commodification is made complete as we read in the *Memoirs* of
how 'all Sects and Sorts of People . . . Jew, Turk, or Infidel' lined up to worship at what
her biographer calls 'The Adoration to WOFFINGTON'S Shrine'. The anonymous
writer then details the 'vast number of young and old Rakes [who] offered themselves to our Heroine, and such a vast number were accepted, that language would
groan beneath the Task of reciting them separately . . . – In a Word, she was true
Actress, and was ready to *act a Part* with every one that Paid her well for it'.[22]

Such notions of sexual access to the person of Mrs Woffington were not
confined to London, where the *Memoirs* was published. Back in her home town
of Dublin, where John Lewis had painted the feigned oval portrait (fig.73), a poem
was published in Latin in the *Universal Advertiser* in 1753 by one Roger O'More,
entitled *Verses to be placed under the picture of the celebrated Mrs Woffington*. Translated,
it reads:

By heav'nly Beauty dazzling Venus pleas'd; And Sappho's learning through
most Climates blay'd: Her shines a nobler Nymph; in her we find The PAPHIAN
Charmer, and the LESBIAN mind.[23]

Such references to the followers of both Paphos and Lesbos, that is, those who engage in heterosexual excess and female homosexual activity, suggest that Woffington was seen as unhesitatingly at the public's disposal. Such liberality had also been observed with regard to her penchant for taking on male roles such as Sir Harry Wildair. One particular male admirer, referred to in the *Memoirs* as 'T-----D T-----FE':

> had seen our Heroine in the Character of Sir Henry Wildair, and concluding from her tender Age (for she was not then more than Thirteen) that she was an untouched Virgin, fancied if he would be so happy to win her, he should be in Possession of a mighty Treasure.[24]

The final portrait (fig.72), of Woffington as a bed-ridden invalid, is an intriguing turnaround for an actress long acclaimed for her ability to 'lear you into a clap'.[25] This crude *double entendre* is now no longer possible. The large eyes, oval face and fine features are still there, but the enticing cleavage and long, delicate fingers, all very visible in the mezzotint and Lewis's oil, are now hidden by bedclothes. Denied an image of a sexually alert actor, we are asked to consider another possibility open to the performer in the mid- to late eighteenth century. Wearing a white lace cap with blue ribbon and surrounded by crimson drapery and a large blue and gold tassel in the centre foreground, the actor has appropriated the iconography of an aristocratic sick-bed portrait. In a tradition limited to the higher ranks of society and stretching back to at least the early seventeenth century, Woffington has been painted in the manner of women who have taken to their bed due either to severe illness or childbirth. There is nothing sexually provocative in this painting, unlike the almost contemporaneous group of bed-scene paintings by Philip Mercier and the Irish-trained artist Matthew William Peters, whose titillating actors and courtesans peer out at the viewer from behind tantalisingly placed bed curtains.[26] Instead of Peg Woffington as the 'Paphian Charmer' or as a 'vermilioned'-cheeked ingénue, we see her as a sympathetic invalid. Instead of the sexually provocative nature of the earlier portraits, the late bed painting conveys baroque grandeur and the respectability of a moneyed lifestyle (Woffington left over £8,000 and some property at her death).

What then are we to make of this final portrait showing Woffington stricken by palsy and bedridden? Some years earlier the Irish entrepreneur and theatre manager Owen McSwiny (fig.74) had left her a legacy of at least £200 a year, but on condition that she change her religion from Roman Catholic to Anglican.[27] With fame, the appropriate religion and an adequate fortune firmly on her side, Woffington was at last in a position to alter her image of the actor as sexual libertarian to the actor as lady, albeit an immobile one. Recently attributed to Pieter Van Bleeck, who had previously painted McSwiny and was a popular artist within theatrical circles,[28] this

74. **Owen McSwiny** (c.1675–1754)
After PIETER VAN BLEECK (c.1737)
Oil on canvas, 768 × 638 cm
(30¼ × 25⅛")
National Portrait Gallery,
London (NPG 1417)

Apart from writing and producing
plays, McSwiny was also an
entrepreneur of the visual arts.
Earlier in the century he had
commissioned a number of
celebrated Italian painters
(Canaletto, Piazzetta, the Ricci
brothers) to produce monuments
or *capricci* honouring the Whig
oligarchy (the Duke of Devonshire,
Sir Cloudesly Shovel and others).

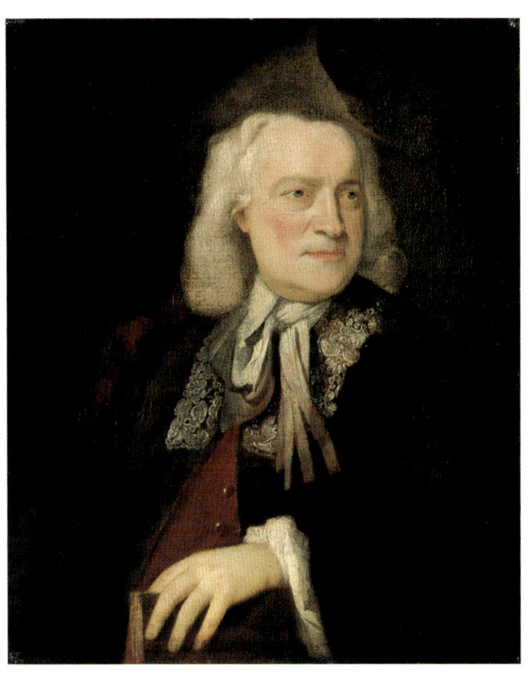

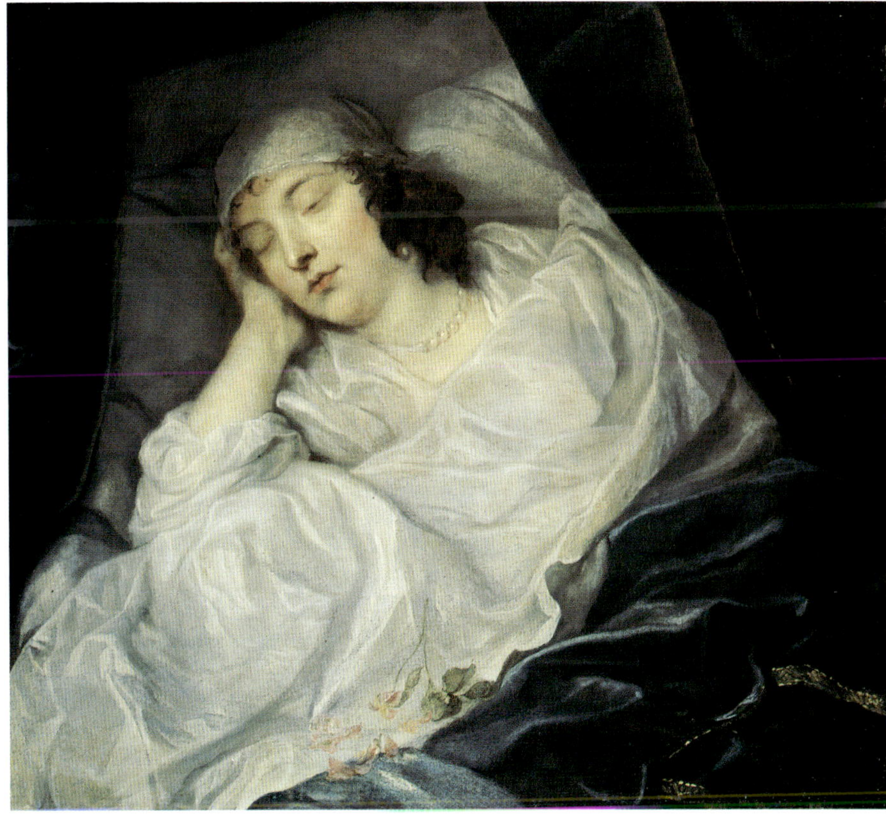

75. **Venetia, Lady Digby**
(1600–1633) **on her Deathbed**
ANTHONY VAN DYCK (1633)
Oil on canvas, 743 × 818mm
(29¼ × 32¼")
Dulwich Picture Gallery, London

painting is a conscious attempt by a mid-eighteenth-century actress to associate herself with the representation of an equally bedridden aristocrat. The most obvious visual similarity is with Anthony Van Dyck's painting of *Venetia, Lady Digby on her Deathbed,* commissioned by her grieving husband in 1633 (fig.75).[29] Both women are depicted in bed with drapes framing the head; while one is dead, the other looks out at the viewer, yet both are visually appealing. As Sir Kenelm Digby wrote of his wife's portrait,

> Vandike . . . hath altered or added nothing about it, excepting a rose lying upon the hemme of the sheete, whose leaves being pulled from the stalke . . . is a fit embleme to express the state of her bodie was then in.[30]

Peg Woffington substitutes a blue and gold tassel for the withering rose. The use of such floral allegory is not appropriate here in a scene of unfortunate disability, but newly acquired wealth can still be flaunted. One is tempted to push further in finding comparisons between Woffington and the character of Venetia Digby. Both were Catholic and both had reputations as lovers of prominent men, yet the Van Dyck painting was not reproduced in print and apart from two miniature copies by Peter Oliver, the only full-scale copy is a version in the Spencer collection at Althorp.[31] Thus it is not known how Woffington or her artist of 1760 made the Van Dyck connection. All the same, the visual similarities are extraordinary: as Kimberly Crouch has suggested, 'by modelling their behaviour on that of fine ladies, actresses [of the eighteenth century] could foster the notion that they were worthy of audience appreciation, both on the stage and off it'.[32] As such, Woffington's visual iconography perfectly illustrates the fluidity of the eighteenth-century actor's identity. From poor Dublin water-carrier to successful interpreter of Shakespeare, from Irish Catholic to Protestant lady of wealth, she could now visually equate herself with the aristocracy and enjoy the pleasures of a rural retreat and a peaceful demise in her home at Teddington, near London.

Finally, can this image of Peg Woffington be described as an Irish portrait? Just as the earlier images of a sexually charged Woffington conform to traditions of representing actresses in the mid-eighteenth century, they also exhibit key aspects of the *Memoirs*: 'a certain racy beauty, wit and talent'. As Siobhán Kilfeather has suggested, all of these attributes were to the mid-eighteenth-century London mind 'associated with economic adventures and moral dubiety, particularly with sexual looseness often supposed to be the product of a Roman Catholic education'.[33] The bed portrait can be read as a reaction to those 'sexual' images, while its aristocratic associations represent a personally chosen iconography as opposed to an imposed imagery that previously dominated so much of Woffington's career. Whereas one could read this portrait as merely depicting a paralysed Englishwoman in an elabo-rate Baroque bed of *c.*1760, contextualisation tells us more. This is a portrait of an

Irishwoman who has achieved success and, despite her ailments, she still needs the oxygen of publicity – in eighteenth-century terms an oil painting on canvas – to advertise her newly acquired wealth and achievement.

The charity sermoniser

One night during the London Blitz a German bomb partially destroyed a house in which hung a large Irish painting of a now forgotten Irish cleric of the late eighteenth century. The lost canvas was *The Rev. Walter Blake Kirwan Pleading the Cause of the Destitute Orphans of Dublin*, painted by Hugh Douglas Hamilton in 1797–8, and its appearance is now known only through a fine mezzotint of 1806 by William Ward (fig.76).[34] Hamilton's portrayal of Kirwan is of a successful celebrity, a Church of Ireland cleric and charity sermoniser who in late eighteenth-century Dublin caught public attention and, through the force of his personality and the emotional intensity of his performances in the pulpit, occasioned a variety of personal and literary responses.

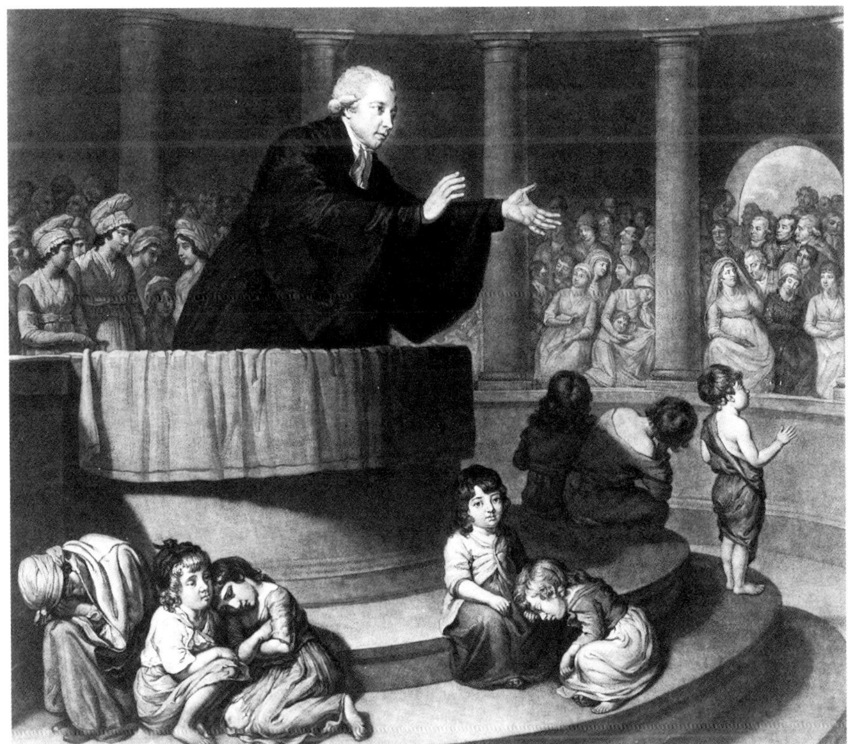

76. **Walter Blake Kirwan** (1754–1805) **Pleading the Cause of the Destitute Orphans**, WILLIAM WARD after HUGH DOUGLAS HAMILTON (1806) Mezzotint, 610 × 680mm (23¼ × 26⅞") National Gallery of Ireland, Dublin

In November 1797 the poet and United Irishman Dr William Drennan visited the Dublin studio of Hugh Douglas Hamilton where he viewed a range of portraits of leading Irish personalities, including a 'full length' of Kirwan preaching. Drennan was intrigued by the range of portraits that Hamilton was working on: Lord Moira (fig.100), Lord Edward FitzGerald (fig.101), Lady Pamela FitzGerald and Arthur O'Connor (fig.112). These portraits of United Irishmen and their supporters will be discussed in Chapter 4. Writing to his sister, Drennan mentioned how Kirwan was painted in an 'attitude of invocation for the poor children, some of whom are at his feet, one sleeping. The tears glisten in his eyes, his lips are touched with fire, yet he resembles his picture as much as it does him – he is painted and it is so.'[35] Drennan seems to be suggesting that there is an unquestionable veracity in Hamilton's depiction of Kirwan – 'his lips are touched with fire'. However, such an uncritical approach to representation is limited: Drennan also said of Kirwan that 'The last sermon I heard from him was a hypocritical adulation of Castle politics'.[36] Kirwan is not 'painted and it is so': rather, he is part of a fabrication, a process where art or visualisation aid the creation of a cult of celebrity.

Hamilton's original painting was large, measuring some 260 × 290cm (102 × 114in). Paid for by members of the wealthy banking family of La Touche, the painting cost 100 guineas[37] and was destined for the Female Orphan House, North Circular Road, Dublin. Kirwan stands in a pulpit and gestures towards an array of Dublin's destitute children. Behind him, dressed in uniform, stand existing members of the Female Orphan House while beyond them Kirwan also addresses his more socially elevated audience, sitting to the right behind a screen of Tuscan columns. As Kirwan's right hand gently blesses the children below, his left hand encompasses this elite, including Ireland's premier peer, the Duke of Leinster (the heavy-set man in the third row on the right). Leinster was the brother of Lord Edward FitzGerald (fig.101), whose portrait Drennan had seen along with the Kirwan canvas in Hamilton's studio in 1797. Also present in the painting, seated just below Leinster, is the Earl of Moira, whose single portrait (fig.100) Drennan had also noted. Moira leans forward to whisper something to Elizabeth La Touche, who is seated prominently in the front row. Wife of Peter La Touche, a major financial supporter of the Orphan House, and having no children of their own, Elizabeth (fig.77) was a dedicated philanthropist: she had even formed a school for orphaned girls in the grounds of her Wicklow estate. It has been suggested that the clearly well-scrubbed orphans in the foreground of the painting were modelled on the children of Elizabeth's brother-in-law, David La Touche the Younger. Exhibited in 1800 at Allen's print shop, Dame Street, Dublin, the painting was favourably received by the local press. One reviewer particularly admired the various ancillary portraits:

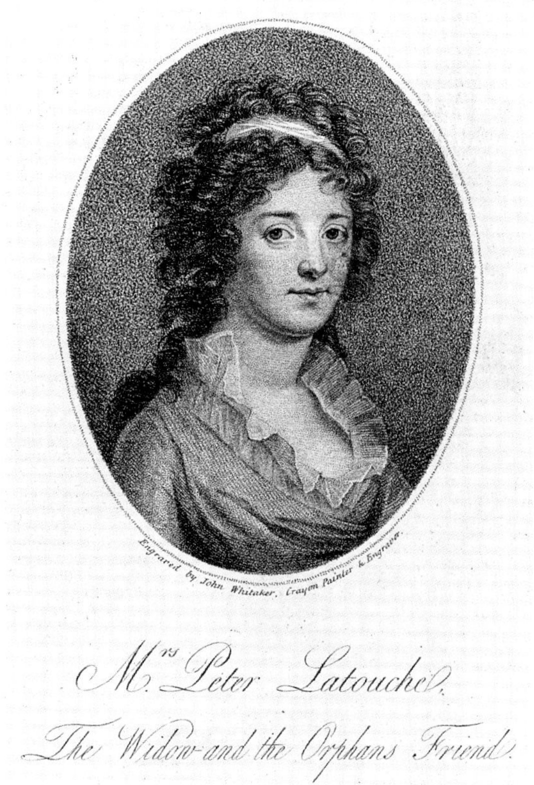

The several groups retain their respective places with the most perfect sub-
ordination. The portraits among the audience are sufficiently made out
for their distance, without drawing the eye from the principal figures. The
children are vigorously coloured, and the lights of the flesh partake more of
the brown olive than the brownish red or purply tint, they do not however
want clearness.[38]

Hamilton's composition is carefully designed for maximum dramatic effect. The
famous orator, in profile and half-length, is caught in an oratorical pose; in the foreground, the three distinct groups of picturesquely dressed indigents are placed in a
frieze-like arrangement, huddled together for comfort and facing their audience.
The large, sad eyes of the little girl in the centre foreground engage the viewer's
emotions, inviting us into what David Solkin has called 'the discursive universe of
. . . eighteenth-century "humanity", alongside the hospitals, theatres, and other sites
of polite assembly dedicated to the cultivation of a sympathetic spectatorship'.[39]

How then should such an image be read, and what does it say about the portrayal of celebrity? Is this simply a portrait of Kirwan himself, or a composite of academic genres – charity scene, history painting or portrait? In fact it could be argued to contain all three. We are invited, both by the stare of the child in the centre foreground and the curved space of the church interior, to play the same role as the painted audience and become involved in a historical moment. Sentiment thus plays a major role in our response to the image. The original painting recorded Kirwan's famed charity sermons that attracted large audiences and even larger profits. Much discussed in the Dublin press and in contemporary memoirs, his sermons, and more importantly his performances, were seen not only as a major attraction but as a phenomenon of their times. Only a few years earlier the liberal writer Joseph Cooper Walker had called for a renewed patronage of Irish artists, recommending that 'Dublin's new buildings of the time should be decorated by native artists with portraits of Irish worthies, or historical paintings of memorable events'.[40]

The Protestant divine

With Hamilton's portrait of Kirwan as an exemplum of a sub-genre of eighteenth-century portraiture, the Protestant divine may be seen as an indicator of the rise of the cleric as a celebrity. From portraits of Jonathan Swift (figs 78 and 79) and George Berkeley (fig.80) in the early eighteenth century to Kirwan and the Earl-Bishop of Derry (fig.83) at its end, the artistic lineage of the Irish prelate is one of celebrated individuals. Swift's iconography, for example, is extensive.[41] The Irish-born artist Charles Jervas painted him the most, and the National Portrait Gallery three-quarter-length, executed in Dublin in 1718 (fig.78), seems to have been the one preferred by the Dean of St Patrick's. We know that Swift carefully supervised the production of prints after Jervas's various oils and this seems to be the case with the engraving by Pierre Fourdrinier (fig.79). In the National Portrait Gallery painting the Dean sits by a table, pen in hand. Four books are discernible on the left: copies of Lucian, Horace and Aesop, with a fourth volume, of *Don Quixote*, only legible when the frame is removed. It has been suggested that this oil may once have shown up to six books, as Fourdrinier's 'accurate' engraving 'extends the left-hand margin to include a slim untitled volume and a volume entitled Milton'.[42]

This image, whether we are looking at the oil or the line engraving, of the bewigged Dean wearing his priestly bands, his greatest literary influences by his side, carries all the information needed to portray the image of an eminently public man to a wider audience. Portraits of Swift by other artists further develop various aspects of his celebrity. One of Francis Bindon's full-lengths of about 1739–40 is an

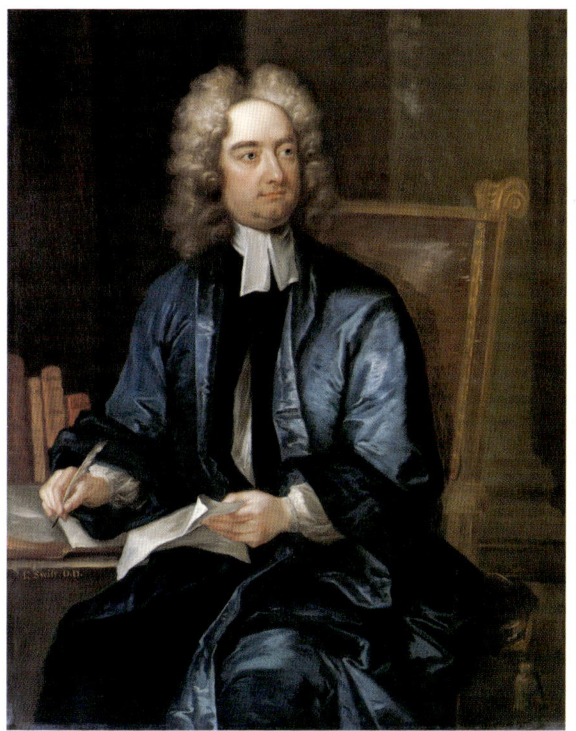

78. **Jonathan Swift** (1667–1745)
CHARLES JERVAS (C.1718)
Oil on canvas, 1232 × 972mm (48½ × 38¼")
National Portrait Gallery, London (NPG 278)

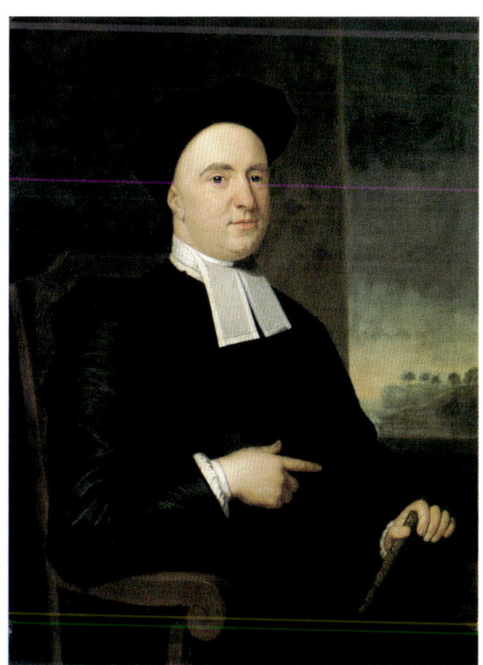

80. **George Berkeley** (1685–1753)
JOHN SMIBERT (1730)
Oil on canvas, 1016 × 749mm
(40 × 29½")
National Portrait Gallery,
London (NPG 653)

79. **Jonathan Swift** (1667–1745)
PIERRE FOURDRINIER after CHARLES JERVAS (C.1718)
Line engraving, 370 × 275mm (14⅝ × 10⅞")
National Gallery of Ireland, Dublin

In 1734 Charles Jervas wrote to Swift of how pleased people
were with the engraving after his oil portrait. Jervas added,
'I do not fail to distribute them to all your wellwishers'
(Falkiner in Scott, vol.12, 1908, pp.17–18).

allegorical celebration of Swift's campaign over Wood's Halfpence, while the well-known marble head by Louis François Roubiliac in the Long Room of Trinity College, Dublin (fig.81), confirms his reputation by placing him within a display of busts of what a Dublin newspaper of 1749 called 'other men eminent for genius and learning'.[43] Commissioned in 1745, the year of Swift's death, and produced without access to the great writer himself, Roubiliac's bust is probably based on a portrait by Jervas. The sculptor retains Swift's determined look as well as his double chin as he turns his head to the right, but he has exchanged the wig for a more informal turban cap. Swift had been about 51 when he was painted by Jervas, and the addition of the fur-lined cap, together with a similarly lined gown, allows Roubiliac to gently age a sitter he may never have met and who had recently died at the age of 73. Paid for by monies raised by Trinity College students, the bust was placed within a set of fourteen ancient and modern heads originally commissioned from Peter Scheemakers, 'but

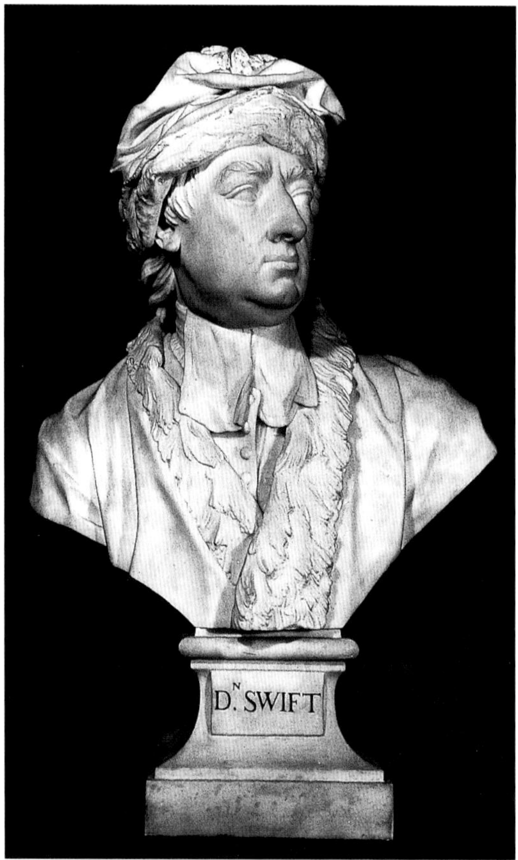

81. **Jonathan Swift** (1667–1745)
LOUIS FRANÇOIS ROUBILIAC
(1749)
Marble bust, ht 851mm (33½")
Trinity College, Dublin

in part sub-contracted to Roubiliac'.[44] This collection of busts had been formed a few years earlier from the bequest of Dr Claudius Gilbert, a former Vice-Provost of the college. The set includes Homer, Socrates, Plato, Aristotle, Demosthenes, Cicero, Shakespeare, Bacon, Milton, Newton, Locke and two Irishmen, the scientist Robert Boyle and James Ussher, Archbishop of Armagh, as well as Thomas Herbert, the 8th Earl of Pembroke.[45] In the nineteenth century the *Dublin University Magazine* celebrated the inclusion of Irishmen amongst the busts on display here:

> for, as there are books for the mind, so there are busts for the memory – and some of them as delineatory of the outward physical features of Ireland's learned sons, as the volumes they appear to sentinel are delineatory of their inward mental faculties.[46]

The Senior Sophisters at Trinity who paid for Roubiliac's bust of Swift wrote a verse that they proposed should accompany the portrait. It never did, but the piece began and ended thus:

> We, youth of Alma, – thee, her pride and grace,
> Illustrious Swift, amid these heroes place; –
> . . .
> All hail, Hibernia's boast! Our other pride –
> Late, very late, may Berkeley grace thy side.[47]

The idea of placing of a bust of Bishop Berkeley next to Roubiliac's bust of Swift was entirely apposite; but again, such an act never took place. As Ireland's greatest philosopher and the country's other great early eighteenth-century prelate, Bishop Berkeley would have found suitable companions amongst the Gilbert busts already listed. A posthumous oil portrait was commissioned by Trinity College in 1782, but it was not until well into the nineteenth century (1865) that an original oil portrait of Berkeley by James Latham, dating from *c*.1737, was finally purchased by the Bishop's alma mater.[48] Almost twenty years later, in 1882, the National Portrait Gallery in London was presented with a portrait of Berkeley by the Scottish-born artist John Smibert (fig.80). Dated a decade earlier than the Trinity portrait, Smibert shows the Dean of Derry, as he then was, seated by an open window and pointing towards an island-like scene, 'possibly intended to represent Bermuda'.[49] Berkeley had attempted to found a college on the island but gave up his ambition in 1732. Many portraits relating to his Bermuda project follow on from the National Portrait Gallery oil, such as the well-known group also by Smibert in the Yale University Art Gallery (1729–31) and others incorporating fountains and water symbolism that have been interpreted as conveying 'Berkeley's hope for the spiritual and moral cleansing of the New World'.[50]

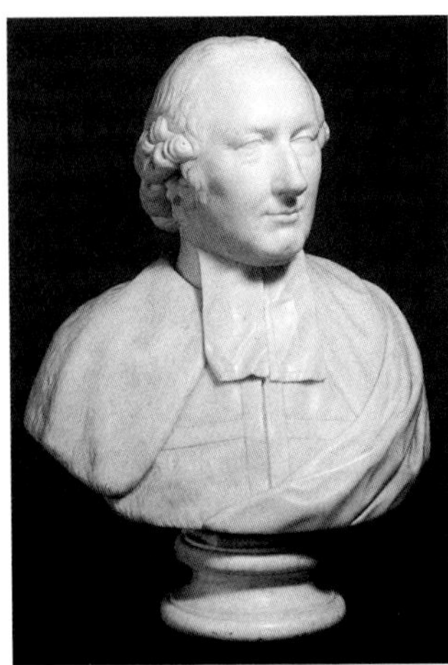

82. **Frederick Hervey, Bishop of Derry and 4th Earl of Bristol**
(1730–1803)
CHRISTOPHER HEWETSON (C.1779)
Marble bust, ht 648mm (25½")
National Portrait Gallery,
London (NPG 3895)

A leading figure among the foreign artists resident in eighteenth-century Rome, Hewetson's sculptures are not hard to find. They include papal portraits in the Vatican as well as busts of leading poets now in the Museo di Roma. He frequently signed himself 'Hibernius Sculp.'.

Later eighteenth-century representations of Irish clerics include the not un-common phenomenon of English-born bishops who were awarded Irish sees. One such individual was the Earl of Bristol and Bishop of Derry. Although committed to religious toleration and to alleviating the hardships of the penal laws against Roman Catholics in Ireland, a topic he even discussed with Pope Clement XIV, the Earl-Bishop actually spent a lot of his time in Italy and became, as Brinsley Ford has aptly put it, 'an eccentric and capricious patron of the arts'. It is not altogether clear if the Earl-Bishop's patronage of a number of Irish artists resident in Italy from the 1770s to the 1790s was either eccentric or capricious, but the portraits they produced are certainly the most compelling images of the man. The fine bust by Christopher Hewetson (fig.82), together with Hugh Douglas Hamilton's later depictions of the Bishop, one a large oil with his granddaughter in the Borghese Gardens (fig.83) and the other a superbly executed pastel of him seated on the Pincean Hill (both c.1790), are important contributions to images of Irish Grand Tourists in Rome.[51] All three show the Bishop in bands and sober clerical garb, yet such a simple costume belies the extravagance that frequently surrounded the Earl-Bishop's public display. The Hewetson bust probably dates from 1779, the same year that the Bishop 'most absurdly' appeared in full Anglican episcopal dress at the Holy Thursday celebrations in the Sistine Chapel. The Irish Member of Parliament Sir Edward Newenham recorded in his diary:

The Bishop of Derry . . . was laughed at by everyone. For this piece of absurdity he was obliged to go to the lowest part of the chapel amongst the common people while my sons and I were in the same upper division with the Cardinals. After this behaviour the eccentric bishop was held in the greatest contempt. Scarcely a nobleman would visit him.[52]

The large portrait of the Earl-Bishop with his granddaughter (fig.83) combines both sides of this extraordinary man's character. He leans against a tree to the right, dressed in clerical black, the only outward show of extravagance being the gold buckles on his shoes and the large carved ring on the little finger of his left hand. Yet leading away from him to the left is the dancing figure of his granddaughter, Lady Caroline Crichton, whose outstretched arms connect her grandfather to the sophisticated artefacts of ancient Rome, and also embrace the beauties of the contemporary city and the natural delights of the Borghese Gardens. Lady Caroline rests her hand on a large classical altar, the Ara Borghese, while in the distance, visible through the gap between the altar's plinth and base, is the modern Temple of Aesculapius, only completed some three or so years before the portrait group was painted. Such an elaborate backdrop to the portrait of an Irish prelate had never been attempted before; given the loss of the Kirwan painting, the Borghese group, with its large size and fluent colouring, gives us a sense of what the Kirwan would

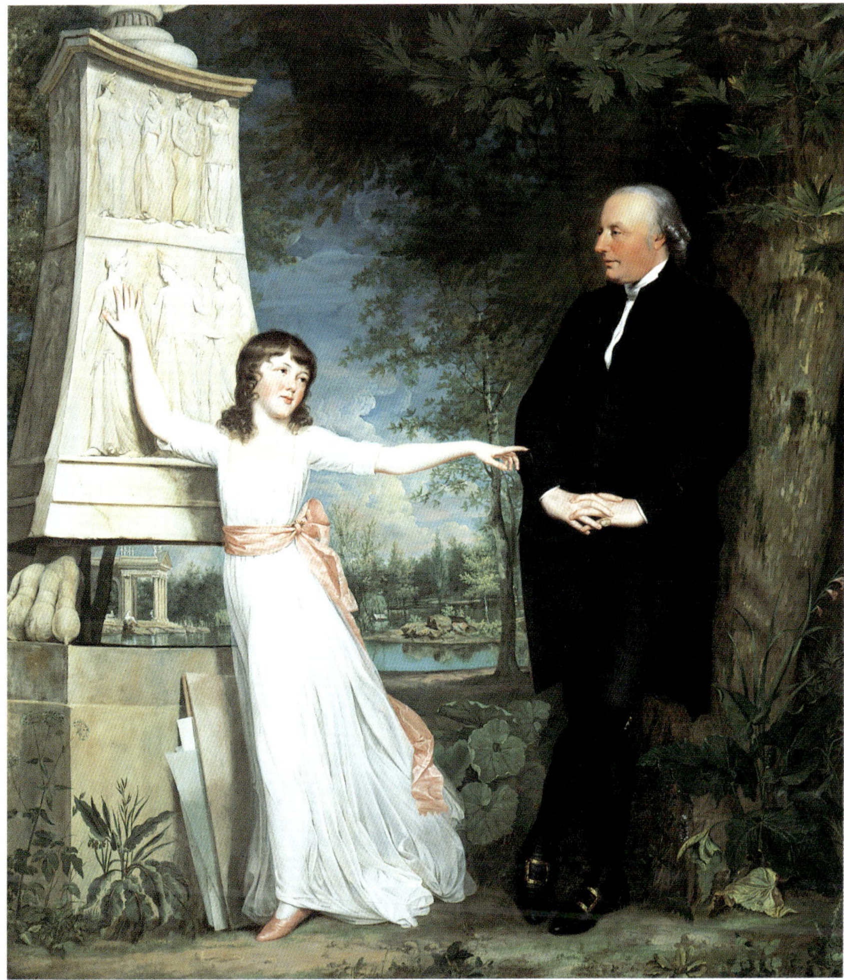

have looked like. Though not as wide as the Kirwan, which boasted at least another 90cm, the scale and assured detail of the Earl-Bishop's Roman portrait hint at the confident capturing of his subject that Hamilton would produce in the Dublin painting of some seven years later.

The Roman prelate

Toby Barnard has recently suggested that the 'incumbents of the Church of Ireland had long been in the vanguard of the campaign to conquer Ireland for England'. Such a proselytising mission features in Hamilton's portrait of Dean Kirwan (fig.76), to which we will return shortly. By contrast, the portraits of Swift, Berkeley and the Earl-Bishop are more concerned with personal celebration than mere 'apologists of the established political order'.[53] Yet at the same time all three men belonged to the established religion, so no barriers were placed before them. Their portraits satisfied their ego and were sought by their admirers. No such freedom was accorded the Roman Catholic clergy. Although a recent study on ecclesiastical art of the Penal Era has suggested that a tradition of episcopal portraiture continued 'even during the difficult years of the early eighteenth century', portraits of Roman prelates hardly exist as a consistent genre in Ireland until the nineteenth century.[54]

Engravings after paintings of such seventeenth-century cult figures as Oliver Plunkett (fig.28) were certainly in circulation throughout the eighteenth century, but few contemporary ecclesiastical portraits were produced. One large-scale example of an episcopal portrait is that of Christopher Butler, Archbishop of Cashel and Emly from 1711 until his death in the late 1750s. This portrait by the young James Latham (who later painted the portrait of Bishop Berkeley now in Trinity College Dublin, c.1737) was possibly produced between 1718 and 1720 and has been preserved due to the fact that Butler was a member of a highly prestigious family and a cousin of the 2nd Duke of Ormonde.[55] In time, and certainly by the early nineteenth century, the portrait was in the collection of the Butler family at Kilkenny Castle. The painting shows Archbishop Butler in his episcopal robes with an adorned altar to his left and a distant view of the Rock of Cashel. Although Butler led a peripatetic life under the Penal Laws, Latham's portrait is known in at least three other versions, indicating that Catholic portraiture was produced but was not very visible. Furthermore, although repeal of the Penal Laws did eventually come in the later eighteenth century, the 'Catholic Church was handicapped by an impoverished clergy and a hierarchy whose authority was often shaky'.[56]

Although portraits of Catholic bishops and prominent clergy continued to be produced over the following century, it is not until after Emancipation that one finds anything like the confident visual assurance previously solely enjoyed by Anglican churchmen. Nicholas Crowley exhibited a full-length of Archbishop Daniel Murray of Dublin at the Royal Academy of Arts in London in 1844, while the following year he showed *Taking the Veil*, a portrait of Murray with Mother Mary Aikenhead, founder of the Sisters of Charity in Dublin in 1815. In Crowley's large painting, which now hangs in St Vincent's Hospital, Dublin (founded by the Sisters of Charity in 1834), Miss Jane Bellew, accompanied by two male pages, is being received as a nun by an open-armed Archbishop Murray.[57]

The ambition of Crowley's *Taking the Veil* is unusual in nineteenth-century Catholic portraiture. More standard fare is offered by the many portraits of Irish bishops painted in Rome by Italian painters. Alessandro Capalti's 1855 portrait of *John MacHale* (fig.84) shows the 64-year-old Irish Archbishop of Tuam in a traditional pose, dressed in episcopal robes and wearing an archiepiscopal pectoral cross.[58] By having his portrait painted in Rome, MacHale, a nationalist prelate who is also remembered as 'the first Irish bishop since the sixteenth century to be educated solely in Ireland',[59] leapfrogs over the English portrait tradition which

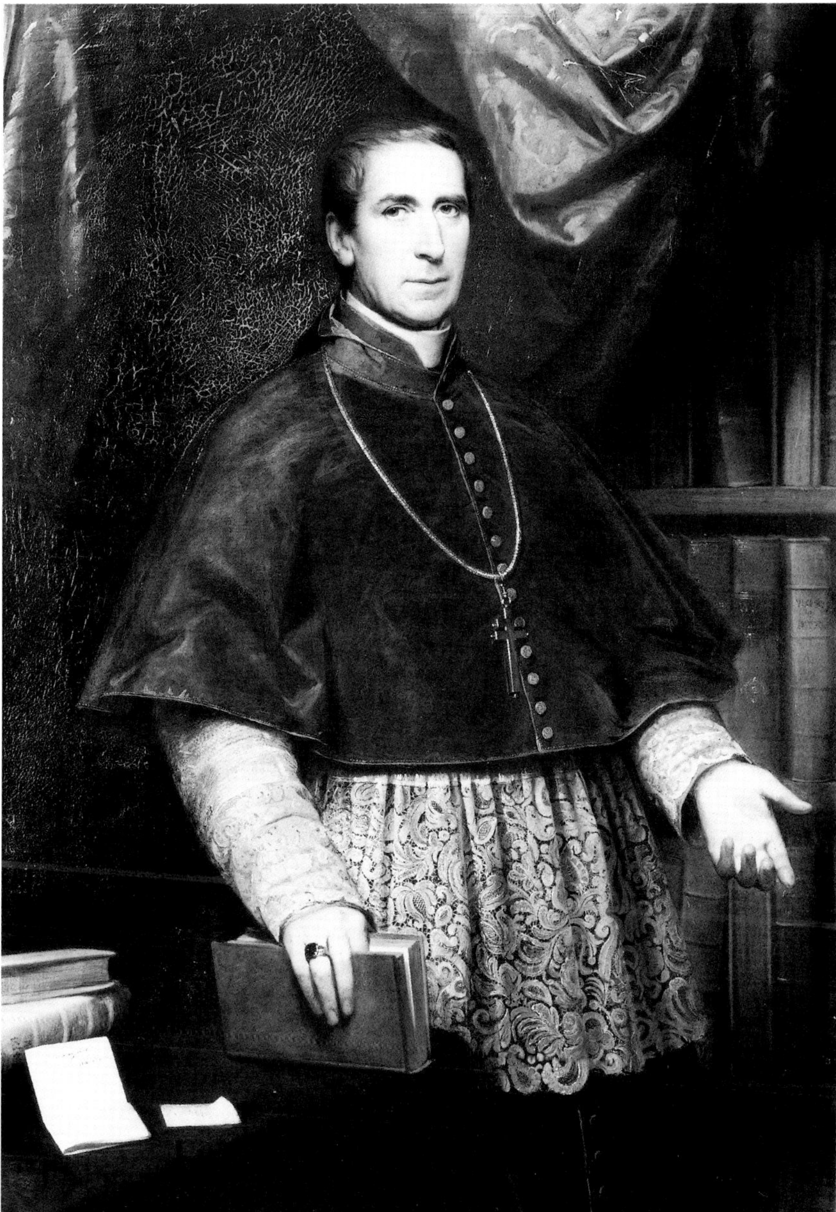

includes any relevant artist working in Ireland in the 1850s. Like post-Emancipation Irish Catholic church design, which was heavily influenced, for obvious reasons, by Roman classicism, such an aesthetic decision was dictated by a desire to distinguish both the visual appearance of the Catholic church and its individual clergy from the Established church.[60]

Such continental assurance was in full swing by the time John Lavery came to paint Michael Logue, the Cardinal Archbishop of Armagh (fig.85), in 1920. In terms of both subject-matter and the application of paint, Lavery's half-length portrait has

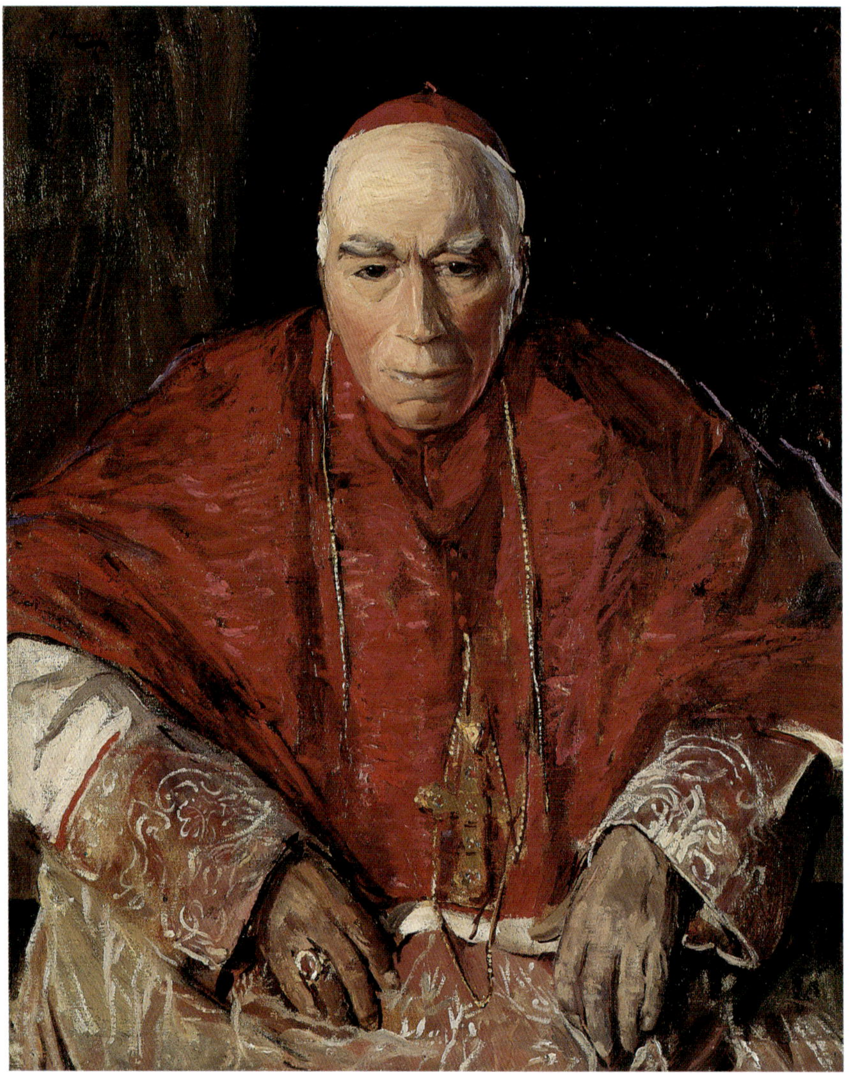

been rightly compared with Velázquez's portrayal of *Pope Innocent X* (1649–50, Galleria Doria Pamphilj, Rome). But there is more to this image than just august art-historical references. It is one of the most insightful Irish twentieth-century portraits of a national figure, yet it is also a portrait of a most unprepossessing individual. The 80-year-old Cardinal leans forward in his chair, his neck has become invisible while his eyes fail to catch the attention of the artist. The portraitist is almost denied access to the sitter, who keeps himself to himself. Despite such reservations from the aged and, by his own admission, 'lonely' prelate, Lavery propels Logue forward, pushing him into our space. The scarlet *mozzetta* and gold pectoral cross, together with the sapphire ring and the delicate lace of his cuffs, declare him to be a prince of the church and an eminent public man. Yet the painter described him as 'a little old man with round shoulders . . . with beetling brows and a long upper lip', while Logue told Lavery of another portrait of him which had made him 'look like a monkey in a bush'.[61]

With such seemingly unlikely material Lavery still creates a surprisingly effective portrait of power and achievement. The tension between sitter and painter has been likened by Seamus Heaney to a 'battle of personalities', and perhaps that is just what it is. Here we have a highly successful portraitist fulfilling yet another official commission and an unwilling client who, according to the artist, initially refused to lift his head to assist the painter's task. Lavery's work is often criticised for a tendency towards slickness and a rather vapid sophistication. This appears in many of his Mediterranean paintings of the wealthy basking in the sun. And yet the Logue portrait, together with some of his other Irish 'political' paintings (fig.141), offers something more. The sitter's bulk combined with the vibrancy of his dress and the dogged force of his unattractive face make this a memorable image of one who has truly succeeded. Educated at a 'hedge school' (an underground, locally organized system) in County Donegal, Logue rose to the Professorship of Theology in the Irish College in Paris, and in 1888 was chosen to run the see of Armagh where he oversaw the completion of St Patrick's Cathedral.[62] Just as J.J. McCarthy's twin west towers of Armagh's Roman Catholic Cathedral dominate in terms of 'scale and hill-top site, the meagre Protestant cathedral across the valley',[63] so, too, Lavery's brooding portrait of Logue challenges the long tradition of Anglican portraiture which, as we have seen, sets the mould for Irish ecclesiastical portraiture from the seventeenth to the nineteenth centuries.

Colonial uncertainty

In the light of the range of portraits of distinguished churchmen, Hamilton's representation of Kirwan performing in his pulpit (fig.76) stands out as an unusual depiction of an Irish clergyman, not just in the eighteenth century. Its varied content – one of the many well-recorded public sermons, the mingling of rich and poor as well as its blatant celebration of a famous name – demand that it be examined in some detail. Hamilton's is not the only oil portrait known of Kirwan. The National Gallery of Ireland's large canvas in the elevated portrait style by Martin Archer Shee (fig.86) was exhibited at the Royal Academy of Arts in 1803. Painted in London by a fellow Irishman and a rising star of fashionable portraiture, the painting shows Kirwan as a learned cleric (opened book, prominent quill and sheet of notes) surrounded by all the stock visual imagery of steadfastness (a classical interior) and elevated social status (dangling drape and richly covered table). Martha McTier, who attended a Kirwan sermon in 1793, described him as 'an awkward plain looking man'.[64] Shee by contrast visualises masculine bulk through the mass of black

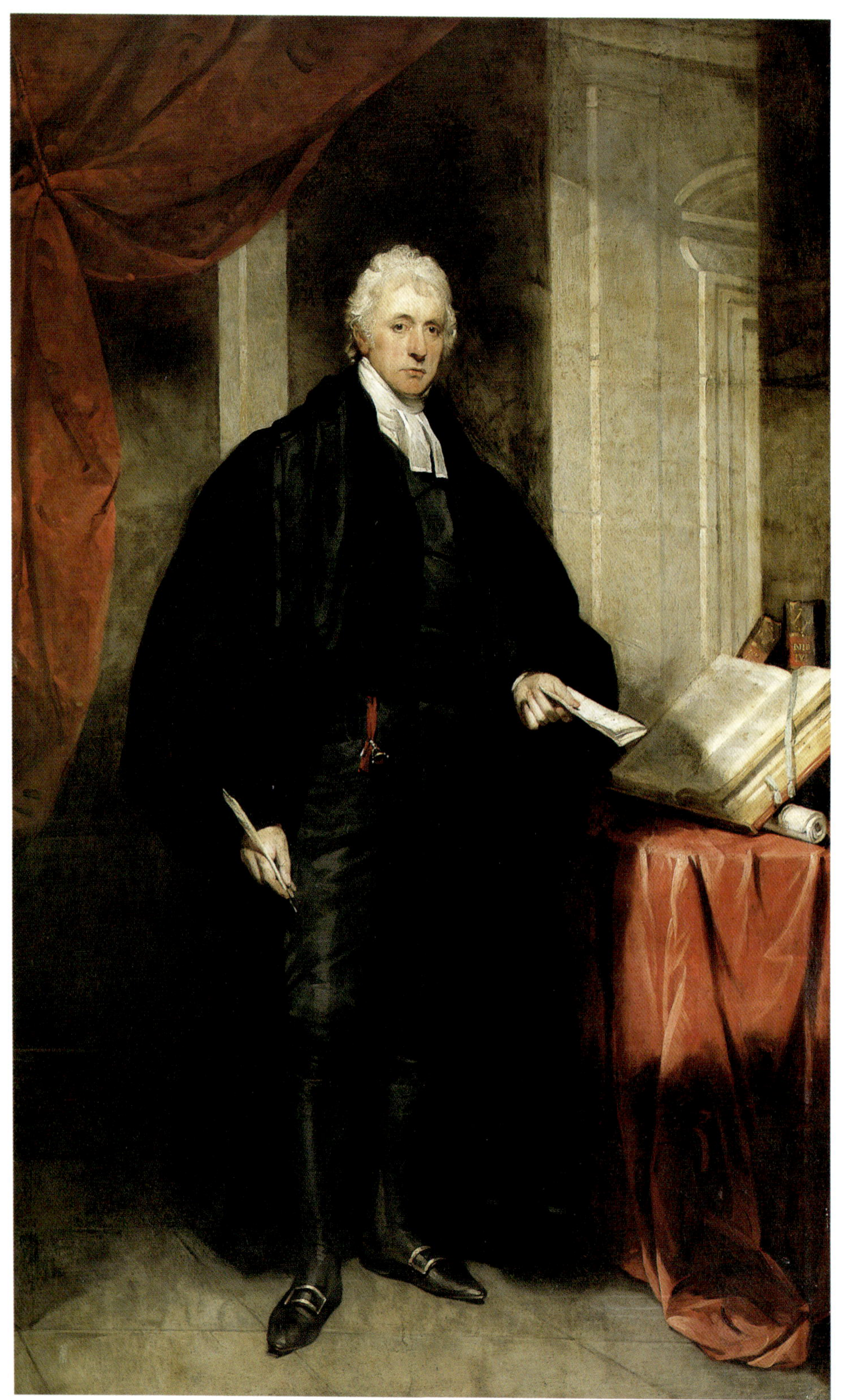

86. Walter Blake Kirwan
(1754–1805)
MARTIN ARCHER SHEE
(c.1800–1803)
Oil on canvas,
2400 × 1480mm
(94½ × 59¼")
National Gallery of Ireland,
Dublin

clerical garb, an elegance of poise and delicate hands. In its conventional formality the Shee differs substantially from Hamilton's more probing examination of celebrity and its relationship with a variety of audiences.

Those audiences, the indigent children in the foreground, the uniformed orphans behind and the society congregation beyond the columns, offer a range of reactions. Some listen and are moved while others whisper and exchange glances. A woman in the centre background is lost in her private thoughts, burying her face in her hand and pulling tightly on her child. As noted above, in a more public gesture, Lord Moira confers with Mrs La Touche. Perhaps affected by Kirwan's expressive delivery, Moira may be wondering how much money he should donate: Kirwan's orations were famed just as much for their financial returns as for the worthiness of their subjects. Accompanying Mrs La Touche, in the front row of Hamilton's painting, are those whom William Drennan refers to in a letter as 'the fair dames of quality whose gentle pressure drew from the general purse'. Jonah Barrington, a rich source of Dublin gossip for the period, records how the usual collection for the charity sermons at St Peter's was £200 but under Kirwan it rose to £1,100: 'I knew a gentleman myself', Barrington wrote, 'who threw both his purse and watch into the plate'.[65]

In 1791, after a Kirwan sermon, Drennan wrote to his brother-in-law of how, despite the fact that,

> The town is thin [...] he got £418. One lady took her purse, and not thinking it enough, threw a watch with trinkets into the plate which was handed round by Lord Clonmell, etc. You may conceive what a sermon it was when I felt the strongest impulse to give a guinea, but somehow or other it was, in falling, transformed into a shilling. I doubt much if St Paul could have preached better.[66]

Drennan's observation is perceptive because it is a famed representation of that apostle that has clearly suggested Hamilton's composition. Raphael's tapestry cartoon of *St Paul Preaching at Athens* (fig.87) offered the Irish artist some very obvious formal suggestions, from the stance and gestures of the preaching saint and the semicircle of listeners to the colonnade of Tuscan columns on the rotunda in the background. Such borrowing was not at all unusual for an artist who had lived in Rome for many years and had in his collection early eighteenth-century prints by Nicolas Dorigny after the famous cartoons which had been in the British Royal Collection since the time of Charles I.[67] Yet it also suggests another visual reference that is closer to Hamilton's own time. The reference here is to William Hogarth, who not only helped found the Thomas Coram Foundling Hospital in London, a precursor of the Dublin Orphanage, but actively used art to bring in funds. In planning his painting of Kirwan, however, Hamilton looked not at one of the Coram paintings,

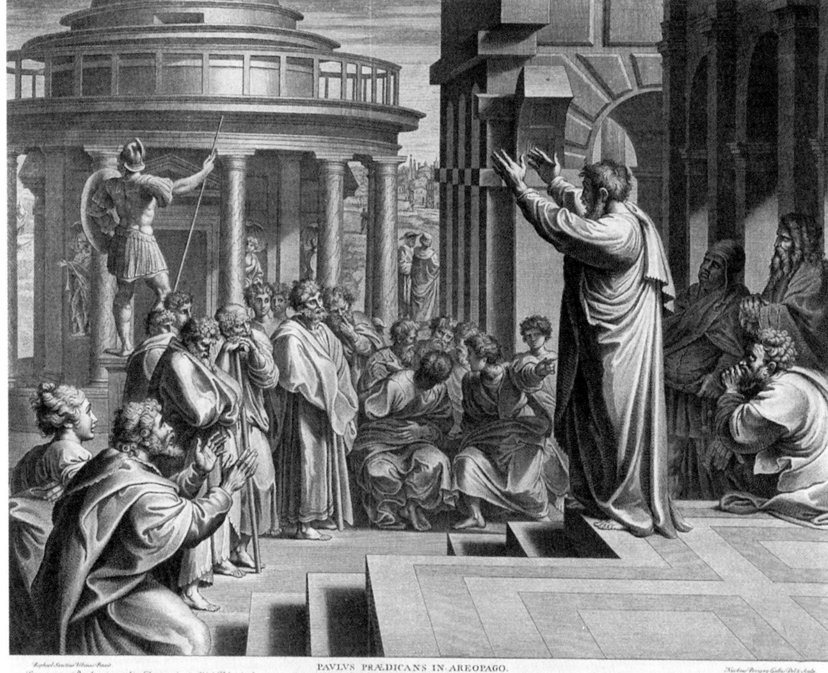

but at Hogarth's *Paul before Felix* (1748), subsequently engraved in a neoclassical style under Hogarth's supervision by Luke Sullivan in 1752 (fig.88). Both the painting and the engraving owe debts to Raphael's *Paul at Athens*. The Hogarth original, which was painted for the Chapel of London's Lincoln's Inn, represents the apostle proclaiming 'to the Roman Governor Felix the transcendence of Divine over temporal justice'. Paul attempts to convert by attacking idolatry and avarice. Equally, Ronald Paulson has suggested that the 'conversion has to do with the role of the artist freeing English painting from "ancient" art and the Continental tradition'.[68]

Hamilton uses his visual sources to convey an Irish 'conversion'. With due acknowledgement of these sources and aware of the paucity of such similar works in Ireland in the closing years of the eighteenth century, his large portrait of the Irish-Anglican clergyman, preaching to a congregation surrounded by children from the majority Catholic religion, offers a refreshing twist to the iconography of the Irish prelate. Kirwan was attached to the strongly Huguenot parish of St Peter's Church, Aungier Street, Dublin, and thus attracted the patronage of the Huguenot La Touche family: yet a contemporary review of the painting claimed that 'The artist has not laid the scene in any particular church. The architecture view appears to be his own fancy.'[69] By placing the indigent children in an imaginary pit-like space below the preacher, while the elite sit behind the rotunda of columns, Hamilton suggests the traditional architecture of a baptistry. This spatial conceit is reinforced by the central placement of the peculiarly font-like pulpit in which Kirwan stands, and the choice of the severe Tuscan order for the colonnade suggests austerity and a return to a simpler form of existence. Thus the painting may be seen as representing

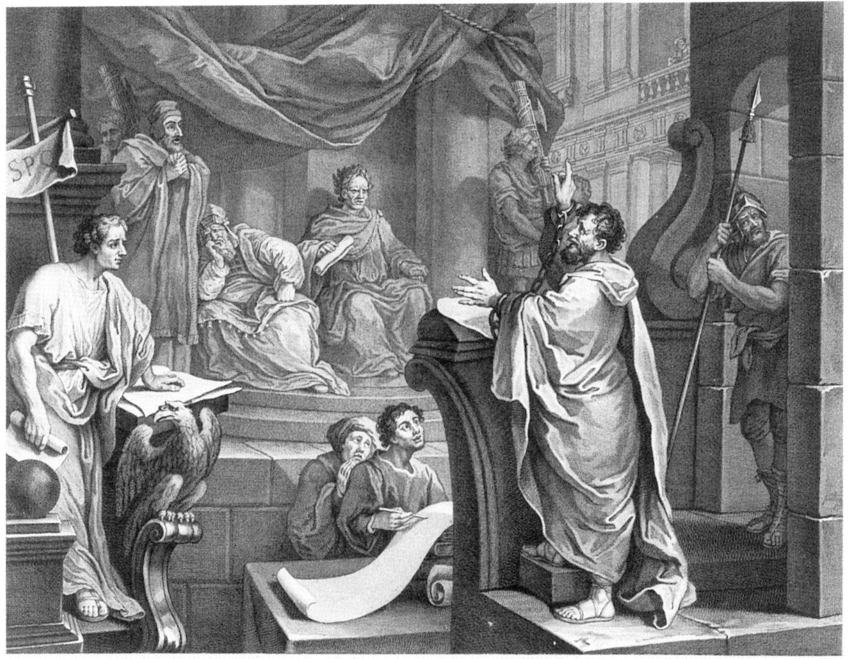

88. **Paul before Felix**
LUKE SULLIVAN after
WILLIAM HOGARTH (1752)
Etching and engraving,
384 × 505mm (15⅛ × 19⅞")
British Museum, London

In Hogarth's composition, Paul addresses the Roman governor Felix, whose gestures suggest fear on hearing the word of God (Acts 24.25). Next to Felix, the Jewish High Priest, Ananias, exhibits extreme discomfort. Hamilton's image of Kirwan (fig.76) borrows these visual reactions in the figures of the two women seated directly below the preacher's left hand.

a quasi-political baptism. Kirwan blesses the Dublin poor and brings them into the Anglican fold, where in time they will grow into responsible citizens like the young women behind the pulpit. Hamilton's image, painted as early as November 1797 and perhaps well into 1798, thus stands for social cohesion, the saving of these destitute children contributing to national unity. The nation as such is represented by the congregation of Dublin's elite gathered behind the columns. In a sermon delivered on 23 December 1798, five months after the collapse of the United Irishmen's rebellion, Kirwan spoke on behalf of the Female Orphan House. His text was from the epistle of St James, 'The wisdom that is from above is full of mercy':

> Never, in any period of our existence, did circumstances more unite to recommend the practice of this great virtue. Scarce breathing from the various and perhaps unparalleled evils of civil dissentions, what a spectacle does our bleeding country present at this moment, what a field for commiseration and the most active benevolence! What exertions will be necessary to repair the direful calamities of war![70]

In another charity sermon of a few months earlier, for 'the Benefit of the Widows and Children of those Yeomen and Militia Men, who fell in the Rebellion', Kirwan spoke of how things had been improving for the Irish peasantry, 'every quarter of the nation making rapid advances of wealth and prosperity … Such was the high ground on which we stood; such the manifest condition of Ireland, when the infernal demon of French liberty and equality came, like Satan into Eden, to attempt to blast our happiness.' Such, indeed, was the success of his appeal that he extracted a total of £1,122 from the fashionable audience that gathered in St Thomas's Church.[71]

Taking such information into account, can this image be interpreted as a comment on late eighteenth-century Irish attitudes to religion and the uncertain state of Irish affairs in the year leading up to the rebellion of 1798? Here is a Protestant clergyman, preaching to a wealthy Protestant audience on behalf of a Catholic multitude. Can Hamilton's painting be read as a metaphor for the religious and cultural divisions of the time: a division implied visually by the pit-like space reserved for the orphans and the screened-off congregation beyond? An added complication is the fact that Kirwan himself had been born a Catholic into a well-to-do Galway merchant family. He had studied with the Jesuits at St Omer and was ordained a Roman Catholic priest in Louvain, where he went on to become Professor of Natural and Moral Philosophy.[72] Eventually, in 1778, he became chaplain to the Neapolitan ambassador in London, where his sermons soon began to attract attention. Ten years later he converted to Anglicanism, and returned to Ireland the following year (1789) to take up a living attached to St Peter's Church, Dublin.

The Female Orphanage on Dublin's North Circular Road, on whose behalf Kirwan frequently preached, had the benefit of receiving funds not only from private benefactors such as Peter La Touche, but also an annual grant from the Irish parliament. A review of the painting when exhibited in Dublin in 1800 commented that the incident depicted 'is founded on an affecting fact of this celebrated Divine's having procured admission for eight destitute female orphans into the orphan-house by an eloquent appeal, in one of his sermons, to the feelings of his audience'. Kirwan had worked hard on his listener's emotions:

> In the very countenances of these children you may read the tender impression which your humanity produces on their hearts. If they love and respect any thing under heaven, it is you, and even me, at this moment. That miserable and humiliating dependence to which the destiny of their birth had reduced them, is forgotten in the tumult of such feelings, every kind and compassionate look we cast upon them, gives them that innocent but happy consequence in their own eyes, which is beyond all expression.[73]

Quoting *A Brief Record of the Female Orphan House* published in 1893, Maria Luddy has discussed how the Female Orphan House took in destitute girls between the ages of five and ten years, and that they 'would be clothed, dieted, lodged and taught reading, writing and common accounts; carefully instructed in the Christian Religion, and habituated to cleanliness and industry . . . to spin, knit and when able to make their own clothes'.[74] The children in Hamilton's image fit such an age group and are clearly in need of clothing.

A study of charity children in eighteenth-century Dublin has counted approximately twenty-seven Episcopalian Protestant charity schools, with no Catholic-run establishments, although there is evidence of informal Catholic schools.[75] Donna Andrew has brought attention to the common practice in such institutions of bringing up female orphans of Irish Catholics as Protestants, and quotes one London philanthropist of the 1750s as saying that such a procedure would, 'render them useful and loyal subjects and strengthen the Protestant cause'. Charity involved both the aristocrat and the pauper because it provided 'similar moral imperatives for both'; in this way, by the end of the eighteenth century, the 'attempt to save the souls of the nation' became 'an attempt to reunite the classes and the nation under the banner of a new and revitalised Christianity'. Andrew cites the example of one London healing charity which claimed that through its work

> The whole population, high and low, become intimately known to each other. The poor labourer is no longer an isolated being, for whose welfare no one seems to care . . . His industry will now be marked and applauded; and in the hour of his need, his wants will be supplied from the pure fountain of his own exertions and his own merits; which he can receive with an unbroken spirit.[76]

The role of charity to restore social connections is emphasised again and again in the literature of the period. In the Ireland of the late 1790s, with religious tensions at their height and the threat of French involvement in Irish affairs only too real, the need for the restoration of social unity was paramount. Hamilton's image is an attempt to visualise the reunification of the nation, in tune with the contemporary fashion for philanthropy, 'under the cloak of charity'.[77]

The nation is under threat and Kirwan asks that charity bring the people together. The enemy is France, the source of revolution. Yet lurking behind all this anti-Gallic fury lies a wonderful irony: despite the strength of Kirwan's attack on French ideas, contemporary sources saw the nature and manner of his preaching as decidedly French. To Jonah Barrington,

> [Kirwan] was vehement for a while, and then, becoming, or affecting to become exhausted, he held his handkerchief to his face, a dead silence ensued; he had skill to perceive the precise moment to recommence – another blaze of declamation burst upon the congregation, and another fit of exhaustion was succeeded by another pause . . . at the conclusion of one of his finest sentences, a 'celestial exhaustion', as I heard a lady call it, often terminated his discussion abruptly.[78]

Equally, the *Anthologia Hibernica* of June 1793 commented on how Kirwan formed himself on the model of the 'French preachers, whose various tone, gestures, and animated manner are sure to catch the attention, and rouse the admiration of their hearers'.[79] In seeing Kirwan's performances as of the French school, these commentators introduce a contradiction in the cleric's public view of himself. If Kirwan was behind Hamilton's painting, why would a man who saw France as Satanic allow distinctly French visual imagery to pervade his pictorial triumph? A striking set of quotations from a number of paintings by Jean-Baptiste Greuze can be found here, both in the depiction of Kirwan himself and of the children in the foreground. The French artist's penchant for heart-wrenching scenes of domestic tragedy is a rich source of figures which here, ironically, stress the negative results of French ideals. Hamilton has adapted Greuze's frieze-like arrangement of emotionally troubled children, maintaining the French artist's array of outstretched arms and pleading faces. Kirwan's animated hand movements recall any number of Greuze's grey-haired patriarchs or, in the case of *The Punished Son* of 1778 (fig.89), the long-suffering mother on the right of the painting. The weeping boy at the foot of his father's bed in Greuze's work reappears as a crouching girl on the far left of the Irish portrait.[80] Echoing Diderot's celebrated praise of Greuze some thirty years earlier, where the critic had admired the painter's varying nuances of grief, the *Hibernian Journal* of 1800 praised Hamilton's portrait saying that the 'appertaining feelings of the

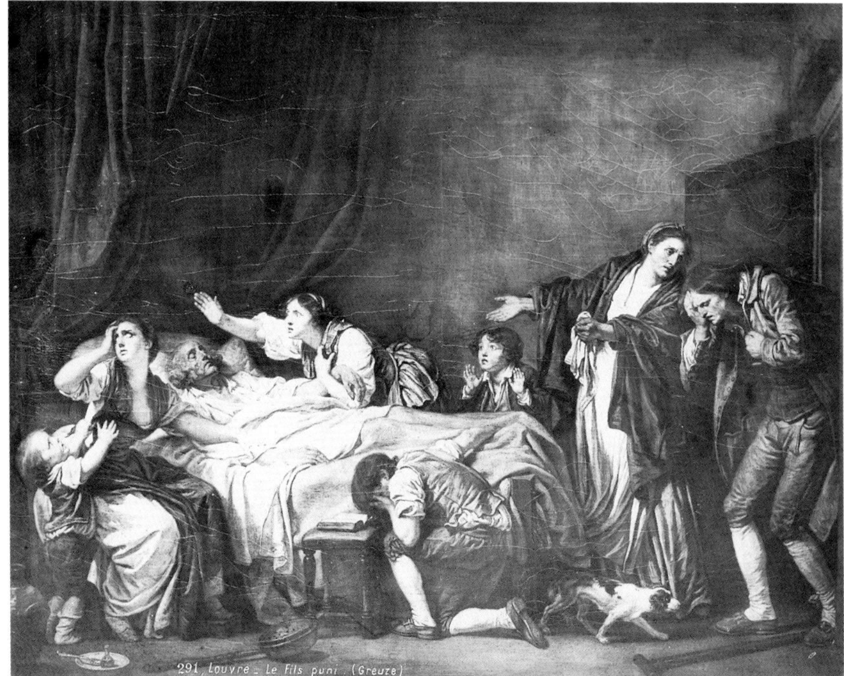

89. **The Punished Son**
JEAN-BAPTISTE GREUZE (1778)
Oil on canvas, 1300 × 1630mm
(51⅛ × 64⅛")
Musée du Louvre, Paris

subordinate personages are happily illustrated, to show not only the subject, but the various impressions made by the Preacher'.[81]

There is a glorious irony in the fact that Hamilton's grand historical portrait of a contemporary Irish figure, who in his sermons demonised the French, is shown here surrounded by visual quotations from a well-known French artist. This is compounded by the fact that the very children that Kirwan seeks to protect from French influence are themselves borrowings from France. Although he was trained in France at a Catholic school and used French oratorical skills to affect his audience, his conversion to Anglicanism was the result of his conviction that he might perform more effectively as a Protestant minister, and therefore be in a position to do more good. He spoke out against the blind credulity advocated by Rome, an oppositional stance that does not seem to have hindered his speedy rise within the Established church: Kirwan was appointed Dean of Killala in 1800, the year in which Hamilton's painting was exhibited in Dublin.

Contemporaries did not hesitate to comment on this meteoric rise. In 1796 Drennan saw him as an 'author, orator and actor', while a year later he criticised him for his 'hypocritical adulation of Castle politics'.[82] A satire on Kirwan published in 1791, entitled *The Kirwanade* by Patt Pindar, the pseudonym of Henrietta Battier, attacked its subject as 'a haughty priest/Who, tho' his tongue was fed with dew from Heav'n,/Sour'd the rich Manna with Ambition's Leaven'. Addressing the issue of Kirwan's conversion, Pindar wrote the following lines:

> Which of thy warm professions shall we b'lieve?
> Or which Archbishop did you best deceive?
> How grossly did you daub the Mother Church,
> And then, as basely, left her in the lurch.
> Say! – was it disappointment, pique or whym.
> That made you amputate so stout a limb?[83]

There is a degree of colonial uncertainty in all aspects of Kirwan's public presentation. His life is one of opportunities grasped, his sermons vigorous defences of the status quo, admittedly with attention focused on the sorry plight of poor children, while Hamilton's painting is a confusing mixture of Protestant philanthropy and references to contemporary French sources. Francis Wheatley is another late eighteenth-century artist who depicted public charity, for example his well-known portrait-cum-genre scene of *John Howard Offering Relief to Prisoners* shown at the Royal Academy in 1788. This displays not only a thematic debt but also a formal acknowledgement to Greuze in its use of a frieze composition and in the orchestration of hand gesture.[84]

Hamilton's debt is more troublesome, for throughout the decade both the Anglican and Roman Catholic clergy in Ireland denounced what was seen as the

'French Disease', that is, the growing support for French republican values.[85] Such support reached crisis point in August 1798 when the French landed in Mayo. In the wake of a violent and potentially French-aided rebellion, Hamilton's painting of Kirwan pleading on behalf of the Dublin poor must be read in a specific context. The poor are the indigenous Catholic Irish, and they too must be converted. The years immediately following the rebellion saw 'a renewed onslaught on Irish Catholicism, a revamped Reformation', as Kevin Whelan has called it.[86] Extra effort was put into setting up and assisting Protestant Charter Schools, foundling hospitals and the creation of strictly Protestant towns. Can we thus read Hamilton's painting as part of a contemporary propaganda exercise on behalf of Irish Protestantism but one that is, ironically, tainted by unwelcome French visual elements? Despite being able to identify a clearly defined enemy, the uncertain ties of colonial life were such that even when trying to celebrate a viable Protestant hero, a number of unwelcome elements crept into the equation.

NOTES

1. *The Guardian*, 18 March 2002, G2 section, pp.2–3 (article by Madeleine Bunting and Oliver Burkeman).
2. Michael O'Dwyer, *The Irish Times*, 31 August 1996, p.1, quoted in Pettitt, 2000, p.256.
3. Highfill et al., 1973–93, vol. 10, 1984, pp.2–27.
4. See Kerslake, 1977, vol.I, pp.176–7, vol.II, pls 499–504; Mackintosh and Ashton, 1973, no.31.
5. West, 1989, pp.3–9.
6. Kirkman, 1799, vol.II, p.107; quoted by West, 1989, p.7.
7. For Macready and Maclise's name changes see Weston, 2001, pp.97–8, 285 n.129 (quoting R. Renton, *John Forster and his Friendships* [London, 1912], p.61); see also Cullen, 1997, p.43 and Cullen, 2000, p.20.
8. For Jackson's portrait see Ormond, 1973, vol.I, pp.296–9, vol.II, pls 587–92. For *Macbeth and the Weird Sisters* (now in the South African National Gallery) see Weston, 2001, pp.95–7.
9. Tomalin, 1994, pp.6, 16, 177; the Beechey (private collection) is reproduced opp. p.320, see also p.340 n.10; Hoppner's *Viola* (Iveagh Bequest, Kenwood House, London) is reproduced between pp.72–3. See also Walker, 1985, vol.I, pp.284–5, vol.II, pls 661–5.
10. Illustrated in Dunbar, 1968, opp. p.54, where unconvincingly attributed to William Hogarth.
11. Gill Perry, 'The Spectacle of the Muse: Exhibiting the actress at the Royal Academy', in Solkin, 2001, p.124.
12. Perry in Solkin, 2001, p.124.
13. Victor, 1761, vol.III, pp.4–5, quoted in Straub, 1992, p.129.
14. For Woffington's iconography see Kerslake, 1977, vol.I, pp.311–14, vol.II, pls 892–900 ; Figgis and Rooney, pp.346–50. See also Highfill et al., 1973–93, vol.16, 1993, List of Images, pp.220–25.
15. W.J. Lawrence, 'The Real Peg Woffington', *The Connoisseur*, vol. 8, Jan. 1904, pp.44–5, quoted in Figgis and Rooney, 2001, p.349.
16. Straub, 1992, p.13.
17. Straub, 1992, p.163.
18. Anon., 1760, p.7, quoted in Bourke et al., 2002, pp.787–8. My thanks to Siobhán Kilfeather for alerting me to this reference.
19. Bourke et al., 2002, p.787.
20. Anon., 1760, p.8.
21. Anon., 1760, pp.14–15; the Latin reference translates as: 'Here this manuscript is powerfully to be wept over', Bourke et al., 2002, p.788.
22. Anon., 1760, pp.22–3, quoted in Straub, 1992, p.99.
23. Quoted in Figgis and Rooney, 2001, p.349, n.51.

Victor, 1761, vol.III, p.4, quoted in Straub, 1992, p.101.

24 Anon., 1760, p.16.

25 Quoted by Kimberly Crouch, 'The public life of actresses: prostitutes or ladies?', in Barker and Chalus, 1997, p.65.

26 For Mercier and Peters see Postle, 1998, pp.19, 86–7.

27 For Woffington's wealth and McSwiny, see Dunbar, 1968, pp.64–5, 186, 219, 222.

28 NPG 650, Registered Packet, suggestion offered by Brian Allen on the basis of comparison with Van Bleeck's painting *Mrs Cibber as Cordelia* (Yale Center for British Art).

29 Sumner, 1995, p.103. I am grateful to Jeremy Wood for suggesting the Van Dyck similarity.

30 Quoted in Sumner, 1995, pp.59–60.

31 Brown and Vlieghe, 1999, no.69.

32 Crouch in Barker and Chalus, 1997, p.71.

33 Kilfeather, 1993, p.42.

34 This section is an extension of Cullen, 1997, pp.66–74. There is also a small monochrome version in oil which may have been done for the engraver, see Cullen, 1984, pp.192–3. For the provenance of the original painting I am grateful to the late R.H. Carew of Ballinamona Park, County Waterford and Rosemary Trewhella of Devon.

35 Agnew, 1998–9, vol.II, 1999, p.348, dated 20 Nov. 1797.

36 Agnew, 1998–9, vol.II, 1999, p.348.

37 Agnew, 1998–9, vol.II, 1999, p.348.

38 *Critical Review*, 1800, p.22. For La Touche family history see Benedetti, 1998, pp.6–12, 34; David Dickson and Richard English, 'The La Touche Dynasty', in Dickson, 1987, pp.17–299. For identity of indigent children see *The Lady of the House*, Christmas 1910, p.47. The painting was also reviewed in *Dublin Evening Post*, 17 June 1800; see Cullen, 2000, p.236.

39 Solkin, 1993, p.199.

40 Walker, 1790. See Kirwan, 1816, dedicated to Mrs Peter La Touche. For an account of Kirwan's sermons, see Martha McTier's comments in Agnew, 1998–9, vol.II, pp.529–30.

41 Frederick R. Falkiner, 'Of the Portraits, Busts and Engravings of Swift and their Artists, with a Note on the Portraits of Stella', in Scott, 1897–1908, vol.12 (1908), pp.1–82.

42 NPG 278, Registered Packet, information from Glynn Wright, 1980. For general discussion of Swift iconography see Figgis and Rooney, 2001, p.310 and Piper, 1963, p.337.

43 For Bindon's Wood's Halfpence portrait see Crookshank and Glin, 1978, pp.36, 41 (illus.); Bindon's other full-length in the Deanery of St Patrick's Cathedral is illustrated in Crookshank and Glin, 2002, p.32. For Roubiliac see Faulkner's *Dublin Journal*, 21 March 1749,

and Anne Crookshank, 'The Long Room', in Fox, 1986, pp.22–3; *Rococo*, 1984, p.293 (entry by Malcolm Baker).

44 Baker, 1995, p.831.

45 Crookshank and Webb, 1990, pp.150–2.

46 *Dublin University Magazine*, vol.LII, Nov. 1858, quoted in Baker, 1995, p.821 n.7.

47 Quoted from Faulkner's *Dublin Journal* in Crookshank and Webb, 1990, p.132.

48 Crookshank and Webb, 1990, p.20.

49 Saunders, 1995, pp.147, 171.

50 Berman, 1982, p.77; for an illustrated account of portraits of Berkeley see Luce, 1949, pp.239–44.

51 Ford, 1974; for the Hewetson see Hodgkinson, 1952–4, p.50; for the Hamilton oil see Figgis and Rooney, 2001, pp.170–2; the pastel of the Earl-Bishop is in the collection of the National Trust, Ickworth.

52 Quoted in Fothergill, 1974, p.68.

53 Barnard, 2003, pp.81–2.

54 McDonnell, 1995, p.5.

55 For the Latham portrait of Archbishop Butler (oil on canvas, 127 × 94cm [50 × 37in]) see Crookshank, 1988 and Fenlon, 2001, p.78; a version is illustrated in colour in Crookshank and Glin, 2002, p.36

56 Foster, 1988, p.207.

57 Illustrated in colour in Crookshank and Glin, 2002, p.235.

58 Wynne, 1986, pp.16–17.

59 Foster, 1988, p. 387.

60 Alistair Rowan, 'Irish Victorian Churches: Denominational Distinctions', in Gillespie and Kennedy, 1994, p.220.

61 For the comparison with Velázquez see McConkey, 1993, p.154; for the sittings see Lavery, 1940, p.209; Cullen, 2000, p.129.

62 Ulster Museum, 1982, no.8.

63 Alistair Rowan, 'Irish Victorian Churches: Denominational Distinctions', in Gillespie and Kennedy, 1994, p.227.

64 Agnew, 1998–9, vol.I, p.529, letter dated 29 April 1793; for the Shee portrait see Figgis and Rooney, 2001, pp.426–8.

65 Agnew, 1998–9, vol.II, p.216, letter dated 24 March 1796; Barrington, 1869, vol.2, p.237.

66 Agnew, 1998–9, vol.I, p.358, letter dated 21 May 1791.

67 *Catalogue of the valuable collections of Engravings . . . the Genuine property of . . . Hugh Hamilton, Esq.*, 1811 (copy in National Art Library, Victoria and Albert Museum, London). Item 50 lists 'The Cartoon, in Seven Pieces, by Dorigny.' For eighteenth-century interest in the cartoons see Shearman, 1972, pp.148–50; Wood, 1999. The *Hibernian Journal* of 1800

also compared the Kirwan portrait to Raphael's St Paul, see Strickland, 1913, vol.I, p.431.

68 Bindman, 1981, p.119; Paulson, 1993, vol.3, pp.43, 45.

69 *Critical Review*, 1800, p.22. No Dublin church interior compares with this painted space, and certainly not St Peter's, Aungier Street. I am grateful to Edward McParland for confirming this fact.

70 Kirwan, 1816, p.157.

71 Kirwan, 1816, p.329; Robins, 1980, p.122; Maxwell, 1956, pp.47–8.

72 *Dictionary of National Biography*, vol.XI, p.230; Kirwan, 1816.

73 Kirwan, 1816, pp.372–3; Robins, 1980, p.120; *Critical Review*, 1800, p.21.

74 Anon., *A Brief Record of the Female Orphan House 1790–1812*, Dublin, 1893, p.6, quoted in Luddy, 1995, p.77.

75 Hayden, 1943, pp.92–107.

76 Andrew, 1989, pp.118 n.202, 195.

77 Rodgers, 1949.

78 Barrington, 1869, p.237.

79 *Anthologia Hibernica*, June 1793, p.416. Barrington also claimed that Kirwan's sermons were 'adroitly extracted from passages in the celebrated discourses of Saurin, the Huguenot, who preached at The Hague', Barrington, 1869, p.238.

80 See also Greuze's *The Drunken Cobbler* of c.1780 (Portland Art Museum, Oregon), where the outstretched arms of the beseeching son are recast by Hamilton for the orphaned girl on the far right of the Kirwan picture. For Diderot on Greuze see Diderot, 1995 edn.

81 *Hibernian Journal*, June 18, 1800.

82 Agnew, 1998–9, vol.II, p.216, letter dated 24 March 1796.

83 Pindar, 1791, pp.7, 13. See also Carpenter, 1998, pp.464–5.

84 See Webster, 1970, pp.68–9, 135–6. The painting of Howard is in Sandon Hall, Staffordshire.

85 Keogh, 1993.

86 Whelan, 1996, p.141.

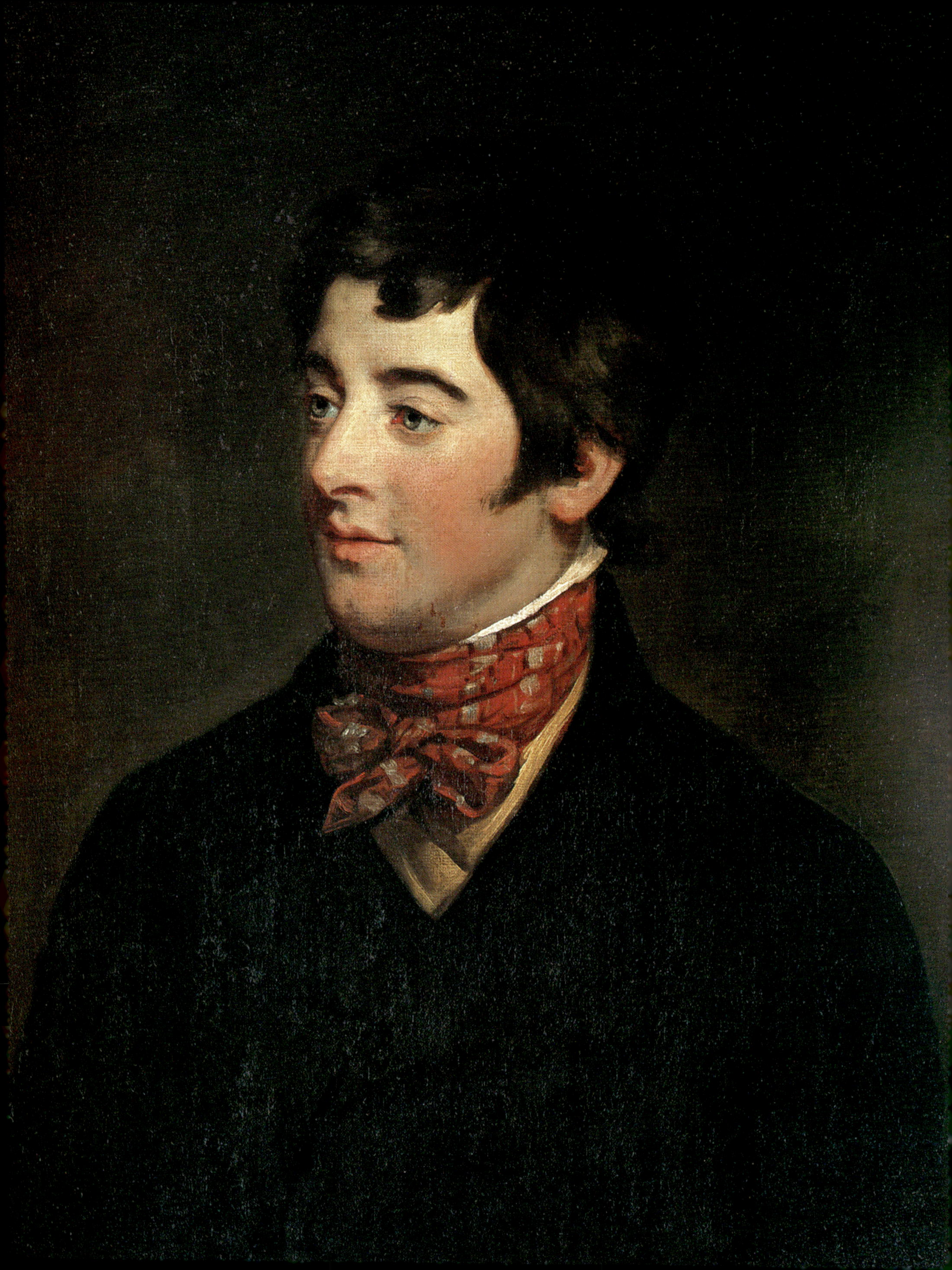

IN 1844 CHARLES GAVAN DUFFY, writing in *The Nation*, recognised the potential for portraiture to inspire national sentiment:

> Except Turnerelli's O'Connell, there is seldom a bust of an Irishmen to be seen in an Irish house. A friend recently mentioned a circumstance curiously illustrative of this dearth of national spirit in Ireland. He called at Nanetti's in Church-lane, to purchase busts for his library. The collection is a very fine one; and he found abundance of Shakespeares, Scotts, Miltons, Byrons, Nelsons ... etc., but not a single Irishman. He enquired in turn for ... Burke, Curran, Banim, Griffin, Lord Edward FitzGerald, and Father Mathew. Not one of them all was to be had. The Duke of Wellington, the genius of military despotism, represented the country in Mr Nanetti's collection. After a curious inspection of the premises, our friend discovered a head of Grattan on a high shelf, and a bust of Thomas Moore under a bench: and when he purchased both, he left the collection ... without one Irishman ... Do we blame the artist for this? Not in the least – it is the fault of the public – a fault that must be amended. If we do not learn to love and cherish the memory of our illustrious countrymen, we will have no more illustrious countrymen to love.[1]

The fact that busts of the poet Tom Moore (fig.25) and the politician Henry Grattan (fig.90) were the only images of contemporary Irishmen available for purchase by Gavan Duffy's friend suggests a decline in Irish political portraiture in the nineteenth century. Apart from the ubiquitous plaster busts of Daniel O'Connell which had been on sale since at least 1828, and that of Henry Grattan, who had been dead for more than twenty years, the status of the contemporary political portrait was clearly very low. This is in sharp contrast to the state of Irish political portraiture during the 1780s and 1790s, the period known as 'Grattan's parliament'.

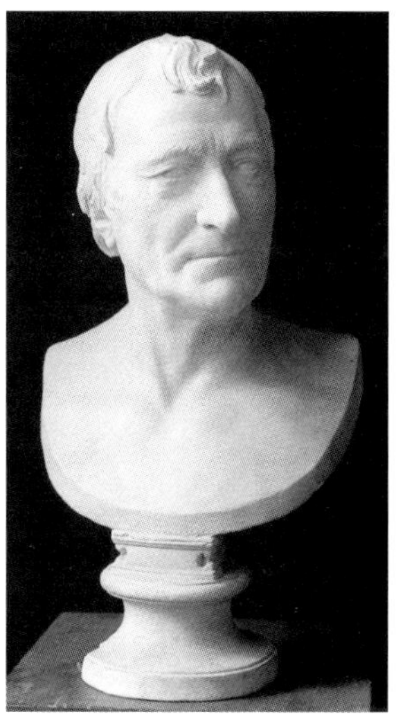

90. **Henry Grattan** (1746–1820)
PETER TURNERELLI (1812)
Marble bust, ht 559mm (22")
National Portrait Gallery,
London (NPG 1341)

A member of the Irish parliament, Grattan in 1779 carried the amendment to the address in favour of Irish free trade. A few years later he spoke in favour of Irish legislative independence, which was successfully achieved in 1782. This action sealed his place in the pantheon of Irish patriots.

The political portrait in the eighteenth century

The Irish political portrait has been in existence since at least 1594, with Gheeraerts's full-length of the Elizabethan adventurer Thomas Lee (fig.5). As discussed in the Introduction (p.20), this portrait may be considered political because it possesses a public role in state affairs. Such large-scale painting of men prominent in Irish life

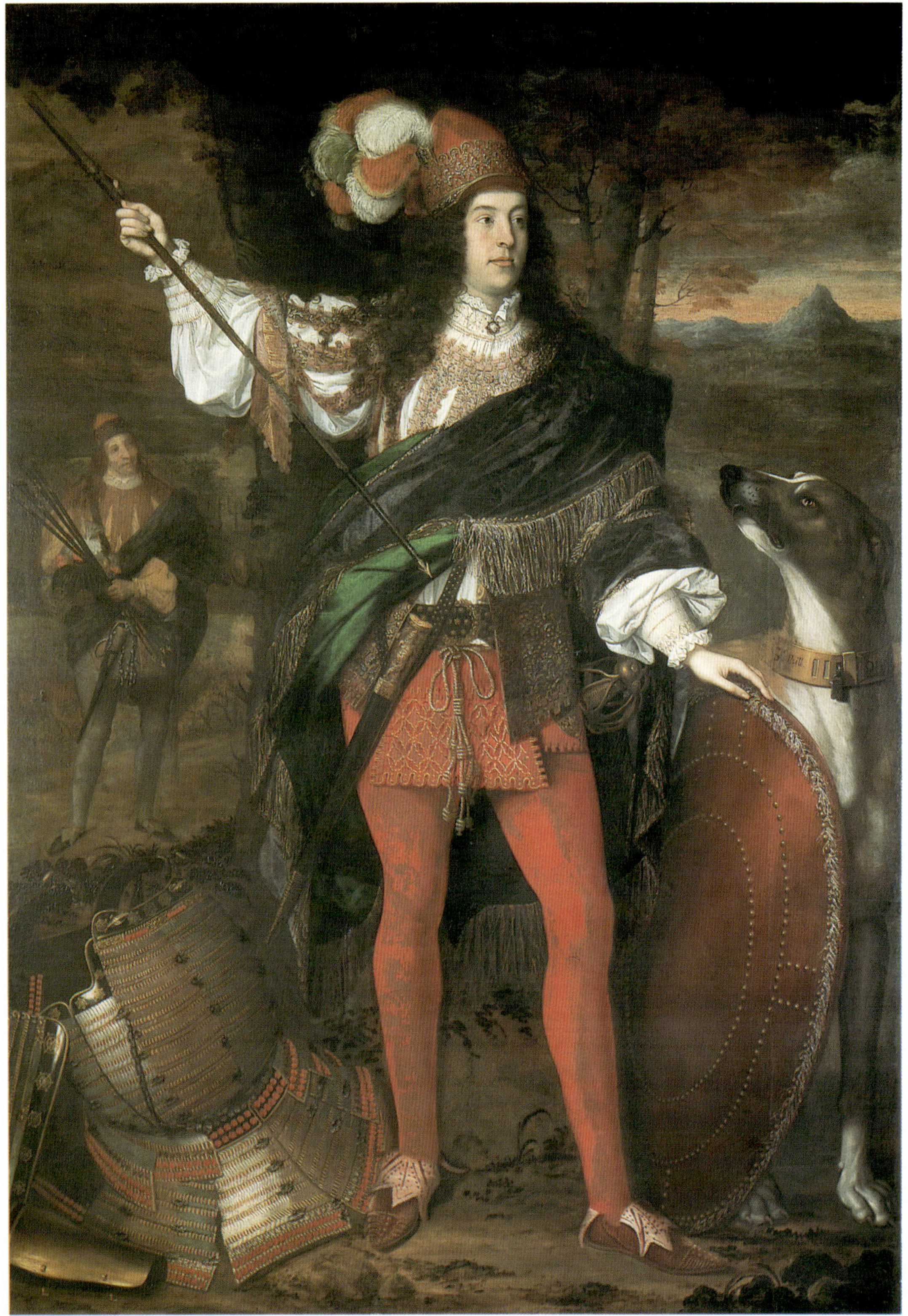

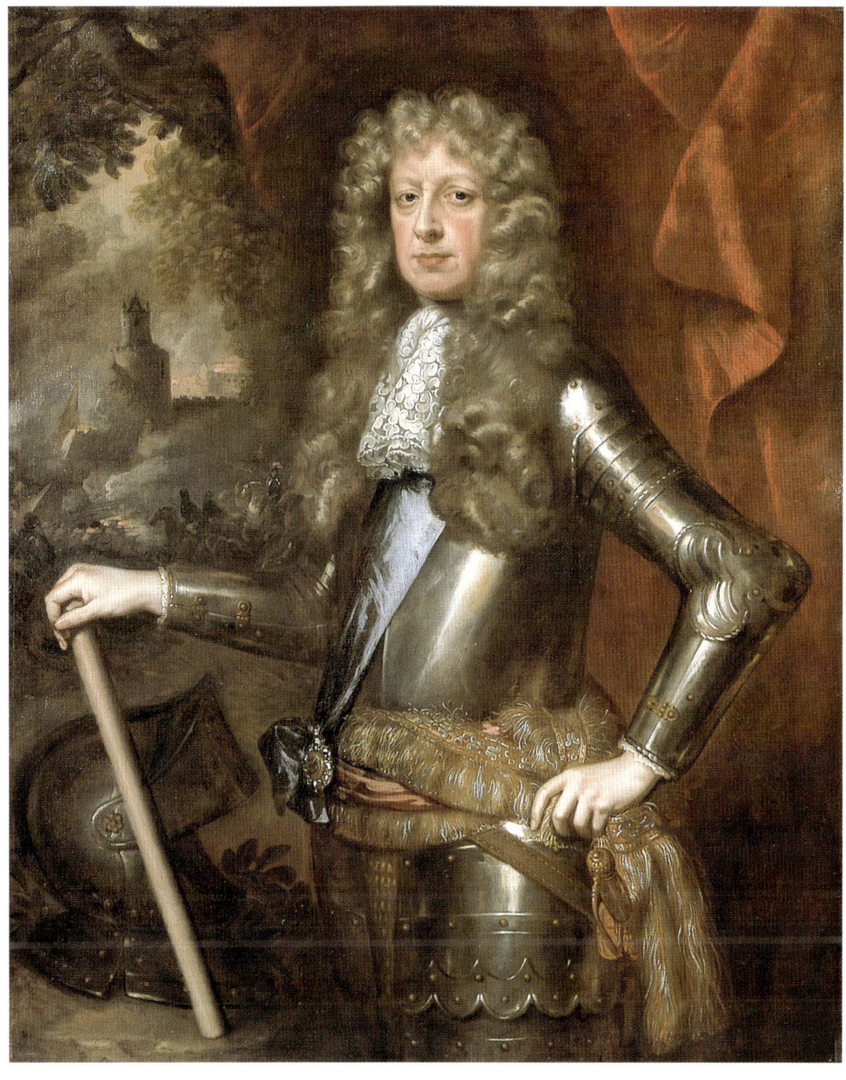

continued throughout the seventeenth century, with the Ormonde collection at Kilkenny Castle becoming an impressive venue for their display. Paintings such as John Michael Wright's portrait of Sir Neil O'Neill in the costume of an Irish chieftain (fig.91) and Sir Peter Lely's portrayal of James Butler, 1st Duke of Ormond, in the robes of the Order of the Garter (1662), or William Wissing's oil showing the duke dressed in armour (fig.92) all hung in Kilkenny.[2] The portrait of the young Neil O'Neill of Killelough, County Antrim, not only resembles Lee in his costume, but also in its aspiration. The Catholic baronet, described in 1706 as 'an Irish Tory in his Country Dress', displays his warrior credentials: spear, arrows, sword, shield and Irish wolfhound, together with the bizarre and not as yet fully explained Japanese armour.[3] Just as Lee was ready to do battle for Elizabeth I, O'Neill would soon do the same for the ill-fated James VII and II at the Battle of the Boyne.

The portraits of the Duke of Ormond are, of course, slightly different. They demonstrate less of a loyalty to Ireland and more of an extended commitment to the English crown and to important alliances with other great families, invariably English. As Jane Fenlon has written:

> At Kilkenny Castle, the principal portraits were displayed in lavishly furnished surroundings in the gallery on the second floor of the main residential block . . . The portraits were carefully displayed to create the maximum impact on the viewer. On the approach from the great stair, and on either side of the great window, were ranged the most important full-length portraits in their elaborate carved frames. Royal portraits included those of Charles I and II and their queens; family were represented by 'the Old Duke of Ormond, the Old Earl of Ossory, the Lady Dowager of Ossory'; marriage alliances by 'The Duke of Richmond and his Dutchess by Van Dyke'.[4]

In 1731 James Latham painted an ambitious full-length of the Member of Parliament for New Ross, Charles Tottenham (fig.93) who on a famous occasion turned up at the Dublin House of Commons in dirty boots to cast his vote against the granting of an Irish surplus of £60,000 to the British government. Latham's portrait celebrates a patriot and shows 'Tottenham in his boots', albeit now cleaned and polished, arriving at a grand entrance.[5] Given the story behind the portrait, one has to ask whether this columned entrance is a direct reference to Edward Lovett Pearce's new Dublin Parliament House, which was being built at that very time. As Edward McParland has shown, 'Parliament sat in the house for the first time on 5 October 1731', while 'by November 1731, most of what remained to be done was on the piazza and colonnade'.[6] Latham's column is on far too high a plinth to correspond to any in Pearce's front, so it may be interpreted as a generalised reference to a parliamentary event. Latham was to reuse this motif in other 'parliamentary' portraits, such as that of Eaton Stannard, Recorder of the City of Dublin, after 1733 (National Gallery of Ireland).[7]

In Francis Wheatley's well-known *Irish House of Commons* of 1780 (fig.94), the political portrait in eighteenth-century Ireland moves inside Pearce's Parliament House, creating one of the most confident Irish public images of the period. The focus is again on a patriotic moment, Grattan's declaration of Ireland's right to make it own laws. And yet Wheatley's painting, like his equally great canvas celebrating a meeting of the Volunteers in 1779, was difficult to sell. In fact, as far as we know, the only commercial spin-offs for Wheatley were prints after his head of Grattan (fig.95), itself a slightly enlarged copy of the head of the patriot in the House of Commons painting.[8] Thus in analysing how the political portrait actually functioned in the eighteenth century it is most constructive to look at images that

93. **Charles Tottenham**
(1685–1758)
JAMES LATHAM (1731)
Oil on canvas,
2275 × 1510mm
(89½ × 50½")
National Gallery of Ireland,
Dublin

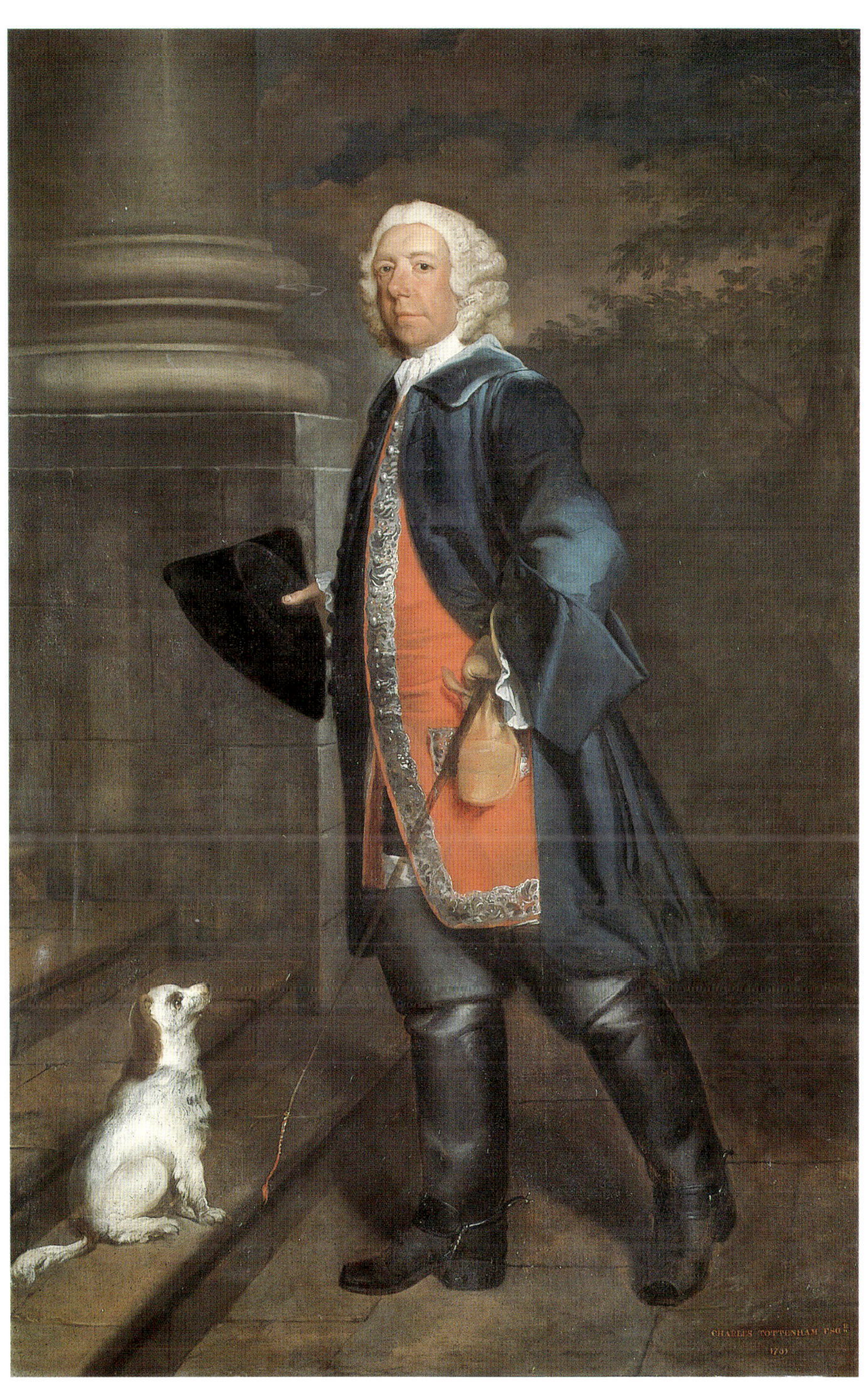

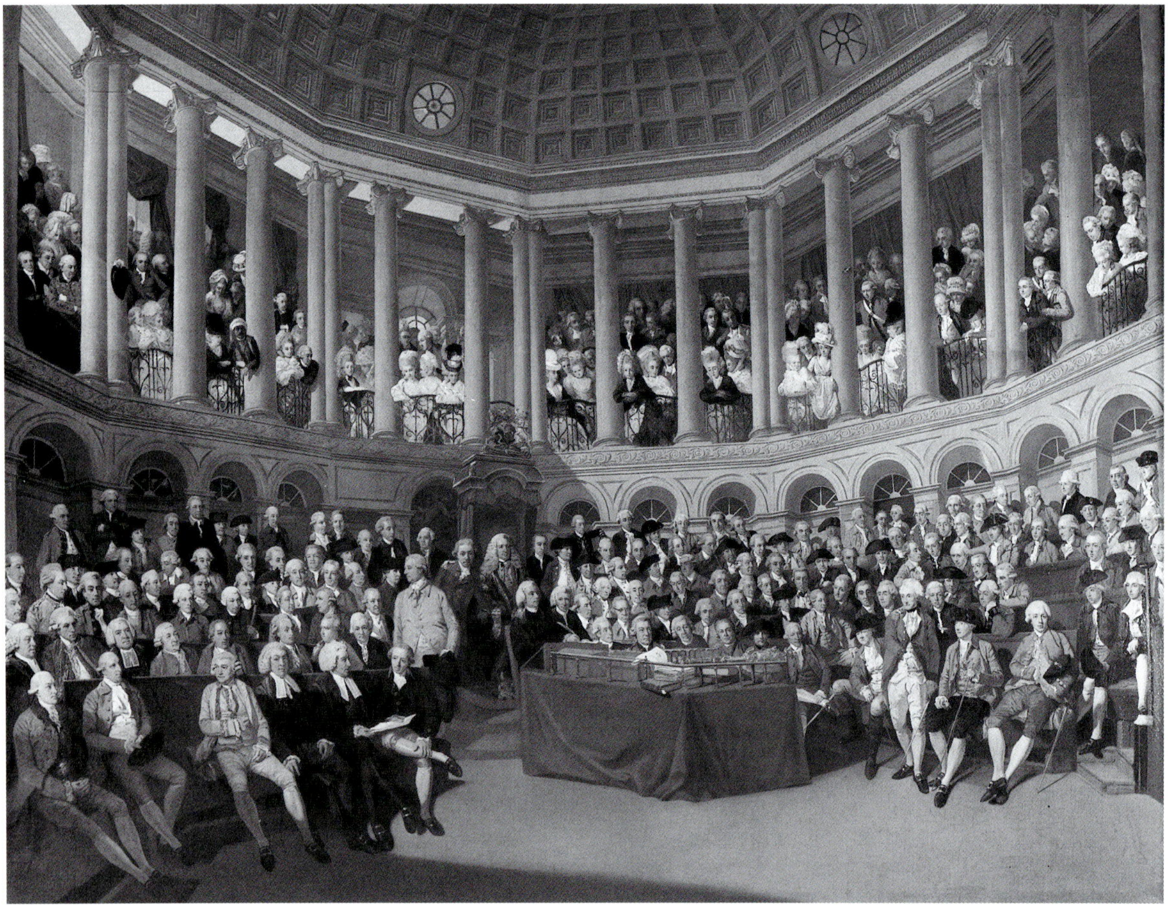

94. **The Irish House of Commons**
FRANCIS WHEATLEY (1780)
Oil on canvas, 1625 × 2159mm
(64 × 85″)
Lotherton Hall, Leeds City Art
Galleries and Museum

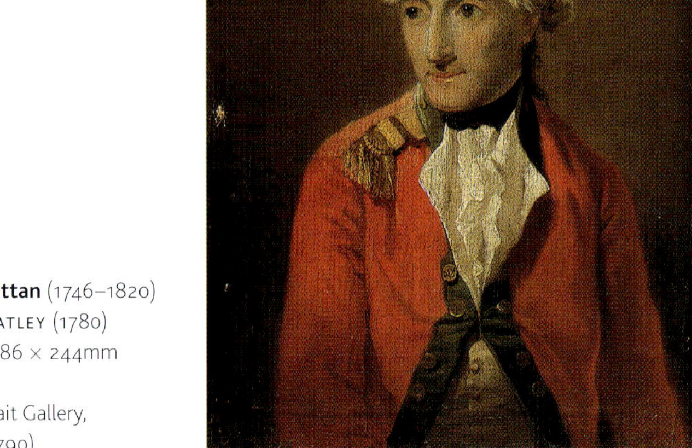

95. **Henry Grattan** (1746–1820)
FRANCIS WHEATLEY (1780)
Oil on panel, 286 × 244mm
(11¼ × 9⅝″)
National Portrait Gallery,
London (NPG 790)

enjoyed the greatest access and mobility. The focus is on the 1790s, a period of political uncertainty following the triumphs depicted in Wheatley's two large works from the previous decade.

The 1790s was also a period that saw portraiture enter a competitive phase, with artists pitting their sitters against each other. An accurate understanding of the political rivalry between William Pitt and Charles James Fox in the 1780s and 1790s, for example, together with the ensuing cult status of the two men well into the nineteenth century, cannot be reached without an acknowledgement of their visual representations. The number and range of representations of the two politicians is huge. In the elevated genre of bust portraiture there was extraordinary demand for plaster copies of Joseph Nollekens's original marble busts.[9] In the more ephemeral world of political satire, in particular in the work of James Gillray, Pitt and Fox were constantly juxtaposed, the difference here being that supporters and rivals alike vied for these images, while only supporters would place a bust of their hero on prominent display. In Gillray's *Promis'd Horrors of the French Invasion* of 1796, both Pitt and Fox hold centre stage: the Prime Minister, tied to a liberty tree is shown as virtuous and thin while Fox, his tormentor, is jowly and vicious. Portraiture, for many late eighteenth-century consumers, was the 'vehicle for politically disputatious issues'.[10]

Moving away from Westminster and back to Ireland, such a dialogue is initially suggested in the portraits of two prominent Irish politicians painted in Dublin by the American artist Gilbert Stuart between 1789 and 1791 (figs 96 and 97). In 1789 John FitzGibbon was promoted to the Lord Chancellorship of Ireland; he duly commissioned a full-length oil from Stuart, who was active in Dublin from 1787 to 1793 and had quickly established himself as a popular portraitist. Taking over from what Wheatley had started in 1780, Stuart brought portraiture more firmly into the confines of the Houses of Parliament. Within a couple of years he had pitched the bravura brushwork of his FitzGibbon against the elegant figure of John Foster, the last Speaker of the Irish House of Commons. It has been suggested that the two portraits should be seen as a pair, FitzGibbon facing to the left and Foster to the right: it was well known at the time that '[they]always hated each other'.[11] Both men are dressed in their robes of office and, if the background to FitzGibbon's portrait is standard Baroque fare (draped column and distant landscape), Foster stands in the columned and domed interior of Pearce's House of Commons. Their respective maces of office balance each other, while the two portraits placed together are defiant images of an institution fighting for its survival. The fight was not with parliament in London alone: it was also with its own members in Dublin. Thus the study of portraiture of the period offers some insight into that culture of conflict.

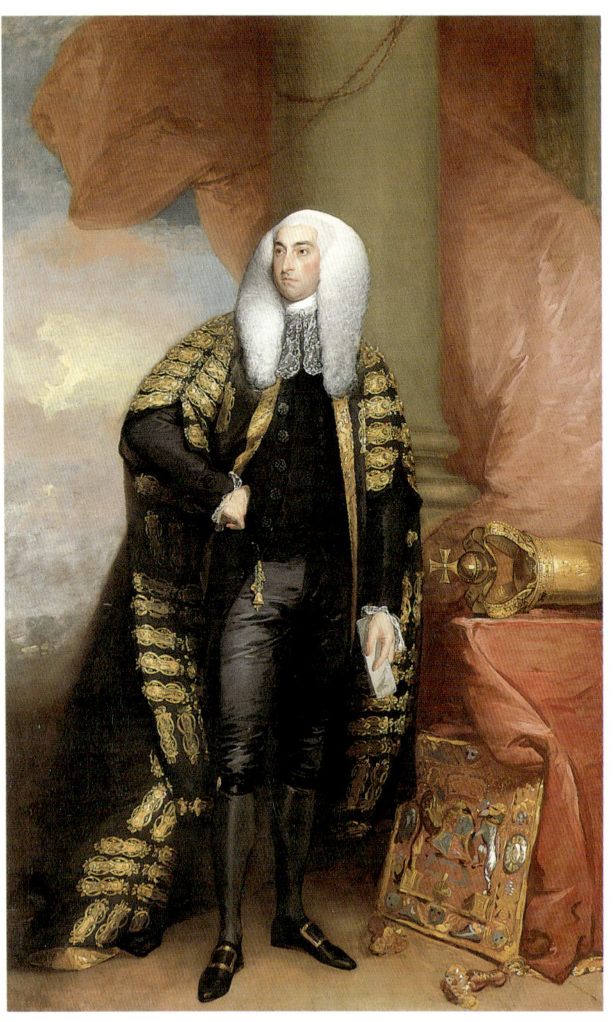

96. **John FitzGibbon, 1st Earl of Clare**
(1749–1802)
GILBERT STUART (1789)
Oil on canvas, 2450 × 1540mm
(96½ × 60⅝")
Cleveland Museum of Art, Ohio

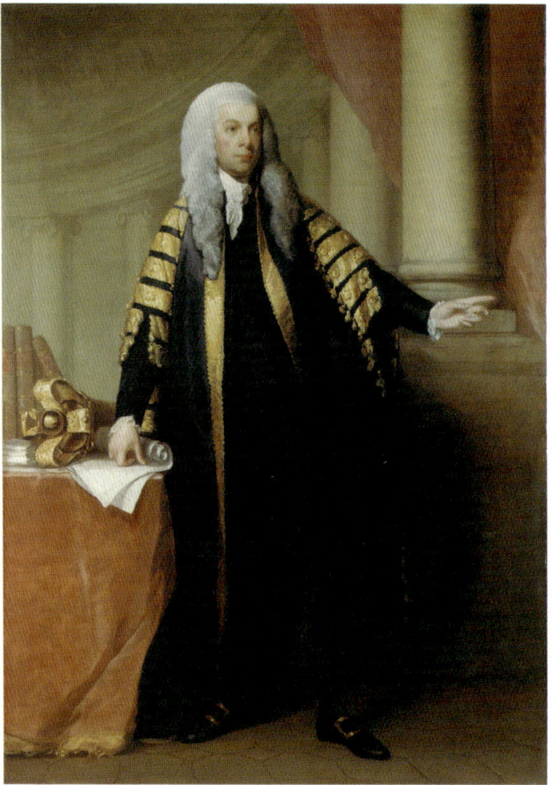

97. **John Foster** (1740–1828),
Speaker of the Irish House of Commons,
later 1st Baron Oriel
GILBERT STUART (1791)
Oil on canvas, 2114 × 1499mm
(83¼ × 59")
Nelson-Atkins Museum of Art,
Kansas City, Missouri

While working in Dublin as a portrait
painter, Stuart received at least five
commissions from Charles Agar, Archbishop
of Cashel (1736–1826). It has recently been
suggested that Agar may have been the
catalyst for Stuart's great pair of full-length
portraits, of FitzGibbon (fig.96) and Foster.

The clash

Many of the studies on the 1790s produced in recent decades are liberally illustrated with portraits of the main protagonists, maintaining a tradition that goes back to the first half of nineteenth century.[12] In the second decade of that century, that staunch voter against the Act of Union Sir Jonah Barrington published his *Historic Anecdotes and Secret Memoirs of the Legislative Union between Great Britain and Ireland*, while a couple of decades later Richard Robert Madden began publishing his exhaustive memoir of the United Irishmen. Both are liberally illustrated with engravings of the leading protagonists of the Union debate and the rebellion respectively. Barrington went on to write further accounts of government corruption, such as *The Rise and Fall of The Irish Nation*. An important feature of these works and of Madden's endeavours on behalf of the United Irishmen is their use of engraved portraits: indeed, these separate volumes are some of the earliest published compilations of Irish contemporary portraits. The images for both Barrington's works and Madden's are derived largely from painted portraits produced in Dublin by artists such as Hugh Douglas Hamilton and John Comerford.[13] It is important to acknowledge the role that portraits may have played in people's residual memories of recent events. Jonah Barrington claimed that 'The life of Lord Clare is the history of Ireland', suggesting that like the hero of a *bildungsroman*, Clare

> appears prominent in every feat of chivalry – the champion in every strife – and, after a life of toil and of battle, falls surrounded by a host of foes – a victim to his own ambition and temerity.

> Thus Lord Clare, throughout these eventful periods, will be seen bold, active and desperate – engaging fiercely in every important conflict of the Irish nation – and at length, after having sacrificed his country to his passions and his ambition, endeavouring to atone for his errors, by sacrificing himself.[14]

Portraiture plays a role in this telling of a 'history of Ireland', Barrington's *Rise and Fall* is lavishly illustrated with heads of the leading characters: on one page are no fewer than seven oval portraits of Lord Clare's contemporaries – himself, the Duke of Leinster, Grattan, Charlemont and others. Further on there are similar arrays of portraits, including radicals such as Lord Edward FitzGerald. In the examples of Barrington and Madden the discussion of a rebellion and a major legislative act are enlivened and enriched by the inclusion of a wide range of portraits from both sides, what Barrington was to call the 'red' and the 'black', those who opposed the Union and those in favour of it.[15]

Students of late eighteenth-century Irish history are well acquainted with the portraits of Wolfe Tone (figs 98 and 99) and Lord Edward FitzGerald, as well as a number of other rebel protagonists; but is there more to the images of these men, and they are always men, than a mere likeness? In exploring the portrait in Ireland at this period it is important to examine both the myriad representations of revolutionaries such as FitzGerald (figs 101, 111 and 115) and the equally prolific depictions at the other end of the political spectrum, such as John FitzGibbon, Earl of Clare and Lord Chancellor of Ireland (figs 96, 106, 108 and 109). As we move from one political group to the other, two things need to be noted: first, the iconography of representation, or how a sitter or subject is visually conceived, and secondly, who saw the images and how they were disseminated.

There is no shortage of material from which to examine the representation of the leading players in the events of the 1790s. Late eighteenth-century Dublin magazines and subsequent nineteenth-century sources were liberally illustrated with engraved portraits. A line engraving entitled *The Unfortunate Theobald Wolfe Tone, Esq.* (fig.98) appeared in Walker's *Hibernian Magazine* in November 1798 'after a drawing taken at his trial'. Based on what the magazine called a 'striking likeness', it was

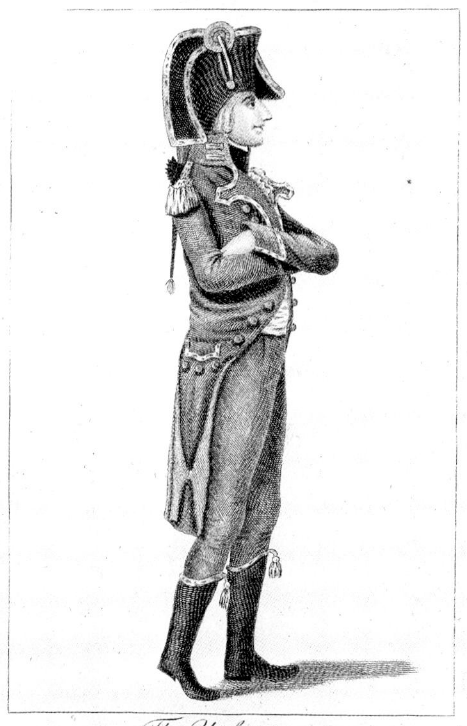

98. **The Unfortunate Theobald Wolfe Tone, Esq**. (1763–98)
ANONYMOUS (1798)
Line engraving from the *Hibernian Magazine*, 208 × 118mm (8⅛ × 4⅝")
National Gallery of Ireland

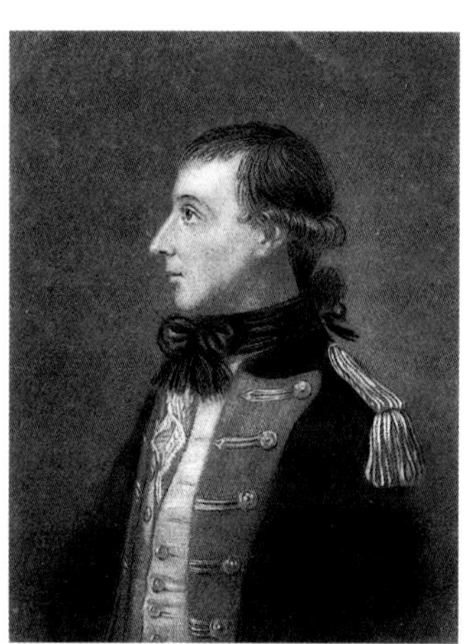

99. **Theobald Wolfe Tone, Esq**. (1763–98)
T.W. HUFFAM after an anonymous oil portrait (1840s)
Mezzotint and etching, 202 × 123mm (8 × 4⅞")
National Portrait Gallery, London (NPG D13755)

accompanied by an account of his court hearing.[16] The technique is not sophisticated, yet its appeal is immediate. The use of 'The Unfortunate' in the inscription adds a touch of late eighteenth-century sentiment, aided by the isolation of the figure on the page. A later mezzotint and etching by T.W. Huffam after an anonymous head-and-shoulder oil portrait (fig.99), possibly dating from around 1790–91, appeared in the 1840s in R.R. Madden's *The United Irishmen, their Lives and Times*, where it is inscribed 'from an original portrait representing him in his volunteer uniform in the possession of Mr Burrowes'.[17] This is an altogether more optimistic portrait of the man and thus a fitting image to accompany Madden's 'fiercely anti-government' discussion of Tone.[18] The inscription here is equally telling, as the owner of the original portrait was Peter Burrowes, an old Trinity College and legal friend of Wolfe Tone. Madden made extensive use of family and close friends of the United Irishmen in assembling his data, an important element of which were the historic portrait engravings that appear in all the volumes with the purpose of increasing the emotional impact of his study. The title pages of the various volumes draw attention to the 'numerous original portraits' which are given equal billing with the 'additional authentic documents'. From 1843, when advertisements began to appear for Madden's enterprise, the emphasis was on the visual juxtaposition of political views: 'Embellished with exquisitely finished portraits of several of the United Irish leaders and some of the most remarkable of their opponents and betrayers'.[19] The implication is that these portraits play an important role in any study of Ireland in the 1790s.

Reference was made in Chapter 3 (p.124) to the visit paid in November 1797 by the poet and United Irishman Dr William Drennan to Hugh Douglas Hamilton's Dublin studio, where he viewed a range of portraits of leading Irish personalities, including his 'full-length' of Kirwan preaching (fig.76). Drennan describes the range of portraiture being produced during the 1790s by this leading portrait painter in the city. A principal founder of the Society of United Irishmen, a group determined to introduce civil and religious liberties, Drennan comments on portraits of political figures. He tells his sister of numerous portraits by Hamilton:

> *three* of Lord Moira, all very like, and all very like Don Quixote – I never saw
> his lordship – O'Connor – Lord Edward very spirited – his lady twice; in one
> likeness or rather sketch (think of it), as a Medusa with snakes round her
> head and falling on her bosom. I think it ill judged, though Medusa was a fair
> lady – perhaps it was a vagary of the painter's.[20]

At least two of these three portraits of Moira have survived. In one, a full-length oil, he sits by a table covered in books – Drennan's allusion to Cervantes is perhaps inspired by Moira's musing aspect here.[21] The only other known portrait of Moira by Hamilton is a smaller head and shoulders (fig.100), while the 'spirited' three-

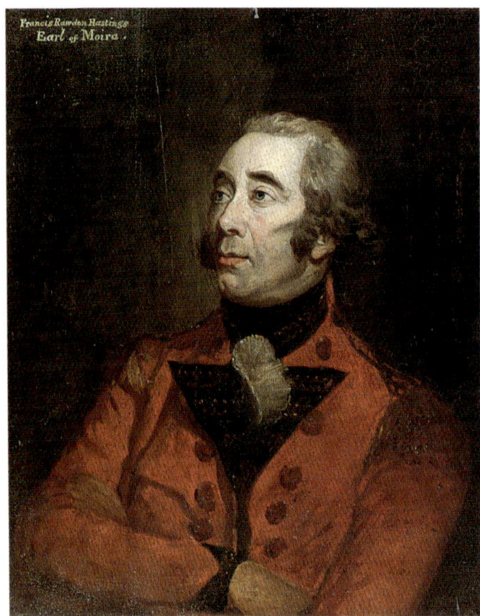

100. **Francis Rawdon-Hastings, 2nd Earl of Moira (later 1st Marquess of Hastings)** (1754–1826)
HUGH DOUGLAS HAMILTON (1797)
Oil on canvas, 730 × 584mm (28¾ × 23″)
National Portrait Gallery, London (NPG 2696)

This head of Moira is based on a full-length portrait by Hamilton that was recently on the London art market. The full-length shows Moira sitting in a high-ceilinged study by a table with large books and a dog sleeping under his outstretched legs.

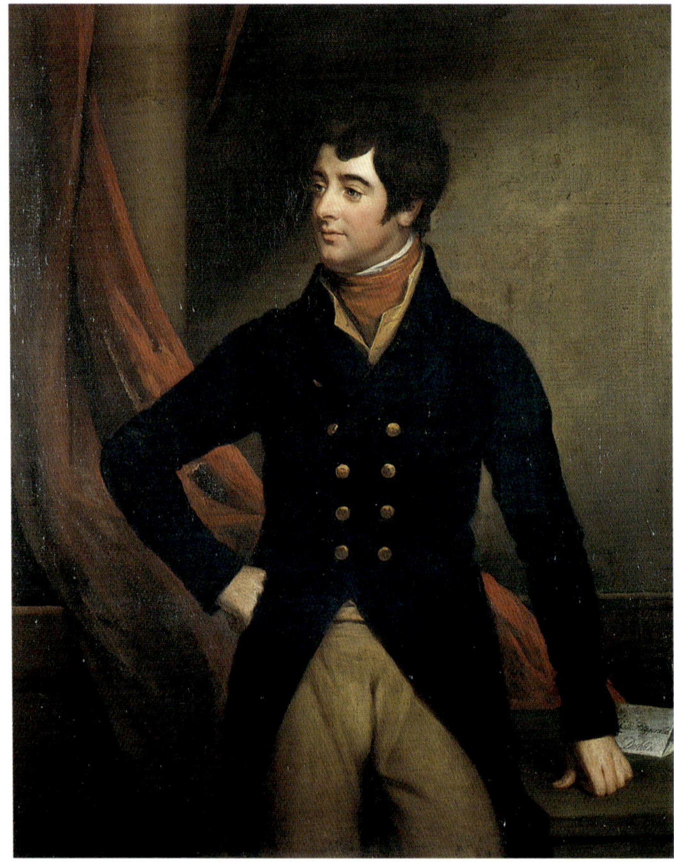

101. **Lord Edward FitzGerald** (1763–98)
HUGH DOUGLAS HAMILTON (1796–98)
Oil on canvas, 1277 × 1020mm (50¼ × 40⅛″)
National Gallery of Ireland, Dublin

quarter-length of Moira's former aide-de-camp, Lord Edward FitzGerald (fig.101), has also survived and is in the collection of the National Gallery of Ireland. Unfortunately the two paintings of Pamela FitzGerald have not been traced. The sketch of her as a Medusa is particularly intriguing given the understandable scarcity of references to women involved in Irish political affairs, let alone commissioned visual representations. The other painting mentioned by Drennan is of FitzGerald's close friend Arthur O'Connor (fig.112), which has only recently come to light. Both of these portraits of committed United Irishmen are discussed below.

As Drennan's letter shows, in late 1797 a successful painter such as Hugh Douglas Hamilton could produce a string of portraits for the moderate Whig Lord Moira, while at the same time attracting the patronage of the pro-French, radical chic FitzGeralds and Arthur O'Connor. A few years earlier, in 1794, even while in prison, another leading United Irishman, Archibald Hamilton Rowan, recognised the need for image-making. Again, Drennan tells us:

Rowan's hobby horse at present seems having his picture taken. [John] Cullen has taken an excellent miniature likeness from which there is to be an engraving, and I believe Hamilton is to paint a prison scene – Mr and Mrs Rowan, his son and his father, on the first entrance into Newgate. The subject is certainly a very good one and all the persons well fitted for the expression except the lady who appears too *embon-point* at present.[22]

Unfortunately for the history of Irish painting, Hamilton had to abandon his potentially ambitious design as Rowan soon escaped from prison and fled to France!

William Drennan's visit to Hamilton's studio demonstrates the late eighteenth-century popularity of portraiture as a social activity, whether commissioning it or viewing it. Drennan's letters and those of his sister, Martha McTier, are a rich archive of references to the relevance of portraiture in the lives of politically aware Irish people in the late eighteenth century. Lacking what we might call a disposable income, neither sibling was in a position to spend extravagantly on portraiture but their correspondence shows them discussing the subject on many occasions. They complain about prices and artistic quality, tell each other of exhibitions and visits to artists' studios, both in Dublin and Belfast, have their own portraits painted and discuss those of their friends. In June 1794 Drennan wrote to his sister about a request for a portrait by the bookseller, printer and fellow United Irishman John Chambers, so that 'my rueful phiz should be exposed in the pillory of the press or the monthly magazine'. Drennan writes that John Walker of the *Hibernian Magazine* 'was determined to coin my countenance, and if he did not get a good impression, he would make it a rap'.[23] In order to avoid such a counterfeit being produced Drennan seems to have arranged for a copy to be made from an oil by Robert Home painted in Belfast almost a decade earlier, in 1786 (fig.102). Five years later, Drennan muses on the business of portraiture. Having seen an engraving of his Belfast friend the merchant and banker Waddell Cunningham in the window of a Dublin print shop, he writes: 'Portraitures always flatter'. Thinking of his own portrait by Home, he tells his sister that: 'posthumous fame is much like another and that fame itself is little else than the oyster shell in my picture which reveals the deep mystery of this my meditation, so long the puzzle of your little public'.[24]

In the foreground of Home's portrait is a shell carrying an inscription in Greek. The letters are not easy to decipher but may read ΦΙΛΙΠΠΩ, 'Philippo', meaning 'to' or 'for Philip'.[25] Drennan clearly delighted, as did his sister, in the enigmatic nature of the portrait. Martha McTier wrote that 'it bespeaks great thought, and a degree of anxiety, that interests the beholder'.[26] The name 'Philip' may refer to Philip of Macedon, the father of Alexander the Great who is remembered, especially through the writings of Demosthenes, as a particularly ruthless opponent of free speech. Home's painting dates from 1786, a year after Drennan had published his

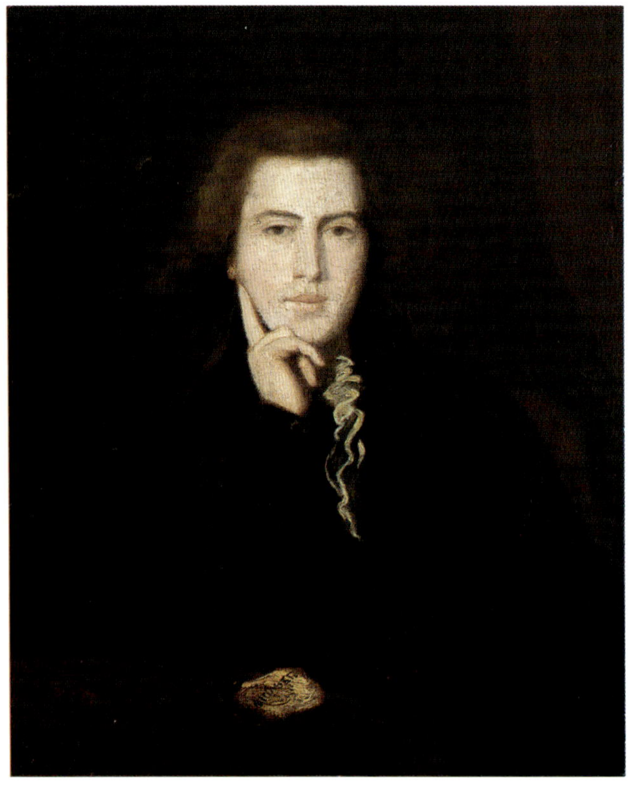

important *Letters of Orellana*. In this series of letters Drennan placed himself in the guise of a slave writing, as he said, to 'fellow slaves', and calling for his countrymen to recognise that freedom was being denied them.[27] Perhaps the shell is intended to symbolise the need to create a new order, 'the shell . . . [being] the mystic symbol of the prosperity of one generation rising out of the death of the preceding generation'.[28] If this is the case, Drennan's modest portrait and the dialogue that it inspired amongst his Ulster friends, 'wondered at by some, and ridiculed by others', as his sister informed him, demonstrates late eighteenth-century Irish concern with portraiture as a conveyor of layers of meaning.

Political opposition

One of the main roles of portraiture has always been to familiarise the spectator with the physical features of particular individuals. Most oil portraits, and virtually all reproductive engravings of the late eighteenth century, were accompanied by a label or inscription, thus demanding a degree of literacy.[29] But in Ireland only a relatively limited audience would have had access to the images or known who was being portrayed, whether in oils on canvas or engraving on paper.

Keeping the educated middle- and upper-class audience in mind, how did portraiture permeate eighteenth-century Dublin culture? Unlike Westminster, the

Irish parliament did not enjoy the production of an annual of engraved portraits illustrating figures in public life. In London, for example, from 1798 to 1807 such annuals as the *British Public Characters* carried a frontispiece of tiered political portraits, presenting 'the distinguished personages who now fill up the drama of public life in the British Empire'.[30] Marcia Pointon has commented that these engraved images 'enabled readers to familiarize themselves with the appearance of figures prominent in the public view'.[31] But Dublin had no such volumes. In the dying days of the Irish parliament, however, and although Irish periodicals of the period have been condemned by Brian Inglis as 'ephemeral, featureless and dull',[32] the short-lived *Dublin Magazine* enlivened Irish political life between late 1798 and late 1799 by publishing three fold-out examples of what they called 'humorous prints of the Union … in which are introduced many well-known characters'.[33] Each sheet contains two tiers of small portraits, many in groups of two or more that appear almost like caricatured vignettes (figs 103 and 104).

103. **The Union**
ANONYMOUS (1798)
Line engraving from the
Dublin Magazine,
432 × 234mm (17 × 9¼")
British Library, London

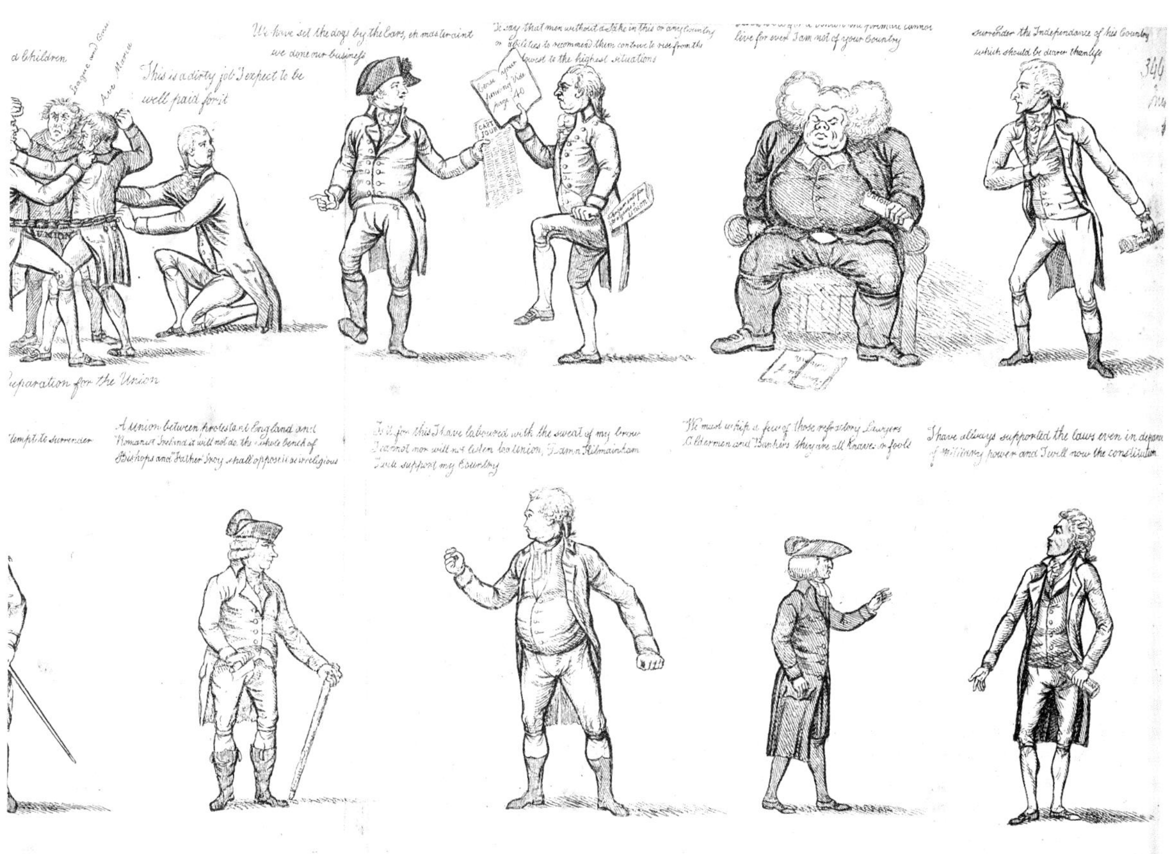

What is most striking about these engraved satires is their visual composition: the vignettes are, on the whole, of men locked in verbal battles. In the earliest of the three, dating from December 1798 (fig.103) and entitled *The Union*, Henry Grattan (top right) confronts a sleeping prelate who will vote for the Union. Grattan exclaims, 'Surely no Irishman can be so base as to surrender the independence of his Country which should be dearer than life.' Directly below him, John Philpot Curran (see Chapter 1, pp.55–60) defends lawyers and the law from an attack by Charles Agar, the Archbishop of Cashel. Left of them are a pair of MPs, both of whom oppose the Union. John 'Bully' Egan, on the right, raises his fist in anger and supports Grattan by taking a purely patriotic stance: 'Is it for this I have laboured with the sweat of my brow. I cannot nor will not listen to a Union.' Placing his position as Chairman of Kilmainham in jeopardy, Egan curses: 'Damn Kilmainham, I will support my country.'[34] To his rival it is more a question of his own religious prejudice. Leaning on his cane, Dr Patrick Duigenan, Member of Parliament for Armagh, suggests plainly that 'A union of protestant England and Romanist Ireland will not do'. A month later, in another print, entitled *Anti-Union*, the British Prime Minister William Pitt confronts Sir John Parnell, the Chancellor of the Irish Exchequer, claiming that he 'will carry the union and if you do not support it I will find them who will'. Parnell replies, 'You may – I love my country better than Office and sooner than surrender its independence will lose my life.'

The final print in the series, *The Vacation or Union Canvas* (fig.104), appeared nine months later, in October 1799. The Union is now inevitable. In the top left, wearing a medallion of Grattan around her neck, Ireland is overcome by despair and left unprotected by the sleeping wolfhounds at her feet. Clearly being maltreated by Lord Cornwallis (Lord Lieutenant of Ireland) and others, a document on Ireland's lap labelled 'Irish Independence' is substituted for one marked 'Article of Union'. All that Ireland has are her dreams, in this case the past glories of 'Charlemont and the old Volunteers', who appear as a shady apparition in the distance. In the top centre, Prime Minister Pitt faces Speaker Foster of the Irish House of Commons across a table, saying 'You have Carte Blanch make what terms you please'; Foster returns a sheet entitled 'No Union', while remarking 'Those are my terms'. Coming in from the right, we see the reaction of the Lord Chancellor, John FitzGibbon, elegant in riding dress, who comments: 'We will carry the measure in spite of his opposition'. This single figure of the Lord Chancellor is carefully balanced by another isolated figure on the bottom left of the sheet, a fearsome bear holding a pike who represents the United Irish, and thence 'One of the Arguments for a Union'.

In the lower centre of the sheet, the Union is further satirised by the juxta-position of the infamous High Sheriff of Tipperary, Thomas Judkin FitzGerald, and Horish, a Dublin master-sweep. A year earlier, over the summer of 1798, FitzGerald had terrified Tipperary by seeking out and flogging United Irishmen. At his trial a

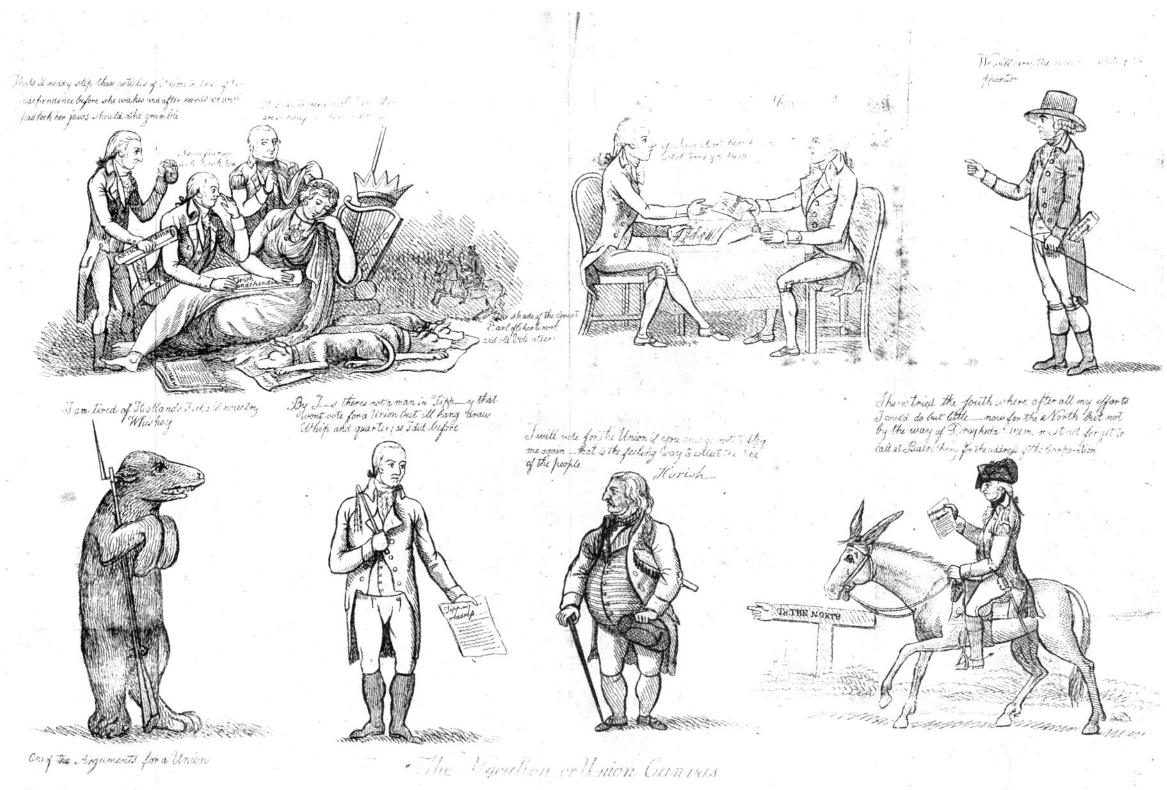

few months prior to the publication of this caricature, FitzGerald had claimed that by whipping fifty he had saved the lives and property of half a million.[35] Here he holds a 'Tipperary Address' and, brandishing his well-used cat-o'-nine tails, threatens that he will 'hang draw whip and quarter as I did before', if the men of his county do not support the Union. Such a stance is ridiculed by the presence of Horish, the Castle sweep (indicated by the brush he carries under his arm), who in 1798 had allegedly tried to burn down the Houses of Parliament; he is now ready to support Union if, as he says, 'you engage not to flog me again'.[36] Finally, referring to the title of the sheet, in the lower right is Cornwallis, the Lord Lieutenant, setting out on a tour of the country to canvas support for the Union.

The dynamism of these sheets is based on confrontation and opposition, pro-Union versus anti-Union and, to a degree, reactionary versus radical. This contrast of opposites was by the end of the 1790s a much-used visual schema and had been particularly effective a few years earlier in satires that compared French and English attitudes to liberty. But in the Dublin sheets the style is of mild caricature. Easily recognisable tropes are used to identify the protagonists: FitzGibbon is dapper while Grattan is identifiable by his sharp nose and prominent chin, features that had been visible in portraits in circulation for some twenty years.[37] Indeed, the concept of confrontational political prints in Ireland goes back to Grattan's heyday in the early 1780s, when James Gillray had depicted him battling over the issue of public expenses with Henry Flood in the Irish House of Commons (fig.105).[38] The popularity

104. **The Vacation or Union Canvas**
ANONYMOUS (1799)
Line engraving from the *Dublin Magazine*,
432 × 234mm (17 × 9¼")
British Library, London

– and economic profitability – of such confrontations is demonstrated by their reappearance in slightly reworked prints. An example is the argument between Duigenan and Egan, which had appeared as a vignette to 'The Union' in the *Dublin Magazine* (fig.103) but resurfaced a year or so later in colour, reversed and entitled *The Rival Orator's* [*sic*]. In the later print Egan is beefier and wears spurs, while he thrusts his fist more firmly in Duigenan's direction. Not to be outdone, the arch-Protestant, easily identifiable by his square-tipped nose, now wields his stick as if involved in a duel.[39]

These Union prints provide in schematised form a view of opposition that suggests a means of exploring the portraiture of the 1790s. It is one thing to know that oil portraits of such figures as John FitzGibbon and Lord Edward FitzGerald (figs 101 and 106) were produced in Dublin; but what is worth examining is how they were represented and who saw the images. The range of portraits produced in 1790s Dublin covered a wide range of media. Late eighteenth-century Irishmen, like their counterparts across Europe, depending on their purse and requirements, could choose from the small, finely crafted miniature portrait to oils on canvas in a variety of sizes. These images could then in turn be engraved and more widely circulated. The list of images of FitzGibbon or FitzGerald is not unimpressive, though understandably not as extensive as that of a prominent politician in London – as was suggested earlier, the likenesses of Pitt and Fox run into the hundreds.

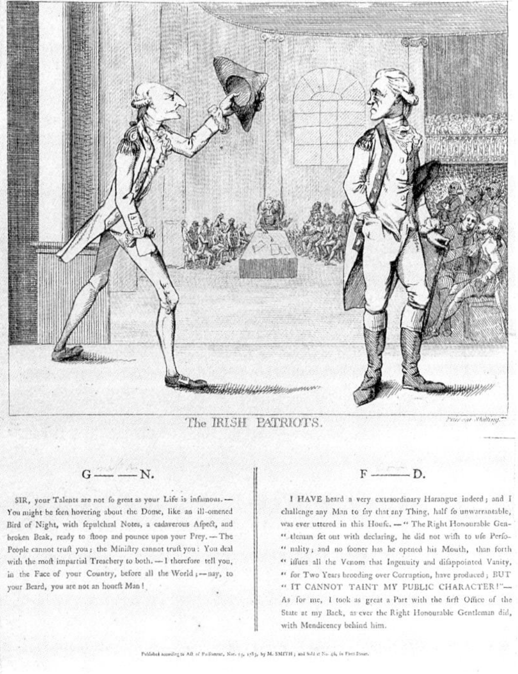

105. **The Irish Patriots**
JAMES GILLRAY (1783)
Engraving, 222 × 279mm
(8¾ × 11")
British Museum, London
(*Political Satires*, no.6272)

Within the Irish Patriot party of the early 1780s the differences of opinion between Grattan (on the left) and Henry Flood were considerable. In 1783, during a debate on retrenchment of public expenses, the pair attacked each other vigorously. To Grattan, Flood was 'an ill-omened Bird of Night'.

Gilbert Stuart's splendid portraits of FitzGibbon and Foster have been discussed (p.153); in 1793 he left Dublin for America with the ambition of painting the first President of the United States. As he told his Irish friend the painter James Dowling Herbert, 'I expect to make a fortune by Washington'.[40] And so he did: but he did not forget Dublin. Of the two key pictures Stuart was to paint of George Washington, the so-called 'Lansdowne' portrait of 1796 (fig.29) is clearly the result of earlier experiments with figures in a grand, portico-like space, most particularly the Foster full-length of 1791 (fig.97).[41] While attempting to ignore the now iconic status given to the Washington image, it is worth noting the close compositional resemblances (albeit in reverse) between the two public portraits, as well as their similar didactic rationale, legislative independence from Westminster.

Back in Dublin, with Stuart gone, the leading painter of the 1790s was Hugh Douglas Hamilton, who headed the city's most successful portrait studios. Hamilton painted everyone. Although a tally of his known output favours the anti-Union/ patriot side of the House of Commons, we should not allow that to deceive us into thinking that he was a Whig, let alone a radical.[42] In painting Lord Edward FitzGerald, Hamilton was the purveyor if not the originator of one of the most ubiquitous representations of a United Irishman and certainly its most celebrated romantic hero, yet the artist's politics were not at all close to those of his famous sitter. In some letters written between 1800 and 1801, to his friend the Italian sculptor Antonio Canova, Hamilton claimed that: 'In this country at the moment we live quietly but between you and me, it is known that the French plan to invade in which case the rebellion will be renewed.' Later he commented that 'a hostile enemy will create a situation of war even more horrible than before because the people here are full of revenge and it is very troubling to me that they seem incapable of forgetting. If peace comes, I wait not without hope, of returning to Italy'.[43]

In comparing portraits of FitzGibbon and FitzGerald (figs 96, 101 and 106), although the two portraits of the Lord Chancellor are in full length and the United Irishman is a three-quarter length, it is evident that both sitters are depicted in the visual language of mainstream Baroque formal portraiture. In all three paintings the men stand by a draped column symbolising steadfastness. As Lord Chancellor, FitzGibbon is shown in his full regalia (figs 96 and 106), standing by the Mace of the House of Lords and holding the Bourse of the Great Seal of Ireland. The portraits are formal and conservative. The Hamilton painting (fig.106) is dated on stylistic grounds to the late 1790s: FitzGibbon probably commissioned the portrait himself, to celebrate the Act of Union with which, of course, he was so closely involved.[44] The papers that FitzGibbon indicates on the right may even be the Act of Union itself, although the words are now illegible. Visual precedent in the portraiture of comparable holders of state office comes to our aid here. In 1707, for example, Sir Godfrey Kneller had painted a portrait of a berobed John Smith, then Speaker of the

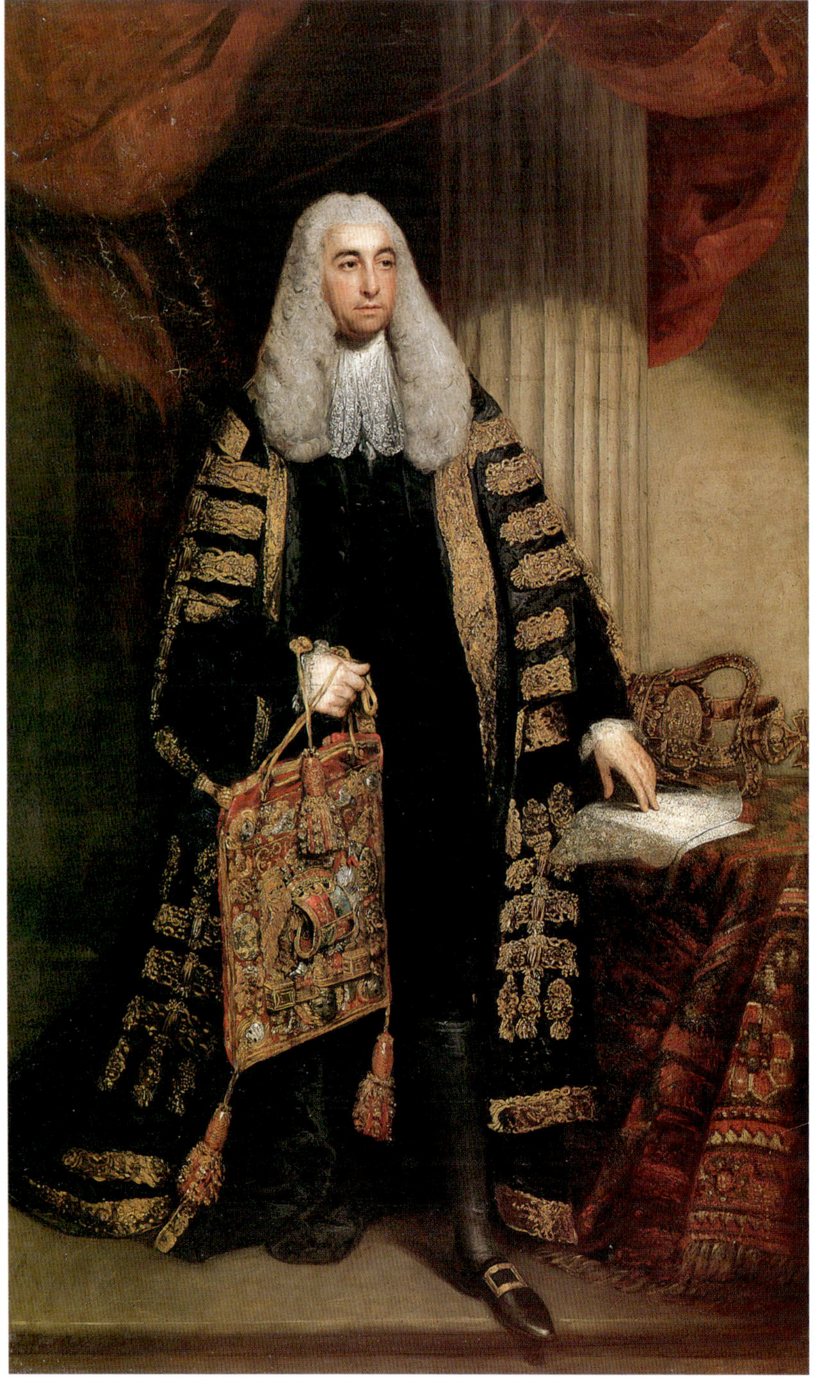

106. **John FitzGibbon, 1st Earl of Clare** (1749–1802)
HUGH DOUGLAS HAMILTON
(c.1799–1800)
Oil on canvas, 2360 × 1450mm
(92⅞ × 57⅛")
National Gallery of Ireland, Dublin

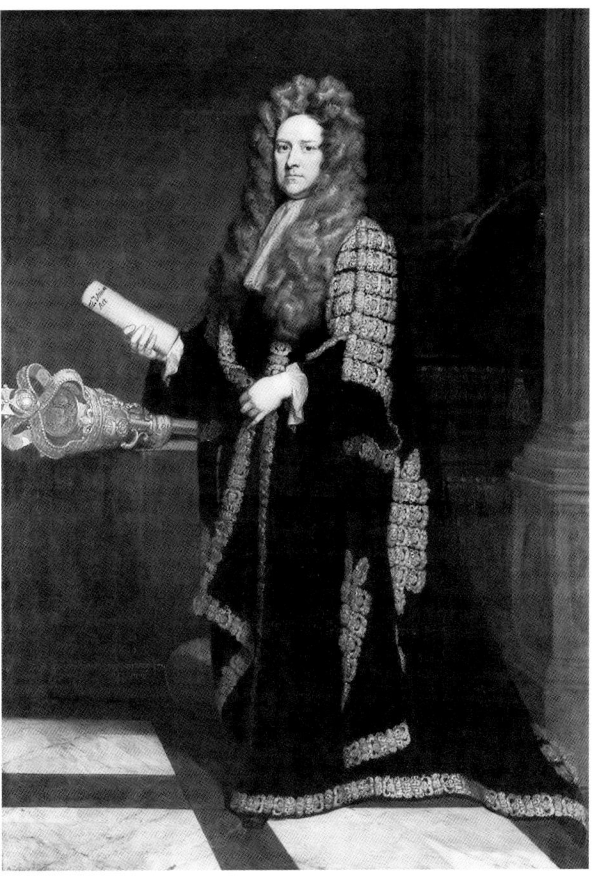

House of Commons in Westminster (fig.107), showing him holding a document inscribed 'The Union Act', clearly a reference to the Union of the Scottish and English parliaments. The conservatism of the Hamilton portrait is further underlined by the fact that his FitzGibbon portrait shows little if any stylistic development from the comparable yet more visually exciting portrait of a decade earlier by Gilbert Stuart (fig.96). If there is little in the way of artistic development in these portraits, they do at least show the extraordinary social advancement of FitzGibbon from the 'middling respectability' of his convert father's Limerick to the dizzy heights of the lord chancellorship.[45]

Portraiture played a significant part in FitzGibbon's self-perception. Wealthy, vain and ambitious, he had himself painted on at least eight occasions between the late 1780s and the turn of the century. Supplying his friends with engraved images of himself was something that he clearly enjoyed, while suppressing unflattering representations was an equally time-consuming occupation. In a letter of November 1794, William Drennan told his brother-in-law of seeing a print in a Dublin shop window 'against' the Chancellor and how 'FitzGibbon . . . was himself ferreting them out through the streets. I should not like to buy one', Drennan continued, 'though perhaps all this delicacy is for fear of my being exhibited myself in Carey's promised caricature'. The specific caricature is yet to be identified but the engraver,

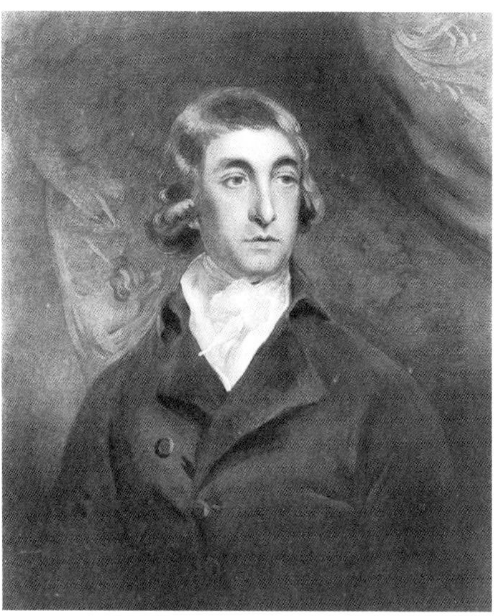

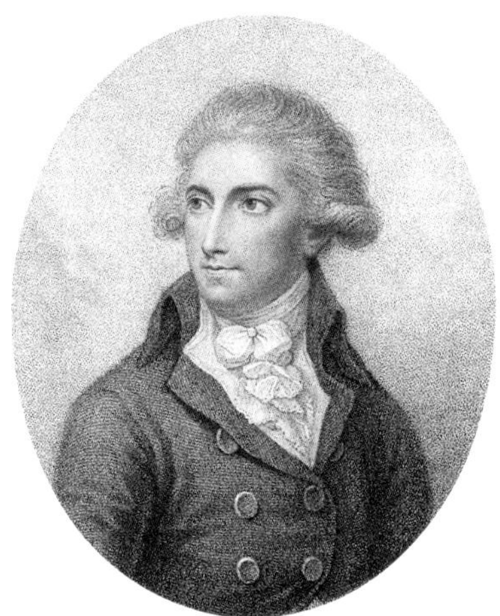

109. **John FitzGibbon, 1st Earl of Clare**
(1749–1802)
FRANCESCO BARTOLOZZI after
RICHARD COSWAY (1790)
Stipple engraving, 253 × 230mm (5 × 4½")
National Portrait Gallery, London
(NPG Archive)

108. **John FitzGibbon, 1st Earl of Clare** (1749–1802)
CHARLES TURNER after JOHN HOPPNER (1802)
Mezzotint, 404 × 287mm (16 × 11¼")
National Gallery of Ireland, Dublin

William Paulet Carey (1759–1839), sold his work at William Allen's shop in Dame Street, Dublin; earlier that year, in June 1794, he had informed against Drennan for being a United Irishmen.[46]

Writing in autumn 1798 to his close friend William Eden, 1st Lord Auckland, the former Chief Secretary for Ireland, FitzGibbon supplied a list of top portraitists of the period who had painted him:

> I sat to Mr Hoppner for a picture of which Hobart's is a copy, and Boydell desires my leave to make an engraving of it. This I gave him, of course, and desired that when the prints were engraved, he would give you a proof impression from me … in the meantime, I will send you a print taken from a miniature by Cosway for which I sat in the days of my youth. There is a vile bad one extant from a full length drawn by Stewart, which I shd be ashamed to sent [*sic*] you.[47]

Of the three portraits mentioned, the 'vile bad' engraving after Gilbert Stuart was a mezzotint produced in Dublin and London in 1790 after the oil of the previous year (fig.96), and is formal and grand. The other two, both of which FitzGibbon approved, are portraits which he would have had made in London by John Hoppner (fig.108) and Richard Cosway. The print after the Cosway miniature (fig.109) was the portrait that Eden initially received. Compared with the other two, it is certainly the most immediate of the portraits he mentions and he was particularly proud of it. The miniature was originally painted in 1788 when, despite his claim in the letter, the sitter was not exactly 'in the days of his youth' but almost forty, the year before he became Lord Chancellor. FitzGibbon had the image engraved in stipple, in both colour and monochrome, by the celebrated engraver Francesco Bartolozzi, and it was published by William Dickinson, one of the most fashionable contemporary print-sellers in London.[48] Formal portraiture such as the Stuart full-length played a role in emphasising one's social position while the exchange of engravings, particularly of more informal images such as the Cosway, acted as a bond of friendship as well as a mark of political allegiance.

Painting United Irishmen

The Lord Chancellor's stated aim was to rescue 'this giddy country from ruin',[49] a political ambition perhaps embodied in both Stuart's lively yet authoritative portrait and in Hamilton's stern representation of FitzGibbon (figs 96 and 106). Turning to a seminal depiction of Lord Edward FitzGerald (fig.101), it might at first seem surprising to view this as, by contrast, a portrait containing radical elements. In many ways the FitzGerald portrait is, as Stella Tillyard has claimed, 'innocuous'.[50] As we have seen (p.165), the draped column and three-quarter view of the face are standard features of late eighteenth-century portraiture, as is the folded paper on the right which here reads: 'Rig[t]. Hon.[ble]/L Edw. FitzGerald/Dublin'. We note from this inscription that there is no dropping of the sitter's honorary title as son of a duke or of his status as a Member of Parliament, which dates the commencement of the portrait to the winter of 1796–7, the last session of the Irish parliament in which FitzGerald sat as Member for County Kildare. Yet despite such traditional visual language, FitzGerald's 'very spirited' portrait, as his fellow United Irishman William Drennan called it,[51] subtly subverts the genre of respectable portraiture by means of a number of discreet inclusions. He is dressed in a cutaway blue coat and buff trousers, the dress and colours of the English opposition, the Foxite Whigs.[52] Visual precedence for such a representation can be found a decade earlier, in a double portrait of Charles James Fox and Edmund Burke (fig.110), where the Irish painter Thomas Hickey depicts Fox, on the left of the painting, in a similar outfit to that worn by his first cousin FitzGerald in the late 1790s. But to all of this in Hamilton's portrait FitzGerald has added a red French cravat, while his hair is combed forward in the French style over the temples. By dressing down, 'he is turned a complete Frenchman', remarked one of his old friends.[53] It would be difficult in 1790s Dublin to find a more palpable contrast with FitzGibbon's official garb (figs 96 and 106): instead of the powdered wig we have natural hair cut democratically short. The elegant arm akimbo is a common feature of male portraiture of the period (see Stuart's portrait of the Lord Chancellor, fig.96), as is the draped column, but the 'swatch of scarlet cloth' that follows the flow of FitzGerald's body and is forced on our attention by the opening of his arms is a provocative visual echo of his red

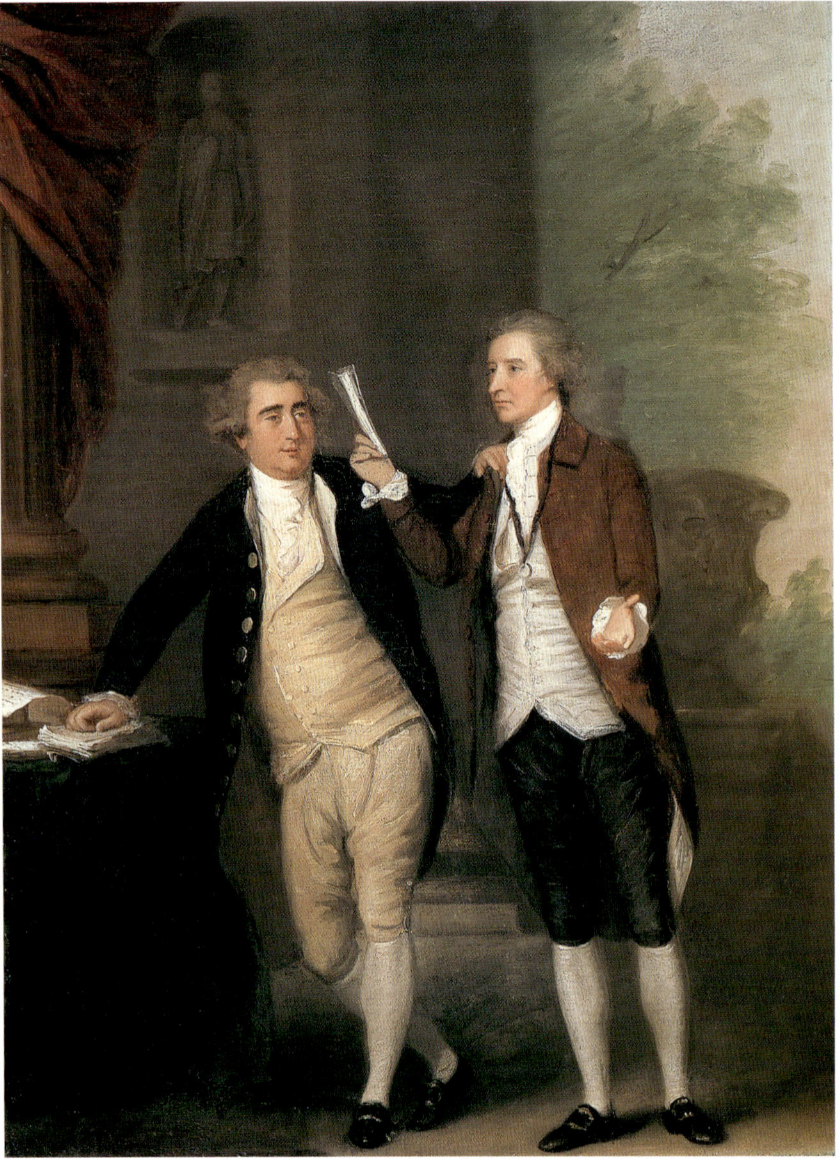

necktie, possibly reminding us of the demotic association that the colour red had in Revolutionary France.[54]

FitzGerald probably sat for Hamilton in 1796 and the painting was worked on throughout 1797.[55] Given his political distractions, FitzGerald was not in a position to sit regularly for the artist, which may explain the close similarity in facial pose and the turn of the head to a number of miniatures produced by Horace Hone. The first of these dates from 1795, with another from 1797 (fig.111).[56] But it was Hamilton who was to produce the majority of variations on these images of the republican hero (fig.115). Hamilton's three-quarter length (fig.101) was seen in his studio by William Drennan in November 1797, and that portrait is the most elaborate image in

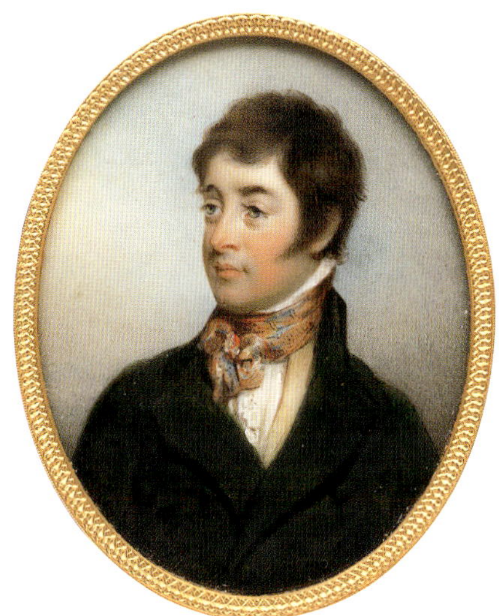

111. **Lord Edward FitzGerald** (1763–98)
HORACE HONE (C.1797)
Watercolour on ivory, 93 × 75mm (3⅝ × 3″)
National Portrait Gallery, London (NPG, 5704)

Wearing a dark green coat, cream waistcoat, and
white shirt with red, blue and gold patterned 'belcher,'
FitzGerald is proclaiming his republican sympathies
more openly than in either of the Hamilton oils
reproduced here (figs 101, 115).

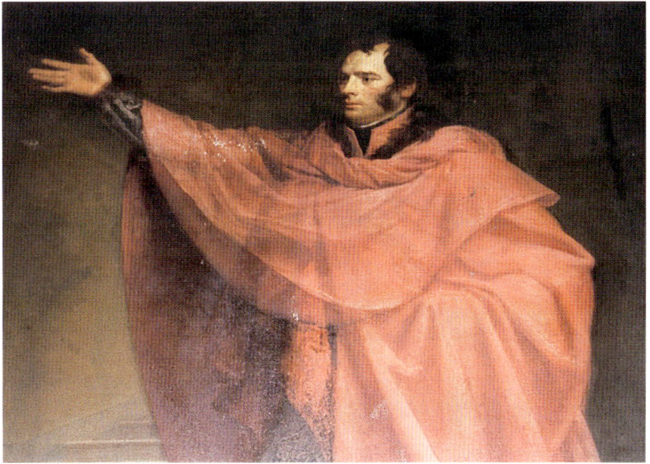

112. **Arthur O'Connor** (1763–1852) detail
HUGH DOUGLAS HAMILTON (1796–7)
Oil on canvas, c.2360 × c.1450mm (93 × 57″) (by sight)
Private collection

Hamilton's full-length of O'Connor is in a very poor state of conservation:
owing to canvas damage and paint loss on the sitter's legs and lower reaches
of his cloak, only the top half of the portrait is reproduced here.

the array of FitzGerald likenesses that have survived. The artist went on to adapt the three-quarter-length to head and shoulder size. In the National Portrait Gallery version of these reduced oil portraits (fig.115 and detail p.146) the sitter wears a green jacket, a sartorial choice that also appears in a number of miniatures by Hone (fig.111).[57] Just as the French spent much of the decade arguing over official revolutionary costume, so too the United Irishmen 'developed a symbology which was exploited for propagandist purposes as well'. They also appropriated the colour green as emblematic of the national cause.[58] Within a short time of being painted by Hamilton, FitzGerald had a suitable commander's uniform designed which incorporated Irish green for the jacket and braiding of revolutionary red, an outfit that was seen by Dublin Castle as being 'manifestly French'.[59]

When discussing FitzGerald's flaunting of the colour red, we should also consider the portrait of his friend and political intimate, Arthur O'Connor (fig.112). Also painted by Hamilton and equally viewed by Drennan in the artist's studio in November 1797, this full-length is now in a very damaged condition and in serious need of major restoration. However, it is still possible to discern a few key features of this ambitious portrait of an Irish radical painted on the eve of the 1798 Rebellion. It appears even more French than the FitzGerald, and as such it is a more striking republican statement. The United Irishman stands in a columned hall as he addresses an invisible assembly. Robed in a toga-like scarlet cloak, his right arm outstretched, his right leg thrust forward, O'Connor's declamatory representation within an assembly may specifically refer to his famous speech made in the Irish House of Commons only two years earlier, in May 1795, on behalf of Henry Grattan's bill to admit Roman Catholics to parliament. Equally, it may reflect his more recent public statements, such as his letter *To the Free Electors of the County of Antrim* which was published in early 1797. At the same time he was writing his most memorable contribution to United Irishmen literature, *The State of Ireland*, a pamphlet that advocated political and economic reform but was not published until the following year, 1798.[60]

In this portrait O'Connor has clearly instructed Hamilton carefully on how he wishes to appear. Like FitzGerald, O'Connor had been to Revolutionary France in August 1796, where he met General Hoche in Angers and discussed a French invasion of Ireland.[61] Infected by a new radical fervour, he has had himself painted in a fashion not far removed from contemporaneous French portraits. The colour red is the key factor in such a comparison, as O'Connor may have been attempting to draw a resemblance between himself and the red cloaks adopted by the Councils of the Directoire (the Cinq-Cents and the Anciens).[62] It was agreed by the National Convention in May 1795 that they should meet 'in costume', and they charged the abbé Grégoire to present a report on the costume to be adopted. This he did by September of that year; the result, amongst other features was a 'scarlet Greek-style cloak decorated with embroideries, in wool', which was not formally worn until late February 1798.[63] The final appearance of this costume, seen at the time as 'something beautiful . . . something imposing and truly senatorial',[64] post-dates Drennan's mention of Hamilton's portrait of O'Connor by at least three months. And yet a similarity of conception exists between the Irish portrait and, for example, a now lost painting by Jacques Sablet of 1797 showing a member of the Cinq-Cents at the tomb of his father. That painting and other illustrative sources from the second half of the 1790s show members of the Cinq-Cents taking up comparable rhetorical poses and sporting scarlet cloaks similar to that worn by O'Connor in Hamilton's portrait.[65]

Earlier in 1796 at the Luxembourg Palace, Wolfe Tone had met with Lazare Carnot, who had appeared 'in the petit costume of white satin with crimson robe, richly embroidered. It is very elegant, and resembles almost exactly the draperies of Van Dyke.'[66] This encounter between an Irish would-be revolutionary and an existing French one, where a consciousness of dress is emphasized, helps us to see the Hamilton portrait of O'Connor as part of a deliberate effort to make a visual point in favour of a radical gesture. Indeed, at his trial a few years later Wolfe Tone wore full ceremonial French military uniform (fig.98). In the case of O'Connor, consciousness of dress was also combined with personal appearance. As observers such as William Drennan tell us on a number of occasions, O'Connor was well aware of his dark,

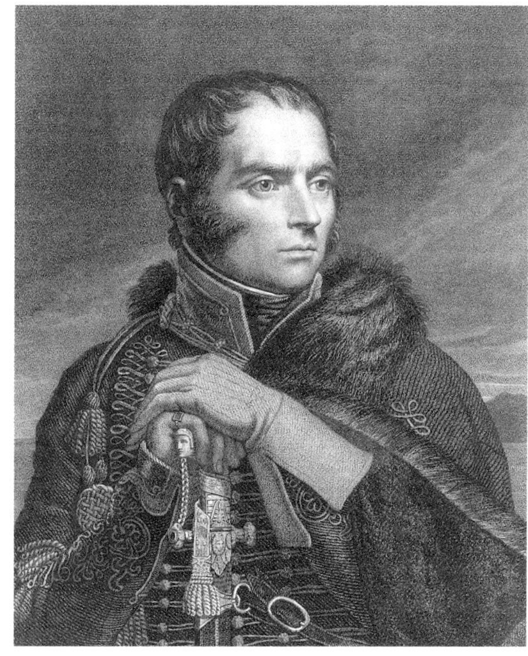

penetrating features. Drennan refers to him as 'a singularly looking man as Grattan is, but the ladies might, and I believe many do think O'Connor singularly handsome'. As suggested in Hamilton's portrait, the sitter's vanity no doubt dictated the brushing forward of his hair to cover up for recent loss due to a fever.[67]

O'Connor's portrait possesses other, more enigmatic features. The sitter wears a cape-like garment reaching from shoulder to shoulder, which differs from the pseudo classical cloak clasped on the right shoulder worn by the Cinq-Cents. On closer inspection, clear pentimenti reveal a series of vertical folds falling from O'Connor's right shoulder that may indicate an original garment closer to that of the French uniform. The roll of material at the neck is also consistent with the appearance of the French cloak, yet pentimenti appear in the lower half of the image suggesting that the cloak was extended to the floor at a later date. These alterations and the fact that O'Connor's left arm is covered and thus constrained by the red cloak (not a feature of the dress of the Cinq-Cents), together with inclusion of a military-style black stock and fur-trimmed collar, suggest that at some later date the painting was reworked. Until a full conservational examination can be made of the painting, it is suggested that the overpainting, probably not by Hamilton but done some years into the nineteenth century, was an attempt to reduce the revolutionary aura of the image.

If Hamilton did not retouch the painting in the nineteenth century, his actual involvement with the original canvas can only have been for a relatively short period of time. Seen by Drennan in November 1797, O'Connor had only been released from jail in Dublin Castle a few months earlier, in August, and left for London in January 1798. He was arrested in Maidstone in February, tried and imprisoned until 1802. O'Connor's sittings for Hamilton must only have been few. On his release he settled in France and in time became a *général de division* in Napoleon's army, gradually distancing himself from his radical past.[68] An engraving by Jean Godefroy after a highly flattering portrait by François, Baron Gérard (fig.113) shows the black stock and fur-lined collar seen in the Hamilton portrait, as well as the assurance of a man who had moved beyond Irish politics.

Having mentally stripped away the overpainting of a more reactionary future, we can now attempt to return to the portrait of O'Connor the radical that Drennan saw in Dublin in 1797. In his youth, possibly even in Hamilton's studio, the painter and biographer Thomas James Mulvany (1779–1845) saw O'Connor's portrait and discussed it, along with other contemporary portraits by Hamilton such as the fine Richard Mansergh St George (National Gallery of Ireland), which was exhibited in 1801. Some forty years later he wrote a useful account of the painter's career and recalls seeing the picture of O'Connor

> addressing a public assembly. He stands firmly erect, with arm raised and stretched forth, as though he had just uttered a sentence of stimulating excitement. His countenance seems the seat of sanguine anticipations. His robe is the Roman toga, and the whole act of the man is that of Brutus. Hamilton judiciously attempts no present action for the orator, but has expressed that momentary pause which presupposes a bygone one. It is historical, in the best acceptance of the term, and, although said to have been a faithful likeness of the individual, yet it possessed all those generalised forms which represent a class; it was a most able production.[69]

Standing in a declamatory manner in a public chamber with steps receding behind him to the left and a great black marble column to the right, O'Connor's portrait, with its radical red cloak and his own inflammatory reputation, offers a direct challenge to the tradition of parliamentary portraits that had been in existence in Ireland since at least Latham's portrait of Tottenham in his boots back in 1731 (fig.93). As has been discussed (p.150), this tradition had continued with Wheatley's interior of the Irish House of Commons in 1780 (fig.94) and, a decade later, with Stuart's portraits of FitzGibbon and Foster (figs 96 and 97). The focus of all of these portraits, be they protagonists of the patriot party or of the executive, was on maintaining a constitutional consensus. But O'Connor's portrait offers a direct challenge to this system.

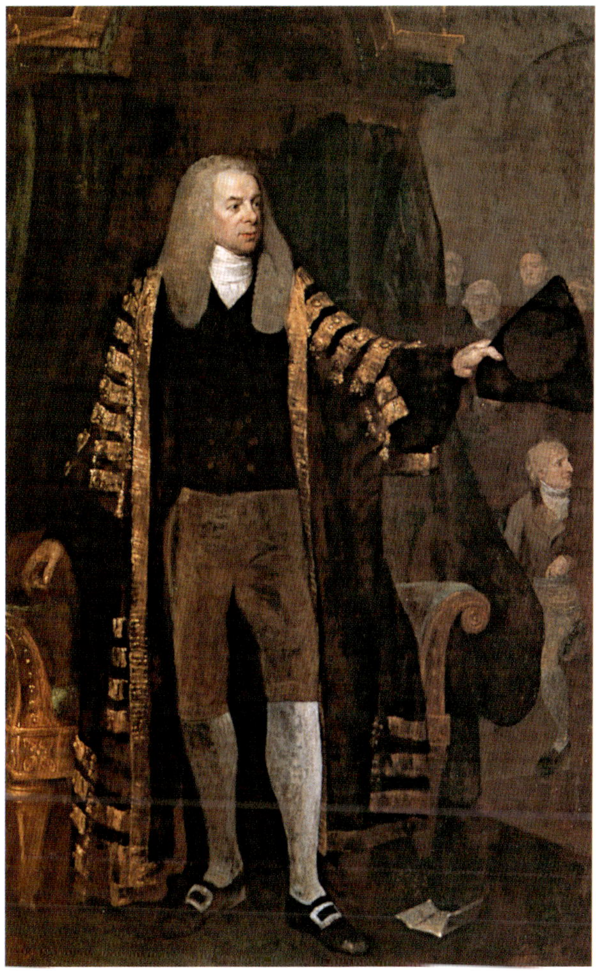

A few years later, in 1799, Hamilton, no doubt unwittingly, underlined the continued oppositional nature of portrait production when he accepted a commission from Dublin Corporation to paint a full-length portrait of the outgoing Speaker of the Irish Commons, John Foster (fig.114). This was to be Foster's second great public portrait and it acts as a fittingly contemporaneous and reactionary rejoinder to the French sentiments expressed in the O'Connor painting. Like the portrait of the United Irishman, Foster stands in a parliamentary setting, dressed in his Speaker's robes, his chair behind him along with a group of men seated in rows. On the floor lies a folded parchment which reads 'Rights and Liberties of the Irish Nation'. When this portrait was exhibited a few years later, in 1802, its sitter was praised for his 'dignity' and commitment to parliamentary procedure.[70] O'Connor's private pictorial outburst had met its match.

The difference between the portraits of members of the executive such as Foster and FitzGibbon and radicals such as O'Connor and FitzGerald is that the former had total control over what was produced, and their portraits stayed in the public domain. Commissioned by the City of Dublin, Foster's portrait by Hamilton still hangs in the Mansion House, while in the autumn of 1798 a copy of Gilbert Stuart's *John FitzGibbon* (fig.96) replaced Robert Home's portrait of Henry Grattan in Trinity College's Examination Hall, due to a suspicion that Grattan was involved in the United Irishmen.[71] Given O'Connor's precarious lifestyle in 1797–8, it is doubtful whether his potentially subversive portrait left Hamilton's studio until after the sitter's release from jail in 1802, and it was then probably transported to France after he had launched a new career. The portrait has never been publicly displayed.

The cult of the portrait

FitzGerald's original three-quarter length (fig.101) had an equally 'hidden' afterlife, and like the portrait of O'Connor it, too, was still in Hamilton's studio in 1802. In fact it was unfinished and Hamilton was nervous about lending it out to be engraved.[72] Although we know that FitzGerald personally sat for Hone and Hamilton, the vast majority of portraits of him are posthumous and as such should be viewed as part of the creation of a cult.[73] It may be argued that FitzGerald initiated this cult himself by having his portrait painted by Hamilton with the intention of presenting it to his mother who, it is known, had for some time before his death in June 1798 been collecting 'memories and objects to remind herself of him'.[74] But the cult of Fitz-Gerald's image was also fostered by his family, in particular his female relatives and friends. Within months of Lord Edward's death his niece, Emily FitzGerald, refers to a Hamilton portrait as 'the Precious Picture', while others describe 'the Divine face' or 'the Angelic Face'.[75] The existing letters suggest that the members of the very large FitzGerald family each shared a determination to have an image of their deceased relative. This familial concern with maintaining Lord Edward's memory was to remain a feature of the FitzGeralds. As late as 1885 a published list of *Pictures, Plate, Antiquities* at various family properties describes innumerable objects associated with the United Irishman. Carton, the family seat in northern County Kildare, boasted a cabinet with objects ranging from fifteenth-century family seals to a 'Pin, with hair of Lord Edward FitzGerald' and a 'Ring … Left on his deathbed to his sister, Lady Lucy', while elsewhere in the house are 'Snow-shoes' and 'a sleigh … brought from Canada … in 1789'. A year before this list was compiled, Hamilton's three-quarter-length portrait (fig.101) had been

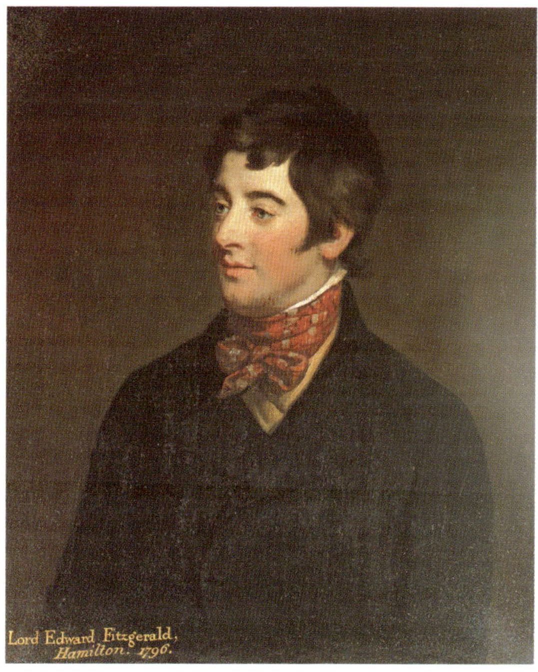

115. **Lord Edward FitzGerald**
(1763–98)
HUGH DOUGLAS HAMILTON
(1796–8)
Oil on canvas,
7620 × 6360mm (30 × 25″)
National Portrait Gallery,
London (NPG 3815)

presented to the National Gallery of Ireland by the 4th Duke of Leinster; a head and shoulders oil, as well as an oval pastel portrait, both by Hamilton, remained. Another head and shoulder portrait hung at Kilkea Castle in the south of the county.[76]

Such private adulation eventually led to a public reclamation of the memory of FitzGerald. Despite Hamilton's initial qualms, numerous engravings were made from both his and the Horace Hone images (fig.111), all of which led to the creation of a nationalist icon. In time this was greatly aided by Thomas Moore's biography of 1831, which Charles Gavan Duffy was to call 'a patriot's offering on a native shrine', to be followed by Madden's 'Memoir', published a decade later.[77] Moore used some of those emotive family letters to inform his readers of the creation of the cult. In one letter, written within days of FitzGerald's death, his aunt tells his brother:

> I have got the watch and chain that hung constantly round his neck, with a locket of hair, which I will send you by the first opportunity, along with his own dear hair. I have been with Hamilton the painter. There are two pictures of him, one for your mother and the other for you, besides one of Lucy, I believe for you also. Mr Hamilton says they are not finished and cannot be ready to go to England these three months; but he will hasten them as much as possible, and I will take care to forward them.[78]

These two copies soon grew to at least seven or eight. In examining these paintings it is clear that shortly after his death small changes began to occur in FitzGerald's iconography. The red necktie and green jacket seen in the earlier variations on the original three-quarter length were to 'tactfully' disappear in the numerous post-humous portraits, and be replaced by a necktie of 'blameless white' and a black jacket.[79] This visual dilution of the image of the radical FitzGerald runs alongside his gradual popular and historical transformation from an impressive political and military strategist to a tragic yet romantic innocent.[80]

Just as FitzGibbon had had his portrait produced in London by the leading artists of the day, so too the image of FitzGerald was available to a London audience. The difference is that by the time this happened he was dead. For at least a year after his death, FitzGerald's name and representation appeared in a number of London-based satires as synonymous with radicalism, but also with lost opportunities. Charles James Fox is frequently the one who has lost out, both politically, in the defeat of the republican cause, and personally, in the loss of a cousin. On 11 June, a week after FitzGerald's death, Fores of Piccadilly published *Tears of Sensibility . . . The Whig Club in Distress*, where Fox and his friends shed tears and sigh, 'Poor Neddy'. Fox exclaims, 'O Dear Lord Edward FitzGerald, the Worthiest, the truest, most <u>hot</u> hearted, the bravest, the best of us All, the most, like myself, and whoever feels for him must feel for me also'.[81]

It is Gillray, though, who can be accredited with one of the earliest depictions of that subtle change of emphasis that affected the transformation of FitzGerald from rebel to victim. *Nightly Visitors at St Ann's Hill* (fig.116) of September 1798 shows Fox at home in bed, again with a *bonnet rouge* on his head, being visited by a Banquo-like apparition of six recently deceased United Irishmen. The bloodstained figure of FitzGerald accuses him of seducing 'my youthful Mind from Virtue/Who plann'd my Treasons, & who caus'd my Death?/Remember poor Lord Edward and despair!!!' The other headless bodies represent the executed Cornelius Grogan, Rev. James Coigly (sometimes Quigley), the Sheares brothers and Bagenal Harvey. Fox echoes Macbeth in his denials: 'Why do'st thou shake thy Goary Locks at me? . . . Thou can'st not say, I did it!' But an open book on the ground by his bed reads 'Plan of the Irish Rebellion'.[82] Gillray maintains the by now much-depicted FitzGerald features of thick hair brushed forward and a youthful, fleshy face.

The pervasive presence of portraits in the culture of the period is exemplified by an amusing anecdote. The *Irish Magazine* was certainly adversarial in its style, but in the context of the subject of this study its proprietor, Watty Cox, was also very aware of the potency of portraiture; indeed, he subtitled his publication *Monthly Asylum for Neglected Biography*.[83] Biographical sketches accompanied by illustrations were frequent and most issues carried an engraved portrait frontispiece, ranging from Oliver Plunkett, Patrick Sarsfield and Robert Emmet to Turlough O'Carolan. In 1810 Cox ran a lengthy yarn on the sale of the hated Major Sirr's renowned art collection. Sirr is, of course, remembered as the man who shot and captured FitzGerald. Cox's rather over-long joke creates a macabre fantasy out of the titles of Sirr's paintings. John FitzGibbon had died eight years earlier and at his funeral, as legend has it, a dead cat was hurled at the coffin – an ironic reminder that FitzGibbon had boasted that he would 'make the seditious as tame as domestic cats'.

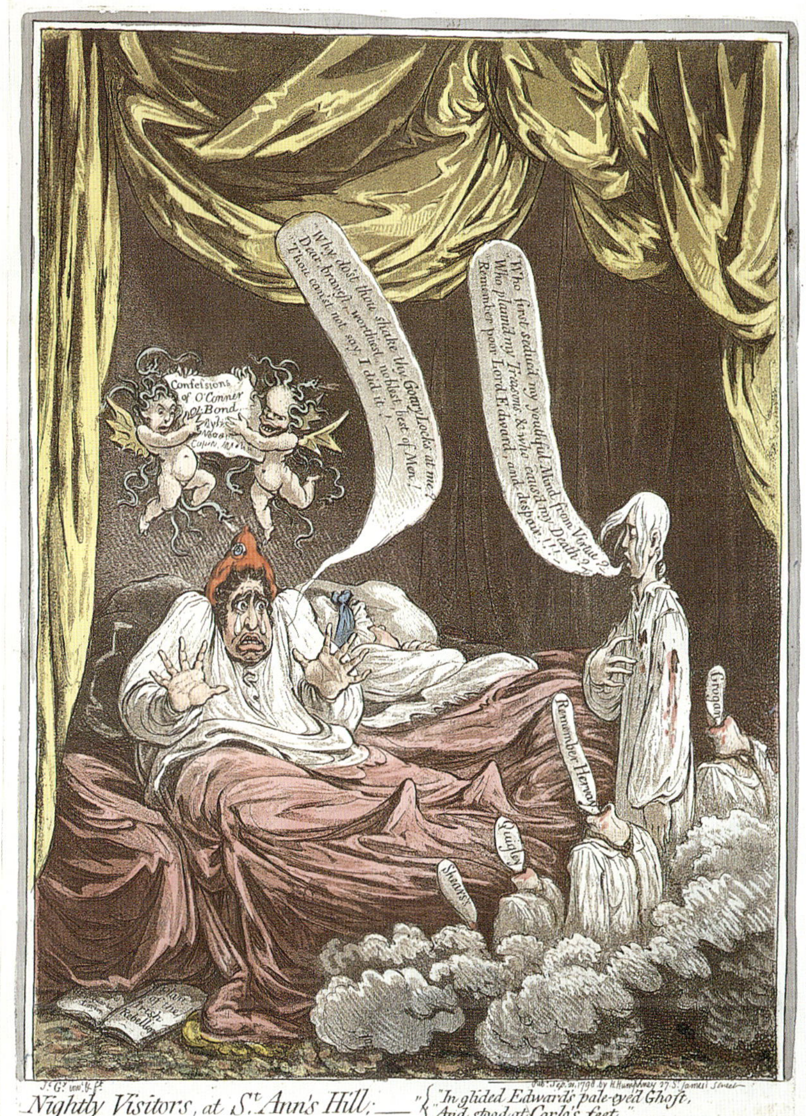

Nightly Visitors, at St. Ann's Hill: — "{ "In glided Edwards pale-eyed Ghost, / And stood at Carlo's feet."

116. **Nightly Visitors at St Ann's Hill**

JAMES GILLRAY (1798)
Hand-coloured aquatint,
360 × 261mm (4⅛ × 10¼")
National Portrait Gallery,
London (NPG D12658)

The recently deceased Lord Edward FitzGerald and other United Irishmen appear, Banquo-like, to Charles James Fox in the privacy of the latter's bedchamber in his house outside central London. Gillray frequently referred to Ireland in his prints of the 1790s.

On his list of the contents of Sirr's collection Cox includes a portrait of 'Lord FitzGibbon, and his favourite cat ... most correctly finished'.[84]

Dissemination

In the immediate aftermath of the 1798 Rebellion the dissemination of nationalist portraiture was not at all easy. Of the five individuals viewed on canvases in Hamilton's studio in November 1797 by William Drennan, only one of them, Francis Rawdon, Lord Moira (fig.100) was to be exhibited publicly, and then not until 1804. A Liberal, Moira had opposed the Union but either for expediency or due to his close friendship with the Prince of Wales, he later withdrew his opposition. The other portraits, one each of Arthur O'Connor and Edward FitzGerald, as well as two of FitzGerald's wife, Pamela, were never seen. During these years other Hamilton portraits of loyalists and members of the executive were given a public airing at the revived Society of Artists of Ireland exhibitions. In keeping with the reactionary content of the exhibitions for 1801 and 1802, the portraits were suitably housed in the now abandoned Parliament House. As a contemporary diarist commented,

> The exhibition of last year was a little better than a closet, the present is in a palace – you pass thro' a magnificent colonnade and Hall into a couple of noble apartments, arched ceilings and lightings at top – the walls hung with green cloth, shew both the paintings and the superb frames which surround them, to the greatest advantage. The first room is appropriated to miniatures, sketches, drawings, elevation, etc. The second to the paintings, the catalogue contains in the whole, 200 pieces.[85]

Later the diarist discusses Hamilton's portrait of the melancholic Lieutenant Richard Mansergh St George, himself a victim of the brutality of the 1798 Rebellion.[86] A year later Hamilton's portrait of Speaker Foster (fig.114) was also shown in Pearce's great building. This latter display had a certain tactlessness about it, given Foster's vehement opposition to the disbanding of the Irish parliament. In 1804, when Moira's picture was exhibited, the venue for the Society's exhibitions had moved down the street to Allen's print shop on Dame Street, where the emphasis again was strongly on the executive. Although the anonymous diarist referred to the exhibition space as being comparable to 'a closet', Moira's portrait somehow shared wall space with portraits of other notables such as Lord Castlereagh, recently Chief Secretary for Ireland, and the late Chief Justice of Ireland, Lord Kilwarden (fig.117), who had been murdered exactly a year earlier on a Dublin street. A victim of the Robert Emmet Rebellion of 1803, Kilwarden is shown *en négligé*, with an open white shirt. His portrayal drove the *Dublin Evening Post* to praise this 'loyalist and patriot – the Christian and the moralist', who, 'when expiring in cruel torture, was only anxious that the law should survive and live in that constitutional vigour which he, himself, had always endeavoured to maintain'. Such sentiments took a long time to die as almost seventy years later, in 1872, spectators at the National Historical Portraits Exhibition were asked to consider Hamilton's 'grave and even sanctified-looking portrait' of Kilwarden.[87]

The many portraits of FitzGerald were all private commissions from his large, aristocratic family, and as such they had limited visibility outside. Apart from the engraving in Madden's book, public access to painted images of FitzGerald was to be very limited for many decades. In 1868 and 1872, head and shoulder variations on the Hamilton original were exhibited in both London and Dublin, while Hamilton's

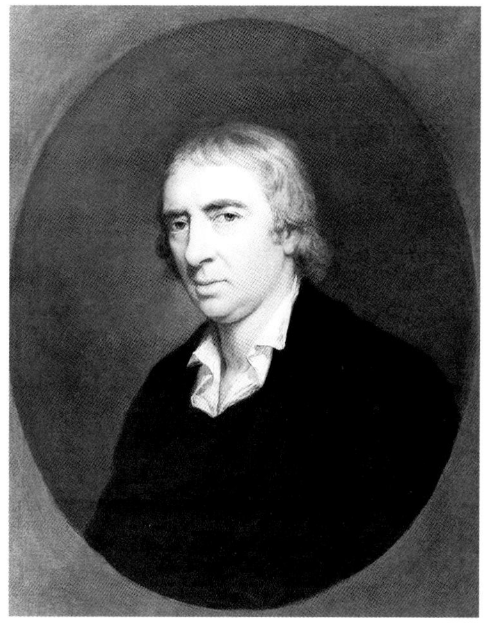

117. **Arthur Wolfe, later 1st Viscount Kilwarden, Lord Chief Justice of Ireland** (1738/9–1803)
HUGH DOUGLAS HAMILTON
(c.1795)
Oil on canvas, 700 × 560mm
(27½ × 22″)
National Gallery of Ireland,
Dublin

three-quarter-length oil (fig.101) only resurfaced when it was presented to the National Gallery of Ireland by the 4th Duke of Leinster in 1884.[88] This removal of the political portrait from the Irish scene was condemned by R.R. Madden in the 1840s when he highlighted an earlier failure of Irish people to subscribe for engravings after a dramatic representations in oils of FitzGerald's arrest by the painter and actor James Dowling Herbert. In time, with no subscriptions forthcoming, neglect led to the deterioration of Herbert's painting. Madden's account of this loss ends with a call on the public bodies of Ireland to exhibit 'sufficient patriotism to secure this representation of the mortal conflict wherein the noblest being that Ireland ever produced received his death wounds'.[89]

Such a call on the nation's conscience echoes Thomas Davis's contemporaneous complaint that 'We have Irish artists, but no Irish, no national art'. Davis went on to supply a list of historical subjects accompanied by suitable textual sources for the creation of such a national art.[90] The topics ranged from 'The Landing of the Milesians' as told by Geoffrey Keating and by Thomas Moore in his *Melodies*, to 1798 itself. All of Davis's 1798 themes are celebratory, invoking stirring, positive moments in the pursuit of nationhood. He ends his list with his own era, the 1840s, and the key figure of Daniel O'Connell. Interestingly, the O'Connellite themes he suggests are no longer the single portraits that are the focus of this chapter. Instead, they are all group events: 'First Meeting of the Catholic Association', 'O'Connell Speaking in a Munster Chapel', 'The Clare Hustings – Proposal of O'Connell' and 'The Dublin Corporation Speech'. Published in 1843, Davis's list was timely: although all his suggested subjects for painters set O'Connell within an Irish setting, and while actual single portraits of 'The Liberator' were being produced in plenty (fig.17), from at least 1833 O'Connell was also being included in large-scale group portraits bringing the discussion of the Irish political portrait to Westminster.

NOTES

1 *The Voice of the Nation. A Manual of Nationality by the Writers of the Nation Newspaper*, Dublin, 1844, 5th edn, pp.122–3: sections quoted in Barrett, 1975, pp.405–6 and Kilfeather, 2002, p.240. 10,000 plaster copies of Peter Turnerelli's bust of O'Connell were supposed to have been sold in Ireland: see Strickland, 1913, vol.II, p.470. This huge sale realised some £50,000: see Gilmartin, 1967.

2 Fenlon, 2001, pp.67–88. For the spelling of Ormond/Ormonde, I am following the sensible approach taken by Fenlon, 2001, p.9.

3 Quote is from Bainbrigge Buckeridge, 1706, p.479. See *Masterpieces of British Art from the Tate Gallery*, exh. cat., Metropolitan Art Museum, Tokyo, and Hyogo Prefectural Museum of Modern Art, Kobe, 1988, cat. no.6, p.214, and, www.tate.org.uk (Collection: Wright: Short Text). As Karen Hearn writes on the Tate website (May 2001), the 'armour . . . is of a style . . . worn during the period c.1350–1530 . . . The Japanese were perceived in the west as persecutors of Catholics, so the armour may have been included in order to represent O'Neill as a defender of his faith, treading on the deflated armour of its enemies. See also Stevenson and Thomson, 1982, pp.88–91; Fenlon, 1988.

4 Fenlon, 2001, p.18.

5 Figgis and Rooney, 2001, pp.326–8.

6 McParland, 2001, p.188.

7 Figgis and Rooney, 2001, pp.328–30.

8 For Wheatley's *A View of College Green with a Meeting of the Volunteers*, 1779–80 (National Gallery of Ireland, Dublin), see Cullen, 1997, chap.2 *passim*. Valentine Green produced a mezzotint of the NPG painting in 1782: see Cullen, 'Radicals and reactionaries', in Smyth, 2000, p.173.

9 There are many references to Nollekens's busts of Pitt and Fox in Farington's 1806 diaries: see Farington, 1978–98 ed., vols 7 and 8 (1982); Godfrey, 2001, pp.101, 151.

10 See Pointon, 1993, pp.103–4. For Gillray's cartoon see Godfrey, 2001, p.115, and Donald, 1996, p.170.

11 Lord Shannon to Lord Boyle, 15 February 1791, quoted in Malcomson, 1978, p.393. See also Crean, 1990, p.262 (the Fitzgibbon portrait is discussed on pp.249–57). The caption comment for fig. 100 refers to Malcomson, 2002, p.64.

12 Elliott, 1982; Elliott, 1989.

13 Barrington, 1809–15; Barrington, 1833; Madden, 2nd edn, 1857–60. For engravings after Comerford and Hamilton that appear in

Barrington, see Le Harivel, 1988, pp.72–5, 196–7; for Hamilton, see also Cullen, 1984, *passim*; for Comerford see also Caffrey, 1999, pp.65–75. For a reassessment of Madden's work on the United Irishmen see Whelan, 1996, pp.167–8 and Elliott, 2003, pp.131–9.

14 Barrington, 1833, pp.15–16. See Claire Connolly, 'Writing the Union', in Keogh and Whelan, 2001, pp.183–4.

15 Quoted by Patrick Geoghegan, 'The making of the union', in Keogh and Whelan, 2001, p.41. The illustrated pages in Barrington, 1833, opp. pp.17 and 413.

16 Walker's *Hibernian Magazine*, Nov. 1798, p.737; see also Le Harivel, 1988, p.281.

17 Madden, 2nd ser., 2nd edn, 1858, opp. p.48. The oil is in the National Gallery of Ireland: see Figgis and Rooney, 2001, pp.288–91.

18 Elliott, 1989, p.400.

19 Advertisement in *The Nation*, 15 July 1843, p.1.

20 Agnew, 1998–9, vol.II, p.348.

21 See Cullen, 1984, pp.195–6.

22 Agnew, 1998–9, vol.II, p.33.

23 Agnew, 1998–9, vol.II, pp.62–3.

24 Agnew, 1998–9, vol.II, p.366.

25 My thanks to Professor Alan Sommerstein of the University of Nottingham for assistance in the translation.

26 Agnew, 1998–9, vol.I, p.281.

27 Drennan, 1785.

28 Cirlot, 1971, p.294.

29 On this topic see Nicholson, 1996, pp.5–21.

30 *British Public Characters*, London, 1798, p.vii, 1798, quoted in Pointon, 1993, p.97.

31 Pointon, 1993, p.97.

32 Inglis, 1954, p.244.

33 *The Dublin Magazine*, vol.1, Dec. 1798, p.1; the other prints appeared in vol.2, Jan. 1799 and vol.3, Oct. 1799. For a comparable image see *The Union Olio*, frontispiece to the *Hibernian Magazine*, Jan. 1799 and Stephens and George, 1870–1954, vol.7, cat. no.9346. *The Dublin Magazine* ran from 1798–1800.

34 For Egan and his outbursts see Geoghegan, 'The making of the union', in Keogh and Whelan, 2001, p.41.

35 McDowell, 1979, pp.579–82; Pakenham, 1969, pp.283–4.

36 For Horish see Pakenham, 1969, pp.101, 126; also, Smyth, 1992, p.177.

37 For Grattan iconography see Cullen, 1997, pp.63, 69.

38 For the Gillray see Stephens and George, 1870–1954, vol.5 (1935), p.736, cat. no.6272.

39 Reproduced in colour in Nicholas Robinson,

'Marriage against inclination: The union and caricature', in Keogh and Whelan, 2001, pl.15, discussed pp.150–51; print in National Library of Ireland.

40 James Dowling Herbert, *Irish Varieties for the last Fifty Years*, London, 1836, quoted in Miles, 1995, p.161.

41 Miles, 1995, p.161 and Evans, 1999, pp.67–9.

42 See Cullen, 1984, p.174. Here I disagree with Crean (1990, p.272), who suggests that while in Ireland the American was the painter of the conservatives while Hamilton attracted the radicals: the situation is not that simple.

43 Letters of 1800 and 1801; for trans. from the Italian see Cullen, 2000, pp.187–8.

44 The portrait hung in FitzGibbon's seat at Mount Shannon, County Limerick, until the 1880s, when it was sold: see Figgis and Rooney, 2001, pp.183–4.

45 Ann C. Kavanaugh, 'John FitzGibbon, Earl of Clare', in Dickson, Keogh and Whelan, 1993, p.116.

46 Agnew, 1998–9, vol.II, p.114. There are a number of Carey prints in the Nicholas Robinson collection, Trinity College Dublin Library, ref.137, nos 503–10. Robinson's 'Marriage against inclination: The union and caricature', in Keogh and Whelan, 2001, pp.149–57, cites many caricatures of a few years later that refer to FitzGibbon. Carey went on to publish *Some Memoirs of the Patronage and Progress of the Fine Arts in England and Ireland*, London, 1826.

47 Kavanaugh, 1997, p.200.

48 For portraits of FitzGibbon see Kilmurray, 1979, p.44 and Elmes, 1937, pp.40–1. The reference to 'Boydell' in FitzGibbon's letter refers to the publisher John Boydell; for London print culture see Clayton, 1997. The Cosway original, signed and dated 1788, was on the London art market in 1979: see *Connoisseur*, vol.CCII, Oct. 1979, p.139.

49 FitzGibbon to William Eden, 1st Lord Auckland, Sept. 1799, quoted in McDowell, 1951–2, p.301.

50 Tillyard, 1997, p.218. For Hamilton's painting see Figgis and Rooney, 2001, pp.179–80.

51 Agnew, 1998–9, vol.II, p.348.

52 Tillyard, 1997, p.140. A dark coat, buff pantaloons and boots were also the 'stock-in-trade' of middle-class intellectual republicans in Paris, where FitzGerald had spent some time earlier in the decade: see Ribeiro, 1988, p.120.

53 Tillyard, 1997, p.158, quoting Robert Jephson.

54 Tillyard, 1997, p.218. For the colour red in France see Wrigley, 1997, p.140, and Geffroy, 1987, pp.119–48.

55 Figgis and Rooney, 2001, pp.179–80

56 See Caffrey, 2000, pp.98–9, and Walker, 1985, vol.1, pp.182–3.

57 For a list of portraits of FitzGerald see Walker, 1985, vol.1, pp.182–4 and Cullen, 1984, pp.187–8, 203. Another oil portrait of FitzGerald in a green jacket (in a private collection) is illustrated in Pakenham, 1997, p.22. For Hone see Strickland, 1913, vol.I, pp.508–13. See also F. Cullen, 'Radicals and reactionaries: Portraits of the 1790s in Ireland', in Smyth, 2000, pp.161–94 and Cullen, 1998, pp.17–20.

58 Curtin, 1994, p.249; see also Hunt, 1984, chap.2.

59 Richard Boyle, 2nd Earl of Shannon to Lord Boyle, 21 May 1798, quoted in Thomas Bartlett, 'Defence, Counter-Insurgency and Rebellion: Ireland, 1793–1803', in Bartlett and Jeffery, 1996, p.278.

60 MacDermot, 1966–7; O'Connor, 1998.

61 Elliott, 1982, p.102.

62 The following reading of the O'Connor portrait is greatly indebted to the suggestions of Tony Halliday, author of *Facing the Public: Portraiture in the Aftermath of the French Revolution*, Manchester, 1999.

63 Wrigley, 2002, pp.80–2. See also Hunt, 1984, pp.78 f., and Delpierre, 1972.

64 Wrigley, 2002, p.82, quoting the *Réimpression de l'Ancien Moniteur*, 21 Feb. 1798.

65 The Sablet is a now lost group portrait of an anonymous member of the Cinq-Cents, 1797 (formerly in the collection of G. Chabert, Paris). See also Ribeiro, 1988, pp.97–107.

66 Bartlett, 1998, p.478.

67 Agnew, 1998–9, vol.II, pp.277, 331

68 MacDermot, 1966–7, p.63.

69 Mulvany, 1842, pp.72–3. The portrait was probably removed to France after O'Connor's release from prison in 1802. It is still in a private collection near Paris.

70 *Dublin Evening Post*, 27 May, 1802. The commission document, dated 30 April 1799 and July 1799, is in the Foster-Masereene MSS, Public Records Office of Northern Ireland, D.207/10/34. My thanks to Dr Anthony Malcomson for this information. See also Cullen, 1984, p.189.

71 Crookshank and Webb, 1990, pp.53, 61; also Curwen, 1818, vol.II, pp.114–15.

72 Lord Wycombe to Lord Holland, 7 Apr. 1802, Holland House Papers, British Library Add MSS 51,685, ff.241–2. My thanks to Richard Aylmer for this information. Figgis and Rooney suggest that Hamilton's daughter Harriott finished the portrait (2001, p.180).

73 For an indication of the range of FitzGerald portraits see note 57 above and Cullen, 1998. For a nineteenth-century listing see Lennox/FitzGerald/Campbell Papers, National Library of Ireland, Dublin, MSS 35,018 (5), 'Oil paintings of Lord Edward , all by Hugh Hamilton'.

74 Tillyard, 1997, p.218.

75 Lennox/FitzGerald/Campbell Papers, NLI MSS 35,005 (7), Emily FitzGerald to Lady Lucy FitzGerald, 2 December 1798; MSS 35,005 (9), Frances Coutts to Lady Lucy Fitzgerald, 21 July 1798; Strutt Papers, Public Record Office of Northern Ireland, Belfast, T/3092 (15) 33, Frances Coutts to Lady Lucy FitzGerald, 16 Nov. 1798. My thanks to Richard Aylmer for leading me to these papers.

76 *Notes on the Pictures*, 1885, pp.7, 11, 14, 25, 34, 49.

77 C. Gavan Duffy, *The Nation*, 1842, quoted in Deane, 1991, vol.1, p.1253. See Moore, 1831 and Madden, 2nd ser., 2nd edn, 1858, portrait opp. p.359

78 Moore, 1831, vol.II, pp.149–50.

79 Tillyard, 1997, p.218; for posthumous alterations to FitzGerald's contribution to the United Irish movement see Tillyard, 1997, pp.311–20. For the colour variations in FitzGerald portraits, see Cullen, 1984, p.188; for a colour illustration of a Hamilton portrait with a white necktie (private collection), see Tillyard, 1997, opp. p.210.

80 For FitzGerald's skill as a strategist see Elliott, 1982, *passim*.

81 Stephens and George, 1870–1954, vol.7, cat. no.9227.

82 Stephens and George, 1870–1954, vol.7, cat. no.9244 (21 Sept. 1798).

83 For a discussion of *The Irish Magazine* see Whelan, 1996, p.164, and Elliott, 2003, pp.110–12.

84 *The Irish Magazine*, Sept. 1810, p.56; for FitzGibbon's boast see Whelan, 1996, p.88. For Sirr's actual collection of some 500 paintings, see *Catalogue of Paintings*, 1841.

85 Dublin, Royal Irish Academy MS 24K14, 3 June 1801, quoted in Cullen, 2000, pp.238–9. For Hamilton's exhibited portraits 1800–04 see Cullen, 1984, p.208.

86 Cullen, 1997, pp.104–15; Figgis and Rooney, 2001, pp.176–9.

87 Cullen, 2000, p.236; Figgis and Rooney,2001, p.174; FitzGerald, 1872, p.42, no.203.

88 For listings of the exhibition history for Hamilton's FitzGerald paintings see Cullen, 1984, pp.187–8.

89 Madden, 2nd ser., 2nd edn, 1858, p.473; the engraving after Herbert's lost oil is discussed and reproduced in Cullen, 'Radicals and reactionaries', in Smyth, 2000, pp.190–93.

90 See Cullen, 2000, pp.70–73; Sheehy, 1980, pp.30–34.

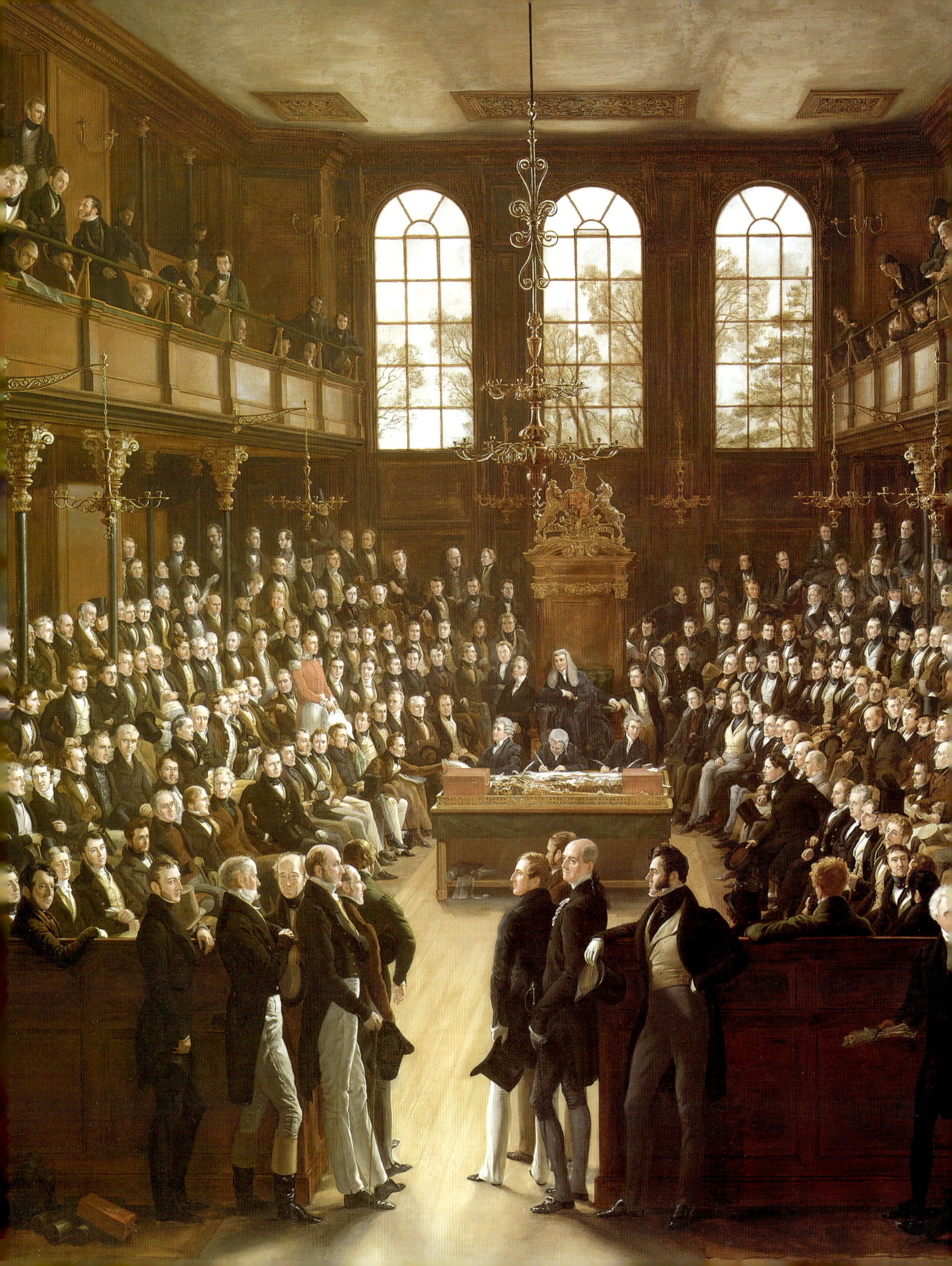

EVEN THOUGH DUBLIN lost its parliament in 1801, the visual representation of an Irish parliamentary presence continued throughout the nineteenth century. Both Daniel O'Connell and later Charles Stewart Parnell, as well as many other political figures, appear continuously in oil paintings, sculpture and more ephemeral media. Starting with the post-emancipation era and the age of Reform, the reappearance of Irish political figures in the genre of public political portraiture celebrates the role played by certain Irish individuals in a larger political environment.

Moving to Westminster

Paintings by George Hayter (fig.118) and Benjamin Robert Haydon (fig.120) focus attention on Daniel O'Connell in the context of major political events, recalling, from an Irish point of view, the equally declamatory tones of Francis Wheatley's *Meeting of the Volunteers* and Grattan addressing the Irish House of Commons in 1779–80 (fig.94).[1] Hayter's colossal canvas of the interior of the House of Commons in Westminster was begun in 1833 but not exhibited until 1843. It features nearly 400 figures, with O'Connell prominent on the Opposition Front Bench (on the right). He leans forward, thus allowing his head to be captured in recognisable profile. The picture represents the moving of the address to the Crown at the opening of the first reformed parliament which took place in St Stephen's Chapel on 5 February 1833. The figure speaking on the left is the 2nd Marquess of Breadalbane, while the Whig Prime Minister, Lord Grey, who had spearheaded the reform bill, leans against the bar of the House on the far left. Hayter's oil study of O'Connell (fig.121), with his hat on his head rather than in his hand as in the finished picture, allows us to explore his features more carefully.[2] He pushes his chin forward, perhaps displaying an eagerness to catch what is being said: or perhaps Hayter uses O'Connell's profile to heighten the political tension in the House. In the finished canvas, O'Connell focuses his gaze upon the bench opposite, and seems to be staring intently at Edward George Stanley, Chief Secretary for Ireland, later 14th Earl of Derby and a future Prime Minister. Stanley, who stares full face out of the picture, sits second to the right of his fellow Cabinet member Lord Russell, who leans forward to leave a sheet of paper on the Commons' table. A deep enmity existed between Stanley and O'Connell. Both were celebrated as masters of debate, and both were supporters of

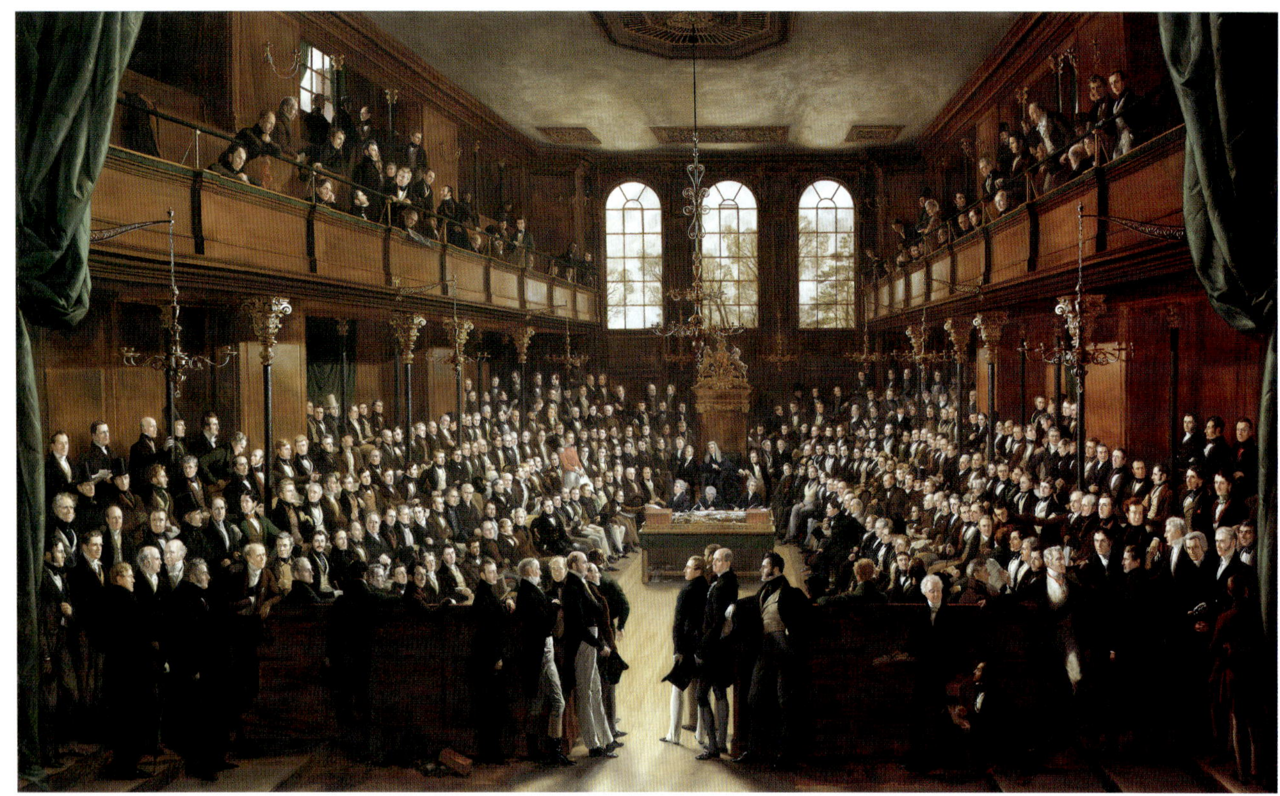

118. **The House of Commons 1833**
SIR GEORGE HAYTER (1833–43)
Oil on canvas, 5420 × 3460 × 135mm
(213⅜ × 136¼ × 5⅜")
National Portrait Gallery,
London (NPG 54)

Daniel O'Connell sits in the centre of
the Opposition Front Bench (on the
right), leaning forward in clear profile.
He holds his open hat in his right
hand, his left hand on the bench
arm allowing him to thrust his torso
forward. Sheil sits a row behind,
possibly seated on the gangway
given his low position.

parliamentary reform, although O'Connell wished to go further than Stanley and had recently begun his great campaign to repeal the Act of Union and the re-establishment of an Irish parliament. By contrast, Stanley did not conceal his 'support for the continuance of Protestant Ascendancy in Ireland'.[3] Celebrated in both Ireland and England as an advocate of the furtherance of democracy, O'Connell's posture is deliberately confrontational, opposite the party that had actually passed the reform bill. While he sits next to William Cobbett, the radical Member of Parliament for Oldham, with the Irish Member for Tipperary, Richard Lalor Sheil, crouched behind them, O'Connell's position in Hayter's great painting offers a direct challenge to the implementation of reform, given the harsh Irish coercion acts soon to be introduced by Grey and his government.

This visual coupling of O'Connell and Sheil was further developed by Daniel Maclise in a contemporaneous caricature for *Fraser's Magazine* (fig.119). Seated on the Commons' benches and jocularly identified on the left as the author of 'Agitation', O'Connell 'paws' Sheil, 'with patronizing hand', as William Maginn wrote in the text accompanying the caricature. On the back of the original drawing, now in the Victoria and Albert Museum, London, Maclise inscribed in pencil that this scene represented the two men 'as they appeared in the house Monday night Feb 10th 1834', that is, only five days after the event depicted in Hayter's painting. 'Sheil', Maclise's inscription continues, 'is supposed to look at Lord Althorp'. This is a reference to

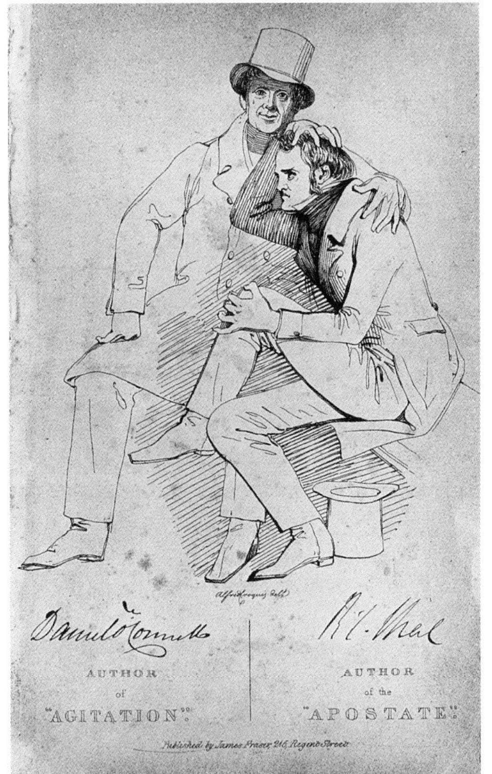

119. **Daniel O'Connell** (1775–1847)
and Richard Lalor Sheil (1791–1851)
DANIEL MACLISE (1834)
Lithograph, 212 × 131mm
(8⅜ × 5⅛″)
National Gallery of Ireland, Dublin

Frequently referred to as 'The Great Agitator', O'Connell is here ridiculed as the 'author' or instigator of agitation. By 1834, after the passing of the Catholic Emancipation Act, agitation referred to O'Connell's efforts to repeal the Act of Union. Sheil by contrast was actually the author of a prose tragedy entitled *The Apostate* (1817).

John Charles Spencer, later 3rd Earl Spencer, but in 1834 still Viscount Althorp and Chancellor of the Exchequer. Not surprisingly, Spencer sits between Stanley and Russell on the Government Front Bench. In keeping with the visualisation of enmity suggested by the O'Connell/Stanley clash, we now see a further confrontation suggested by Sheil's 'agonized' stare, supposedly directed at the Chancellor.[4] As O'Connell's biographer has pointed out, 'the king's speech [of 5 February 1834] . . . at Stanley's direction, threatened throughgoing repression in Ireland'.[5] The ensuing tension between O'Connell and Stanley is palpably visualised in Hayter's painting, which shows the beginning of the debate on the king's speech. The debate lasted the whole of the following night and, as Denis Le Marchant, a young liberal, noted in his diary,

> O'Connell's speech, artful and persuasive in a very high degree, made a deep impression. It required a very skilful answer, and certainly did not receive it from Stanley. His invective upon O'Connell, though pointed and forcible, did more injury to himself than to his opponent. It was not accompanied by a proper confutation of O'Connell's charges, so it looked liked invective alone, and the evening ended by O'Connell standing in a much higher position than in the last Parliament. The new members thought he had much right on his side.[6]

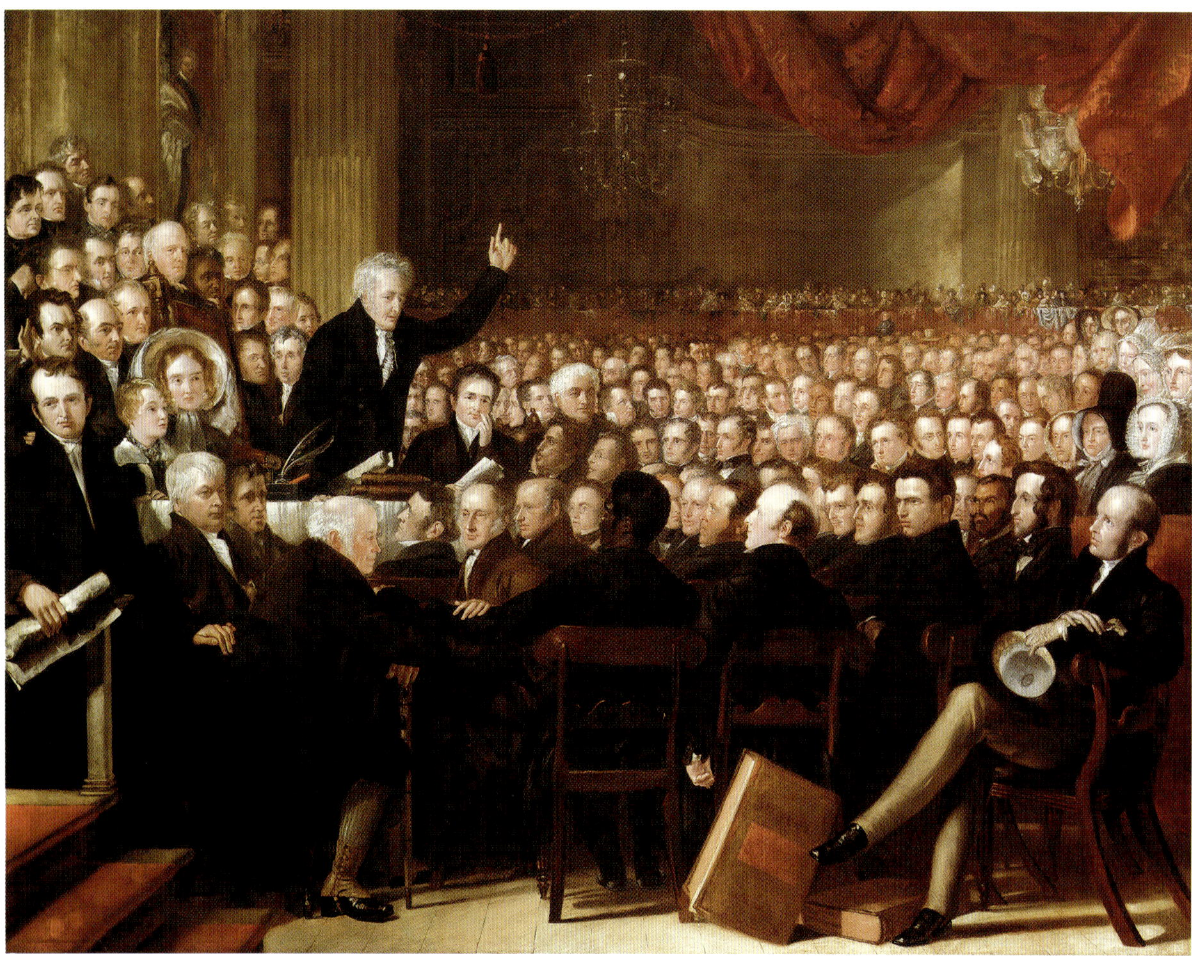

Although facing the Whigs and sitting next to some radical members, O'Connell is also seated, as Hayter himself wrote, 'in the midst of the high conservative members',[7] and thus offers a comparable check to that side of the house. Sir Robert Peel sits further along the front bench from O'Connell, in a yellow waistcoat, while the Liberator's fellow Irishman, the former Prime Minister, the Duke of Wellington (fig.16), stands this side of the bar on the far right, in a white waistcoat. Hayter referred to his painting as 'a national document'[8] and, given O'Connell's prominent position and the confrontational aspects implied by his 'eager attitude', it is entirely reasonable to include it in a discussion of the Irish portrait.[9]

Another important group portrait of the period that celebrates a liberal agenda and includes O'Connell is Benjamin Robert Haydon's painting of the delegates at the Anti-Slavery Society Convention (fig.120), which took place in London in June 1840. The painting was exhibited a year later, in May 1841, in the Egyptian Hall, Piccadilly.[10] This 'waggon load of heads', as one journalist described it, and Hayter's House of Commons interior reveal the Irish politician in the imperial parliament and on a world stage, participating in the parliamentary procedures of the United Kingdom

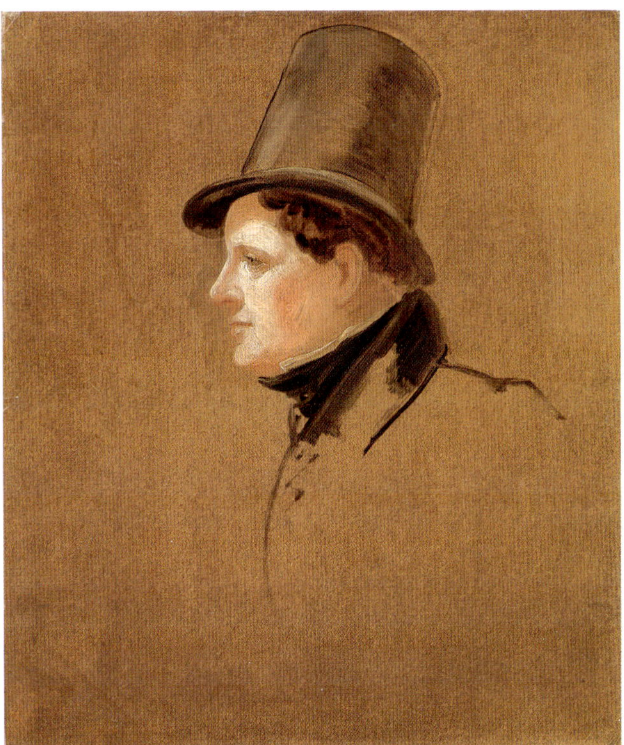

and lending an Irish voice to the condemnation of slavery.[11] Haydon includes O'Connell in the top left-hand corner of the painting, some distance behind Thomas Clarkson, the 'father of anti-slavery', who addresses the delegates. In the front centre, with his back to the viewer, sits the African-Jamaican former slave Henry Beckford, whose prominence in the painting was intended 'to demonstrate . . . the success of emancipation'.[12] To 'deafening' applause, O'Connell had 'made a speech of great power', as one American delegate wrote, 'and denounced American slave-holders in blistering language – at the same time paying the highest compliments to American abolitionists'.[13] His relationship with Haydon was less rapturous: when the artist visited him in London in February 1841 to paint his sketch they discussed politics and religion. Haydon found in him 'a keen, lynx look, and a great good nature, but cunning & trick[y]'. Although they agreed to differ over religion, the Irishman's less than respectful comments on whether Wellington had been 'wounded in the bum in Spain' made the painter want to 'put my fist in his face'.[14]

Ireland in court

The Hayter and Haydon canvases represent what one art historian has called 'an uneasy coalition of group portraiture and history painting'. Ironically, given the fact that Haydon spent a year on his picture and lost a lot of money on its exhibition, he went on to criticise such large group paintings, saying that 'The Time is fast coming

when we shall get sick of these bastard "High Art Works".[15] He was right. Such a
time may not have been imminent but, jumping almost fifty years and turning to
Charles Stewart Parnell, that other great Irish parliamentarian in London in the
nineteenth century, a series of decidedly non-'High Art Works' record an important
Irish political event in pencil, on the pages of a popular illustrated journal.

Portraiture is not only the preserve of the elite. On the contrary, any discussion
of it as an artistic genre must involve exploring the full range of output, rich
and poor, known and unknown. As we have seen with political portraits since the
eighteenth century, representation in both Dublin and London was visually mixed,
from the grand oil exhibited at a public exhibition to an appearance in a popular
journal. In the case of Daniel O'Connell, portraiture played a vital role in his own
development; and also, more importantly, that of a growing Irish presence in
London. But in analysing the Irish face it is important that we draw upon a wider
array of Irish portraits.[16]

In turning to the representation of Irish witnesses at the hearings of the Special
Commission on Parnellism and Crime as they appeared in the *Graphic*, an illustrated
London journal published between autumn 1888 and autumn 1889 (fig.122), a new
type of personage enters our discussion. In the nineteenth century the ordinary
Irishman and woman appear for the first time. The line drawings to be discussed
here are the work of the journalistic illustrator Sydney Prior Hall (1842–1922), who
sat through the interminably long speeches of the Special Commission held at the
Royal Courts of Justice on London's Strand. Hall produced hundreds of pencil
drawings, many of which appeared within days of execution on the pages of the
Graphic. A highly-paid draughtsman whose coverage of royal tours and the like had
brought him considerable renown, Hall's drawings for the Parnell Commission
have been referred to by one historian of printing as 'quite outstanding'.[17]

Parnell had been accused, in a series of special articles in *The Times*, of being associated with intimidation and of sanctioning murder connected with the activities of
the National League, founded some years earlier to alleviate the plight of the Irish
rural tenantry from the dominance of landlords. *The Times*, with the support of the
ruling Conservative party led by the Prime Minister, Lord Salisbury, also wished to
taint the reputation of Gladstone's Liberals by allying them with terrorism. The
newspaper had run three articles on the topic of 'Parnellism and Crime', starting in
March 1887. Within a month, three facsimile letters were reproduced in the newspaper suggesting that Parnell was implicated in the Phoenix Park murders in Dublin
in 1882, when Lord Frederick Cavendish, the Irish Chief Secretary, and his assistant
had been brutally assassinated. Parnell called for an inquiry into the allegations but
the government chose to set up a special commission.[18]

Over the course of a year and 128 days of hearings, more than 450 witnesses
appeared in Probate Court Number 1, answering almost 100,000 questions. The

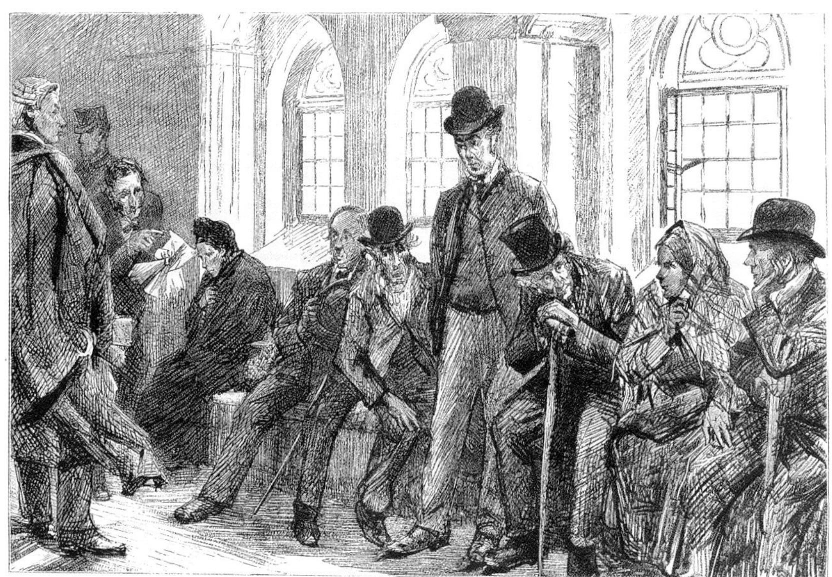

122. **The Parnell Commission:
Irish Peasants Subpoenaed by
the 'Times'**
SYDNEY PRIOR HALL
Wood engraving from the
Graphic, 17 November 1888,
page 293 × 114mm (11½ × 4½")
National Portrait Gallery, London

Commission came to a dramatic crux in February 1889, when the letters were proved to be forgeries and Parnell was vindicated. At the same time he was also wounded by the unfounded allegations of involvement with intimidation and rural violence, and this is where the testimony of the Irish peasantry was particularly important. Nothing tangible was proven against Parnell or his fellow Irish Members of Parliament, but the stories of secret societies and murder told by the Irish witnesses fascinated the court and the public at large. Indeed, at the start of the proceedings in November 1888 the *Graphic* referred to its own coverage as being of interest to the 'idle sensation-loving public'.[19]

One of Sydney Prior Hall's earliest drawings illustrated in the *Graphic* is *Irish Peasants Subpoenaed by the 'Times'* (fig.122). Occupying one-third of a page in the journal, it shows a man labelled 'The Next Witness' who has just stood up to go into court at London's Royal Courts of Justice, to testify against Parnell and his Parliamentary Party.[20] These Irish peasants had been brought over from rural Ireland to give their accounts of intimidation, brutality and sometimes murder perpetrated by the supporters of the Land League and, by association, Charles Stewart Parnell. These transplanted country folk are wide-eyed and open-mouthed, while also respectful of the pseudo-Gothic corridor in which they wait. But the illustrations in the *Graphic* carry a range of portrait vignettes of an otherwise unseen Irish: this column of witnesses is not typical. A more usual ploy used by Hall was to name his subject as he or she appeared in the witness box, providing an unrivalled array of as authentic a range of portraits as one could hope to assemble: drawn in court, only feet away from the artist, named, recorded and then reproduced in the pages of a leading metropolitan journal. Hall does not, of course, focus on the Irish peasantry alone. All those who appeared in court are represented, from prominent defendants such as Parnell himself (fig.129) to the three presiding judges, the various

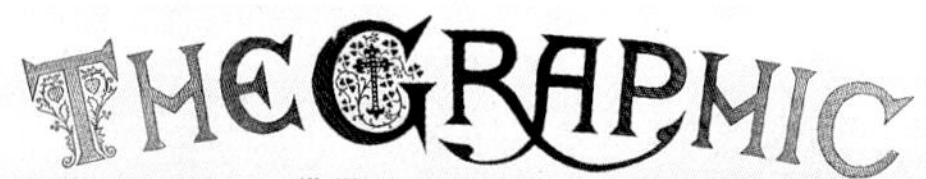

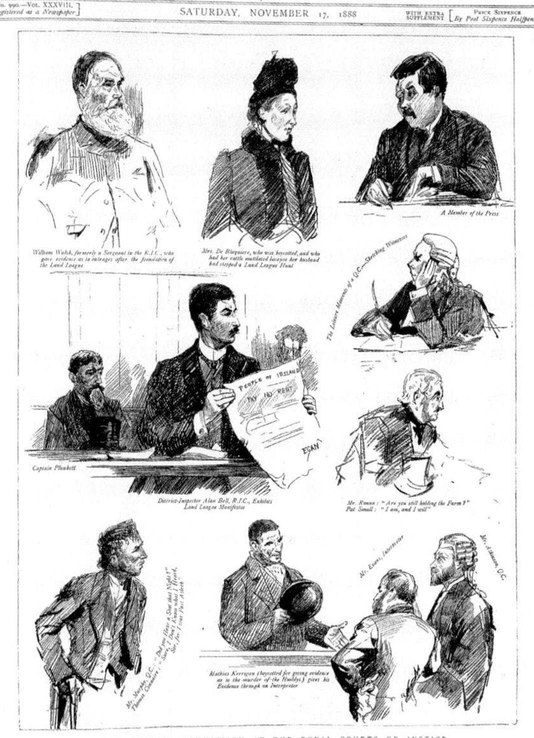

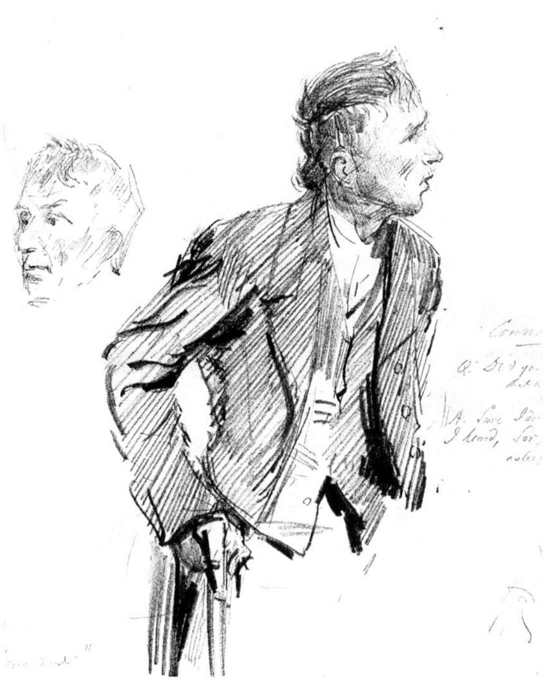

123. **The Parnell Commission**
SYDNEY PRIOR HALL
Wood engraving from the *Graphic*, 17 November 1888,
page 293 × 114mm (11½ × 4½")
National Portrait Gallery, London

124. **The Parnell Commission: Thomas Connaire**
SYDNEY PRIOR HALL (1888)
Pencil on paper, 252 × 200mm (9⅞ × 7⅞")
National Gallery of Ireland, Dublin

Queen's Counsels and their junior Counsels, District Inspectors and innumerable witnesses and members of the audience. Fig.123 illustrates a full page from the *Graphic* of 17 November 1888: in the centre left a District Inspector named Alan Bell exhibits evidence, while above, Mrs de Blaquiere, a middle-class woman who was boycotted, tells of her ordeal. Below, a trio of vignettes show three Irish peasants in discussion with their legal interrogators: the sharp-featured Pat Small (centre right) shows his determination to hold his farm, while Mathias Kerrigan, being an Irish speaker, answers questions through an interpreter. In the bottom left, Thomas Connaire (also spelt Connair), a tenant of Sir Henry Burke at Shrahananta, County Galway, creates some amusement by admitting, as the caption informs us, that he was fast asleep when he heard some shots fired at his house. In Hall's original drawing of Connaire, now in the National Gallery of Ireland (fig.124), the artist annotated the sheet with this humorous exchange: the curved caption that wraps itself around Hall's illustration in the *Graphic* abbreviates an even fuller account of this exchange with the QC for *The Times* newspaper elsewhere in the journal.[21]

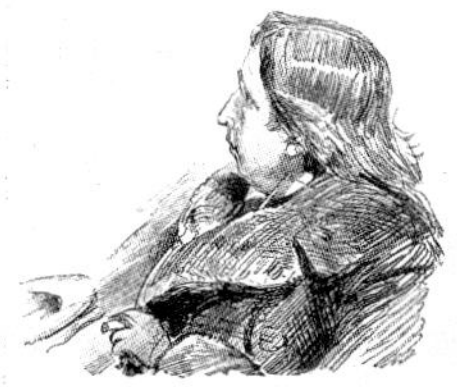

THE PARNELL COMMISSION

MAJOR LE CARON, otherwise Beach, is decidedly the most interesting witness who has hitherto appeared before the Commission, and the reproduction of much of his evidence by the Irish-American newspapers shows that it is considered to be important in revolutionary circles on the other side of the Atlantic. On Thursday, February 7th, the Major's examination-in-chief was concluded. Several noteworthy items were elicited. The United Brotherhood in America decided to provide for the family of one Lomasney, who, with another, was, it is said, killed in trying to blow up London Bridge. Patrick Egan and Brennan (the latter of whom was walking in the Strand with the present Lord Mayor of Dublin when he first learnt his danger) very narrowly escaped being arrested. If Gallagher had had forty-eight hours more in London, some of the best buildings would have been blown up. "Though French by name and descent, he has ever proved himself one of the most devoted friends of the Irish national cause." These were the generous terms (they aroused some laughter in Court) in which Patrick Egan introduced "my friend, the Major," formerly T. W. Beach, of Colchester, to his brother-Leaguers in the Southern States of America. It was not until 3.35 P.M. that Sir C. Russell's cross-examination began. The witness rapped out his answers with a sharp metallic twang. He was first questioned about his previous career. He had been a clerk and draper's assistant both in this country and in France. He

MR. OSCAR WILDE IN COURT

went to America in 1861, and at once joined the Federal Army, in which he served throughout the Civil War. In 1865 he became a member of the Fenian organisation, which, he frankly declared, he entered with the view of ascertaining its secrets and betraying them. He never had any sympathy with their cause, and regarded himself as a military spy, who was acting as he did for the good of his country. Since 1868 he had sent hundreds and even thousands of despatches to the British Government, but for the first three years of his espionage he had received no remuneration for his services. Some squabbling subsequently arose among the counsel engaged respecting these documents, from which, for the purposes of the trial, a selection had been made by the Major aided by Mr. Houston, Secretary to the Irish Loyal and Patriotic Union. Sir Charles Russell demanded power to inspect all these documents. Sir H. James demurred to this, but undertook to look through the papers, to see if there were any others relevant to the issue. On Friday, February 8th, many questions were put to Major Le Caron for the purpose of establishing the fact that many respectable Americans (often of other than Irish origin) countenanced the meetings of the League and other similar organisations. For the proceedings of the Court during the present week the reader is referred to our "Legal" column.

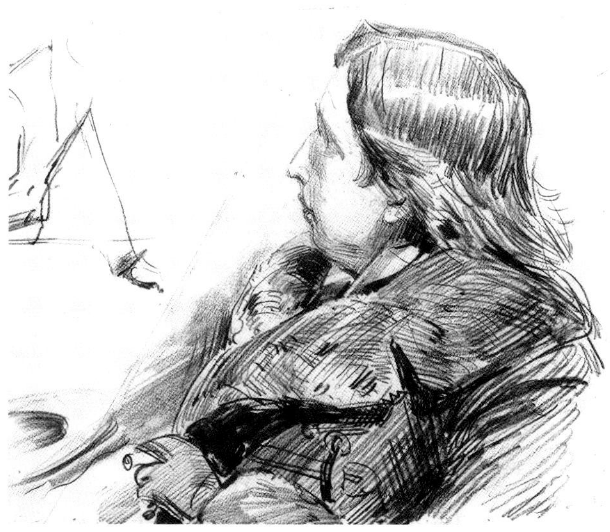

125. **The Parnell Commission: Oscar Wilde** (1856–1900)
SYDNEY PRIOR HALL
Wood engraving from the *Graphic*, 16 February 1888,
page 293 × 114mm (11½ × 4½")
National Portrait Gallery, London

126. **The Parnell Commission: Oscar Wilde** (1856–1900)
SYDNEY PRIOR HALL (1889)
Pencil on paper, 172 × 204mm (6¾ × 8")
National Portrait Gallery, London (NPG 2265)

A surprising cross-section of elite society went to the Royal Courts of Justice to hear the proceedings of the Parnell Commission: ambassadors, prominent politicians and leading celebrities. Parnell's compatriot Oscar Wilde (figs 125 and 126) was spotted by Hall in February 1889, while he also drew Sir Edward Burne Jones, William Gladstone and many others. Wilde attended the Commission on a number of occasions with his brother, Willie, who wrote articles on Parnell's behalf in the *Daily Chronicle*." In Hall's drawing Oscar Wilde appears highly attentive to the proceedings, yet it can also be said that the original sketch, pencilled on a single sheet of paper now in the National Portrait Gallery, focuses on the writer's individualism, his beautifully profiled head, his flowing hair and fur-lined collar. By contrast, the line-drawing of Wilde in the *Graphic* (fig.125) is placed in the centre of a long column describing the testimony of the government spy Thomas Miller Beach ('Major Le Caron'). Wilde himself does not feature in the text; he is but an element of a larger design.

What is of particular interest and relevance to Ireland is that apart from sketching Wilde, Hall also drew a range of otherwise ordinary Irish men and women to be reproduced in the pages of the *Graphic*. Although ostensibly pressed to attend the Commission in order to speak against Parnell, such individuals had not been represented so publicly before. Sydney Prior Hall's original drawings for the Parnell Commission are now in the possession of the National Portrait Gallery in London and the National Gallery of Ireland in Dublin. In the late 1920s, when the artist's son decided to bequeath the drawings to the London Gallery, it was thought appropriate, given the founding remit of the National Portrait Gallery, that London receive only the drawings of the prominent individuals such as Oscar Wilde, or a series of well-observed sketches showing the famous figures involved in the evolving court drama. Dublin inherited the rest.[23]

The best drawings of Parnell himself were left to the National Portrait Gallery. In one sheet (fig.127), Hall captures the tension and excitement of the daily events as Parnell, dressed in an old coat, is accompanied by his solicitor, Sir George Henry Lewis. The two men, wonderfully framed by the arched entrance to the Courts of Justice (with its business as usual notice of 'Chambers to be Let') and absorbed in discussion, ignore the spy Major Le Caron, standing off to the right. The empty space between Le Caron and the central pair neatly captures the seismic gulf between the leader of the Irish Party and this government spy. Testifying against Parnell, Le Caron was revealed as having been 'at the heart of fenian and Clan na Gael activity in the U.S.A.' and had, in 'revolutionary guise [. . .] conferred with Parnell in the very palace of Westminster'.[24] In time, Le Caron's exposure would be one of the key events of the Commission.

Another drawing in the London collection (fig.128) shows the continuing tension inside the courtroom as Parnell's team are observed by '*The Times* party' (John Patrick Murphy and Sir Henry James) during the cross-examination of the forger Richard

127. **The Parnell Commission: Charles Stewart Parnell** (1846–91)**, Sir George Henry Lewis, 1st Baronet** (1833–1911) **and Thomas Miller Beach (Major Le Caron)** (1841–94)
SYDNEY PRIOR HALL (1889)
Pencil on paper, 292 × 457mm (11½ × 18″)
National Portrait Gallery, London (NPG 2244)

The National Portrait Gallery's acquisition of the Hall drawings was marked by an exhibition in 1929 and this drawing was reproduced on the cover of the *Graphic*, 24 August 1929, together with laudatory comment on Hall's 'lively sketches'.

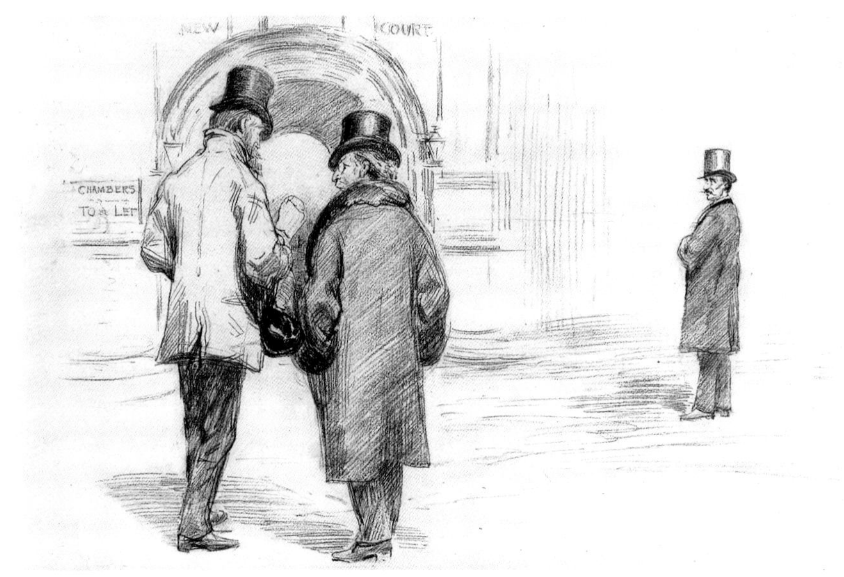

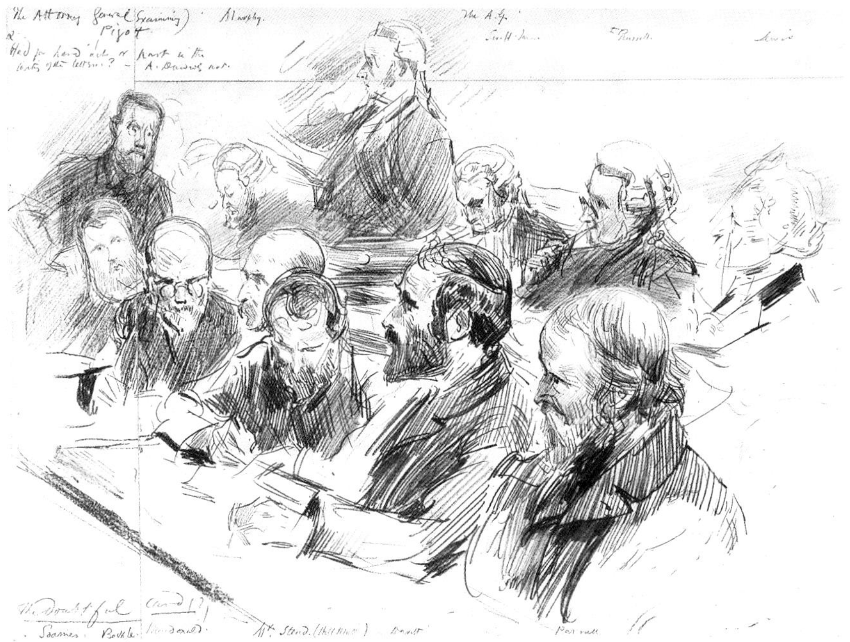

Pigott. Parnell sits in the foreground, his eyes apparently focused on the witness box, while to his right sits his fellow Irish Member of Parliament Michael Davitt (see also fig.43) and the London journalist William Thomas Stead.[25] Towards the end of the Commission, in May 1889, Hall produced a finely-wrought full-page portrait of Parnell in the witness box (fig.129) during his cross-examination.[26] The old coat and downcast look have been discarded (although not his ubiquitous black bag) in favour of a defiant stance as he answers questions from Sir Richard Webster, the Attorney-General. In these drawings, as in reality, Parnell triumphs. Yet ironically, by placing William J. Walsh, the Roman Catholic Archbishop of Dublin, directly behind Parnell, Hall unwittingly suggests a more potentially threatening but still silent prosecution: only six months later, when the details of Parnell's private life were finally revealed, it was the Irish bishops who turned on him so vehemently.

Hall's three-quarter-length drawing of Parnell, which he later turned into an oil (fig.130), shows an artist sympathetic to his subject. The posthumous oil portrait was clearly the artist's own idea, as he later confessed that 'Mr Parnell never consciously sat for me, but I sketched him for many hours in all sorts of poses'.[27] Such sympathy may later have led Hall's son, a curator of Egyptian and Assyrian Antiquities at the British Museum, to give Dublin a huge collection of over 300 drawings relating to the Commission. Although Parnell features in many of them, they are largely portraits of the 'unspectacular' Irish. A page from the *Graphic* for 8 December 1888 (fig.131) indicates the range of Hall's portrait drawings of the ordinary witnesses; it is important to note that the original pencil drawings for all of these images are in the Dublin collection.[28] Here, interspersed with advertisements for exhibitions and Mediterranean tours, we find an account of the Commission

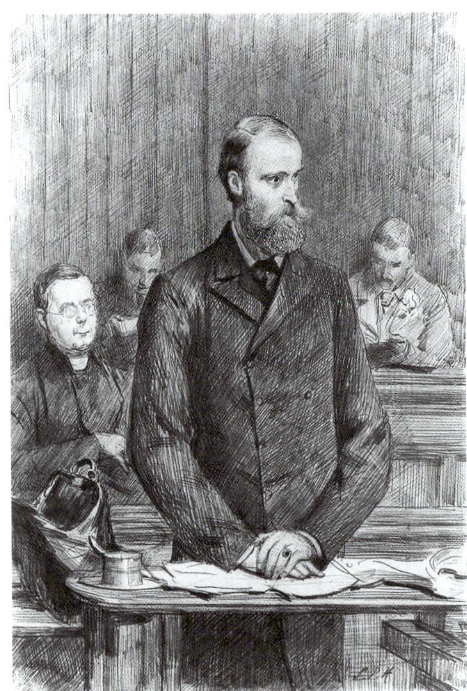

129. **The Parnell Commission: Group including Charles Stewart Parnell** (1846–91), **and William J. Walsh** (1841–1921)

 (1889)
Pencil on paper, 483 × 333mm (19 × 13⅛")
National Portrait Gallery, London (NPG 2229)

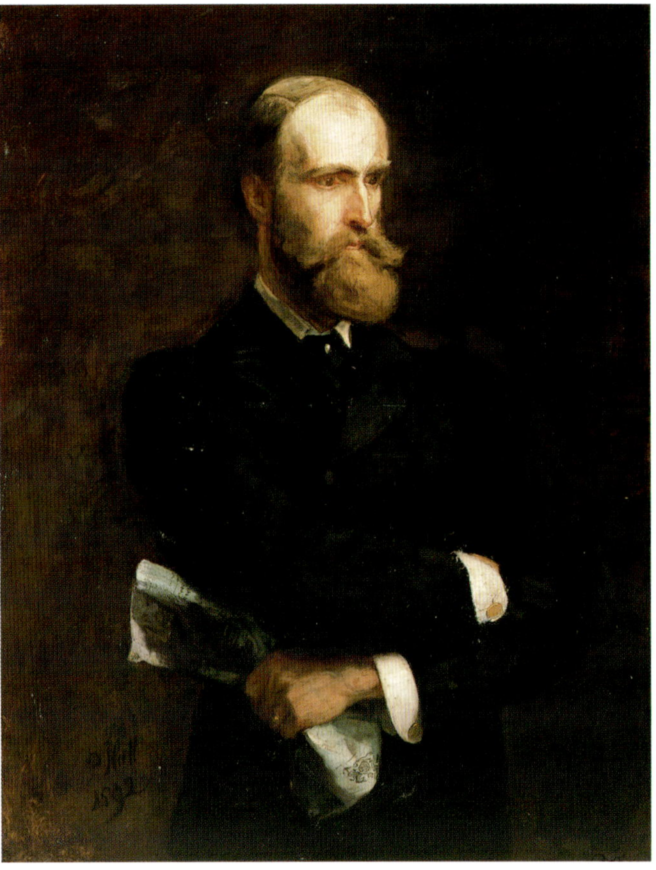

130. **Charles Stewart Parnell** (1842–1922)
 (1892)
Oil on canvas, 1120 × 860mm (44 × 33⅞")
National Gallery of Ireland, Dublin

In this portrait Parnell's head is clearly derived from Hall's drawings taken on the spot at the Royal Courts of Justice (see fig.129). Presumably, so as to convey determination and post-Special Commission vigour, Parnell crumples a sheet of parliamentary order papers which prominently displays the royal crest.

broken by no less than nine vignettes of victims of intimidation, all of whom had been subpoenaed to attend the court in London to speak against Parnell. Tenant farmers mix with shopkeepers and tell of their ordeals, while an ex-Moonlighter and the Rev. Canon Griffin from Castleisland, County Kerry, stand in the witness box and inform on the Land League. The textual accounts that surround them are straightforward: 'Pat Murphy' (whose portrait in profile appears at the bottom of the page) is described as 'a fine-looking white-haired man, who had part of his ear cut off, and had been boycotted for two years for taking an evicted farm'. By contrast, Hall's drawing is sharply drawn and controlled, while Murphy's strong face and his confidently placed arm on the bar of the witness box convey a dignity new to the representation of the ordinary Irish in British nineteenth-century imagery.

SYDNEY PRIOR HALL

Wood engraving from the
Graphic, 8 December 1888,
page 293 × 114mm (11½ × 4½")
National Portrait Gallery,
London

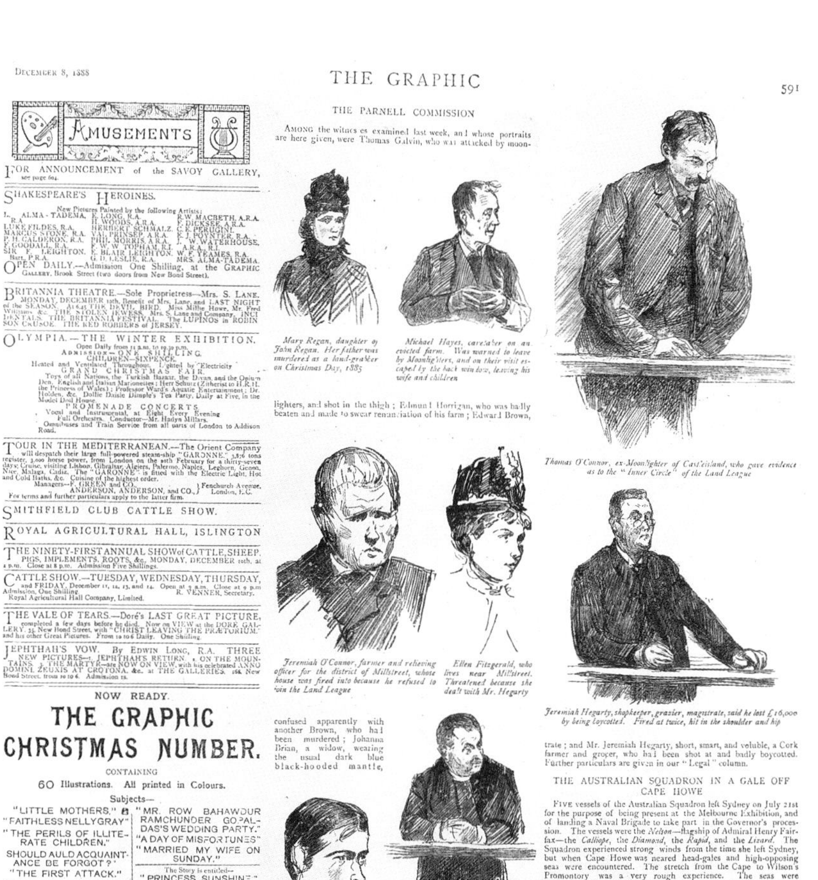

THE GRAPHIC

591

THE PARNELL COMMISSION

AMONG the witness examined last week, and whose portraits are here given, were Thomas Galvin, who was attacked by moon-

Mary Regan, daughter of John Regan. Her father was murdered as a land-grabber on Christmas Day, 1885

Michael Hayes, caretaker on an evicted farm. Was warned to leave by Moonlighters, and on their visit escaped by the back window, leaving his wife and children

lighters, and shot in the thigh; Edmund Horrigan, who was badly beaten and made to swear renunciation of his farm; Edward Brown,

Thomas O'Connor, ex-Moonlighter of Castleisland, who gave evidence as to the "Inner Circle" of the Land League

Jeremiah O'Connor, farmer and relieving officer for the district of Millstreet, whose house was fired into because he refused to join the Land League

Ellen Fitzgerald, who lives near Millstreet. Threatened because she dealt with Mr. Hegarty

Jeremiah Hegarty, shopkeeper, grazier, magistrate, said he lost £16,000 by being boycotted. Fired at twice, hit in the shoulder and hip

confused apparently with another Brown, who had been murdered; Johanna Brian, a widow, wearing the usual dark blue black-hooded mantle,

Cornelius Kelleher, beaten by Moonlighters because he worked for Mr. Hegarty

Rev. Cannon Griffin, a Castleisland priest who was opposed to the Land League

Patrick Murphy, who took a farm from which Widow Lennahar was evicted. His house was visited by Moonlighters; he was beaten, fired at, and had part of his ear cut off

whose husband was murdered by Poff and Barrett, who were afterwards hanged for it; Maurice Kennedy, a farmer at Enniskillen, whose horse had been mutilated because he had bought hay at a boycotted auction; John Kennedy, whose voluble mutterings were only understood by Mr. Atkinson, himself an Irishman; and Daniel Cronin, an old man who had been shot in the legs for paying his rent. Next day (Thursday), the witnesses were Jeremiah Sullivan, whose house was attacked because his wife had paid part of the rent; Pat Murphy, a fine-looking white-haired man, who had had part of his ear cut off, and been boycotted for two years for taking an evicted farm; and Mary Regan, John M'Auliffe, and Michael Hayes, who respectively gave evidence of sundry outrages. On Friday, the witnesses were persons of a higher social grade namely, Mr. Samuel Hussey, for thirty-seven years a Kerry magistrate; and Mr. Jeremiah Hegarty, short, smart, and voluble, a Cork farmer and grocer, who had been shot at and badly boycotted. Further particulars are given in our "Legal" column.

THE AUSTRALIAN SQUADRON IN A GALE OFF CAPE HOWE

FIVE vessels of the Australian Squadron left Sydney on July 21st for the purpose of being present at the Melbourne Exhibition, and of landing a Naval Brigade to take part in the Governor's procession. The vessels were the *Nelson*—flagship of Admiral Henry Fairfax—the *Calliope*, the *Diamond*, the *Rapid*, and the *Lizard*. The Squadron experienced strong winds from the time she left Sydney, but when Cape Howe was neared head-gales and high-opposing seas were encountered. The stretch from the Cape to Wilson's Promontory was a very rough experience. The seas were stupendous, and the *Rapid* and the *Diamond* each lost a boat, washed off the davits by the violence of the waves. After passing the promontory the weather moderated, and the Squadron anchored inside Port Phillip Heads off Queenscliffe on the night of July 25th, with the exception of the *Rapid*, which had been left lying-to during the heavy weather, but she joined her consorts next day, when all the vessels proceeded to Hobson's Bay.

A CRUISE IN THE MEDITERRANEAN ON BOARD THE STEAM-YACHT "VICTORIA." XI.

THE PROPER THING TO DO AT GIBRALTAR

THE altitude of the Rock of Gibraltar is great; equally so is the heat of the sun during the small hours of the afternoon, while the energy of the hero of these sketches is small. It is, perhaps, rather shabby behaviour to give a friend the ship who is providing for your amusement; but then, some friends will not take a refusal, and leave no loophole for escape save in such a proceeding. We must, however, lament that there is any one who could find greater satisfaction in idly promenading, and endeavouring to what is vulgarly termed "mash" the fair portion of the promenaders, than in serious contemplation of the work of science in the galleries and the work of Nature from the summit of the Rock.

THE BATTLE OF KOTKAI

THIS sharply-contested action was fought on October 5th. The general advance of the Black Mountain Expedition was made on October 3rd, and the Fourth Column of the force, under the command of the late Colonel Crookshank, was ordered to advance upon and take Kotkai, a rocky stronghold, lying between mountain spurs on the Indus, about fifteen miles north from Darband and the same distance west of Oghi, whence the main portion of the Expedition started. Kotkai had previously been destroyed in the Expedition of 1852-3. Our troops consisted of the Royal Irish Regiment, 14th Punjab Infantry, the 29th Punjab Infantry's Headquarters' wing, and 241 men of the Scottish Division Royal Artillery, and met with some opposition from the enemy, which consisted of the Hassanzais, a branch of the Yusufzais, a section of the Pathans. After the Royal Irish had carried the enemy's position, about two miles from Kotkai some Ghazi fanatics delivered a countercharge, but were repulsed and killed to a man. On our side Captain Beley, one native officer, two privates of the Royal Irish Regiment, and one sepoy were killed, two officers and twelve men being wounded.

DECEMBER 8, 1888

AMUSEMENTS

FOR ANNOUNCEMENT of the SAVOY GALLERY, see page 604.

SHAKESPEARE'S HEROINES.

New Pictures Painted by the following Artists: L. ALMA-TADEMA, R.A., E. LONG, R.A., R.W. MACBETH, A.R.A., LUKE FILDES, R.A., H. WOODS, A.R.A., F. DICKSEE, A.R.A., MARCUS STONE, R.A., HERBERT SCHMALZ, C.E. PERUGINI, P.H. CALDERON, R.A., VAL PRINSEP, A.R.A., E.J. POYNTER, R.A., F. GOODALL, R.A., PHIL MORRIS, A.R.A., J.W. WATERHOUSE, A.R.A., R.I., SIR F. LEIGHTON, Bart., P.R.A., F.W.W. TOPHAM, R.I., F. BLAIR LEIGHTON, W.F. YEAMES, R.A., G.D. LESLIE, R.A., MRS. ALMA-TADEMA. OPEN DAILY.—Admission One Shilling, at the GRAPHIC Gallery, Brook Street (two doors from New Bond Street).

BRITANNIA THEATRE.—Sole Proprietress—Mrs. S. LANE. MONDAY, DECEMBER 10th, Benefit of Mrs. Lane, and LAST NIGHT of the SEASON. At 6.45 THE DEVIL BIRD. Miss Millie Howe, Mr. Fred Williams &c. THE STOLEN JEWESS, Mrs. S. Lane and Company, INCIDENTALS. THE BRITANNIA FESTIVAL. The LUPINOS in ROBINSON CRUSOE. THE RED ROBBERS of JERSEY.

OLYMPIA.—THE WINTER EXHIBITION. Open Daily from 11 a.m. to 10.30 p.m. ADMISSION—ONE SHILLING. CHILDREN—SIXPENCE. Heated and Ventilated Throughout. Lighted by Electricity GRAND CHRISTMAS FAIR. Toys of all Nations, the Turkish Bazaar, the Divan, and the Opium Den, English and Italian Marionettes; Herr Schutz (Zitherist to H.R.H. the Princess of Wales); Professor Ward's Aquatic Entertainment; Dr. Holden, &c. Dollie Daisie Dimple's Tea Party, Daily at Five, in the Model Doll House. PROMENADE CONCERTS Vocal and Instrumental, at Eight Every Evening Full Orchestra. Conductor—Mr. Hadyn Millars. Omnibuses and Train Service from all parts of London to Addison Road.

TOUR IN THE MEDITERRANEAN.—The Orient Company will despatch their large full-powered steam-ship "GARONNE." 3,876 tons register, 3,000 horse power, from London on the 20th February for a thirty-seven days' Cruise, visiting Lisbon, Gibraltar, Algiers, Palermo, Naples, Leghorn, Genoa, Nice, Malaga, Cadiz. The "GARONNE" is fitted with the Electric Light, Hot and Cold Baths, &c. Cuisine of the highest order. Managers—F. GREEN and CO., ANDERSON, ANDERSON, and CO., Fenchurch Avenue, London, E.C. For terms and further particulars apply to the latter firm.

SMITHFIELD CLUB CATTLE SHOW.

ROYAL AGRICULTURAL HALL, ISLINGTON

THE NINETY-FIRST ANNUAL SHOW of CATTLE, SHEEP, PIGS, IMPLEMENTS, ROOTS, &c., MONDAY, DECEMBER 10th, at 1 p.m. Close at 8 p.m. Admission Five Shillings.

CATTLE SHOW.—TUESDAY, WEDNESDAY, THURSDAY, and FRIDAY, December 11, 12, 13, and 14. Open at 9 a.m. Close at 9 p.m. Admission, One Shilling. R. VENNER, Secretary. Royal Agricultural Hall Company, Limited.

THE VALE OF TEARS.—Doré's LAST GREAT PICTURE, completed a few days before he died. Now on VIEW at the DORÉ GALLERY, 35 New Bond Street, with "CHRIST LEAVING THE PRÆTORIUM." and his other Great Pictures. From 10 to 6 Daily. One Shilling.

JEPHTHAH'S VOW. By EDWIN LONG, R.A. THREE NEW PICTURES—1, JEPHTHAH'S RETURN, 2, ON THE MOUNTAINS, 3, THE MARTYR—are NOW ON VIEW, with his celebrated ANNO DOMINI, ZEUXIS AT CROTONA, &c. at THE GALLERIES, 168, New Bond Street, from 10 to 6. Admission 1s.

NOW READY.

THE GRAPHIC CHRISTMAS NUMBER.

CONTAINING

60 Illustrations. All printed in Colours.

Subjects—

"LITTLE MOTHERS," "FAITHLESS NELLYGRAY," "THE PERILS OF ILLITERATE CHILDREN," SHOULD AULD ACQUAINTANCE BE FORGOT?" "THE FIRST ATTACK." "'TWIXT TWO WORLDS,"

"MR. ROW BAHAWDUR RAMCHUNDER GOPALDAS'S WEDDING PARTY." "A DAY OF MISFORTUNES" "MARRIED MY WIFE ON SUNDAY."

The Story is entitled—
"PRINCESS SUNSHINE," By Mrs. J. H. RIDDELL.

THERE ARE ALSO

Two Presentation Plates

From the Pictures of Shakespeare's Heroines in "The Graphic" Collection.

Sweet Anne Page,
By G. D. LESLIE, R.A.
"The dinner is on the table; my father desires your worships company."

Juliet,
By P. H. CALDERON, R.A.
"O Romeo, Romeo! Wherefore art thou Romeo?"

Price One Shilling; by Parcels Post 3d. extra.

190, STRAND, LONDON.

NOTICE.——*With this Number is issued an EXTRA COLOURED SUPPLEMENT, entitled "LOVE THE CAPTIVE," from the Picture by Angelica Kauffmann.*

Our Illustrations

THE CHINESE SQUADRON UNDER SAIL.

"My sketch," writes an officer, "represents four ships of the Squadron making their way across the Sea of Japan to the Siberian coast without the aid of steam. In this age of mastless ships, such a reminiscence of the old days is interesting, as in a few years the spectacle of a fleet of men-o'-war under sail with fires banked and screws hoisted will be impossible, and the old tea cries of 'Helm a lee' and 'Mains'l haul,' as the ship is put about, will be heard no more in the Royal Navy. The sister-corvettes the *Constance* and the *Cordelia* are leading the way, and very lively craft they are in anything of a seaway."

Prominent individuals such as W.B. Yeats and Oscar Wilde, and many others, have all been discussed in terms of their positions as displaced Irish in London.[29] But what of the thousands of other Irish men and women who took the Holyhead boat in the second half of the nineteenth century? Much has been written about the Irish diaspora in England and the post-Famine hordes who occupied ghastly tenements in St Giles, Holborn and similar London locations.[30] The visual representations of these displaced populations are at best generic types, whether in negative images such as those perpetrated by *Punch* or more benign references to the post-Famine poor, such as those that appear in Ford Madox Brown's painting *Work* (City of Manchester Art Galleries) that dates from 1852–63.[31] By definition such generic types do not represent real people. The importance of Hall's illustrations in the *Graphic* is that he names his subjects and they are individualized, their stories retold both in the journal itself and in the multi-volumed official records of the Commission.

John Macdonald, a journalist for the London *Daily News* reporting on the Parnell Commission, saw the proceedings in stark terms. 'Ireland is in the Strand', he wrote:

> and behind the light and play of her contemporary life looms, perpetually, a dark background . . . This is a legal trial. It is also the *viva voce* history of a people – one of the dreariest, saddest histories in the world. And when one listens to it, one feels, with something like despair, how little Englishmen know of this mournful Ireland, which is only twelve hours journey from London.[32]

Macdonald may well have been indulging in hyperbole, but the fact remains that Ireland was on trial in the Strand for almost a year from late 1888 to late 1889. The *Daily News* was thus not exaggerating the appeal of the Special Commission. In also suggesting that the history of Ireland was on trial, it was only repeating a well-worn trope of the nineteenth century that Ireland was permanently in the dock. Equally, in drawing his spirited vignettes of the Commission's participants and audience, Sydney Prior Hall was also perpetuating a visual tradition that had started almost a hundred years earlier with the trials of the rebel republicans Wolfe Tone (1798; fig.98) and Robert Emmet (1803; figs 132 and 133). These images, like Hall's, are supposedly based on drawings made while the accused stood in the dock.

Rebels in the dock

The image of Wolfe Tone (fig.98), discussed in Chapter 4 (pp.156–7), shows him at his trial in 1798 in full ceremonial uniform, dignified and assured of his position as a member of the French army. Yet it is also quite a crude piece of imagery and was quickly produced for the *Hibernian Magazine* within the same month as Tone's court appearance. By contrast, Robert Emmet's head by John Comerford (fig.132) of a few years later is a very sophisticated miniature produced by a highly experienced artist who, as a recent historian has suggested, 'was particularly adept at painting the fashionable windswept men's hairstyles current in the early years of the nineteenth century'.[33] Comerford's watercolour on ivory miniature shows a sharply profiled young man whom the artist observed in the dock at Dublin's Green Street Court House. Emmet's abortive rebellion of 1803 occurred only five years after the far bloodier outbreak of 1798, but unlike the earlier event, this one centred round the youthful figure of Emmet, the son of a Dublin physician.[34] Comerford's miniature is a later reworking of a sketch made in court. Possibly commissioned by his brother-in-law, the radical barrister Robert Holmes, Emmet's profiled head with hair brushed forward in the French revolutionary style soon took on iconic status, just like the comparable images of his rebellious predecessor, Lord Edward FitzGerald (figs 101 and 111).[35]

Apart from Comerford, a number of other artists produced images of Emmet at his trial on 19 September 1803. James Petrie, father to the more famous artist and antiquarian George, produced drawings not only of Emmet himself but also of the presiding judge, Lord Norbury, and various lawyers, and at least one of the judicial benches.[36] Another leading Dublin artist/engraver, Henry Brocas Senior, was commissioned by the Government to attend the trial and makes sketches of Emmet. The result is a profiled head, remarkably similar to Comerford's miniature, made:

> at an early hour and not later than ten o'clock, when the blank wall of the
> court room to the right of Emmet was yet bright from reflected light which
> showed his erect figure in bold relief, emphasizing his freshness of bodily
> vigor and defiant air.

While at work Brocas stood about twelve feet to the west of the prisoner, several feet below him at the corner of the dock, and a little behind him. As a friend of the Government and once employed for this purpose, he was able to work to the best advantage.[37]

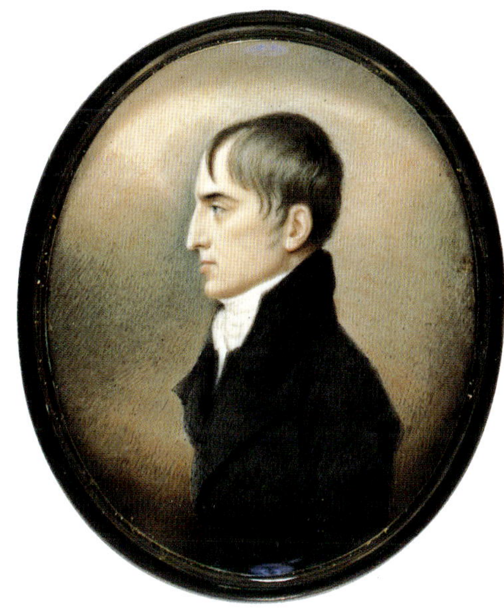

132. **Robert Emmet** (1778–1803)
JOHN COMERFORD (1803)
Watercolour on ivory,
69 × 57mm (2¾ × 2¼")
National Gallery of Ireland, Dublin

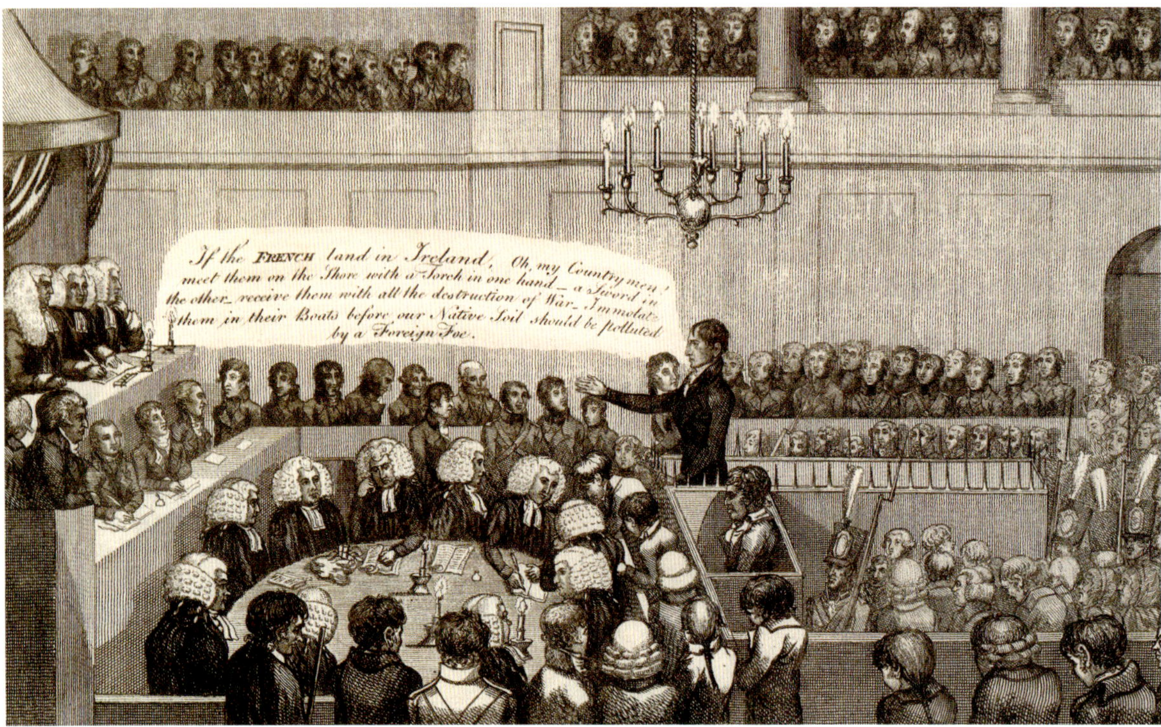

133. **The Speech from the Dock by Robert Emmet** (1778–1803) **at his Trial, 19 September 1803**

Line engraving, 218 × 325mm
(8½ × 12¾")
National Library of Ireland, Dublin

Brocas's government connection meant that his portrait of Emmet was reused, immediately after Emmet's execution, in a Government broadside showing the rebel at his trial, apparently speaking against the French and ridiculing a possible French invasion (fig.133). Instead of the memorable passage from his much-reported speech, in which Emmet requested that his epitaph not be written until 'my country takes her place among the nations of the earth', a crude balloon of words comes from the prisoner's mouth. 'Immolate them in their Boats', he says, 'before our Native Soil should be polluted by a Foreign foe'. A century later, Emmet's great-nephew, Thomas Addis Emmet, published a two-volume account of his illustrious kinsman, referring to this broadside in emotive, anti-British, terms:

> The issue of the large broadside by the Government was a most important political move and their sagacious trick in printing a false report of Emmet's speech was the means of quickly changing the whole prospect of Ireland by breaking up all good feeling between United Irishmen and the French Government.[38]

In fact, the reported words in the Brocas broadside were not false but taken out of context. As Marianne Elliott has suggested, Emmet 'was not proclaiming a rupture with France; he was simply qualifying a standing invitation . . . Ireland was willing and able to win her own independence without exchanging one foreign tyranny for another'.[39]

In time these court-based images resounded throughout the nineteenth-century Irish visual imagination. In 1872 the iconic status of Robert Emmet was demonstrated by the display of Comerford's miniature at the Dublin Exhibition. Due to the small size of the object and its 'precious' aspect 'to his kindred in the United States', the then owner of the ivory, Hon. Judge Robert Emmet, the rebel's nephew (and father of the author of the above cited memoir), offered to exhibit a photograph of the miniature 'on an enlarged scale' which he assured was an accurate recording of his uncle's likeness: 'features', he wrote, that 'never have been, and never can be effaced from my memory'. But luckily for Dublin, Henry Doyle, then Director of the National Gallery of Ireland, seems to have prevailed on the Emmet family in New York and the original was on display by late June 1872. As we learned in Chapter 1 (p.34), 1872 was a busy year for Doyle as only a few months later he was attempting (eventually unsuccessfully) to extract financial aid from the Treasury in London for Dublin's fledgling National Portrait Gallery. But with the Emmet miniature he was successful and he told the readers of the *Irish Times* that it was visible 'on the walls of the National Portrait Gallery, in the corridor where I am sure it will be an object of great public interest'.[40]

As cultural artefacts of Irish nationalism that still resonated with the Irish public seventy years after the event, the various portraits of the captured Emmet are comparable to published anthologies such as Timothy Daniel Sullivan's 1867 collection, *Guilty or not Guilty?: Speeches from the Dock*. Many editions of this volume quickly followed, until the title was reduced to just *Speeches from the Dock* and its editorial team expanded to include two more Sullivan brothers, A.M. and D.B.[41] Recent discussion of popular nationalism in Ireland in the second half of the nineteenth century has reminded us of the immense contemporary success of one of those Sullivans, the Cork journalist and politician Alexander Martin Sullivan (1830–84), whose *Story of Ireland* first appeared in 1867. Roy Foster states that Sullivan 'helped create the popular Irish concept of nationalism through his newspaper the *Nation* and his oft reprinted *Speeches*'.[42] In the latter, the Sullivans included orations by a wide variety of speakers, from Tone and Emmet to a raft of Young Irelanders and future Fenians such as John Mitchel (fig.134), Terence Bellew McManus (fig.135) and John O'Leary (figs 37–9). It has also been suggested that in organising their pantheon the Sullivans orchestrated their biographical details around 'the social status, education and background of the heroes. All of them were men of independent means and good education.' Excluding the peasant witnesses to the Parnell Commission, such 'eloquent patriotism' is also a key aspect of the visual trope of the Irish in the dock.[43]

More felons

In Ireland today the circulation of images of political prisoners from both sides of the cultural divide is a fairly common phenomenon. Twenty or so years ago photographs, painted portraits and wall murals depicting the emaciated form of the IRA hunger striker Bobby Sands were much in evidence. More recently, newspaper photographs of a newly released Unionist paramilitary leader following the edicts of the Good Friday Agreement enable us to confront the face of the terrorist in a very immediate way. The circulation of portraits of 'state prisoners', as such men were called in the nineteenth century, is not at all new, but rather a present-day manifestation of an old tradition.

Edward Chandler, the historian of Irish nineteenth-century photography, has shown that the entrepreneurial studio of Leone Glukman at 24 Upper Sackville Street, Dublin, exploited popular interest in Young Ireland prisoners such as John Mitchel (fig.134), William Smith O'Brien and Terence Bellew McManus (fig.135), following their aggressive anti-government journalism and then the dismal 'cabbage-patch' revolution of July 1848.[44] Glukman reproduced portraits of most of the imprisoned leaders, not as photographs but as lithographs based on daguerreotypes. It is entirely conceivable that, as many of the Young Ireland portraits 'carried facsimile signatures' as well as dedications to their friends, some of these daguerreotypes were actually 'taken in prison'. Chandler reproduces a lithographic portrait of Smith O'Brien, which is signed and dated 'Kilmainham Gaol, Aug 31. 1848', while the National Gallery of Ireland has two portraits of the younger rebel Terence Bellew McManus (fig.135), both of which carry named dedications. Glukman's daguerreotype was taken on 11 October 1848 as McManus stood in the dock at Clonmel Court House, while the lithograph sheets were addressed over the next couple of months, from Dublin's Richmond Prison, to Smith O'Brien and others.[45]

This circulation of portraits of prisoners was, of course, not all one-way: portraits of loved ones outside also entered the prison cell. In his famous *Jail Journal*, John Mitchel (fig.134) records how on 4 August 1848 he received 'a large trunk from home, with some clothes, a few books, and, what I value most highly, four exquisite coloured daguerreotypes of Gluckmann's [*sic*]'. Having been convicted for sedition, at the time of writing Mitchel was in a prison ship, *The Dromedary*, awaiting passage to Bermuda and thence to Van Diemen's Land (Tasmania). He describes the four daguerreotypes thus:

> my wife in profile, another has my mother and wife together; a third, John Martin, my staunch and worthy friend – by this time, I suppose, my fellow-felon. What a mild and benevolent looking felon! The convict Jesus was hardly purer, meeker, truer, more benignant than this man is. The fourth likeness illuminates my cell on the right mainly and noble countenance of Father Kenyon. He is

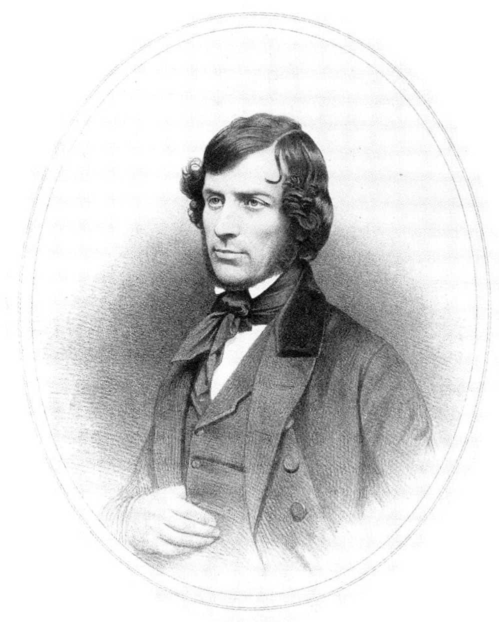

134. **John Mitchel** (1815–75)
M. and N. HANHART after LEONE GLUKMAN (1848)
Lithograph after a daguerreotype,
433 × 358mm (17 × 14")
National Gallery of Ireland, Dublin

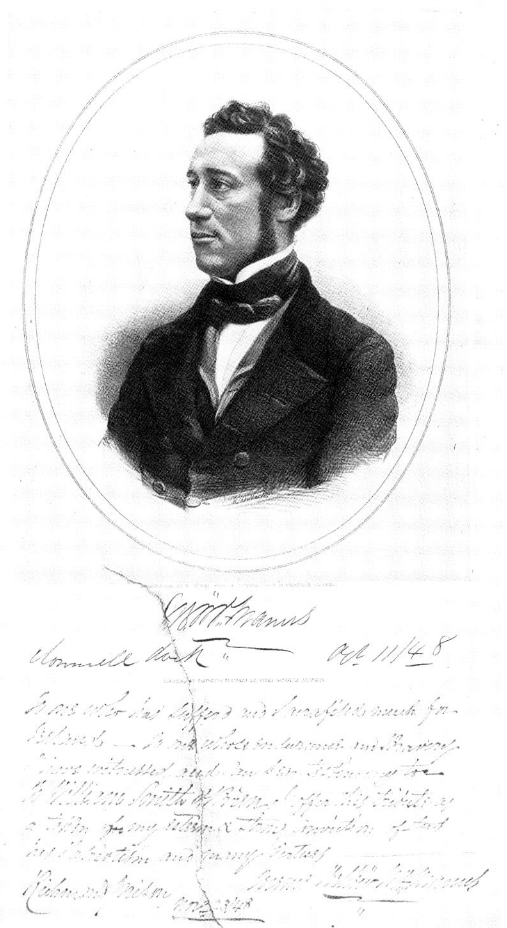

135. **Terence Bellew McManus** (1823–60)
HENRY O'NEILL after
LEONE GLUKMAN (1848)
Lithograph after a daguerreotype,
547 × 379mm (21½ × 15")
National Gallery of Ireland, Dublin

The original daguerreotype of this image was probably taken while the sitter was in the dock in Clonmel. The eventual lithograph reproduction carries a dedication later written by McManus while in Richmond Prison, Dublin, to his fellow Young Irelander, William Smith O'Brien (see note 45 for text of dedication).

standing with his arms folded, and a look of firmness, almost scornful defiance, but tempered and subdued, in his compressed lips and clear grey eye. Now, the speaking images of two such friends as there – to say nothing of the first two – will be high and choice companionship for me in my den. But what do they now? Where are they? How fare they?[46]

Some decades later, an equally limited circulation was accorded to the large number of Fenian convict photographs taken by the Dublin Castle authorities during the second half of the 1860s. These individual portraits of seated men show shopkeepers and farmers, as well as the occasional foreign mercenary or university student who had been arrested and charged with conspiracy. Some were later discharged, while others were sentenced to penal servitude.[47] Possibly restricted for security use, some of these prison photographs did in fact become collectors' items. The Samuel Lee Anderson Album is one such example, collected by an intelligence officer who operated out of Dublin Castle. Although it includes such Fenian luminaries as James Stephens and John O'Leary, its main focus is on members of secret societies like the Westmeath Ribbonmen who were held in Kilmainham Jail.

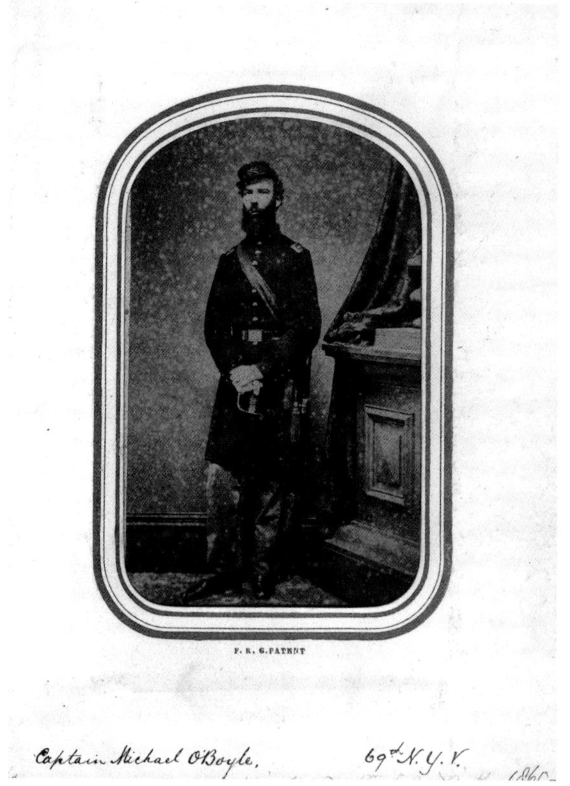

136. **Captain Michael O'Boyle**
Carte-de-visite (1865–6)
Albumen print on card,
image 86 × 55mm
(3⅜ × 2⅛")
National Library of Ireland,
Dublin

Another collection is that formed by Sir Thomas Larcom, Under-Secretary for Ireland from 1853 to 1868, who pasted portraits of Fenians into a scrapbook.[48]

At the same time that official convict images were being processed by the Castle authorities, photographs of the more elite members of the Fenian Brotherhood were available in sophisticated and commercially attractive forms. With advances in the collodion process of photography, the carte-de-visite had by the 1860s become as popular in Dublin as it was throughout most other major European cities. It is thus not surprising to find advertisements in the *Nation* in December 1865 for images of 'state prisoners' such as O'Leary, Charles J. Kickham and Jeremiah O'Donovan Rossa, the 'incarcerated scribes of [the Fenian newspaper] the *Irish People*', as one historian has called them.[49] The anonymous compiler of a small carte-de-visite album dating from the late 1860s, the so-called Fenian Album in the collection of the National Library of Ireland, is a good example of the new fashion for collecting such easily available images of prisoners and displaying them in manufactured pre-cut slots. As well as Stephens, Kickham and company, the Dublin album also carries images of American Fenians such as Captain Michael O'Boyle of the 69th New York Volunteers, dressed in the uniform of the Union Army (fig.136). The inclusion of a Fenian dressed as a participant in the recent American Civil War was highly significant because such a portrait carried with it the key Fenian values of social liberty and equality. With its tooled leather cover and brass clasps enclosing a gallery of national heroes, the Fenian Album mimics the contemporaneous family Bible. But instead of a sacred text the Irish album contains identified and dated portraits of prominent revolutionaries. The bound album was also a fashionable way to display a family's history. However, tradition and continuity are subverted in the Fenian Album by its collection of unlikely national heroes, many of whom at the time the album was being collated were serving harsh prison sentences in English jails such as Portland and Chatham.[50]

'High Treason'

Representations of the Irish in court, prison portraits and accounts of speeches from the dock had by the late 1880s and the Parnell Commission become potent visual symbols of Anglo-Irish relations and would continue as such well into the twentieth century. A final case in point, before we return to the Special Commission of 1888–9 in the Strand, is John Lavery's large court scene, *High Treason, Court of Criminal Appeal: The Trial of Roger Casement* (fig.137). Lavery's oil has none of the immediate and personal qualities of the Emmet imagery, nor does it suggest the camaraderie of the Young Ireland lithographic portraits. Equally, and despite its size, it does not present the array of figures of Sydney Prior Hall's drawings for the Parnell Commission. Casement's appeal against his conviction for high treason and his sentence of execution took place on 17–18 July 1916. Lavery, a well-established society painter, seems to have been encouraged to record the proceedings by Sir Charles Darling, the presiding judge at the appeal. On a very large scale, we are presented with painted reportage: Sergeant Sullivan KC from the Irish Bar, acting on Casement's behalf, stands on the right facing Justice Darling (in the centre, head raised in perfect profile). The painter sat in the unused jury box sketching the scene and apparently taking snapshots.[51] In the centre distance the prisoner sits, cross-armed behind bars, stoically listening to the proceedings. Everyone in the court is intent on what Sullivan is saying: heads turn, people listen and just above Casement, the clock goes on ticking and summer morning light falls on the Irishman in the dock.

Only a few months earlier Casement had been speedily removed from County Kerry, where he had landed from a German U-boat in an attempt to deter the eventual Easter Rising.[52] In Lavery's oil (fig.137) he is painted at a distance, and transformed into a hero. Despite the dramatic red of the judges (Darling included) on the left and the tall, black-gowned figure of Sullivan on the right, Casement is the focus of the painting. Framed as he is by iron bars, the prisoner draws the viewer's eye towards him and steadily meets our gaze. This visual connection between the prisoner and the viewer contradicts the focus of the moment being captured on canvas. Although Sullivan delivers his argument against the prosecution's use of the

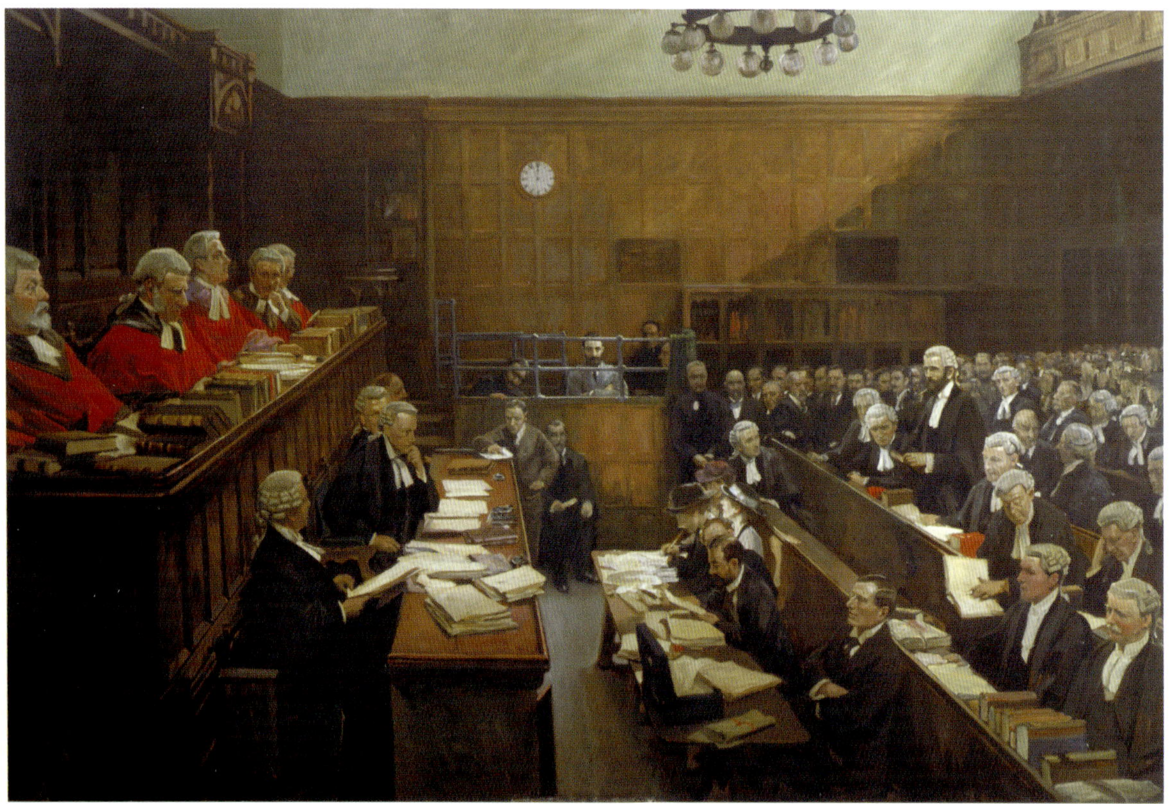

137. **High Treason, Court of Criminal Appeal: The Trial of Roger Casement** (1864–1916)
JOHN LAVERY (1916–1930s)
Oil on canvas, 2140 × 3220mm
(84¼ × 126¾")
Government Art Collection, London

Lavery's painting remained in the artist's studio until his death in 1941. After having been turned down by the National Portrait Gallery it was accepted by the Royal Courts of Justice, but was eventually placed on loan to the Honourable Society of King's Inns, Dublin, where it still hangs.

1351 Statute of Treason, we do not at first heed his words or concern ourselves with the judges' reactions: instead, we are compelled to stare at Casement in the dock. Years later, in 1937, W.B. Yeats was equally struck by this visual ploy when in 'The Municipal Gallery Revisited', he comes across Lavery's smaller oil-sketch of *High Treason* which had been bequeathed to the Dublin Gallery a few years earlier:

> Casement upon trial, half hidden by bars,
> Guarded.

Only one person in the painting actually looks at Casement: on the solicitor's bench, a woman's brightly lit face turns towards the dock and acknowledges the prisoner. She has been identified as Gertrude Bannister (later Parry), Casement's cousin and close supporter. The only other person in court looking at the prisoner is of course the artist, Lavery, who excludes himself from the scene. But he does not exclude his sympathies: these are conveyed through the subtle organisation and composition of the canvas, and were also expressed retrospectively in his autobiography. While awaiting his inevitable sentence, Casement noticed the artist at work and, puzzled as to Lavery's identity and that of his wife Hazel (fig.138), wrote to his cousin: 'I thought I knew her face. It was very sad – and I kept on trying to remember.' Gertrude Bannister later wrote to the artist of the amusement that her cousin took from watching Lavery at work. To Casement,

I should think he came dangerously near 'aiding and comforting' if not indeed 'compassing' from the way he eyed Mr. Justice Darling delivering judgement. Surely it is treason to take a Judge's head off on the Bench!

She ends her letter with the observation: 'I cannot be too thankful that it is an Irishman who is painting the picture.'[53]

Whether painted at Justice Darling's suggestion or not, the judge certainly gave Lavery every assistance. The two men had known each other for some time and in 1907 Lavery had painted a dramatic image of the judge known as *The Black Cap*, showing him about to deliver the death sentence.[54] Darling visited the artist's studio and even allowed him to return to the courtroom after Casement's trial. Surprisingly, Darling also seems to have been in a position to summon Sullivan and others to return to the court to pose for Lavery. And yet, Darling did not acquire the painting and nor did anyone else; in the 1930s a number of proposals were made to purchase the painting, but nothing came of them.[55] The painting was still in Lavery's studio at his death in 1941 and, despite the intentions in his will, the National Portrait Gallery declined to accept it. H.M. Hake, the then Director of the Gallery, wrote that the painting had been 'duly considered by the Trustees who do not consider the occasion important enough for representation here'.[56] After the War and a period

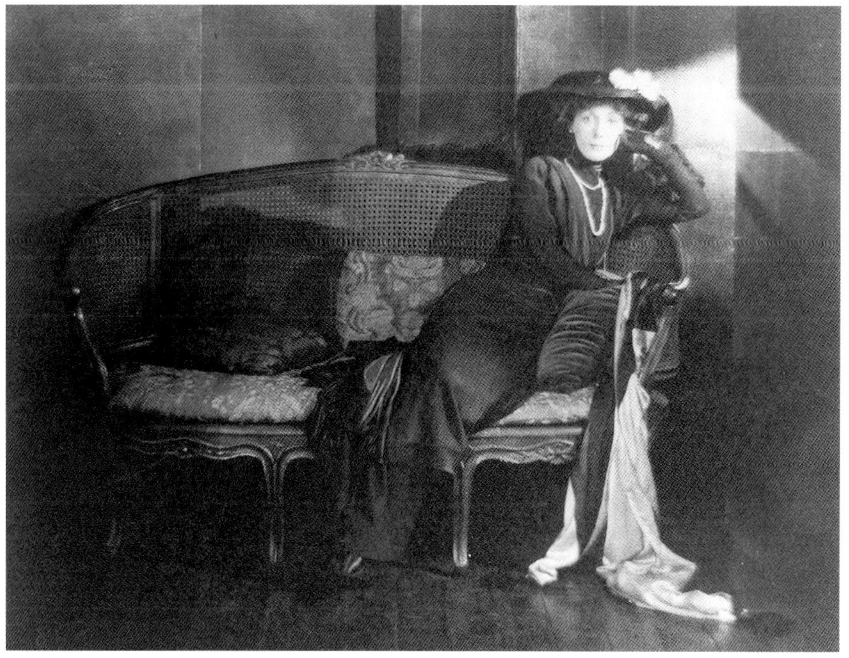

138. **Hazel, Lady Lavery**
(1880–1935)
BARON ADOLF DE MEYER (1910)
Bromide print, 171 × 222mm
(6¾ × 8¾")
National Portrait Gallery,
London (NPG P164)

The American-born Hazel Martyn was the second wife of the artist John Lavery. She is now remembered for two things: a possible affair with Michael Collins, and as the model for Lavery's design for the first Irish Free State banknotes, where she appears as Kathleen Ní Houlihan, an allegorised representation of Ireland.

of storage in the National Portrait Gallery, and following the further dictates of Lavery's will, the canvas was finally accepted by the Royal Courts of Justice and thus eventually became part of the Government Art Collection. Yet for the past fifty years Lavery's painting has hung in King's Inns, Dublin, after having become what the elderly Sergeant Sullivan came to call 'an unwanted work' to the post-war London authorities.[57] Although it had been hanging rather forlornly for a number of years in the office of the Senior Clerk of the Court of Criminal Appeal, the Lord Chancellor's Office was concerned lest any public exhibition of the painting should create 'undesirable demonstrations by people who considered Casement a martyr'. So as a gesture of goodwill to the government of the new Republic of Ireland, the painting was finally placed on long-term loan to Dublin and was duly unveiled by President Seán T. O'Kelly in 1951.[58]

The saga of the Casement painting is not dissimilar to the fate of his bodily remains. Ignoring international pleas for clemency, the British authorities executed him on 3 August 1916 in Pentonville Prison. His body was unceremoniously buried in quicklime. In 1965, on the eve of the fiftieth anniversary of the 1916 Rising, the Irish Government prevailed on the Wilson administration to transfer the bones to Ireland, where they were eventually reinterred in Glasnevin cemetery, Dublin. Both the painting and the body had been kept out of sight and out of Ireland for their first thirty-five and forty-nine years respectively; then they were given to Dublin.

In contrast to the plight of Casement's remains which had, according to Harold Wilson, 'soured Anglo-Irish relations for almost half a century',[59] the display of Lavery's painting was hardly an international concern. And yet, in cultural if not in diplomatic terms, the location of a painting – and in particular a politically-charged portrait – can indicate important attitudes prevalent in a society. Back in 1918, in a letter congratulating Lavery on being awarded a knighthood, Justice Darling had written: 'You will I hope take it as an expression of the will of HM's Government that you should complete your picture of Casement's trial, one of their victories over the Benches.'[60] But instead the picture was to be ignored or seen as an embarrassment. As such, Britain maintained its ambiguous attitude towards things Irish. By refusing to accept the painting in 1941, albeit a quarter of a century after the event depicted, the National Portrait Gallery, in the midst of another World War, may well have been concerned about the inappropriateness of displaying the portrait of a traitor, particularly one who had had dealings with Germany. Yet by doing so the Gallery was turning its back on a key event in early twentieth-century British-Irish history, although not one which the Director saw as 'important enough'. Such an attitude reminds one of the tortuous series of letters referred to in Chapter 1 that Henry Doyle, Director of the National Gallery of Ireland, had written to Her Majesty's Treasury in 1872–3 when attempting to set up an Irish Portrait Gallery. In the eyes of the late Victorian civil servant writing to Doyle, Irish portraits were of 'local' interest, not 'national' – let alone 'imperial'. The *Irish Times* had indeed summed it up well in 1865, when one of its journalists had toured the then newly formed National Portrait Gallery in London with what he called 'an Irish eye':

> It seems to me that the trustees have sought to secure statues or portraits of men who have stamped their name on the history of England or of Scotland, and have not dealt equal-handed justice to Ireland.[61]

George Bernard Shaw, in an attempt to reprieve Roger Casement's order of execution, highlighted the ambiguities of Anglo-Irish relations in a letter to the *Manchester Guardian* in July 1916:

> In Ireland [Casement] will be regarded as a national hero if he is executed, and quite possibly as a spy if he is not. For that reason it may well be that he would object very strongly to my attempt to prevent his canonisation. But Ireland has enough heroes and martyrs already, and if England has not by this time had enough of manufacturing them in fits of temper experience is thrown away on her, and she will continue to be governed, as she is at present to so great an extent unconsciously, by Casement's countrymen.[62]

And yet the story does not end there. Within a couple of years of the return of his bones to Ireland in 1965, Dublin's Office of Public Works, together with the Arts Council and the Department of External Affairs, commissioned a bronze statue of Casement from Oisín Kelly, one of Ireland's leading sculptors of the day. Intended for Casement's burial place in Glasnevin, the 2.2-metre-high statue was never unveiled in its intended spot due to State sensitivities over the outbreak of violence in Northern Ireland at the end of the 1960s. Kelly's unashamedly heroic figure of Casement has him standing alone, his head held high, his wrists bound with rough rope. Below the figure Casement's name appears in Irish, *Ruairi Mac Easmainn*, a linguistic fantasy that took much research and imagination by various Government agencies. Yet such a republican and Gaelicised representation could not rescue the statue from a form of mistreatment comparable to what happened to the Lavery painting: kept in storage for thirteen years, the bronze was finally banished to the windy wastes of Ballyheigue Park, County Kerry, where it overlooks Banna Strand, the site of Casement's arrest by the Royal Irish Constabulary on the eve of the Easter Rising in 1916.[63]

Back at the Special Commission

Having looked at a range of images of well known Irish political prisoners in the dock, it is time to finally return to the Special Commission in the Strand and to the plight of the Irish peasants who acted as witnesses in Probate Court Number 1. Hall's rapid pencil drawings, reproduced in the pages of the *Graphic*, capture what Costas Douzinas has referred to as the law's organisation 'of its own operation [as being] in a highly spectacular and visual manner'.[64] The 'viewpoint' of the sketch is 'everywhere and nowhere: from the dock, the judge's bench, the public gallery'.[65] To return to fig.123, a full page from the *Graphic*, it can be seen that Hall has drawn portraits of six individuals, policemen and farmers, in the witness box; on the same page he has included 'A Member of the Press', who would have been situated elsewhere in the courtroom. This is in fact a portrait of T.P. O'Connor, editor of the newly founded *Star* and a well-known nationalist Member of Parliament. Below him on the page, and doubtless positioned at a different angle again from the artist, would have been the doodling QC. Hall is concerned with conveying what Lynda Nead calls, 'the general impression of presence within the courtroom'.[66]

Combined with the notion of 'presence within the courtroom', and taking account of the extraordinary visual dominance given to the Parnell Commission over the course of a year in the pages of the *Graphic*, one could interpret the fascination with protagonists and witnesses as a kind of spectacle. Indeed only a decade earlier, a New York commentator, Frederic Hudson, in surveying illustrated newspapers in the US, saw them as:

> a feature. Every newspaper stand is covered with them. Every railroad train is filled with them … they make the battlefields … the corruption of politicians, the balls … familiar to everyone. They are in brief, the art gallery of the world. Single admission, ten cents.[67]

Or in the case of the *Graphic*, 'single admission' sixpence. This 'gallery of the world' idea is no better illustrated than in Hall's depiction of the witnesses in the Strand. In moving away from what Joshua Brown has called 'the safety of official portraiture', the illustrated journal of *c*.1880 began presenting 'character sketches that conveyed facial expression, gesture, and the idiosyncrasy of personalized poses appropriate to the high emotions of the event'.[68] Hall was following a contemporary trend to move away from tableaux, inspired by history-painting to draw images 'that distinguish the pose of unconscious subjects'.[69] If we compare a page from the *Graphic* (fig.123) with the traditional tableau arrangement of a nineteenth-century group portrait such as George Hayter's *The House of Commons, 1833* (fig.118), we notice that as opposed to a uniformity of heads, Hall's Parnell Commission is captured in a series of 'fractured' vignettes displaying frustration, exasperation, humour and concern – all suitable emotions in what was an urgent and important event in the political life of both Britain and Ireland.

By focusing on the witnesses subpoenaed to London from rural Ireland, Hall presents us with a gallery of Irish men and women placed on display. Although

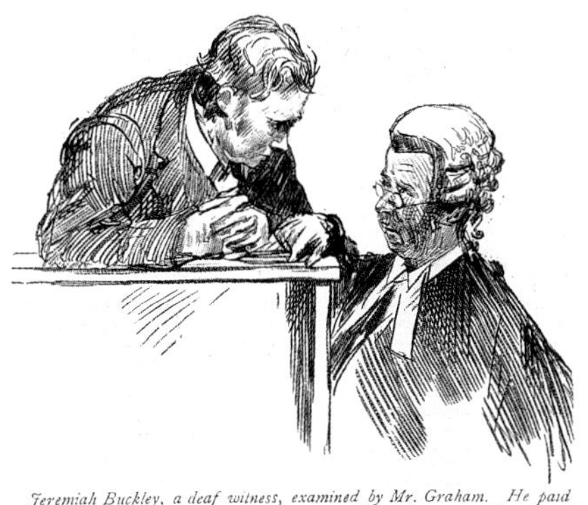

Jeremiah Buckley, a deaf witness, examined by Mr. Graham. He paid his rent, and Moonlighters cut off the lobe of his right ear. " What sort of scissors did they use ?" " I don't think they were good ones"

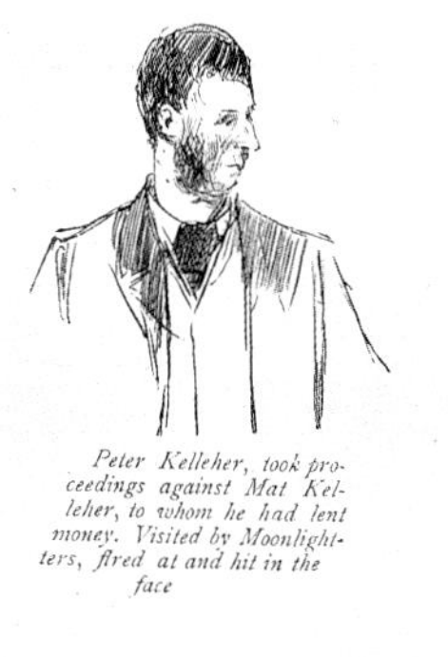

Peter Kelleher, took proceedings against Mat Kelleher, to whom he had lent money. Visited by Moonlighters, fired at and hit in the face

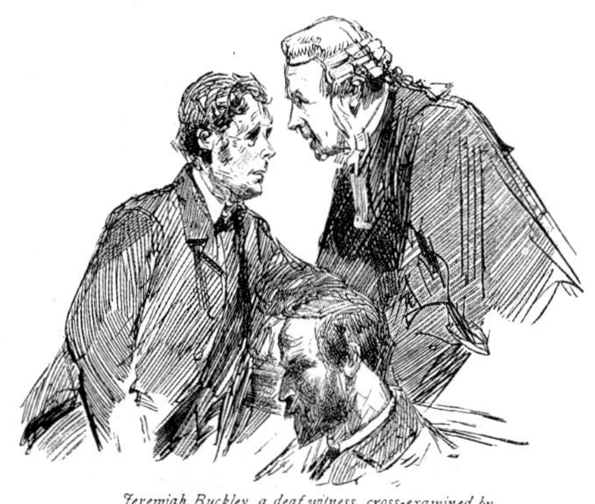

Jeremiah Buckley, a deaf witness, cross-examined by Sir C. Russell. " You have joints of roast meat every day ?" " What's that ?"

139. **The Parnell Commission**
SYDNEY PRIOR HALL
Wood engraving from the
Graphic, 15 December 1888,
page 293 × 114mm (11½ × 4½")
National Portrait Gallery, London

Ireland can be described as having been 'in the Strand', as the *Daily News* put it, for just a year, the nation became the centre of metropolitan spectacle. A rare moment of public exposure was granted to an otherwise hidden population of the United Kingdom. This displaced group of Irish rural tenantry was put under pressure to travel from many parts of Ireland to a city, let alone another island to which most of them had never travelled before. The Royal Irish Constabulary 'obtained, examined or escorted witnesses, and paid their expenses, and, in one instance, threatened a delinquent witness with gaol for his past offences if he refused to testify' against Parnell.[70] The notion of displacement is important here because the Irish witnesses were only brought to London for the duration of their appearance before the Commission. It is articulated both visually and orally in one of Hall's vignettes for the *Graphic* on 15 December 1888, where at the top of the page (fig.139) we are presented with two conversations between rival counsels with the same West Cork tenant farmer, Jeremiah Buckley, who had given evidence ten days earlier. As Buckley was hard of hearing, the counsels spoke loudly into his ear. The court had been informed that in 1881 Buckley had been the victim of an attack on his house by moonlighters who had beaten him with furze bushes and asked whether he had paid his rent. Buckley replied in the affirmative and the lobe of his right ear was cut off. Although the Report of the Special Commission reprints some thirty questions asked of Buckley, Hall reduces it all to just two humorous incidents: on the left, Mr Graham, counsel for *The Times*, asks what sort of scissors was used to cut off his ear, to which Buckley replies 'I don't think they were good ones'. The other sketch shows Buckley with Sir Charles Russell, counsel for Parnell and the Irish parliamentarians, who asks the Corkman about his diet: 'You have joints of roast meat every day?' 'What's that?' replies the deaf witness.[71]

As with his portrayal of Thomas Connaire (fig.124), the original drawing of Jeremiah Buckley (fig.140) shows Hall's attention to the farmer's pinched features. To ensure accuracy, Hall drew Buckley's profile twice on a single sheet. The Irish countryman is clearly out of his depth: he is being made a fool of, despite the fact

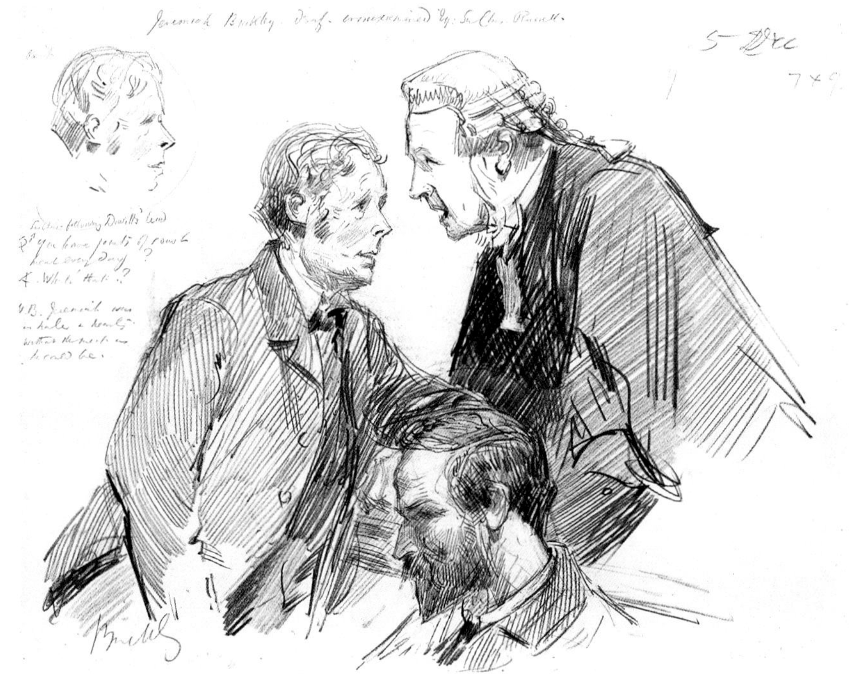

140. **Jeremiah Buckley cross-examined by Sir Charles Russell (later 1st Baron Russell of Killowen)** (1832–1900) **with Michael Davitt** (1846–1906) **in the foreground**
SYDNEY PRIOR HALL (1888)
Pencil on paper, 202 × 260mm
(8 × 10¼")
National Gallery of Ireland, Dublin

that his journey to London had been paid for jointly by *The Times* and the Irish Constabulary. The court transcripts of these sections of dialogue are slightly different from the speech captions recorded in the *Graphic*. While he was being questioned by Sir Charles Russell on behalf of the Parnellites, the focus of the discussion was indeed on Buckley's diet, but due to the tenant farmer's hearing difficulties there is much repetition of questions and the answers are full of convoluted sentences. Finally, Russell asks Buckley, 'Do you see fresh meat often?' The reply, 'Fresh meat, be gad, I do not', is quite different from 'What's that?'[72]

Ironically, the witness ostensibly appearing for the forces of Unionism against the Irish nationalism of Parnell is treated with the same racial buffoonery as had been the hallmark of the Irish throughout the nineteenth century. Despite his existence as a named witness, Buckley, and many of his fellow witnesses throughout the Special Commission, became victims of traditional stereotyping that had been the distinguishing feature of the generic types created most infamously by *Punch*.[73]

Hall's repetition of Buckley (fig.139) on the same page is a common feature of his reporting of the events at the Special Commission. Parnell himself and many other witnesses frequently appear and reappear on a single page of the *Graphic* in a fashion that is almost cinematic in its immediacy. The intensity of Hall's original pencil portraits (fig.123), together with the care with which they have been translated on to the pages of the journal and then framed by curvaceous captions, suggests comparisons with the organisation of a carefully inscribed photograph album. Just as the album can reveal a sense of development in the lives of individuals, a narrative or a story, so too Hall's drawings, and most particularly these portrait sketches for the

Graphic, encapsulate the witnesses in an experimentation with time. The 'fractured' vignettes of Jeremiah Buckley in fig.139 show concentration on the left and a wish to oblige on the right. The Irish peasantry move across the pages of the *Graphic*, suggesting both the passing of time and repetition: the original event (in this case, the cutting off of Buckley's ear) of some years previously is remembered; the retelling in court and the encounters with legal counsels are recorded as they happen in Hall's sketch pad; and then finally, perhaps up to a week later, the scenes appear as line drawings in a popular weekly journal.[74]

Despite this combination of realism and journalistic innovation, Hall's experiment with realism only goes so far. The *Graphic*'s transplanted Irish peasantry are in effect the victims of cultural displacement: while never visually represented in their own culture, they had to undergo the process of metropolitan reinvention in the pages of a London pictorial newspaper to satisfy the popular expectations of that dominant culture. In addition, the elite and the historically significant are invariably treated differently from these ordinary witnesses. As Margaret O'Callaghan has recently argued, the crude tactic used by *The Times* and the Tory party of equating Parnellism and crime, actually worked.[75] Even though Parnell was personally vindicated, the tales of intimidation prised from the motley array of witnesses, stuck. The Commission was summed up by Arthur Balfour, the Irish Chief Secretary and Lord Salisbury's nephew, who claimed that Irish politicians always lie: their antics may be amusing but fundamentally they cannot be taken seriously. Equally, as Sydney Prior Hall's illustrations in the *Graphic* demonstrate, the same might be said of all the witnesses that appeared before the Special Commission. Ireland, as the journalist for the *London Daily News* had said, may have been in the Strand but the participants in the Commission 'dismantled' any form of nationalist alliance that might have existed by washing Ireland's dirty laundry in public.[76]

Neutral ground?

It was two Irish artists, John Lavery and William Orpen, who dominated society portraiture in both Dublin and London in the early decades of the twentieth century. Both artists were highly successful in official circles and both received knighthoods in 1918. Lavery, a Belfast Catholic from humble circumstances, explored *pleinairisme* in France and Tangiers; by 1913 he was painting George V and his family against the backdrop of the sumptuous White Drawing Room in Buckingham Palace (fig.9). Orpen's Dublin background was solidly unionist and Protestant middle class, and, although he dallied with Irish themes such as his strange *The Holy Well* (1916, National Gallery of Ireland), he was an official war artist from 1917–19 and is chiefly remembered for his series of portraits of the political and military leaders who gathered in Paris for the Versailles Peace Conference.[77] Before the Great War, as was mentioned in Chapter 1, Orpen had painted individuals from conflicting sides in Irish politics. His portraits of the nationalist Michael Davitt (fig.43), whom we met earlier in the front row of the Parnell Commission (figs 128 and 140), and the unionist Sir Anthony MacDonnell (fig.42) hung together in Dublin's original Municipal Gallery of Modern Art in 1908.

As we have seen with the Casement experiment (fig.137) and regardless of the grandeur of the Royal Family group, Lavery was not one to shy away from revealing his interest in Irish affairs. His Anglo-Irish Treaty portraits (figs 141 and 142) of the early 1920s represent both sides of the negotiations and they represent perhaps the last great series of painted celebrations of opposing Irish political groups. Among the ten or so portraits painted, the Irish sitters included Arthur Griffith (fig.141), who headed the Irish delegation and was later elected President of the Dáil, while from the British side Lavery painted a portrait of the Prime Minister, David Lloyd George (fig.142). In examining this series and moving from the portrait of one Treaty negotiator to another, one recalls William Drennan's description of Hugh Douglas Hamilton's studio in Dublin on the eve of the United Irishmen's rebellion of 1798. The range of political opinions assembled in both artists' studios is indeed comparable. In November 1797 Drennan had told his sister that she 'would like to see these pictures': a couple of United Irishmen (Lord Edward FitzGerald and Arthur O'Connor, figs 101 and 112, as well as portraits of Lady Pamela FitzGerald), a possible sympathiser (Lord Moira, fig. 100) and a supporter of the Castle (Dean Kirwan, fig.76).[78] Such a visual spectrum of political loyalties was also created by Lavery from the summer of 1921 through to 1922. Like O'Connell's inclusion in Hayter's and Haydon's large London-based group portraits (figs 118 and 120), and in the same way that Sydney Prior Hall's drawings focus on an Irish influx to the capital of the Empire, so too the Treaty portraits introduce the Irish political portrait into a larger political environment.

In Lavery's series, we move from individual paintings of Arthur Griffith and Michael Collins to representations of other signatories such as Robert Barton and George Gavan Duffy, David Lloyd George, Winston Churchill and Austen Chamberlain, as well as the Lord Chancellor, Lord Birkenhead.[79] These paintings present the range of personalities involved in the lengthy negotiations that came to a head on the night of 5 and 6 December 1921; the Anglo-Irish Treaty was eventually signed at 2.20 in the morning.

The paintings of the Irish delegates were painted quickly and under pressure. They are more a series of recordings than measured considerations of the sitters. In all of them the canvas is usually clearly visible, though the faces are enlivened by a thick use of impasto. In fact the whole process was perfunctory: Lavery requested no more than three hours of each sitter and just a day's notice by telephone that they

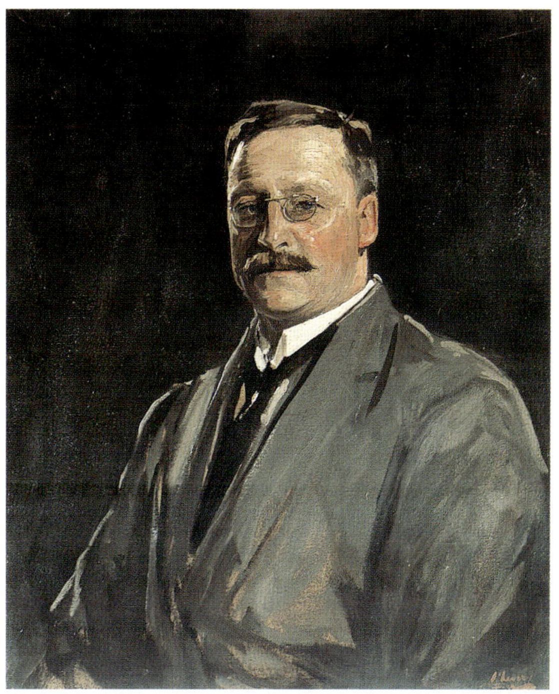

141. **Arthur Griffith** (1871–1922)
JOHN LAVERY (1921)
Oil on canvas, 769 × 639mm (30¼ × 25⅛")
Dublin City Gallery, the Hugh Lane

In his 1937 poem 'The Municipal Gallery Revisited', W.B. Yeats uses
the portraits on display in the Dublin gallery to recall his friends.
The portraits mentioned include three illustrated here, Synge
(fig. 41), Casement on trial (an oil sketch for fig.137) and Lavery's
Griffith, above.

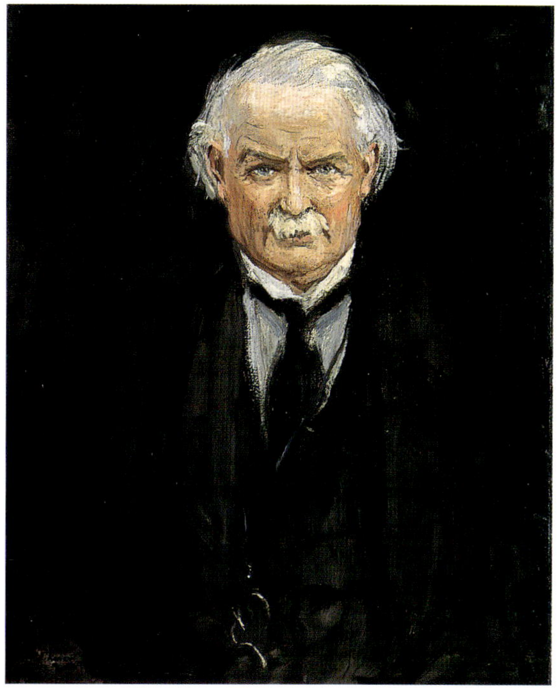

142. **David Lloyd George** (1863–1945)
JOHN LAVERY (1922)
Oil on canvas, 762 × 636mm (30 × 25")
Dublin City Gallery, the Hugh Lane

could make it to his studio. Again one is reminded of the equally hurried sittings
that Hamilton must have had to accept when painting Lord Edward FitzGerald
in 1797. Lavery later attributed the inspiration for the series to his American wife,
Hazel Martyn (fig.138):

> When the Great War came and the Black and Tans were given <u>carte blanche</u>
> to do their damnedest – which they did – the desire to fight stirred in my
> blood for the first time. Yet I very much doubt if it was patriotism and a love
> of country so much as a sense of justice. There was nothing much I could
> do. So when Hazel asked me why I did not do something for my country
> I replied, 'I cannot see that I can do anything without mixing myself with
> religion or politics, and I have no time to differ with people'. 'Don't differ', she
> replied. 'Just agree with them all, as you do anyway'. So it struck me that
> I might be some use in making my studio neutral ground where both sides
> might meet.[80]

'Hazel and John', as Lady Lavery's biographer has suggested, 'developed a rapport with the Irish delegates, who were dining frequently at Cromwell Place by mid-November'. Soon the Laverys had all the Treaty protagonists except Erskine Childers calling into the painter's studio. 'Collins', Lavery observed, 'was a patient sitter, but I noticed that he liked to sit facing the door. He was always on the alert'.[81] The Laverys clearly thrived on the excitement of the occasion. Years later, in 1935, the artist bequeathed thirty-four paintings to Dublin's Municipal Gallery, which included Treaty portraits and miscellaneous others, as well as a number of subject pictures.[82] Of the Treaty portraits, the most memorable are those of Griffith and perhaps Lloyd George. With his tight mouth and suspicious look at the artist and hence us, Griffith (fig.141) does indeed stare, perhaps not in 'hysterical pride', as W.B. Yeats described the portrait in 'The Municipal Gallery Revisited'.[83] The image of Lloyd George (fig.142), who did not sit until 1922, also conveys the intensity of his stare and the self-assurance of a man who was always in a position to threaten war if the Treaty was not signed.

The post-modern portrait

Much of the political portraiture of the last generation has focused on the individual, whether in the mainstream or as an outsider. Robert Ballagh, a leading figurative artist based in Dublin, has spent his career attempting to merge his art with his personal commitment to Irish republicanism and socialism.[84] Two portraits of opposing politicians from the 1980s provide a useful conclusion to the discussion of the role of oil portraits in image making in a multi-media society. Both are political images of men with prominent public profiles. The first is of Charles Haughey (fig.143), a former Taoiseach (Prime Minister) who became leader of Fianna Fáil (Soldiers of Destiny) in December 1979. Fianna Fáil see themselves as a centrist republican party and are the biggest and most effective political machine in modern Ireland. The other Robert Ballagh portrait is of Noël Browne (fig.145), a political radical who as a Labour minister in a post-war coalition government assisted in the eradication of tuberculosis from Ireland. Browne went on to break away from the moderate Irish Labour Party, always maintaining an individual radicalism that is now seen as a major contribution to Irish parliamentary politics.

Ballagh's paintings are interesting experiments in the historicising of the genre of portraiture; they are also very much part of his delight in visual games and tricks. In *The Decade of Endeavour* he portrays Haughey speaking at the February 1980 Fianna Fáil Árd Fheis (annual party conference), his first as Taoiseach and as leader of his party. Ballagh creates the witty juxtaposition of a portrait within a portrait by placing Haughey in front of his own hugely enlarged photographic image, with

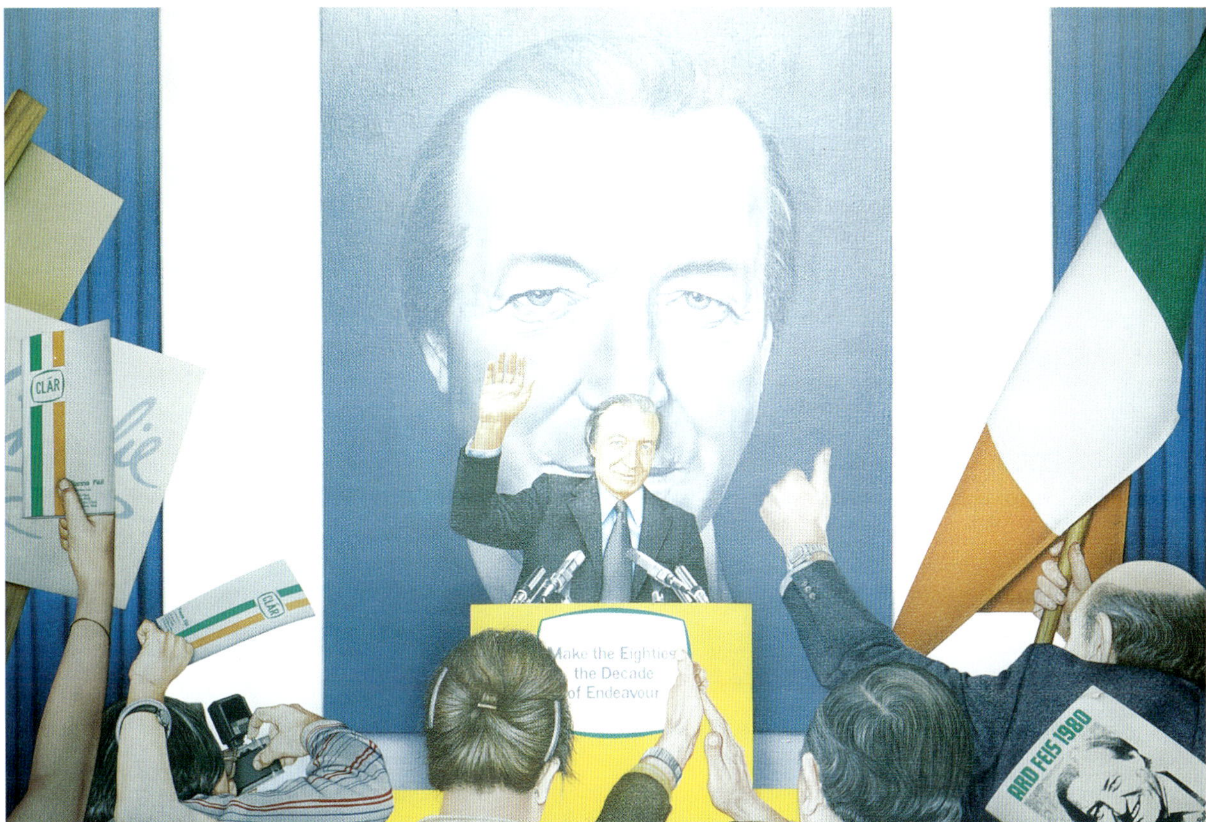

143. **The Decade of Endeavour: Portrait of Charles Haughey**
(b.1925)
ROBERT BALLAGH (1980)
Oil on canvas, 1220 × 1920mm
(48 × 75⅝")
Private collection

Celebrating 'Charlie' Haughey's return to the centre of Irish politics, Ballagh's portrait pictures the then Taoiseach at the Fianna Fáil Árd Fheis (annual party conference). Enthusiastic party members cheer and wave the tricolour and copies of the conference programme (Clár). In the bottom left the artist includes himself as a photographer.

supporters and journalists waving in the foreground. Some years earlier Ballagh had established his reputation as an ironic commentator on the public act of looking at twentieth-century art. He had produced a large number of paintings of people standing in front of canvases by celebrated modern artists such as Matisse and Lichtenstein. In the Haughey painting he brings a similar element of visual surprise. As viewers, we wonder if we too are participating in the conference hysteria, the flag-waving and the cheering.

In refreshing contrast to the myriad static images of Irish politicians that have become the norm since the foundation of the Irish State, *The Decade of Endeavour* actively plays with the business of political portraiture. Compare it, for example, with Seán O'Sullivan's war-time oil of Taoiseach Éamon de Valera (fig.144). The visual emphasis of this large painting is on the small areas of flesh, the face and hands, three areas of light which emerge from the dark surroundings of the sitter's suit, the polished hard wood of the chair and the draped background. Now in Áras an Uachtaráin (de Valera was President of Ireland for fourteen years), this painting of the defender of Ireland's controversial neutrality during the Second World War hangs in the President's dining room, a totemic reminder of Irish traditionalism. By contrast, Ballagh's portrait of Haughey is less about keeping the status quo and

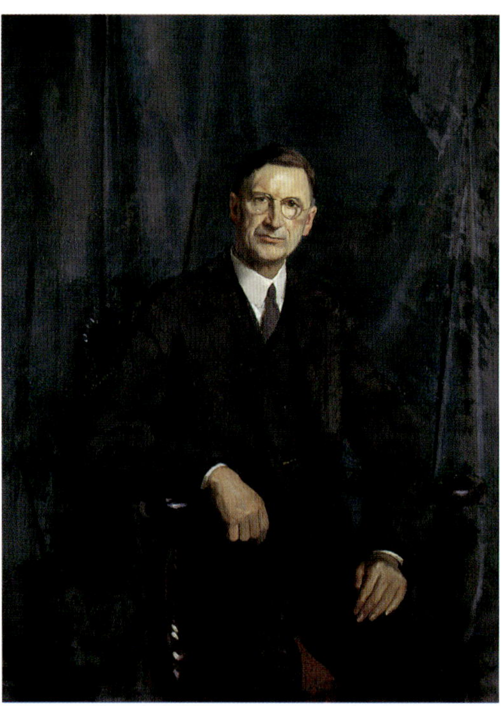

144. **Éamon de Valera**
(1882–1975)
SEÁN O'SULLIVAN (1943)
Oil on canvas, 1880 × 1470mm
(74 × 57⅞")
Office of Public Works, Áras an
Uachtaráin, Dublin

more about change. The lectern at which Haughey stands carries the legend 'Make the Eighties the Decade of Endeavour', an uplifting slogan that is echoed by raised arms and the towering face and hooded eyes of the leader on the backdrop. De Valera's sober portrait is the archetypal representation of a Taoiseach who acts on behalf of the public, whereas Haughey's image, also a portrait of a prime minister in office, is more about personal celebration and oozes the politics of individual success. With its presidential-style razzmatazz, the portrait was personally commissioned by Haughey to hang in the grand setting of his eighteenth-century home. Ballagh himself, one hopes somewhat tongue-in-cheek, has likened his relationship with 'The Boss' to the alliance that existed between Jacques Louis David and Napoleon.[85] If by that the artist sees some similarity between this privately commissioned portrait of Haughey and David's *Napoleon at the Saint-Bernard Pass* (1800, Musée National de Château, Versailles), then he might have a point. Both images, despite the age difference of the two sitters, are at key moments in their respective careers. Napoleon is at the beginning of his, while Haughey is relaunching himself after the 'murky manoeuvres' of a decade earlier.[86] Haughey's lectern slogan, like the historical names of Hannibal and Charlemagne carved in the rocks in David's painting of Napoleon, acts as a foretaste of the (possible) victories to come.[87]

By contrast, the portrait of Noël Browne (fig.145) is less bombastic but equally public. Browne is portrayed in a cross-shaped canvas made up of six equal squares. He wears an Aran sweater and wooden clogs, while the barren soil of his Connemara home is symbolised by the pebbles that fall out of the painting onto the

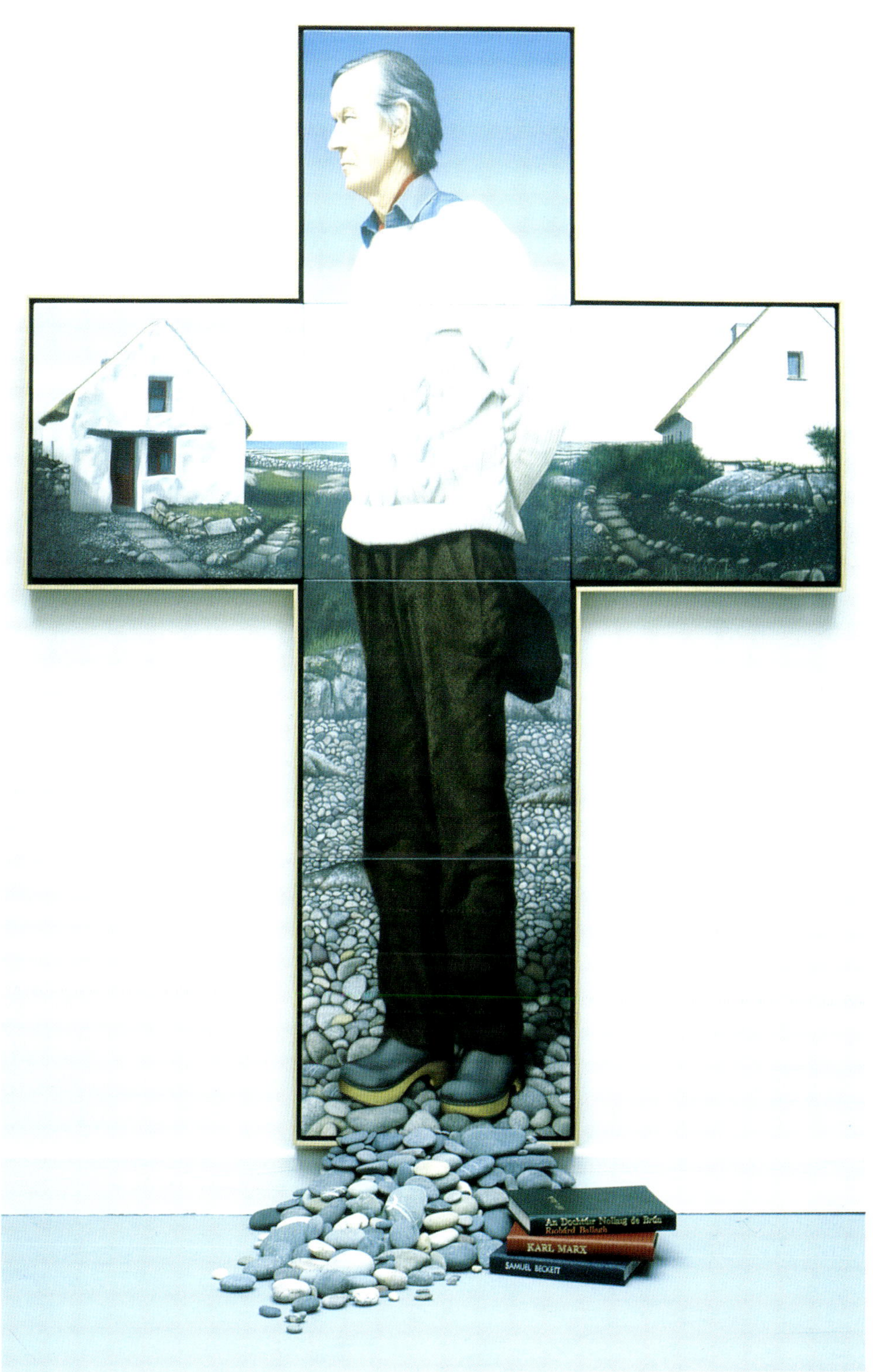

145. **Dr Noël Browne**
(1915–97)
ROBERT BALLAGH (1985)
Oil on canvas and
mixed media,
1830 × 1370mm
(72 × 54")
National Gallery of
Ireland, Dublin

floor of the Gallery. Browne's commitment to unbreakable ideals are implied both
by his dress and by Ballagh's placement of three books on the floor next to the
spilling pebbles. Two of these represent the works of Karl Marx and Samuel Beckett,
European socialism and Irish literature, a mixture of political drive and personal
honesty. The third book is a suitably witty Ballagh joke: the spine carries the artist's
name in Irish, along with the name of his sitter; the book itself is entitled *Fód a bháile*,
a fisherman's traditional expression for coming ashore.[88] According to Ballagh, the
choice of a cross-shaped composition was not intentional but evolved from his
own reluctance to painting 'acres of stones'.[89] Be that as it may, the verticality was
doubtless suggested by Browne's height, while the cross evokes an emotional
reaction appropriate to a politician who, as Minister of Health from 1948 to 1951, had
taken on the Roman Catholic hierarchy in attempting to introduce a Mother and
Child health scheme. Encountering total religious opposition, and not supported
by his Cabinet colleagues, Browne resigned. His future political career was solitary,
perhaps most especially his position from 1977 to 1982 as the sole Member of the
Dáil for the Socialist Labour Party.[90] A single, unpretentious figure on a cross is thus
a suitable visual trope for a man who took on the establishment, while the West of
Ireland setting adds a late twentieth-century visual twist to the portrayal of the
political patriot. Just as Ballagh's portrait of Charles Haughey can be compared
with David's *Napoleon*, so too his West Galway representation of Browne may be
contrasted with earlier twentieth-century romantic images that merge the West of
Ireland and political action.

Seán Keating's *Men of the West* (fig.146) of 1915 is both a self portrait (figure on
the left) and a statement of allegiance to a political cause. Painted a year before the
Easter Rising of 1916, three men dressed in Aran costume pose with guns and
the Irish tricolour. Keating himself is the only one who is shown in full face, yet the
exotic dress and readiness to fight cause us to pause. Is this a political statement or a
romantic posture? In comic mode, Ballagh himself was to refer to Keating's painting
as 'more reminiscent of being west of the Rio Grande than west of the Shannon'.[91]
Ballagh avoids such artificiality in his portrait of Noël Browne. Connemara is no
longer the locus of a civilisation needing cultural acknowledgement; instead, it is
a landscape of clarity. Browne's parents had come from the West, 'So in a sense',
Ciaran Carty suggests in his book on Ballagh,

> [Browne] has come back to his roots. But without any sentimental illusions.
> Meet him in Dublin and he is apt to be wearing a *crios* around his waist.
> Ballagh shows him in an Aran sweater. But that's as far as that kind of
> 'Irishness' goes. That is part of the irony of the portrait.[92]

One of Keating's gunmen also wears a *crios* (a hand-knitted belt) and in the foreground of the painting its multi-coloured knotted strands ostentatiously dangle

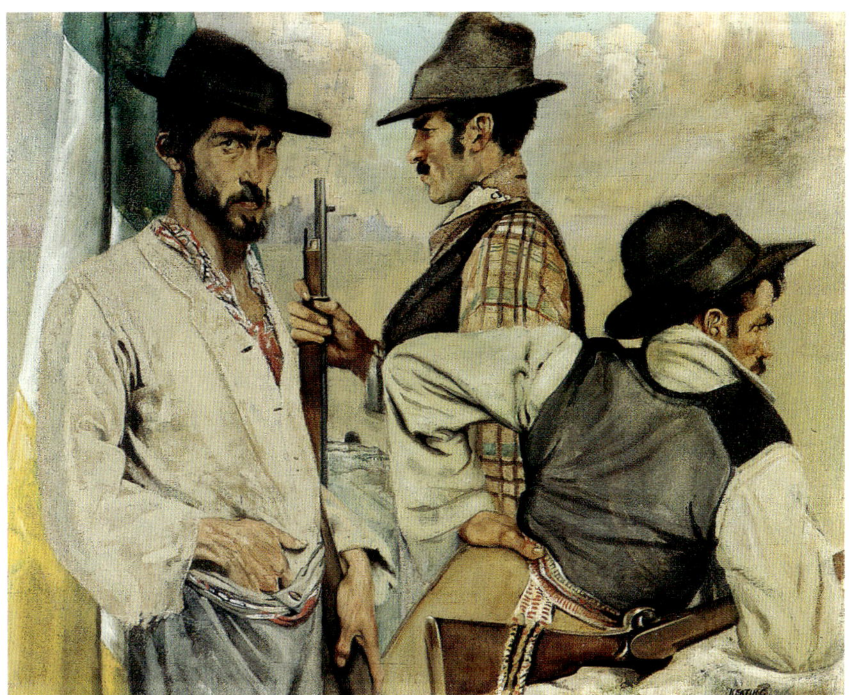

over the butt of a gun. When we return to Ballagh's portrait of Browne, we see him in an unromanticised Connemara setting that suggests that his late twentieth-century politician is as real as the stones that fall out of the painting and as relevant as the writings of Marx and Beckett.

With their wit and illusionistic trickery, Ballagh's late-twentieth-century political portraits are a long way from the solid classicism of Grattan's marble bust (fig.90) or the rhetorical competitiveness of Stuart's portraits of FitzGibbon (fig.96) or Foster (fig.97). Equally, by playing with art-historical associations (whether echoing a world-renowned artist such as Jacques Louis David or a painter such as Seán Keating, whose fame is more Irish-based), Ballagh asks that we view portraiture less as a literal representation of the individual (as in the case of Sydney Prior Hall's numerous drawings of the Parnell Commission) and more as a cultural construct. Unlike the more didactic political portraiture of the past, Ballagh's images invite us to make up our own minds about how politicians have fared in their respective contexts. At the same time, despite his penchant for visual games, much of his portraiture is traditional in its focus on the individual as expressed through oil on canvas.

In the final section of this book we will consider the more radical ways in which an artist develops portraiture using more innovative media.

1 Discussion of O'Connell's visual iconography is steadily growing: see Ormond, 1973, vol.I, pp.346–9 and vol.II, pls 680–4; Fergus O'Ferrall, 'Daniel O'Connell, the "Liberator", 1775–1847: Changing Images', in Gillespie and Kennedy, 1994, pp.91–102; Cullen, 1997, pp.90–101.

2 Ormond, 1973, vol.I, pp.526–36 and vol.II, especially pl.1028 with key; for oil sketch, see vol.I, p.346. I am grateful to Hazel Armstrong for information on the wearing of hats by MPs in the House of Commons in the nineteenth century. For information on dress in Parliament see <www.parliament.uk> HC Factsheets – Series G no. 7 ('Some Traditions and Customs of the House of Commons').

3 MacDonagh, 1991, p.338.

4 Arts Council of Great Britain, 1972, pp.48–9. The caricature was published in *Fraser's Magazine*, IX (1834), facing p.300. In the accompanying text Maginn refers to Sheil's face as 'agonized'.

5 MacDonagh, 1991, p.371.

6 Quoted in MacDonagh, 1991, pp.371–2, 'Diary of Denis Le Marchant', Feb. 1833 in Aspinall, 1952, p.295.

7 Hayter to W.E. Gladstone, 1854, quoted in Ormond, 1973, vol.I, p.526.

8 Hayter to Sir Robert Peel, 1845, quoted in Ormond, 1973, vol.I, p.528.

9 *Athenaeum*, no. 806, Apr. 1843, p.340, quoted in Ormond, 1973, vol.I, p.528.

10 Ormond, 1973, vol.I, pp.538–44 and vol.II, pls pp.1035–7.

11 William Lucas, *A Quaker Journal*, vol.1, 18 May 1841, p.241, quoted in Ormond, 1973, vol.I, p.542.

12 Hall, 2002, p.159.

13 W. Lloyd Garrison to Helen Garrison, 29 June 1840, quoted in Taylor, 1974, p.92.

14 Haydon, 1960–63, vol.V, pp.31–2; see Cullen, 2000, pp.194–5.

15 Richard Ormond discussing Haydon and then quoting from the artist's *Diary* (vol.V, p.259): Ormond, 1973, vol.I, p.542.

16 The following section is an extension of research for a forthcoming exhibition, *Conquering England: Ireland in the Victorian Metropolis*, National Portrait Gallery, London, 2005, curated by Fintan Cullen and R.F. Foster.

17 Twyman, 1970, p.100; Lusk, 1905. My thanks to Peter Funnell of the National Portrait Gallery for information on Hall and the Commission drawings. There are a large number of drawings and sketches by Hall in the Royal Collection: see Millar, 1995 vol. 1, pp.409–37. My thanks to Tracy Anderson for this information.

18 *Report of Special Commission Act*, 1890. For recent reassessments see T.W. Moody, 'The Times versus Parnell and Co., 1887–90', in Moody, 1968, pp.147–75; Lyons, 1974, pp.123–40; see also O'Callaghan, 1994, chap.5.

19 The *Graphic*, vol.38, 10 Nov. 1888, p.486.

20 17 Nov. 1888, vol.38, p.512: unlike many of the other *Graphic* illustrations no known drawing of this scene exists.

21 The *Graphic* usually carried textual commentary on the scenes depicted: the Murphy/Connair(e) exchange is reported vol.38, p.514.

22 Ellmann, 1987, p.273.

23 Bequest of Dr H.R. Hall FSA, National Gallery of Ireland, Dublin 1927; National Portrait Gallery, London, Dec.1928. All NPG drawings are illustrated under Sydney Prior Hall on www.npg.org.uk. The Dublin drawings are illustrated in Le Harivel, 1983, pp.191–230.

24 R.V. Comerford, in Vaughan, 1996, p.75, published in the *Graphic*, vol.39, 16 Feb. 1889, p.161.

25 The *Graphic*, vol.39, 2 March 1889, p.205.

26 The *Graphic*, vol.39, 11 May 1889, p.500.

27 Quoted in Stewart, 1984, p.42; the painting was presented to the NGI in 1898.

28 Starting top left, NGI 6131, 6208, 6202, 6207, 6206, 6204, 6205, 6264, 6154; all reproduced in Le Harivel, 1983, pp.215, 218, 224, 225.

29 For Yeats in late nineteenth-century London see Foster, 1997, *passim*; for Wilde see Kiberd, 1996, pp.33–50, and Kiberd, 2000, pp.325–39.

30 For the growing body of scholarship on the Irish diaspora in London see Swift and Gilley, 1989; MacRaild, 1999; Swift, 2002.

31 For a discussion of the Irish peasant immigrant in England, see Cullen, 1997, pp.135–46; for *Punch* cartoons see Curtis, 1997; Foster, 1993, pp.171–94.

32 Quoted in Lyons, 1977, p.390; see also Macdonald, 1890. The *Graphic* was not the only illustrated journal to cover the Parnell Commission: see also the *Illustrated London News*, 1888–9.

33 Caffrey, 2000, p.114; see also Caffrey, 1999.

34 For Emmet's rebellion see Geoghegan, 2002. See also Elliott, 2003; O'Donnell, 2003.

35 Emmet, 1915, vol.II, pp.253, 257.

36 George Petrie tells a story of Emmet's lover, Sarah Curran, visiting his father's studio c.1805 and being overcome with emotion on seeing a portrait of the dead rebel: see Geoghegan, 2002, p.23 (quoting from William Stokes, *The Life and Labours in Art and Archaeology of George Petrie,* London, 1868, p.389). Caffrey, 2000, reproduces a commemorative print, p.115. For portraits of Emmet see Emmet, 1915, vol.II, pp.253–9; O'Donnell, 2003a. For Petrie's drawings see Le Harivel, 1983, p.642; Emmet, 1915, vol.II, illus. opp. pp.211, 253.

37 Emmet, 1915, vol.II, pp.256–7.

38 Emmet, 1915, vol.II, p.258; for Emmet's speech from the dock see Geoghegan, 2002, pp.244–54.

39 Elliott, 1982, p.315.

40 *Official Catalogue*, 1872, p.186; FitzGerald, 1872, pp.62–3, who quotes the *Irish Times*, 28 June 1872; see also O'Donnell, 2003a, p.113 n.17. The *Nation* advertised reproductions for sale, 14 Sept. 1872: see Elliott, 2003, p.182, who also discusses post-Emmet fictional portraits, chaps 7–8 *passim*.

41 Sullivans, 1887.

42 Foster, 2001, p.6; Elliott, 2003, pp.176–8. Thirty-nine editions of *Speeches from the Dock* appeared between 1868 and 1887: see Gary Owens, 'Constructing the martyrs: The Manchester executions and the nationalist imagination', in McBride, 1999, p.20.

43 Goldring, 1993, pp.52, 54.

44 Foster, 1988, p.316; Chandler, 2001, pp.19–28.

45 Chandler, 2001, pp.23–5. For the NGI lithographic portraits see Le Harivel, 1988, pp.176–82. McManus's handwritten dedication reads: 'To one who has suffered and sacrificed much for Ireland – To one whose endurement and Bravery I have witnessed and can bear testimony to. To William Smith O'Brien, I offer this tribute as a token of my esteem and strong conviction of his Patriotism and many Virtues.' Signed and dated 'Nov 23/48, Richmond Prison'.

46 Mitchel, 1982 ed., pp.55–6.

47 See Fenian files, 'r' series, 1868, National Archives, Dublin, 1639R; for published illustrations see Vaughan, 1989, vol.V, pls 32–3 and xxxv–vi; Sexton, 1994, pp.162–3, 170–3 and Sexton, 2002, pp.16–17.

48 Samuel Lee Anderson Album, 1865–71, National Library of Ireland, MS 5957; see Rouse, 1998, pp.2–3; Larcom Papers, National Library of Ireland, MS 7698; see also Slattery, 1992, vol.II, p.96.

49 Comerford, 1985, pp.129–30. For the advertisement see Slattery, 1992, vol.II, p.96, and the *Nation*, 30 Dec. 1865.

50 National Library of Ireland, Album no.37; for the discussion of carte-de-visite albums see Hamilton and Hargreaves, 2001, p.46. For Fenian jail terms see Comerford, 1985, pp.146–7, 170–3.

51 I am very grateful to Alison Fuller of the Government Art Collection, London (GAC), for help on the origins of the commission, the painting's provenance and the identification of the individuals. The commission is discussed in Lavery, 1940, pp.189–90; McConkey, 1993, pp.152–3, who reproduces an oil study given to what is now the Dublin City Gallery, the Hugh Lane in 1935 (pl.188, p.150). See also McGuiggan, 1999, pp.157–9. This article is accompanied by a key identifying many of the people in the courtroom, which is based on information provided by John H. Morgan who acted as Counsel for Casement: see file on oil sketch in Dublin City Gallery, the Hugh Lane. Identification is also supplied by inscriptions on the back of the finished painting and the sketch. Further information on the history of the making of the painting has been gained from NGI Archive, Lavery file: memo from Sergeant Sullivan to Lavery (artist's use of snapshots) and Tate Archive (TA), T18 7245.

52 For the last months of Casement's life see Inglis, 1973; Reid, 1976; Montgomery Hyde, 1964.

53 Lavery, 1940, pp.189–90.

54 For the Darling portrait see Lavery, 1940, pp.188–9. The portrait of Darling was thought by the Attorney General, F.E. Smith to be 'in the worst possible taste' (Lavery, 1940, p.189).

55 TA 7245/214; 648-650, letters from Darling to Lavery, and 7245/215; 652-653. F.E. Smith (soon elevated to 1st Earl of Birkenhead), who had led the Prosecution against Casement and refused a second appeal, was a friend of Lavery's and later expressed an interest in having the painting purchased for the Law Courts; but the painter's delay in finishing it meant this never happened (TA 7245/4A). Others interested in purchasing the canvas included John H. Morgan, Junior Counsel for the Defence (TA 7245/4-7).

56 Department of Culture, Media and Sport, (DCMS) GAC AA 696/1, letter from H.M. Hake to M.W. Bennitt, Ministry of Works and Buildings, 11 Nov. 1941.

57 DCMS, GAC AA 696/1, Memo from Lord Chancellor's Office (Sir Albert Napier) to Sir Eric de Norman (Ministry of Works and Buildings), 27 June 1950. See also McGuiggan, 1999, p.159.

58 DCMS, GAC AA 696/1, Memo and ongoing correspondence between Ministry of Works and Commonwealth Relations Office, 1951–55; NPG file on Casement, Offer 44/2003. My thanks to Kate Eustace for her assistance.

59 Wilson, 1974, p.110.

60 TA 7245/215; 652-653, Darling to Lavery, 1 Jan. 1918.

61 Irish Times, 20 Oct. 1865. The Lavery painting returned to London in 2003 for cleaning and was displayed at the NPG.

62 George Bernard Shaw, 'Shall Roger Casement hang?', Manchester Guardian, 22 July 1916, quoted in Inglis, 1954, p.416.

63 See Art in State Buildings, 1998, pp.98, 110; for saga of the Kelly statue see Office of Public Works file A99/94/1, Roger Casement (1) Burial Plot (2) Memorial Statue. Casement's pose in Kelly's statue may be based on a Daily Mirror photograph of Casement leaving the Law Courts after his appeal had been dismissed, illustrated in Inglis, 1954, opp. p.385.

64 Costas Douzinas, 'The Legality of the Image', Modern Law Review, 2000, quoted in Nead, 2002, p.135.

65 Nead, 2002, p.136.

66 Nead, 2002, p.136.

67 Frederic Hudson, Survey of the illustrated newspapers – 1873, journalism in the United States, from 1690 to 1872, New York, 1873, p. 705, quoted in Brown, 2002, p.7.

68 Brown, 2002, p.167.

69 Brown, 2002, p.167.

70 Ó Broin, 1971, p.152.

71 Buckley appeared in court on 5 December 1888; the outrage perpetrated against him was described in the Attorney General's speech, see Report of Special Commission, 1888, vol.1, p.115. From Ballyvereen, near Bantry, Buckley's assault had taken place on 22 June 1881. For the interrogation by the two counsels, see Report of Special Commission, 1888, vol.3, pp.87–90.

72 Report of Special Commission, 1888, vol.3, p.89.

73 See Cullen, 1997, chap.4; Curtis, 1997, passim.

74 I am grateful to Deborah Cherry and Colin Cruise for some helpful suggestions regarding Hall's use of repetition.

75 O'Callaghan, 1994, p.119.

76 O'Callaghan, 1994, p.120.

77 See Arnold, 1981, part 4.

78 Agnew, 1998–9, vol.II, p.348.

79 Gavan Duffy and Birkenhead (then F.E. Smith and Attorney General) also appear in Lavery's High Treason (fig.137). As Solicitor for the Defence, Gavin Duffy is the bearded figure seated in the front row while Smith is the clean-shaven Counsel for Prosecution in the bottom right-hand corner.

80 Lavery, 1940, pp.207–8. Included in Cullen, 2000, pp.128–9. For Lavery's hurried painting of sitters see McCoole, 1996, p.74 (for illustrations of the whole series see plates between pp.116–17 and discussion pp.215–26).

81 Lavery, 1940, pp.214–15 and McCoole, 1996, p.75. The original Collins portrait, painted in 1921, is now lost.

82 Lavery, 1940, pp.256–7, lists the 1935 bequest. For a more sceptical view of the Laverys' behaviour see Dolan, 2003, p.76.

83 Yeats's poem is discussed in relation to the paintings by Roger McHugh in Rosc, 1971, p.29: McHugh sees Griffith as 'resolute' not hysterical, adding that 'a consideration of the factual relationship of the poem to the paintings is unlikely to be rewarding'. For a more recent reading see Foster, 2003, p.598. For Lavery's sale of prints after his portraits of Griffith and Collins see Dolan, 2003, p.76.

84 See Carty, 1986.

85 Ballagh, 2001. See also Moroney, 2001; Carty, 1986, pp.172–4. Ballagh's direct admiration for David is suggested by his silkscreens after The Rape of the Sabines, 1973.

86 In 1970 Haughey and other ministers were implicated in 'a plan to import arms to be used by the IRA in the North (of Ireland) "for defence purposes"', see Lee, 1989, p.459. Terry Keane has spoken of Haughey's admiration for Napoleon: Keena, 2001, p.99.

87 For Haughey's speech at the 49th Fianna Fáil Árd Fheis in February 1980 see The Spirit of the Nation. The Speeches and Statements of Charles J. Haughey (1957–1986), ed. Martin Mansergh, Cork and Dublin, 1986, speech 92, pp.327–38.

88 Carty, 1986, p.200.

89 Carty, 1986, p.198.

90 For the background see Browne, 1986.

91 Quoted in Gibbons, 1996, p.23. For some comments on Ballagh's use of parody see Kearney, 1988, pp.202–7.

92 Carty, 1986, p.200.

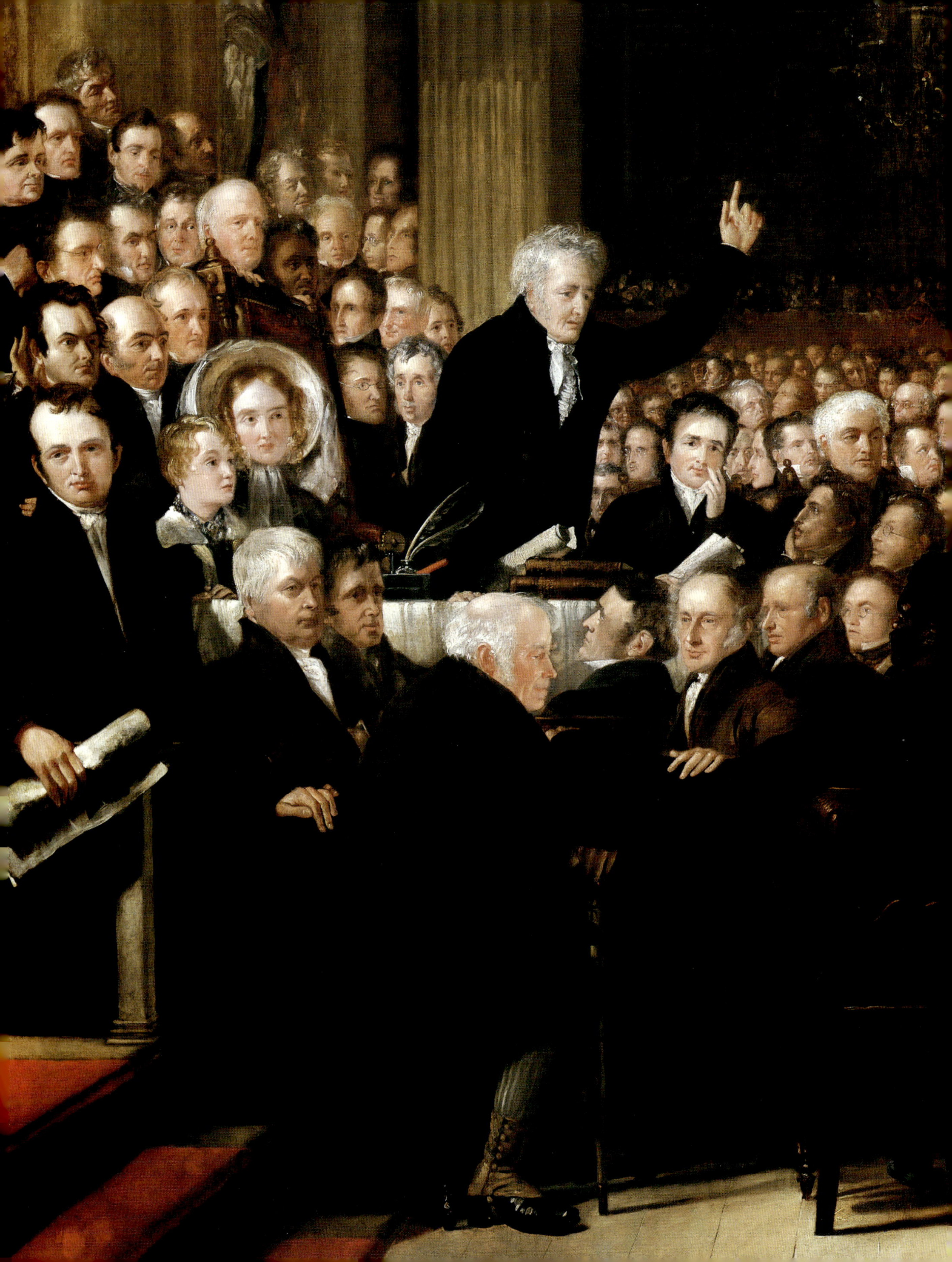

THE EMPHASIS OF much of this book is on portraits from the eighteenth and nineteenth centuries. The portrait as traditionally defined played a far greater artistic and social role in pre-twentieth-century society than it does in our own day. Peg Woffington (fig.73) and Lord Edward FitzGerald (fig.101), James Barry (fig.58) and Lady Morgan (fig.13), as well as Daniel O'Connell (figs 17, 118–20) and Charles Stewart Parnell (fig.130) all benefited from the oil portrait, its engraved aftermath or the pencil drawing that started it all off. Today's actors such as Liam Neeson (fig.67) or public figures from Charles Haughey (fig.143) to Mary Robinson (fig.47) do not need the oil portrait: it has become an additional luxury, not a *sine qua non* of public life.

Admirers of Peg Woffington who wished to be reminded of her likeness and could afford it had no choice but to buy a print after the oils by Lewis (fig.73) or Eccard (fig.71); by comparison, the grieving family of Lord Edward FitzGerald had the financial capabilities to commission a large number of oil copies and variations of the 'Divine face' of their dead relative. As we have seen, James Barry (fig.58) used the portrait, regardless of his disdain for it as a genre, to pursue his own ends and to conduct a personal vendetta against the forces of the establishment in late eighteenth-century London. The presence of oil portraits of writers such as Lady Morgan (fig.13) or politicians such as O'Connell or Parnell (figs 17 and 130) on the walls of an Irish national portrait gallery is a natural outcome of the Victorian preoccupation with the taxonomy of national history.

With the emergence of a modicum of national confidence comes a concern with national display; the 1872 Dublin Exhibition provided the perfect vehicle with which to launch an Irish collection of portraits. One hundred years later, such a display was not in the same demand. The historical portrait had become marginalized – and in Dublin's case, the national collection was relocated for a time to a country seat north of the city. Meanwhile, the contemporary portrait as traditionally defined did not carry the same value as it had for the clients of John Butler Yeats and others of the Literary Revival period. With so many other visual media offering us images of our favourite film stars or familiarising us with the distinguishing features of the politicians and leaders of the day, who needed a gallery of yet more faces?

The private patronage of Robert Ballagh by Charles Haughey (fig.143) or the combined state and private sector sponsored 'national portrait' series that began with Mark Shields's portrait of the Robinsons (fig.47) are examples of interesting yet regressive contributions to a nation's visual culture. Although both works inform

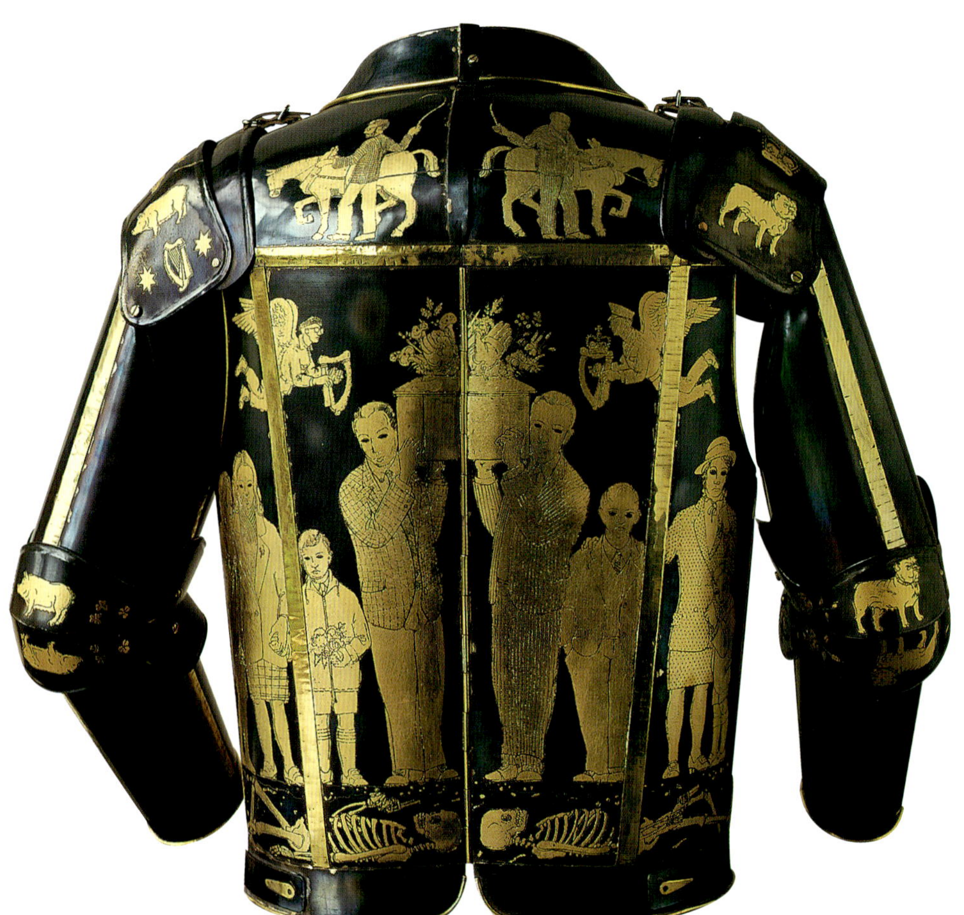

147. **Sectarian Armour
(back and front)**
JOHN KINDNESS (1995)
(Steel fabrication by
Peter Rooney)
Etched gilded steel,
584 × 406 × 305mm
(23 × 16 × 12″)
Imperial War Museum,
London

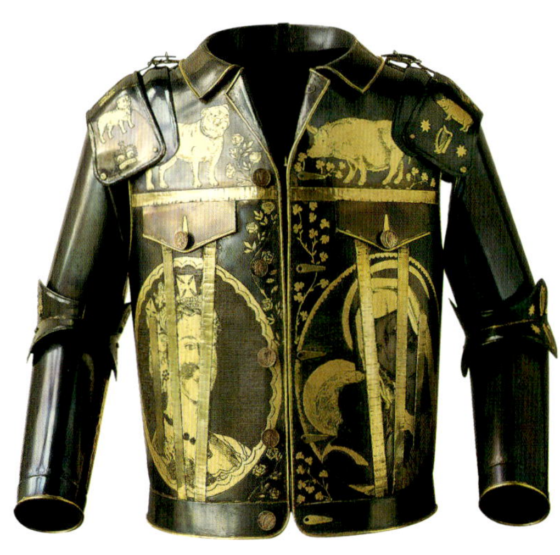

us about the sitters and have contributed to our analysis of the Irish face, their significance as cultural artefacts is not comparable to Lawrence's portrait of George IV (fig.6) given to the city of Dublin in 1821 or Yeats's portrait of John O'Leary (fig.38) displayed at the 1904 Irish exhibition in London's Guildhall. In both of these examples the portraits carried political influence: Ireland's involvement in the Union in the case of George and, a century later, in Yeats's O'Leary a heroic and ancient Ireland merges in the features of a modern republican. The problem with the Haughey and Robinson portraits is that they carry little political or even cultural weight. In the twenty-first century we have so many ways of gaining access to the faces of our prominent individuals that the traditionally defined portrait is no longer a key medium for visual dissemination. Instead, the portrait needs to be redefined if it is to be relevant in a multimedia age. A final example will suggest one new role for the Irish portrait.

Humour tends to be the dominant characteristic of the work of John Kindness, who works in many media: *Sectarian Armour* (fig.147) is just one example of his abiding focus on the divisions within the Irish story. Using sheets of gilded steel he has etched images from Ireland's two cultural groups to create a decorated, denim-like jacket that urges the viewer to consider the futility of cultural divisions. On the front is the banknote effigy of Queen Elizabeth II juxtaposed with a haloed Madonna and Child while a British bulldog faces an Irish pig; on the rear, across the shoulders Gerry Adams, President of Sinn Féin, turns his back on Ian Paisley, leader of the Democratic Unionist Party, both associated with republican and loyalist extremist positions. 'In a parody', Kindness writes, 'of the famous Levis' logo', Adams and Paisley lead a horse each but are in fact pulling 'the whole garment apart at the seams'.[1]

John Kindness is not solely interested in the political tensions and divisions that exist in Belfast or Northern Ireland in general; he also focuses on key social concerns. In *Sectarian Armour* the world being depicted is working-class Belfast, where deep-seated fear and serious violence are rife. This is not simply the Northern Ireland of the elected politicians as seen on television and in the political statement, although Adams and Paisley are important references in Kindness's piece: instead, this is political comment about life on the street. He creates his visual juxtapositions on the sartorial emblem of the working-class youth, the denim jacket, 'the livery of the Belfast "hard man" . . . often emblazoned with symbols and slogans identifying the wearer's political/religious allegiance'. In the long history of the Irish face as it can be traced from the seventeenth century to the late twentieth century, the elite have finally given way to the proletariat and, unlike the witnesses at the Parnell Commission in 1889, they are no longer figures of fun.

1 John Kindness, *Circa*, vol.76, Summer 1996, p.6; see also Ziff, 1994, pp.69–71; Cullen, 1996, p.22.

Chronology

1601	Battle of Kinsale: Irish and their Spanish allies defeated by English forces
1607	'Flight of the Earls': Irish Catholic aristocracy leave for the Continent
1649	Execution of Charles I; Cromwell in Ireland
1661	James Butler created Duke of Ormond
1678	Popish Plot
1681	Execution of Oliver Plunkett, Catholic Archbishop of Armagh
1688	Birth of James Stuart (the Old Pretender)
1690	Battle of the Boyne: James II/VII defeated by William of Orange
1695	'Penal Laws' enacted restricting rights of Catholics
1720	Birth of Charles Stuart (the Young Pretender)
1731	First sitting of Irish parliament in Edward Lovett Pearce's Parliament House
1739–40	Jonathan Swift's campaign over Wood's Halfpence
1740	Birth of Hugh Douglas Hamilton
1741	Birth of James Barry
1768	Royal Academy of Arts founded in London; Frederick Hervey appointed Bishop of Derry
1774	Edmund Burke elected MP for Bristol
1777	James Barry begins painting mural cycle on the Progress of Human Culture in (Royal) Society of Arts, London
1782	Repeal of Declaratory Act (1720) which allowed British parliament to legislate for Ireland (leading to so-called 'Grattan's Parliament')
1791	Foundation of United Irishmen in Belfast: seeking parliamentary reform, Catholic emancipation and a bringing together of Protestants and Catholics
1792–5	French National Convention: body set up to draft new Constitution after fall of monarchy
1795–9	Establishment of 'Cinq-Cents', Council of the Five Hundred (lower house of the French Revolutionary legislature) and Councils of Ancients (upper house of French Revolutionary legislature)
1796	Theobald Wolfe Tone negotiating in France with Lazare Carnot, member of the Directory (five men who governed France, 1795–9)
1797	Arthur O'Connor's *To the Free Electors of the County Antrim* followed by his *The State of Ireland* (1798)
1798	United Irish rebellion in Dublin and elsewhere; both Lord Edward FitzGerald and Wolfe Tone arrested and die in custody
1801	Act of Union
1803	Robert Emmet's rising
1806	Death of James Barry
1808	Death of Hugh Douglas Hamilton; Thomas Moore begins publishing *Irish Melodies*
1821	George IV visits Ireland
1823	Royal Hibernian Academy founded, Dublin
1828	Daniel O'Connell MP for County Clare
1829	Catholic Emancipation Act
1831	Thomas Moore's *The Life and Death of Lord Edward FitzGerald*
1834	Debates on Repeal of the Union at Westminster
1838	Father Mathew's abstinence movement
1842	The *Nation* newspaper is founded to broadcast view of Young Ireland
1845	Potato blight leading to famine
1847	Death of Daniel O'Connell
1848	Rising in Balingarry, County Tipperary, by William Smith O'Brien
1853	Irish Industrial Exhibition, Dublin
1854	Establishment of National Gallery of Ireland by Act of Parliament (opens 1864)
1856	National Portrait Gallery opens in London
1867	Disturbances in England and elsewhere caused by Fenians composed of a group of conspiratorial societies intent on winning Irish independence by force
1869	Disestablishment of the Church of Ireland (Anglican)
1872	Exhibition of Arts, Dublin (including National Historical Portraits)
1879	Irish National Land League founded
1882	Phoenix Park murders of Lord Frederick Cavendish and T.H. Burke
1882	Scottish National Portrait Gallery opens in Edinburgh
1882	John Henry Foley's O'Connell monument unveiled in Dublin
1888–9	Special Commission, Royal Courts of Justice, London
1891	Charles Stewart Parnell dies
1901	John Butler Yeats and Nathaniel Hone exhibition, Dublin
1904	Hugh Lane's exhibition of so-called Irish artists in London
1908	Municipal Gallery of Modern Art opens in Dublin
1915	Sir Hugh Lane dies on the torpedoed *Lusitania*
1916	Easter Rising in Dublin
1919	First Dáil (Parliament) meets in Mansion House, Dublin
1919–21	Anglo-Irish War (Black and Tans sent by British Government)

1921–2	Anglo-Irish Treaty negotiations leading to establishment of Irish Free State and separate government for Northern Ireland	**1971**	Ian Paisley founds Democratic Unionist Party
1922	Michael Collins assassinated; Arthur Griffith dies	**1972**	Thirteen killed in Derry during a banned civil rights march
1929	Sir John Lavery presents a collection of his paintings to Belfast	**1973**	Ireland becomes a member of the European Economic Community
1935	Lavery presents a collection of his paintings to Dublin	**1979**	Charles Haughey elected leader of Fianna Fáil and Taoiseach
1937	Éamon de Valera's constitution of Ireland approved (he becomes Taoiseach or 'leader')	**1982**	National Self-Portrait Collection of Ireland opens in Limerick
1938	Douglas Hyde inaugurated as first President of Ireland (official residence is former Vice Regal Lodge in Phoenix Park, renamed as Áras an Uachtaráin)	**1983**	Gerry Adams becomes President of Sinn Féin
1939	Éire (official name of country until 1949) declares neutral status during Second World War; death of William Butler Yeats	**1990**	Mary Robinson elected President of Ireland
1949	Ireland declared a Republic and leaves Commonwealth	**1995**	Seamus Heaney awarded Nobel Prize for Literature
1951	Roman Catholic hierarchy condemns Noël Browne's 'Mother and Child' scheme	**1998**	Belfast Agreement (also known as Good Friday Agreement)
1959	Éamon de Valera elected President of Ireland	**1998**	National Portrait Gallery of Australia opens in Canberra
1961	Radio Telefís Éireann (RTE) begins broadcasting (national television station)	**2003**	Louis le Brocquy paints portrait of Bono for National Gallery of Ireland/Irish Life and Permanent Portrait series; Ian Paisley's Democratic Unionist Party and Gerry Adams's Sinn Féin become largest unionist and nationalist parties, respectively, in Northern Ireland
1967	First Rosc exhibition, Dublin		
1968	Civil rights marches in Northern Ireland		
1968	National Portrait Gallery, Smithsonian Institution opens in Washington DC		
1970	Charles Haughey and others sacked as Government ministers on suspicion of importing arms to assist Catholics in Northern Ireland. Arms Trials follow		

Bibliography

Agnew, Jean (ed.), *The Drennan-McTier Letters*, 3 vols, Dublin, 1998–9

Alexander, David, 'The Dublin Group: Irish mezzotint engravers in London, 1750–1775', *Quarterly Bulletin of the Irish Georgian Society*, vol.XVI no.3, 1973, pp.73–93

— and Richard Godfrey, *Painters and Engraving: The Reproductive Print from Hogarth to Wilkie*, New Haven, 1980

Andrew, Donna T., *Philanthropy and Police: London Charity in the Eighteenth Century*, Princeton, 1989

Anon., *Memoirs of the celebrated Mrs. Woffington, interspersed with several theatrical anecdotes; the amours of many persons of the first rank; and some interesting characters drawn from real life*, 2nd edn, London, 1760

Arnold, Bruce, *Orpen: Mirror of an Age*, London, 1981

Arnold, Dana (ed.), *Cultural Identities and the Aesthetics of Britishness*, Manchester, 2004

Art in State Buildings 1970–1985, Dublin, 1998

Art in State Buildings 1922–1970, Dublin, 2000

Arts Council of Great Britain, *Daniel Maclise, 1806–1870*, exh. cat., London, 1972

Aspinall, A. (ed.), *Three Early Nineteenth-Century Diaries*, London, 1952

Baker, Malcolm, 'The making of portrait busts in mid-eighteenth-century England: Roubiliac, Scheemakers and Trinity College, Dublin', *The Burlington Magazine*, vol.CXXXVII, 1995, pp.821–31

Ballagh, Robert, 'How a painting was born', *Magill*, April 2001, p.19

Bardon, Jonathan, *A History of Ulster*, Belfast, 1992

Barker, Hannah and Elaine Chalus (eds), *Gender in Eighteenth-Century England: Roles, Representations and Responsibilities*, London and New York, 1997

Barnard, Toby, *A New Anatomy of Ireland: The Irish Protestants, 1649-1770*, New Haven and London, 2003

Barrell, John, *The Political Theory of Painting from Reynolds to Hazlitt*, New Haven and London, 1986

— *The Birth of Pandora and the Division of Knowledge*, London, 1992

Barrett, Cyril, 'Irish Nationalism and Art 1800–1921', *Studies*, Winter 1975, pp.393–409

Barrington, Sir Jonah, *Historic Anecdotes and Secret Memoirs of the Legislative Union between Great Britain and Ireland*, 2 vols, London, 1809–15

— *The Rise and Fall of the Irish Nation*, Paris, 1833

— *Personal Sketches of His Own Times*, 2 vols, 3rd edn, London, 1869

Barry, James, *The Works of James Barry*, ed. Edward Fryer, 2 vols, London, 1809

Bartlett, Thomas (ed.), *Life of Theobald Wolfe Tone, compiled and arranged by Theobald Wolfe Tone*, Dublin, 1998

— and Keith Jeffery (eds), *A Military History of Ireland*, Cambridge, 1996

Benedetti, Sergio, *The Milltowns: A Family Reunion*, Dublin, 1997

— *The La Touche Amorino: Canova and His Fashionable Irish Patrons*, Dublin, 1998

Berman, David and Jill, 'The Fountain Portraits of Bishop Berkeley', *Apollo*, February 1982, pp.76–9

Bindman, David, *Hogarth*, London, 1981

Black, Eileen, *Ulster Museum. Irish Oil Paintings 1572–c.1830: A Catalogue of the Permanent Collection*, vol.3, Belfast, 1991

— (ed.), *Museums and Galleries of Northern Ireland. Drawings, Paintings and Sculptures: The Catalogue*, Belfast, 2000

Bodkin, Thomas, 'John Butler Yeats RHA', *Dublin Magazine*, vol.1 no.6, January 1924, p.483

— 'Some problems of national portraiture', *Burlington Magazine*, December 1936, pp.246–51

Bourke, Angela, et al. (eds), *Field Day Anthology of Irish Writing*, vol. 4: *Irish Women's Writing and Traditions*, Cork, 2002

Bowen, Elizabeth, *Bowen's Court*, London, 1942

— *The Last September*, London, 1998; 1st pub.1929

Boyd, Andrew, *Holy War in Belfast*, Tralee, 1969

Brady, Ciaran (ed.), *Ideology and the Historians*, Dublin, 1991

British Public Characters, London, 1798

Brown, Christopher and Hans Vlieghe, *Van Dyck, 1599–1641*, exh. cat., London and Antwerp, 1999

Brown, Joshua, *Beyond the Lines: Pictorial reporting, everyday life, and the crisis of Golden Age America*, Berkeley, Los Angeles and London, 2002

Browne, Noël, *Against the Tide*, Dublin, 1986

Buckeridge, Bainbrigge, *The art of painting and the lives of painters*, London, 1706

Caffrey, Paul, *John Comerford and the Portrait Miniature in Ireland c.1620–1850*, exh. cat., Kilkenny, 1999

— *Treasures to Hold: Irish and English Miniatures 1650–1850 from the National Gallery of Ireland Collection*, exh. cat., Dublin, 2000

Carpenter, Andrew, *Verse in English from Eighteenth-Century Ireland*, Cork, 1998

Carty, Ciaran, *Robert Ballagh*, Dublin, 1986

Catalogue of the valuable collections of Engravings . . . the Genuine property of . . . Hugh Hamilton, Esq., Christie's, London, 1811

Catalogue of Paintings, now exhibiting at the Long Room in the Rotunda, collected by the late H.C. Sirr, Dublin, 1841

Chaloner Smith, John, *British Mezzotinto Portraits*, 4 vols, London, 1883

Chandler, Edward, *Photography in Ireland: The Nineteenth Century*, Dublin, 2001

Cirlot, J.C., *A Dictionary of Symbols*, 2nd edn, London, 1791

Clark, Anthony M., *Pompeo Batoni: A Complete Catalogue of his Works*, ed. Edgar Peters Bowron, New York, 1985

Clayton, Timothy, *The English Print, 1688–1802*, New Haven and
    London, 1997

Clifford, Timothy, Anthony Griffiths and Martin Royalton-Kisch,
    Gainsborough and Reynolds in the British Museum, exh. cat.,
    London, 1978

Coleman, John, 'Sir Joshua Reynolds and Richard Robinson, Archbishop
    of Armagh', *Irish Arts Review Yearbook,* 1995, pp.131–6

Colley, Linda, *Britons: Forging the Nation, 1707–1837*, New Haven and
    London, 1992

Comerford, R.V., *The Fenians in Context: Irish Politics and Society
    1848–82*, Dublin, 1985

Cooper, Helen A., *John Trumbull*, New Haven, 1982

Corns, Thomas N. (ed.), *The Royal Image: Representations of Charles I*,
    Cambridge, 1999

Crean, Hugh R., 'Gilbert Stuart and the Politics of Fine Art Patronage
    in Ireland 1787–1793: A Social and Cultural History', unpublished
    PhD dissertation, New York University, 1990

*Critical Review, of the First Annual Exhibition of Paintings, Drawings and
    Sculptures, the Works of Irish Artists*, Dublin, 1800

Crookshank Anne, 'James Latham 1696–1747', *Irish Arts Review
    Yearbook*, 1988, pp.56–72

— and the Knight of Glin, *Irish Portraits 1660–1860*, exh. cat.,
    London, 1969

— and the Knight of Glin, *The Painters of Ireland c.1660–1920*,
    London, 1978

— and the Knight of Glin, *The Watercolours of Ireland: Works on paper
    in pencil, pastel and paint, c.1660–1914*, London, 1994

— and the Knight of Glin, 'Some Italian Pastels by Hugh Douglas
    Hamilton', *Irish Arts Review Yearbook*, 1997, pp.63–9

— and the Knight of Glin, *Ireland's Painters 1600–1940*,
    New Haven and London, 2002

— and David Webb, *Paintings and Sculptures in Trinity College Dublin*,
    Dublin, 1990

Cullen, Fintan, 'The Oil Paintings of Hugh Douglas Hamilton', *Walpole
    Society*, vol.50, 1984, pp.165–208

— *The Drawings of John Butler Yeats (1839–1922)*, Albany, 1987

— 'The Art of Assimilation: Scotland and its Heroes', *Art History*,
    vol.16 no.4, December 1993, pp.58–73

— 'Confronting Multiculturalism', *Circa,* vol.75, Spring 1996, pp.20–24

— *Visual Politics: The Representation of Ireland, 1750–1930*, Cork, 1997

— (1997a) ' "The Cloak of Charity": The politics of representation in late
    eighteenth-century Ireland', *The Irish Review*, vol.21, 1997, pp.66–74

— 'Lord Edward FitzGerald: The creation of an icon', *History Ireland*,
    vol.6, no. 4, Winter 1998, pp.17–20

— (ed.), *Sources in Irish Art: A Reader*, Cork, 2000

— and John Morrison (eds), *A Shared Legacy: Essays on Irish and
    Scottish Art and Visual Culture*, Aldershot, forthcoming

Curtin, Nancy J., *The United Irishmen: Popular Politics in Ulster
    and Dublin, 1791–1798*, Oxford, 1994

Curtis, L. Perry, Jr, *Apes and Angels: The Irishman in Victorian Caricature*,
    Washington DC and London, 1997

Curwen, J.C., *Observations on the State of Ireland . . .* , 2 vols,
    London, 1818

Deane, Seamus (ed.), *The Field Day Anthology of Irish Writing*,
    3 vols, Derry, 1991

Delpierre, Madeleine, 'A propos d'un manteau de représentant du
    peuple de 1798 récemment offert au musée du costume',
    Bulletin du Musée Carnavalet, 1972, no.1, pp.13–23

Dickson, David (ed.), *The Gorgeous Mask: Dublin 1700–1850*,
    Dublin, 1987

— Dáire Keogh and Kevin Whelan (eds), *The United Irishmen:
    Republicanism, Radicalism and Rebellion*, Dublin, 1993

Diderot, Denis, *Diderot on Art*, 2 vols, trans. John Goodman,
    New Haven and London, 1995

Dolan, Anne, *Commemorating the Irish Civil War: History and Memory,
    1923–2000*, Cambridge, 2003

Donald, Diana, *The Age of Caricature: Satirical Prints in the Reign
    of George III*, New Haven and London, 1996

Doyle, Henry, *Catalogue, Descriptive and Historical, of the Works
    of Art in the National Gallery of Ireland*, Dublin, 1882

Drennan, William, *Letters of Orellana, an Irish Helot*, Dublin, 1785

Dunbar, Janet, *Peg Woffington and her World*, London, 1968

Duncan, Ellen, 'The Irish National Portrait Collection', *Burlington
    Magazine*, October 1907, pp.6–20

Dundee City Art Gallery, Catalogue of Paintings, Dundee, 1973

Dunne, Tom, 'Haunted by History: Irish romantic writing 1800–50',
    in *Romanticism in National Context*, eds Roy Porter and
    Mikulás Teich, Cambridge, 1988, pp.68–91

Elliott, Marianne, *Partners in Revolution: The United Irishmen and
    France*, New Haven and London, 1982

— *Wolfe Tone: The Prophet of Independence*, New Haven and
    London, 1989

— *Robert Emmet: The Making of a Legend*, London, 2003

Ellmann, Richard, *Oscar Wilde*, London, 1987

Elmes, Rosalind, *Catalogue of Engraved Irish Portraits*, Dublin, 1937

Emmet, Thomas Addis, *Memoir of Thomas Addis and Robert
    Emmet with Their Ancestors and Immediate Family,* 2 vols,
    New York, 1915

Erffa, Helmut von and Allan Staley, *The Paintings of Benjamin West*,
    New Haven and London, 1986

Evans, Dorinda, *The Genius of Gilbert Stuart*, Princeton, 1999

Fallon, Brian, *Edward McGuire, RHA*, Dublin, 1991

Farington, Joseph, *The Diary of Joseph Farington*, 17 vols, New Haven
    and London, 1978–98

Fenlon, Jane, 'John Michael Wright's Highland laird identified', *Burlington Magazine*, vol.cxxx, 1988, pp.767–9

— 'Garret Morphy and his circle', *Irish Arts Review Yearbook*, 1991–2, pp.135–48

— *The Ormonde Picture Collection*, Kilkenny, 2001

Figgis, Nicola and Brendan Rooney, *Irish Paintings in the National Gallery of Ireland*, vol.1, Dublin, 2001

Finlay, Sarah (ed.), *The National Self-Portrait Collection of Ireland*, Limerick, 1989

Firenze e l'Inghilterra, exh. cat., Florence, 1971

FitzGerald, Percy, *Handbook to the National Portrait Gallery*, 2nd edn, Dublin, 1872

Ford, Brinsley, 'The Earl-Bishop: An eccentric and capricious patron of the arts', *Apollo*, June 1974, pp.426–34

Foster, R.F., *Modern Ireland 1600–1972*, London, 1988

— (ed.), *The Oxford Illustrated History of Ireland*, Oxford and New York, 1989

— *Paddy and Mr Punch: Connections in Irish and English History*, London, 1993

— *W.B. Yeats: A Life*, vol.1: *The Apprentice Mage, 1865–1914*, Oxford and New York, 1997

— *The Irish Story: Telling Tales and Making it Up in Ireland*, London, 2001

— *W.B. Yeats: A Life*, vol. 2: *The Arch-Poet, 1915–1939*, Oxford and New York, 2003

Fothergill, Brian, *The Mitred Earl: An Eighteenth-Century Eccentric*, London, 1974

Fox, Peter (ed.), *Treasures of the Library: Trinity College Dublin*, Dublin, 1986

Fraser, T.G. and Keith Jeffery (eds), *Men, Women and War*, Dublin, 1993

Friends of the National Collections of Ireland, *The City's Art – the original Municipal Collection, Catalogue*, Dublin, 1984

Garlick, Kenneth, *Sir Thomas Lawrence: A Complete Catalogue of the Oil Paintings*, Oxford, 1989

Geffroy, A., 'Études en rouge, 1789–1798', *Cahiers de lexicologie*, no.51, 1987, pp.119–48

Geoghegan, Patrick M., *Robert Emmet: A Life*, Dublin, 2002

Gibbons, Luke, *Transformations in Irish Culture*, Cork, 1996

— *Edmund Burke and Ireland: Aesthetics, Politics and the Colonial Sublime*, Cambridge, 2003

Gilbert, Sir John T. and Lady (eds.), *Calendar of Ancient Records of Dublin*, 19 vols, Dublin, 1889–1944

Gillespie, Raymond and Brian P. Kennedy (eds), *Ireland: Art into History*, Dublin, 1994

Gilmartin, John, 'Peter Turnerelli: Sculptor 1774–1839', *Irish Georgian Studies*, vol.10 no.4, October–December 1967, pp.1–19

Godfrey, Richard, *James Gillray: The Art of Caricature*, exh. cat., London, 2001

Goldring, Maurice, *Pleasant the Scholar's Life: Irish Intellectuals and the Construction of the Nation State*, London, 1993

Hall, Catherine, *Civilising Subjects: Metropole and Colony in the English Imagination, 1830–1867*, Cambridge, 2002

Halliday, Tony, *Facing the Public: Portraiture in the Aftermath of the French Revolution*, Manchester, 1999

Hamilton, Peter, and Roger Hargreaves, *The Beautiful and the Damned: The Creation of Identity in Nineteenth-century Photography*, Aldershot, 2001

Haskell, Francis, *Patrons and Painters: A study in the relations between Italian art and society in the age of the Baroque*, New Haven and London, 1980

Haughey, Charles, *The Spirit of the Nation: The Speeches and Statements of Charles J. Haughey (1957–1986)*, ed. Martin Mansergh, Cork and Dublin, 1986

Hayden, Mary, 'Charity Children in Eighteenth Century Dublin', *Dublin Historical Record*, vol.5 no.3, March–May 1943, pp.92–107

Haydon, B.R., *The Diary of Benjamin Robert Haydon*, ed. W.B. Pope, 5 vols, Cambridge, Mass., 1960–63

Haydon, Colin, *Anti-Catholicism in eighteenth-century England: A political and social study*, Manchester, 1993

Hazlitt, William, *The Complete Works of William Hazlitt*, ed. P.P. Howe, after the edn of A.R. Waller and Arnold Glover, 21 vols, London, 1930–34

Heaney, Seamus, *North*, London, 1975

— *Seeing Things*, London, 1991

Hearn, Karen (ed.), *Dynasties: Painting in Tudor and Jacobean England 1530–1630*, exh. cat., London, 1995

Highfill, Philip H., Jr, Kalman A. Burnim and Edward A. Langhans, (eds), *A Biographical Dictionary of Actors, Actresses, Musicians, Dancers, Managers and other Stage Personnel in London, 1660–1800*, 16 vols, Carbondale, 1973–93

Hill, Jacqueline, *From Patriots to Unionists: Dublin Civic Politics and Irish Protestant Patriotism, 1660–1840*, Oxford, 1997

Hodgkinson, Terence, 'Christopher Hewetson, an Irish Sculptor in Rome', *Walpole Society*, vol.34 (1952–4), pp.42–54

Holmes, C.J., *Self and Partners (mostly Self): Being the Reminiscences of C.J. Holmes*, London, 1936

Hunt, Lynn, *Politics, Culture, and Class in the French Revolution*, Berkeley and London, 1984

Ingamells, John, *A Dictionary of British and Irish Travellers in Italy 1701–1800*, New Haven and London, 1997

— and John Edgcumbe (eds), *The Letters of Sir Joshua Reynolds*, New Haven and London, 2000

Inglis, Brian, *The Freedom of the Press in Ireland 1784–1841*, London, 1954

— *Roger Casement*, London, 1973

Kavanaugh, Ann C., *John FitzGibbon, Earl of Clare: Protestant Reaction and English Authority in Late Eighteenth-Century Ireland*, Shannon, 1997

Kearney, Richard, *Transitions: Narratives in Modern Irish Culture*, Manchester, 1988

Keena, Colm, *Haughey's Millions: Charlie's Money Trail*, Dublin, 2001

Kennedy, Róisín, *Dublin Castle Art: The Historical and Contemporary Collection*, Dublin, 1999

Kennedy, S.B., *Irish Art and Modernism, 1880–1950*, Belfast, 1991

Keogh, Dáire, *The French Disease: The Catholic Church and Irish Radicalism, 1790–1800*, Dublin, 1993

— and Kevin Whelan (eds), *Acts of Union: The Causes, Contexts and Consequences of the Act of Union*, Dublin, 2001

Kerslake, John, *National Portrait Gallery: Early Georgian Portraits*, 2 vols, London, 1977

Kiberd, Declan, *Inventing Ireland: The Literature of the Modern Nation*, London, 1996

— *Irish Classics*, London, 2000

Kilfeather, Siobhán, 'Look Who's Talking: Scandalous Memoirs and the Performance of Gender', *The Irish Review*, vol.14, 1993, pp.40–49

— 'Oliver Plunkett's head', *Textual Practice*, vol.16 no.2, 2002, pp.229–48

Kilmurray, Elaine, *Dictionary of British Portraiture*, vol.2, London, 1979

Kirkman, James Thomas, *Memoirs of the Life of Charles Macklin*, 2 vols, London, 1799

Kirwan, W.B., *Sermons by the late Rev. W.B. Kirwan, Dean of Killala with a Sketch of His Life*, London, 1816

Koerner, Leo, 'Albrecht Dürer and the Moment of Self-Portraiture', *Daphnis*, vol.15, 1986, pp.409–39

— *The Moment of Self-Portraiture in German Renaissance Art*, Chicago and London, 1993

Kornhauser, Elizabeth Mankin, *Ralph Earl: The Face of the Young Republic*, New Haven and London, 1991

Lavery, Sir John, *The Life of a Painter*, London, 1940

Lawrence, William, *Dublin Exhibition, 1872: List of Photographs of National Historical Portraits, executed with the sanction of the loan portrait committee*, Dublin, 1872

Lawrence, W.J., 'The Real Peg Woffington', *The Connoisseur*, vol. 8, January 1904, pp.44–5

Lee, J.J., *Ireland 1912–1985: Politics and Society*, Cambridge, 1989

Le Harivel, Adrian (ed.), *National Gallery of Ireland, Illustrated Summary Catalogue of Drawings, Watercolours and Miniatures*, Dublin, 1983

— *National Gallery of Ireland, Illustrated Summary Catalogue of Prints and Sculpture*, Dublin, 1988

— *The Monarch's Head*, Dublin, 2002

Levey, Michael, 'The Exiled Stuarts', in *The Later Italian Pictures in the Collection of Her Majesty The Queen*, London, 1964

— *Sir Thomas Lawrence*, exh. cat., London, 1979

Lovell, Margaretta, 'Reading eighteenth-century American family portraits: Social images and self-images', *Winterthur Portfolio*, vol.22 no.4, 1987, pp.243–64

Luce, A.A., *The Life of George Berkeley, Bishop of Cloyne*, London, 1949

Luddy, Maria, *Women and Philanthrophy in Nineteenth-Century Ireland*, Cambridge, 1995

Lusk, Lewis, 'A famous journalist, Sydney P. Hall, MVO', *Art Journal*, 1905, pp.277–81

Lyons, F.S.L., 'Parnellism and Crime, 1887–90', *Transactions of the Royal Historical Society*, 5th ser., vol.24, 1974, pp.123–40

— *Charles Stewart Parnell*, Oxford, 1977

McBride, Lawrence (ed.), *Images, Icons and the Irish Nationalist Imagination*, Dublin, 1999

McCarthy, Michael (ed.), *Lord Charlemont and his Circle*, Dublin, 2001

McConkey, Kenneth, *Sir John Lavery RA, 1856–1941*, exh. cat., Belfast and London, 1984

— *Sir John Lavery*, Edinburgh, 1993

McCoole, Sinéad, *Hazel: A Life of Lady Lavery 1880–1935*, Dublin, 1996

Mac Craith, Mícheál, 'Review Article on Ó Buachalla's *Aisling Ghéar*', *Eighteenth-Century Ireland: Iris an dá chultúr*, vol.13, 1998, pp.166–71

MacDermot, Frank, 'Arthur O'Connor', *Irish Historical Studies*, vol.15, 1966–7, pp.48–69

MacDonagh, Oliver, *O'Connell: The Life of Daniel O'Connell 1775–1847*, London, 1991

Macdonald, John, *Diary of the Parnell Commission (from The Daily News)*, London, 1890

McDonnell, Joseph, *Ecclesiastical Art of the Penal Era and Art and Transcendence*, exh. cat., Maynooth, 1995

McDowell, R.B., *Ireland in the Age of Imperialism and Revolution 1760–1801*, Oxford, 1979

— 'Some FitzGibbon Letters from the Sneyd Muniments in the John Rylands Library', *Bulletin of The John Rylands Library*, vol.34 no.2, 1951–2, pp.296–311

McDunphy, Michael, *Collection of Historical Pictures, etc., established by Dr Douglas Hyde, President of Ireland*, Dublin, 1945

McGuiggan, John, 'A rare document of Irish history: "High Treason" by Sir John Lavery', *Irish Arts Review*, vol.15, 1999, pp.157–9

Mackintosh, Iain and Geoffrey Ashton (eds), *The Georgian Playhouse. Actors, Artists, Audiences and Architecture 1730–1830*, exh. cat., London, 1973

McParland, Edward, *Public Architecture in Ireland 1680–1760*, New Haven and London, 2001

MacRaild, Donald M., *Irish Migrants in Modern Britain, 1750–1922*, Basingstoke and London, 1999

Madden, Richard R., *The United Irishmen: Their Lives and Times*, 4 vols, Dublin and London, 2nd edn, 1857–60

Malcomson, A.P.W., *John Foster: The politics of the Anglo-Irish Ascendancy*, Oxford and New York, 1978

— *Archbishop Charles Agar: Churchmanship and Politics in Ireland, 1760–1810*, Dublin, 2002

Mannings, David, *Sir Joshua Reynolds: A Complete Catalogue of his Paintings*, 2 vols, New Haven and London, 2000

Marshall, P.J. (ed.), *The Oxford History of the British Empire: The Eighteenth Century*, Oxford and New York, 1998

Maxwell, Constantia, *Dublin Under the Georges 1714–1830*, London, 1956

Miles, Ellen G., *National Gallery of Art, American Paintings of the Eighteenth Century*, Washington DC, 1995

Millar, Delia, *The Victorian Watercolours and Drawings in the Collection of Her Majesty The Queen*, 2 vols, London, 1995

Mitchel, John, *Jail Journal*, reprint with intro. by Thomas Flanagan, Dublin, 1982

Monod, Paul Kléber, *Jacobitism and the English People, 1688–1788*, Cambridge, 1989

Montgomery Hyde, H., *Famous Trials, 9: Roger Casement*, Harmondsworth, 1964

Moody, T.W. (ed.), *Historical Studies*, vol.6, London, 1968

— F.X. Martin and F.J. Byrne (eds), *A New History of Ireland*, vol.8: *A Chronology of Irish History to 1976*, Oxford, 1982

Moore, Andrew and Charlotte Crawley, *Family and Friends: A Regional Survey of British Portraiture*, London, 1988

Moore, Thomas, *Life and Death of Lord Edward FitzGerald*, 2 vols, London, 1831

Morash, Christopher, *A History of Irish Theatre 1601–2000*, Cambridge, 2002

Morgan, Hiram, 'Tom Lee: The posing peacemaker', in *Representing Ireland: Literature and the origins of conflict, 1534–1660*, eds Brendan Bradshaw, Andrew Hadfield and Willy Maley, Cambridge, 1993, pp.132–65

Moroney, Mic, 'Painting Charlie', *Magill*, April 2001, pp.16–18

Mulvany, T.J., 'Memoirs of Native Artists, Hugh Hamilton', *Dublin Monthly Magazine*, January–June 1842, pp.65–76

Murphy, Paula, 'The politics of the street monument', *Irish Arts Review Yearbook*, 1994, pp.202–8

— 'John Henry Foley's O'Connell Monument', *Irish Arts Review Yearbook*, 1995, pp.155–6

— 'The O'Connell Monument in Dublin: The political and artistic context of a public sculpture', *Apollo*, March 1996, pp.22–6

— 'Rejecting public sculpture: Monuments in Dublin', *Apollo*, September 2001, pp.38–43

Murphy, William M., *Prodigal Father: The Life of John Butler Yeats (1839–1922)*, Ithaca and London, 1978

National Gallery of Ireland, *Catalogue of Pictures and Other Works of Art in the National Gallery and National Portrait Gallery, Ireland*, Dublin, 1898

— *Illustrated Summary Catalogue of Paintings*, Dublin, 1981

National Library of Ireland: One Hundred and Twenty Five Years, Dublin, 2002

Nead, Lynda, 'Visual culture of the courtroom: Reflections on history, law and the image', *Visual Culture in Britain*, vol.3 no.2, 2002, pp.119–41

Nicholson, Eirwen E.C., 'Consumers and Spectators: The public of the Political Print in Eighteenth-Century England', *History*, vol.81, January 1996, pp.5–21

Nicholson, Robin, *Bonnie Prince Charlie and the Making of a Myth: A study in portraiture, 1720–1892*, Lewisburg, and London, 2002

Northcote, James, *The Life of Joshua Reynolds*, 2 vols, 2nd edn, London, 1819

Notes on the Pictures, Plate, Antiquities, Etc at Carton, Kilkea Castle, 13 Dominick Street, Dublin and 6, Carlton House Terrace, London, Dublin, 1885

Ó Broin, Leon, *The Prime Informer: A Suppressed Scandal*, London, 1971 (trans. of *Comhcheilg sa Chaisleán*, Dublin, 1963)

Ó Buachalla, Breandán, *Aisling Ghéar: na Stíobhartaigh agus an t-aos léinn 1601–1788*, Dublin, 1996

O'Callaghan, Margaret, *British High Politics and a Nationalist Ireland: Criminality, Land and the Law under Forster and Balfour*, Cork, 1994

O'Connor, Arthur, *The State of Ireland*, ed. James Livesay, Dublin, 1998

O'Connor, Cynthia, *The Pleasing Hours: The Grand Tour of James Caulfeild, First Earl of Charlemont (1728–1799), Traveller, Connoisseur and Patron of the Arts*, Wilton, Cork, 1999

Ó Ciardha, Éamonn, *Ireland and the Jacobite Cause, 1685–1766: A fatal attachment*, Dublin, 2002

Ó Cuív, Ruairí (ed.), *Artists' Century: Irish Self-Portraits and Selected Works, 1900–2000*, exh. cat., Dublin and Belfast, 2000

O'Donnell, Ruán, *Robert Emmet and the Rising of 1803*, Dublin and Portland, OR, 2003

— (2003a) 'Propaganda and iconography: Images of Robert Emmet', *Irish Arts Review*, Spring 2003, pp.108–13

— (2003b) *Remembering Emmet: Images of the life and legacy of Robert Emmet*, Bray, 2003

O'Donoghue, Freeman, and Henry M. Hake, *Catalogue of Engraved British Portraits preserved in the Department of Prints and Drawings in the British Museum*, 6 vols, London, 1908–25

Official Catalogue, Dublin Exhibition of Arts, Industries and Manufactures and Loan Museum of Works of Art, Dublin, 1872

Ormond, Richard, *National Portrait Gallery: Early Victorian Portraits*, 2 vols, London, 1973

Pakenham, Thomas, *The Year of Liberty: The Story of the Great Irish Rebellion of 1798*, London, 1969

— *The Year of Liberty: The Great Irish Rebellion of 1798*, abridged, London, 1997

Pasquin, Anthony, *An Authentic History of the Artists of Ireland, and the Royal Academicians*, London, 1796

Paulson, Ronald, *Hogarth*, 3 vols, New Brunswick, NJ, 1993

Payne Knight, Richard, *The Edinburgh Review*, vol.XVI, 1801

Penny, Nicholas, (ed.), *Reynolds*, exh. cat., Royal Academy of Arts, London, 1986

Pepper, Terence, *High Society Photographs 1897–1914*, London, 1998

Perry, Lara, 'Facing Femininities: Women in the National Portrait Gallery 1856–1899', unpublished DPhil dissertation, University of York, 1998

Pettitt, Lance, *Screening Ireland: Film and Television Representation*, Manchester, 2000

Pindar, Patt (Henrietta Battier), *The Kirwanade*, Dublin, 1791

Piper, David, *Catalogue of the Seventeenth-Century Portraits in the National Portrait Gallery 1625–1714*, Cambridge, 1963

— *The English Face*, London, 1957; 2nd edn, London, 1992

Pointon, Marcia, *Hanging the Head: Portraiture and Social Formation in Eighteenth-Century England*, New Haven and London, 1993

— '1968 and all that: The founding of the National Portrait Gallery, Washington, DC', in *Art Apart: Art Institutions and Ideology across England and North America*, ed. Marcia Pointon, Manchester, 1994, pp.50–68

— *Strategies for Showing: Women, Possession, and Representation in English Visual Culture 1665–1800*, Oxford, 1997

Pompeo Batoni and his British Patrons, exh. cat., London, 1982

Postle, Martin, *Angels and Urchins: The Fancy Picture in Eighteenth-Century British Art*, exh. cat., London, 1998

Pressly, William L., *The Life and Art of James Barry*, New Haven and London, 1981

— *James Barry: The Artist as Hero*, exh. cat., London, 1983

Prinz, Wolfram, *Die Sammlung der Selbstbildnisse in den Uffizien, Band I: Geschichte der Sammlung*, Berlin, 1971

Prown, Jules David, *American Painting from its Beginning to the Armory Show*, Geneva, 1969

— *Art as Evidence: Writings on Art and Material Culture*, New Haven and London, 2002

Pullan, Ann, 'Head to Head Encounters', *Oxford Art Journal*, vol.17 no.2, 1994, pp.103–12

Pyle, Hilary, *Yeats: Portrait of an Artistic Family*, London, 1997

Reid, B.L., *The Lives of Roger Casement*, New Haven and London, 1976

Report of Special Commission Act 1888: Reprints of the shorthand notes of the speeches, proceedings and evidence taken before the Commissioners, 12 vols, London, 1890

Reynolds, Sir Joshua, *Discourses on Art*, ed. Robert R. Wark, New Haven and London, 1981

Ribeiro, Aileen, *Fashion in the French Revolution*, New York, 1988

Robins, Joseph, *The Lost Children: A Study of Charity Children in Ireland, 1700–1900*, Dublin, 1980

Rococo: Art and Design in Hogarth's England, exh. cat., London, 1984

Rodgers, Betsy, *Cloak of Charity: Studies in Eighteenth-Century Philanthropy*, London, 1949

ROSC, *The Irish Imagination 1959–1971*, exh. cat.,Dublin, 1971

Rouse, Sarah, *Into the Light: An Illustrated Guide to the Photograph Collection in the National Library of Ireland*, Dublin, 1998

Saumarez Smith, Charles, *The National Portrait Gallery*, London, 1997

Saunders, Richard H., *John Smibert: Colonial America's First Portrait Painter*, New Haven and London, 1995

Scott, Temple (ed.), *The Prose Works of Jonathan Swift*, 12 vols, London, 1897–1908

Scottish National Portrait Gallery Catalogue, Edinburgh, 1977

Sexton, Sean, *Ireland in Old Photographs*, London, 1994

— *The Irish: A Photohistory 1840–1940*, London, 2002

Shearman, John, *Raphael's Cartoons in the Collection of Her Majesty the Queen*, London, 1972

Sheehy, Jeanne, *The Rediscovery of Ireland's Past: The Celtic Revival, 1830–1920*, London, 1980

Slattery, Peadar, 'The Uses of Photography in Ireland, 1839–1900', unpublished PhD dissertation, University of Dublin, 3 vols, 1992

Smailes, Helen, *A Portrait Gallery for Scotland*, Edinburgh, 1985

Smith, Alistair, *Louis le Brocquy Paintings 1939–1996*, Dublin, 1996

Smith, J.T., *Nollekens and his Times*, 2 vols, 2nd edn, London, 1829

Smyth, Jim, *The Men of No Property: Irish Radicals and Popular Politics in the Late Eighteenth Century*, London, 1992

— (ed.), *Revolution, Counter-Revolution and Union: Ireland in the 1790s*, Cambridge, 2000

Solkin, David H., *Painting for Money: The Visual Arts and the Public Sphere in Eighteenth-Century England*, New Haven and London, 1993

— (ed.), *Art on the Line: The Royal Academy Exhibitions at Somerset House 1780–1836*, New Haven and London, 2001

Stephens, F.G. and M. Dorothy George, *Catalogue of Political and Personal Satires Preserved in the Department of Prints and Drawings in the British Museum*, 12 vols, London, 1870–1954

Stevenson, S. and D. Thomson, *John Michael Wright*, exh. cat., Edinburgh, 1982

Stewart, Ann, *Fifty Irish Portraits*, , Dublin, 1984

— *Irish Art Loan Exhibitions 1765–1927: Index of Artists*, 3 vols, St Owen, Jersey, 1990–95

Stewart, Bruce (ed.) *Hearts and Minds: Irish Culture and Society under the Act of Union*, Gerrards Cross, 2002

Straub, Kristina, *Sexual Suspects: Eighteenth-Century Players and Sexual Ideology*, Princeton, NJ, 1992

Strickland, Walter G., *A Dictionary of Irish Artists*, 2 vols, Dublin
    and London, 1913
— *A Descriptive Catalogue of the Pictures, Busts and Statues in Trinity
    College Dublin. . .*, Dublin, 1916
Strong, Roy, *National Portrait Gallery: Tudor and Jacobean Portraits*,
    2 vols, London, 1969
Sullivan, T.D., A.M. and D.B., *Speeches from the Dock: Or, protests
    of Irish patriotism. Containing introductory sketches & biographical
    notices*, Dublin and Waterford, 39th edn, 1887
Sumner, Ann (ed.), *Death, Passion and Politics: Van Dyck's Portraits of
    Venetia Stanley and George Digby*, London, 1995
Swift, Roger (ed.), *Irish Migrants in Britain 1815–1914: A Documentary
    History*, Cork, 2002
— and Sheridan Gilley (eds), *The Irish in Britain 1815–1939*,
    London, 1989
Tayler, Henrietta, *Prince Charlie's Daughter: Being the Life and Letters
    of Charlotte of Albany,* London, 1950
Taylor, Clare, *British and American Abolitionists: An Episode in
    Transatlantic Understanding*, Edinburgh, 1974
Temple, A.G., *Art Gallery of the Corporation of London, Catalogue
    of the Exhibition of Works by . . . Irish Painters*, London, 1904
Tillyard, Stella, *Citizen Lord: Edward FitzGerald 1763–1798*, London, 1997
Tomalin, Claire, *Mrs Jordan's Profession*, London, 1994
Twyman, Michael, *Printing 1770–1970: An Illustrated History of
    its Development and Uses in England*, London, 1970
Ulster Museum, *Seamus Heaney: A Personal Selection*, exh. cat.,
    Belfast, 1982
Vaughan, W.E. (ed.), *A New History of Ireland*, vol.5: *Ireland Under the
    Union, I, 1801–70*, Oxford, 1989
— *A New History of Ireland*, vol. 6: *Ireland Under the Union, II,
    1870–1921*, Oxford, 1996
Victor, Benjamin, *The History of the Theatres of London and Dublin
    From the Year 1730 to the Present Time,* 3 vols, London, 1761
Walker, Dorothy, 'Sailing to Byzantium: The Portraits of Edward
    McGuire', *Irish Arts Review*, vol.4 no.4, Winter 1987, pp.21–9
— *Modern Art in Ireland*, Dublin, 1997
Walker, Joseph Cooper, *Outlines of a Plan for Promoting the Arts of
    Painting in Ireland, with a List of Subjects for Painters, drawn from
    the Romantic and Genuine Histories of Ireland*, Dublin,1790
Walker, Richard, *National Portrait Gallery: Regency Portraits*, 2 vols,
    London, 1985

Webster, Mary, *Francis Wheatley*, New Haven and London, 1970
West, Shearer, 'Zoffany's "Charles Macklin as Shylock" and Lord
    Mansfield', *Theatre Notebook*, vol.43 no.1, 1989, pp.3–9
— 'The public nature of private life: the conversation piece and
    the fragmented family', *British Journal for Eighteenth-Century
    Studies*, vol.18 no.2, 1995, pp.153–72
— 'Framing hegemony: Economics, luxury, and family continuity in
    the country-house portrait', in Paul Duro (ed.), *The Rhetoric of the
    Frame: Essays on the boundaries of the artwork*, Cambridge, 1996,
    pp.63–78
Weston, Nancy, *Daniel Maclise: Irish artist in Victorian London*, Dublin,
    2001
Whelan, Kevin, *The Tree of Liberty: Radicalism, Catholicism and
    the Construction of Irish Identity 1760–1830*, Cork, 1996
— *Fellowship of Freedom: The United Irishmen and 1798*, Cork, 1998
Whelan, Yvonne, *Reinventing Modern Dublin: Streetscape,
    iconography and the politics of identity*, Dublin, 2003
Wilson, Harold, *The Labour Government 1964–70: A Personal Record*,
    Harmondsworth, 1974
Wood, Jeremy, 'Raphael Copies and Exemplary Picture Galleries
    in Mid-Eighteenth-Century London', *Zeitschrift für Kunstgeschichte*,
    vol.3, 1999, pp.394–417
Woodall, Joanna (ed.)., *Portraiture: Facing the Subject*, Manchester,
    1997, pp.219–38
Woods-Marsden, Joanna, *Renaissance Self-Portraiture: The Visual
    Construction of Identity and the Social Status of the Artist*,
    New Haven and London, 1998
Wrigley, Richard, 'Transformations of a Revolutionary Emblem:
    The Liberty Cap in the French Revolution', *French History*,
    vol. 11 no. 2, June 1997
— *The Politics of Appearances: Representations of Dress in
    Revolutionary France*, Oxford and New York, 2002
Wynne, Michael, *Later Italian Paintings in The National Gallery of
    Ireland: The Seventeenth, Eighteenth and Nineteenth Centuries*,
    Dublin, 1986
Yeats, J.B., *Essays Irish and American*, Dublin, 1918
Yeats, W.B., *Memoirs*, ed. Denis Donoghue, New York, 1972
Ziff, Trisha (ed.), *Distant Relations: Chicano, Irish, Mexican Art
    and Critical Writing*, Santa Monica, CA, 1994

The publisher would like to thank the copyright holders for kindly giving permission to reproduce the works illustrated in this book. Locations and lenders are given in the captions, and further acknowledgements are given below. Every effort has been made to contact copyright holders; any omissions are inadvertent, and will be corrected in future editions if notification is given to the publisher in writing.

Alte Pinakothek, Munich – Artothek: fig.65

Ashmolean Museum, Oxford: fig.61

With kind permission of Robert Ballagh: fig.143

British Library: figs 103, 104

Trustees of the British Museum: figs 29, 48, 50, 60, 64, 87, 88, 105

The Cleveland Museum of Art (General Income Fund, 1919.910): fig.96

The Crawford Municipal Art Gallery, Cork: fig.63

Dublin City Council: Mansion House: figs 6, 114

Dublin City Gallery, the Hugh Lane Municipal Gallery of Modern Art: figs 40, 41, 42, 43, 146

Dublin City Gallery, the Hugh Lane, by courtesy of Felix Rosenstiel's Widow & Son Ltd, London, on behalf of the Estate of Sir John Lavery: figs 141, 142

By permission of the Trustees of Dulwich Picture Gallery: fig.75

Getty Images: fig.66

With kind permission of John Kindness: fig.147

Leeds City Art Galleries & Museum (Lotherton Hall): fig.94

University of Limerick, The National Self-Portrait Collection of Ireland: fig.46

National Gallery of Art, Washington DC: fig.57

National Gallery of Ireland: figs 12, 13, 14, 15, 16, 17, 18, 21, 23, 32, 33, 35, 36, 37, 38, 39, 52, 53, 58, 76, 79, 83, 84, 86, 93, 98, 101, 106, 108, 110, 117, 119, 124, 130, 132, 134, 135, 140

National Gallery of Ireland/ Mark Shields: fig.47

National Gallery of Ireland/Robert Ballagh: fig.145, back cover

Courtesy of the National Library of Ireland: fig.133

National Portrait Gallery, London: frontispiece, figs 2, 3, 9 (& detail p.10), 19, 20, 22, 24, 25, 26, 27, 28, 30, 31, 34 (& detail p.32), 49, 55, 56, 62 (& detail p.78), 69, 70 (& detail p.8), 71, 72 (& detail p.110), 73, 74, 77, 78 (& detail p.6), 80, 82, 90, 92, 95, 99, 100, 109, 111, 113, 115 (& detail p.146), 116, 118 (& detail p.184), 120 (& detail p.224), 121, 122, 123, 125, 126, 127, 128, 129, 131, 138, 139, front cover

The Nelson-Atkins Museum of Art, Kansas City, Missouri (Photo: Jamison Miller): fig.97

Michael O'Boyle, Fenian Album courtesy of the National Library of Ireland: fig.136

Reproduced by permission of the Office of Public Works, Dublin: fig.11

Reproduced by permission of the Office of Public Works, Dublin (Áras an Uachtaráin): fig.144

Reproduced by permission of the Office of Public Works, Dublin (Dublin Castle): fig.10

Reproduced by permission of the Office of Public Works, Dublin (Leinster Lawn): fig. 7

Private collection: fig.112

Photograph copyright RMN-Hervé Lewnadowski: fig.89

Copyright Felix Rosenstiel's Widow & Son Ltd, London, on behalf of the Estate of Sir John Lavery, reproduced with the kind permission of the Trustees of the National Museums & Galleries of Northern Ireland: fig.85

By courtesy of Felix Rosenstiel's Widow & Son Ltd: fig.137

Royal Academy of Arts, London: fig.59

Tate, London: figs 5, 68, 91, 107

Photograph reproduced by kind permission of Trimark Pictures: fig.4

Trinity College, Dublin: fig.81

Uffizi Gallery, Florence (Photo – Scala): fig.45

Photograph copyright Ulster Museum, reproduced with the kind permission of the Trustees of the National Museums & Galleries of Northern Ireland: figs 1, 51, 102

Photograph reproduced with the kind permission of the Trustees of the Victoria and Albert Museum, London: fig.8

Warner Brothers/The Kobal Collection: fig.67

Yale Center for British Art, Paul Mellon Collection: fig.54

Yale University Art Gallery: fig.44

The author and publishers are grateful to the following individuals and institutions for permission to quote extracts:

Curtis Brown Group Ltd., London on behalf of the estate of Elizabeth Bowen for permission to quote from *The Last September* and *Bowen's Court* (copyright © Elizabeth Bowen 1929 and copyright © Elizabeth Bowen 1942)

Faber and Faber Limited, Publishers and to Seamus Heaney for quotations from *Seeing Things* (1991)

The Government Art Collection, London

Courtesy of the National Gallery of Ireland Archives for material from the National Gallery of Ireland

Tate Archives

A.P. Watts Ltd on behalf of Michael B. Yeats for quotations from W.B. Yeats

Index

Figures in italics refer to illustrations